# Romance and
the Rock

# FORTRESS TEXTS IN
# MODERN THEOLOGY

## IN THE SERIES

Protestantism and Progress
Ernst Troeltsch

What Is Christianity?
Adolf von Harnack

Faith and Understanding
Rudolf Bultmann

Servant of the Word: Selected Sermons
of Friedrich Schleiermacher

Christian Caring: Selections from
*Practical Theology*
Friedrich Schleiermacher

Confessions of an Inquiring Spirit
Samuel Taylor Coleridge

The So-called Historical Jesus
and the Historic Biblical Christ
Martin Kähler

Romance and the Rock: Nineteenth-Century
Catholics on Faith and Reason
Edited by Joseph Fitzer

FORTRESS TEXTS IN MODERN THEOLOGY

# Romance and the Rock

## Nineteenth-Century Catholics on Faith and Reason

**Edited by Joseph Fitzer**

**Fortress Press**     **Minneapolis**

ROMANCE AND THE ROCK

Nineteenth-Century Catholics on Faith and Reason

Cover design: Jim Churchville.

Library of Congress Cataloging-in-Publication Data

Romance and the rock: nineteenth-century Catholics on faith and
    reason / edited by Joseph Fitzer.
            p.     cm.—(Fortress texts in modern theology)
        Bibliography: p.
        ISBN 0-8006-3207-9
        1. Faith and reason.  2. Catholic Church—Doctrines.  I. Fitzer,
    Joseph, 1939–  .  II. Series.
    BT50,R64      1989
    230'.2—dc20                                                89-34197
                                                                    CIP

The paper used in this publication meets the minimum requirements of American National Standard for Information Sciences—Permanence of Paper for Printed Library Materials, ANSI Z329.48-1984.

Manufactured in the U.S.A.                                    AF 1-3207
93    92    91    90    89    1    2    3    4    5    6    7    8    9    10

In memory of
*René Dosogne,*
Christian Gentleman, Romantic Musician
†2.28.86

# Contents

# Acknowledgments

For their kind permission to reprint selections from Matthias Scheeben's *The Mysteries of Christianity* and from J. F. Clarkson's compilation, *The Church Teaches,* I wish to thank TAN Books. For permission to reprint Edouard LeRoy's *What Is a Dogma?* I am grateful to Open Court Press.

I especially wish to thank Professor B. A. Gerrish, of the University of Chicago, who urged me to undertake this project, and J. Michael West, Academic Editor of Fortress Press, than whom I cannot imagine a more gracious co-worker. Librarians who helped and to whom I am therefore much indebted include Sister Marie Melton, R.S.M., Director of Libraries, St. John's University, in New York, and her staff, particularly Beatrice de Franc; the Reverend David E. Green, Director of the Library of General Theological Seminary, in New York; and Seth Kasten, Research Librarian of Union Theological Seminary, in New York. I am similarly indebted to Carol Hodgman Deming, who checked my French translation, and to Professor Frederick Lang, of St. John's University, who checked my German translations, though I am responsible for the final form of all my translations. Finally, I offer affectionate thanks to my wife, Mary Molina Fitzer, an astute reader of theological literature, who offered many useful suggestions, who put up with numerous book stalagmites in a smallish house, and who in moment of serendipity suggested the title of the volume.

# Introduction

This volume is a partial introduction to nineteenth-century Roman Catholic theology. There are, I believe, three main reasons why a reader might be interested in this period and style of theological reflection. In the first place, the reader, whether a Catholic or a member of some other religious or quasi-religious tradition, might want to understand better how the Catholic Church has arrived at its present state. I hope the volume will advance such understanding. Second, the reader might want to search the nineteenth century for remedies for what he or she takes to be weaknesses in present-day Catholicism. In that case the volume may not be quite so helpful—for reasons that will be explained in due course—though some emphasis will fall on certain abiding characteristics of Catholicism up to the Second Vatican Council, characteristics that would seem to be criteria for further developments. Third, there is what I consider the best reason for studying nineteenth-century Catholicism: it is *there*. It is the product of fellow human beings wrestling, often with talent and sometimes with genius, with problems that deeply concern them. The better sort of nineteenth-century Catholic theological writing is intrinsically interesting as a human product. The very best of such writing, because of the integration in it of writer, problems, and solutions, can, I believe, lay claim to not only theological but literary merit.

Whatever the reader's concerns, he or she will find a certain tension or opposition running through all the selections in the volume, the polarity between what I call *romance* and the *Rock*. Catholicism considers itself the great, the universal church, the people of God, or at least

1

the very sizable central sector of the people of God. One would expect it, as such, to be animated by a common spirit, a spirit of the people, a *Volksgeist*—and to be moved by that spirit in such a way that each individual would stand in a quasi-biological, *organic* relationship to the whole. In short, *there is romance in Catholicism*: space and time are less boundaries for the individual than vehicles for the free play of intuition, speculation, and prayer. In the organic Catholic people of God the stories, the *romans*, of the hero saints happened only yesterday, perhaps still happen today; and by a similar working of hidden forces the faraway, the exotic, is close.[1]

And yet the romance welling up from the people confronts another constant of Catholicism: the Rock, the papacy, the institution that claims to be chartered in Matt. 16:18: "You are Peter, and on this rock I will build my church." It is certainly arguable that Peter's rock, in the course of the Dark Ages, took the form of a renewal of Roman governance. To the spirit of the people, romance, was opposed Romanness, *Romanità*, the Rock. Here, then, are two conceptions of the church, both of them, arguably, rooted in the Dark Ages: a church arising out of the spirit of the people, and a church that heeds the voice of Peter. This polarity continued, of course, into the nineteenth century; indeed, it was intensified by the challenges then facing the church. So whether the reader's interests are religious and pastoral or humanistic and literary, the reader's attention, in the pages to follow, will largely be directed to the opposition of the romantic spirit of the people and the Petrine rock. The nineteenth was, after all, the century of self-conscious literary, historical, and political romanticism, and also of increasing agitation for, and ultimately the definition of, papal infallibility.

How, then, can nineteenth-century studies help us understand the present state of Roman Catholicism? Catholicism as we now find it is in many ways the result of the Second Vatican Council. Still, that assembly took as its point of departure what was, in many respects, the Catholicism of 1914, the year many would regard as marking the end of the nineteenth century. I say *in many respects*, because there was one very significant change: the qualified acceptance, in Pope Pius XII's 1943 encyclical letter *Divino Afflante,* of modern biblical criticism. With this one exception the period 1900–1960, embracing Pius X's condemnation of Modernism and, of infinitely greater import, the upheavals of two World Wars, was as a whole a period of relative stasis in Catholic thought—though clearly the elements that broke into the open at Vatican II in historical, biblical, liturgical, and social studies were quietly being prepared. More accurately, in the period 1900–1960 Catholic scholars quietly continued the work begun well before the condemnation of Modernism in 1907, waiting, so to say, for the chance of wider publicity. One often senses, in rereading historical or liturgical books of the period, that the motivation that produced them was in good part a concern for doctrinal development, though this concern is not overtly stated.[2] On the whole, then, 1960 leads us back to 1914, and 1914 leads us to consider the process that produced the thoughts and sentiments of that year. It would appear that to understand present-day Catholicism we must study Catholicism in the century stretching from 1800 up to 1914.

At first the task seems almost limitless and uncontrollable. Catholics know, but sometimes Protestants and humanists need to be reminded, how large the Catholic Church is and was. Since the American Civil War it has become by far the largest denomination in the United States. In 1914, Catholicism was the religion of France, Spain, Portugal, Italy, most of the Austro-Hungarian Empire, Belgium, and "occupied" Ireland and Poland, and much of the German Empire, with important Catholic bodies in Britain, Canada, and Australia. It was the religion of the enormous Hispano-Portuguese empire in Central and South America that early in the nineteenth century declared its political but not its cultural independence. Missionaries were quite successfully at work around the globe in the British, French, Spanish, Portuguese, Belgian, German, and American colonial empires.[3] But here the Rock aspect of Catholicism is a help. It is the relative centralization of Catholicism that enables it to be studied: wherever Catholic theologians were, they felt called to deal with the same range of issues, and to deal with them in a fairly uniform manner. (Sometimes, one might add, the "family resemblance" of the Catholics leads to their not being studied very carefully. In all too many textbooks there is considerable attention given to great Protestant *individuals,* such as Schleiermacher and Ritschl, with a unitary discussion of "the Catholics," as if they were lemmings all running off to drown in papal prerogative.)

The centralizing tendency of Catholicism in the period 1800–1914 left us, moreover, a stunning monument and point of reference: Pius IX summoned the First Vatican Council to meet in 1869–70. Universally—I invite you to make your own examination—the literature commenting on nineteenth-century Catholicism sees Vatican I as its center point or high point. It is important to note that *within* the period under discussion, specifically from 1870 to 1914, Catholic writers took the same view, conceptualizing theological work as either leading up to Vatican I or having to take account of the dogmas defined there. We could, to be sure, essay a new conceptualization of nineteenth-century Catholicism, trying to see in it the preparation of our current point of view and concerns, be they devotion to the Sacred Heart of Jesus or liberation theology or whatever. I shall address this endeavor in somewhat more detail later in this introduction, but for the moment suffice it to say that this would not be a nineteenth-century interpretation of the Catholic nineteenth-century. After 1870, Catholics saw perfectly clearly where the church had gone: Vatican I. By all accounts late-nineteenth-century Catholics were intelligent enough, and they were not, I submit, so far removed from us in their general cultural outlook. In short, there simply does not seem to be a convincing reason not to accept the majority self-interpretation of post–Vatican I Catholicism.

The interpretation I propose is found also in Adolf von Harnack's *History of Dogma*. Harnack, who was scarcely a friend of Catholicism, cannot be read as favoring the Catholic self-estimate I have suggested. Nevertheless, he writes,

> In the storm of the [French] Revolution it became apparent that the old lion [Catholicism] still lived, and in their alarm the princes then hastened to impart to it on their side still more vigour. The collapse of the Imperial Church, with which the State Church of Joseph II also disappeared, was a fortunate occurrence for Rome. How the Curia succeeded in suppressing what remained of Episcopalist and State Church thought in Germany, in constructing the Church anew by means of concordats, and in gradually training for itself an Ultramontane Episcopate and an Ultramontane clergy, after the National Church tradition had, as in France been abolished; how in this work there co-operated not only the Jesuits, but above all the princes, the Romanticists, and the unsuspecting Liberals—has been fully narrated quite recently [to which narrations Harnack refers in a footnote]. *The Vatican Decrees were the culmination of this development.*[4]

Some pages later Harnack repeats, "All lines of development, those from within and those from without, converged upon this goal."[5] I should add that there was malice aforethought in my quoting these lines of Harnack. He upholds the view I take here, but in so doing he mentions Joseph II, the French national church, liberals, and suchlike, with the apparent conviction that doctrinal matters cannot be understood without our delving into (institutional) church history. That is indeed so, and the reader unfamiliar with church history, particularly the beginning student, should take the hint and read the pertinent chapters in the one-volume texts of Williston Walker and Paul Johnson.[6]

Let us stay with church history for a moment. The "Vatican Decrees"—above all, the assertion in them of a papal-monarchy as opposed to an episcopal-collegial form of church governance—were meant by their framers as the solution to problems. What problems? Harnack's mention of revolution puts us on the right track, though we can certainly broaden the concept. Vatican I was the Catholic answer to the *many* revolutions affecting the nineteenth century. There was the French Revolution but also the American Revolution—the latter leading to a stable democracy and a religiously neutral state that was not, however, anticlerical. There was the Industrial Revolution, with all the social dislocation it produced. There was what we might call the Scientific Revolution: trains, Darwin, vaccination, and Freud. No life was untouched by the triumphs of applied science, which seemed, in an optimistic glow, about to address every human need. Better nutrition, sanitation, and medical care ushered in a demographic revolution, and in developed countries the drive toward universal education bid to direct its future. (There was a darker side to all this: what today we call the Third World was being "developed" by Europeans and Americans, and powerful revolutions would appear there too, but after the period under discussion.) All these revolutions created enormous problems for organized religion; Vatican I was the Catholic response, or more exactly, the center point of Catholic response.

If I were to sum up that Catholic response in a silly little formula it would be, We're still here. The Catholic Church, drawing on its traditions, has something pertinent and useful to say to moderns. What it wants to say, substantively, is that humankind is not self-sufficient, human reason and good intentions are not a sufficient resource for dealing with modern problems. Divine grace is needed—for daily life but also as the preparation for human beings' true goal, heaven. If divine grace is needed, then all conditions necessary for the effective preaching of grace must be fulfilled. If gospel preaching seems to call for a strong papacy, then strong papacy there must be, a papacy freed from the ever-growing power of the nation-state. If to hear the gospel and respond to grace modern men and women must be disabused of mistaken philosophical notions, then there must even be an ecclesiastical witnessing of the philosophical truth. In the standard history of nineteenth-century Catholic theology, Edgar Hocedez writes,

> The history of theology in the nineteenth century presents a strikingly unified character, which gives it especial interest. Without, but one adversary counted—rationalism; within, one might say, minds were occupied with but one problem—the fundamental problem of the relations between nature and supernature. Under its theoretical aspect it is the question of the relations between faith and reason, in the practical domain, that of the relations between church and state, church and nationalism.[7]

So the Catholic Church in the nineteenth century certainly did not *change* the doctrines defined at the Council of Trent and earlier councils. God forbid! Instead it asserted that those doctrines were still relevant,

indeed, crucial to human happiness. What it set out to do was to add
such doctrinal refinements as would aid in its preaching of the earlier
deposit of doctrine, or would reemphasize its moral authority to engage
in such preaching. As both Harnack and Hocedez recognize, then, there
is a certain logic in what Vatican I actually taught. Its two *constitutions,*
or formal teaching documents (which are included in this volume), deal
with faith and reason and with the authority of the pope. As a result, so
does the present volume as a whole.

To stress the centrality of Vatican I is by no means to suggest that
the paths to it or from it were paved with roses. They were not. As the
name itself suggests, the Vatican Council was held literally *on* the rock
of Peter. Farther away from the Rock, but never forgetful of it, were
those who sought in the spirit of the people the resources to deal with
the problems of the age, the romantic Catholics. The "romance" of
Catholicism figures in a number of the selections in this volume; introducing them, very briefly, gives me a chance to discuss its content and
organization.

Part 1 of this anthology, "The New Romantic Vision," includes selections by François-René de Chateaubriand, Johann Sebastian Drey, and
Johann Adam Möhler. All three writers stress that the church and, with
it, Europe must be restored to something akin to the medieval "age of
faith." That is, the selections are *apologetic,* in the sense of giving an
account of the faith to those who do not share it, in the hope of
persuading them to share it. Chateaubriand is concerned about faith as
the basis of public order and civilization generally. Drey concerns himself with the restoration of the discipline of theology. Möhler aims at
restoring Catholicism to its rightful place in German intellectual and
institutional life. These writers are all imbued with a sense of Catholicism as an organic whole, a whole that is intuitively perceived, and a
whole that will attact precisely in and through its beautiful wholeness in
variety. This whole arises out of the spirit of the people; Möhler goes so
far as to note that in some eras the spirit of the people called for a strong
central authority but in other eras found a weak papacy quite sufficient.

At this point even the reader who has studied some church history
needs to be reminded of the really wretched state of the Catholic Church
in the earlier part of the nineteenth century. Consider what C. S. Phillips
says of the church in France after the revolutions of 1789 and 1830:

> Time was when the great Gallican Church had been proudly self-sufficient
> and needed neither support nor direction from the outside. If she allowed
> herself to be unduly deferential to the civil power, it was largely because
> she chose to have it so and because it suited her purposes. Her clergy
> formed the First Estate of the Realm; she had her own diocesan, provin-

cial and national assemblies; in the Sorbonne she possessed the most
famous school of theological thought and learning in the world, before
which even Rome itself might tremble. But all that had passed with the
*ancien régime.* Her servitude to the State remained, but none of the
prestige and resources that had made that servitude tolerable.[8]

The church had lost its financial endowment, its institutions of higher
learning, even the right to appoint its own bishops. Moreover, many
educated Frenchmen thought this situation *right:* the situation had re-
sulted not from some awful barbarian invasion but from the will of
successive national legislative assemblies. Though the church, in its
apologists, claimed to be rooted in the depths of the national character,
to many at the time it must have seemed a hoary outsider looking in to
the new order of things. What was true of France, rightly called the
eldest daughter of the church, was true elsewhere as well. Not only at its
beginning but throughout the nineteenth century the church throughout
Europe labored under severe financial, educational, and political dis-
abilities. Compared with what was happening in Europe, the course of
the church in the United States was sweetness and light. American
episcopal sees did not go vacant for years, as was the case in Europe; the
Know-Nothing movement seems trivial when compared with Napoleon
III's cynical manipulation of the church, Bismarck's *Kulturkampf,* or the
oppression of the Irish and the Poles. So the first part of this book takes
up romantic apologetics to an unfriendly world. We should note, however, that in working up his apologetic Möhler develops also a romantic
ecclesiology that has become a lasting ingredient of the Catholic style of
religion.

In part 2, we shall consider a kind of spinoff of the romantic vision of
a renewed church, albeit an extremely important one: part 2 deals with
philosophies of religion. An important reason that educated nineteenth-
century people thought the church an anachronism was that their thinking, or philosophy, was materialistic, rationalistic (i.e., disposed to deny
grace and miracle), or idealistic (i.e., disposed to deny that the mind
knows external, objective reality *as it is,* without introducing subjective
limitations of perception and understanding). We live in a time when, to
many, philosophy is either unimportant or restricted to mostly logical
problems, but our nineteenth-century forebears could not bring themselves to accept a church founded by a historical Redeemer sent by his
Father—and promising eternal heavenly happiness with Father, Son,
and Spirit—without having the *philosophical* way prepared for them.
Perhaps their way to religion was more clearly thought out, more truly
human, than ours.

    Catholic thinkers, therefore, busied themselves with the philosophy

of religion. In so doing, however, they ran afoul of a problem that has increasingly beset apologists as Western societies become secular and pluralistic, societies where religion is increasingly treated as the private business of the individual. It is as though the apologist or philosopher of religion has two heads: one of them is that of the advocate of old-time Catholicism, but the other belongs to a man or woman of his or her own time. Hence there arises the question of how much contemporaneity, and therefore apologetic persuasiveness, is compatible with what is being advocated. In this part of the anthology we shall find Georg Hermes modifying Kant for Catholic use, Anton Günther similarly modifying Hegel, Louis Bautain making lighter demands on philosophy though emphasizing a kind of critique of the societal transmission of knowledge, and finally, John Henry Newman striking a balance between empiricism and "reasoning" done in the service of faith.

Part 3 of the anthology is the Rock section. First we shall meet Joseph de Maistre, who argues for papal infallibility on the basis of a general theory of government. Then comes the American convert Orestes Brownson, who in discussing the apparitions at Lourdes argues that a Catholic understanding of salvation emphasizes the participation of the human in God's work. Next is another American, Peter Richard Kenrick, archbishop of St. Louis, who in a pamphlet distributed at Vatican I states that defining papal infallibility would be a mistake, too much emphasis on the Rock at the expense of local rights and sensibilities. Finally, part 3 includes the two dogmatic constitutions of Vatican I, wherein at the feet of Peter the Catholic episcopate affirms binding Catholic positions on faith and reason and on the role of Peter's successors, affirming, in the words of the title of this part, the "church as bearer of revelation."

Part 4 is entitled "Toward an Uncertain Future: Americanism, Neo-Scholasticism, and Modernism." To set a brake on witless reinterpretation of the Catholic nineteenth century, we must never forget that the Catholic episcopate, and after it the Catholic world, accepted the new dogmas of Vatican I with surprisingly little dissent. (That one of the dissenters was quite famous, the church historian Ignaz von Döllinger of Munich, should not blind us to the fact that dissent was minimal; for that matter, Döllinger would not even join the Old Catholic Church.)[9] Nevertheless, modernity did continue to assert itself; not even an ecumenical council could transport Catholics out of their daily lives. Committed Christians would necessarily seek to respond to the social problems of the later nineteenth century. In their doing so, however, would a fresh approach to society result in new *doctrines*? From the first selection in this part, a speech by John Ireland, archbishop of St. Paul, one senses

that this American prelate thought no. But in condemning "Americanism," Pope Leo XIII evidently thought yes. More to Leo's liking was the kind of theology represented by the second selection, in which Matthias Joseph Scheeben gives a modernized version of Thomas Aquinas's teaching on theological method. Still, could neo-scholasticism really be grafted onto modernity? Scheeben thought yes, but Edouard LeRoy thought no—and for his pains had his Modernism condemned by Pope Pius X. LeRoy, it is true, is not so well known as his fellow Modernists Alfred Loisy and George Tyrrell, but this Gallic logician in a short essay, the third selection, penetrates to the heart of the Modernists' difficulties with traditional Catholicism.

The volume, then, includes thirteen theologians and an ecumenical council. I do not overlook the fact that the thirteen are all Caucasian males. I can only say, That is how the nineteenth century was; we would come up with the same result if we were reviewing ministers of state or chefs. Among the thirteen, however, we can find the three who are arguably the greatest Catholic theologians of the century: Möhler, Newman,[10] and Scheeben. I make this claim on the basis of the volume of what they wrote, its range of subject matter, its orthodoxy and technical proficiency, and not least, its *literary* attractiveness and, not infrequently, power.

Can we find in nineteenth-century Catholic writers some remedies for what, at least to some readers, are weaknesses in present-day Catholicism?

The conservative Roman Catholic will no doubt reply that nineteenth-century Catholicism has much to tell the present. After all, in the conservative view, what the present-day church lacks, and what is the source of its other deficiencies, is proper respect for and obedience to the pope, our rock amid increasingly threatening currents of secularity, pluralism, and permissiveness generally. We must, it is said, return to the faith witness of the later nineteenth century, which gave us the Vatican decrees. On the other hand, the more liberal Catholic will also tell us to return to the nineteenth century, but to the *earlier* nineteenth century, where we can find alternatives to the Catholicism of 1914 that were too quickly passed over—above all, philosophies of religion that were more open to post-Kantian thought and, as regards church polity, a fully collegial understanding of the episcopate. Or the more liberal Catholic might turn to *very late* nineteenth-century Catholicism and find yet more alternatives to the Catholicism of 1914: an orientation to social action as providing not only needed service to fellow human beings but a new infusion of meaning to Christian existence, or the relative removal of the work of the historian, exegete, or theologian from papal or episcopal guidance. The conservative undeniably cherishes some of the romance of Catholicism, but the liberal cherishes much more.

It is difficult to prove the nonexistence of something, but I find no reason to disagree with the majority Catholic self-interpretations of 1870 and 1914. The (of necessity) late-nineteenth-century understanding of the nineteenth century must be honored and accepted. It cannot too much be stressed that after some initial scuffling the dogmas of Vatican I *stood,* and with them Leo XIII's condemnation of Americanism and Pius X's condemnation of Modernism. The sanction for nonacceptance was excommunication, which in some cases was actually applied, as with Döllinger and Loisy though not with LeRoy. Here the double bind that beset Archbishop Kenrick applies: how can you disagree in the name of the church if a "morally unanimous" church accepts what you disagree with? So Kenrick accepted Vatican I, and so, I think, must we—as, of course, the Catholic church's self-interpretation at a certain stage of history. It is perhaps worth noting that all the writers in this volume died in communion with Rome, even though Rome had given some of them a great deal of difficulty.

To be sure, there is no limit to possible twentieth-century schemes for reinterpreting the nineteenth century, provided that one recognizes that these, as some would have it, "illuminations" of the nineteenth century were not consciously shared by those of our forebears lucky to be so illumined. This open-endedness of subsequent revision is an additional reason why in an introductory volume of this kind I have thought it wiser to emphasize the traditional interpretation of the Catholic nineteenth century. I must recognize, nonetheless, that some readers will think this emphasis has limited in an unfortunate way the selection of readings. True, the divergent views of Hermes, Günther, Bautain, Kenrick, and LeRoy are presented, but all the selections in the volume deal with faith and reason and church polity. The contemporary Christian who sees in socially beneficial action not only a consequence of belief and polity but a determinant of a subsequent stage of belief and polity might well want to see included some selections devoted to "Catholic social teaching."

As I have noted, the historian is more comfortable with the nineteenth century's overt interpretation of the nineteenth century. But there are other pertinent considerations. We in the twentieth century have got so used to the functioning of the disestablished church in contemporary democracies that we tend to forget that *an enormous amount of effort on the part of the nineteenth-century Catholic Church went into fighting for its very right not only to act but even just to speak in social matters.* And apologetics, the philosophy of religion, and a tightening-up of church organization are precisely the preparation of the basis and of the chance of social commentary and action. If there were a second volume to this anthology, that volume might quite properly be devoted to social questions. But first some consideration must be given to how the church's mandate and right to speak and act were argued for. Hence the contents of this volume. Vatican I's insistence that the pope's teaching cannot be interfered with by any civil government must be understood in the context of, for example, the French sentiment that led to the Law of Associations in 1901 and the separation of church and state in 1905.[11] (Paradoxically, in the United States, where separation of church and state was the law of the land, Catholics had to argue through the whole nineteenth century—and beyond—that Catholicism is not un-American and hence can in actual practice participate in public debate and in movements for social reform. Even today some Americans would agree with Samuel F. B. Morse, who in 1836 wrote that "the modes of influencing elections which the priests adopt in France correspond with facts already multiplying on this side of the Atlantic.")[12] It is above all the pervasive governmental interference that the nineteenth-century church experienced that explains the triumph of the Rock and of ultramontanism. The French priest and writer Félicité de Lamennais, too early in the century for his own good—he ended up excommunicated—proposed that disestablishment at home, and even a measure of democracy, could be counterbalanced by a strong, supranational papacy.[13] To maintain the possibility of Christian witness, and perhaps for lesser motives, the papacy was only too happy from mid-century on to receive the pleas arising from its embattled flock for its own enhancement—without, however, the enthusiasm for democracy that some of the flock cherished.[14]

Another factor influencing the exclusion from this volume of social questions is the complexity of nineteenth-century Catholic social teaching. It is a large subject, in that it logically includes not only church disestablishment and the relations of capital and labor but also education, family matters (mixed marriages, birth control), temperance (the nineteenth-century drug problem), art and culture generally (including liturgical reform),[15] science, war, race, and colonialism. Perhaps not just another volume but a wheelbarrow full of volumes would be needed. Moreover, Catholics were far from being of one mind on these issues. Pius IX actually had a papal army, though it did not fight very much.[16] Then as now, some Catholics, loyal to the papacy in other matters, had great difficulty hearing papal teaching on social justice. After, though not because, the Catholic general P. T. Beauregard of the Confederacy fired the first shot of the American Civil War many Americans considered the Catholic church pro-Southern, and so on and on. Nineteenth-century Catholic social teaching is highly complex, with many topics, on which there were many shades of opinion. For the moment, at least, it is enough to attend to how Catholics based their right to speak and act publicly.

But even though the nineteenth century—or at least this collection of nineteenth-century documents—is of limited use in twentieth-century problem-solving, there remain some constant, enduring traits of Catholicism that call for attention. This is true no matter whether, out of pastoral concerns, one sees in these traits criteria for the authenticity of future developments in Catholicism or, out of humanist or literary interests, one wishes to sharpen one's ability to discern the essence of the Catholic style of being religious.

In the first place, then, Catholicism is *realistic;* it is, if you will, "thingy." However mystical it may become in an individual life, it never loses its absorption with or love for the sensuously immediate: for sacraments, a tendency toward biblical literalism, vestments, candles, incense, all of this. In Hegelian terms, it moves contentedly in the realm of the *Vorstellung.* Speaking of the principal Catholic sacrament, the eucharist, Miguel de Unamuno in his *Tragic Sense of Life* says,

> The sacrament is genuinely realist—*dinglich,* as the Germans would say—which may without great violence be translated "material." It is the sacrament most genuinely *ex opere operato,* for which is substituted among Protestants the idealistic sacrament of the word.

With all due reverence, he continues, the sacrament is concerned with the "eating and drinking of God, the Eternalizer." Unamuno's Spanish Catholic background notwithstanding, he finds this perplexing:

> The Catholic solution of our problem, of our unique vital problem, the problem of the immortality and eternal salvation of the individual soul, satisfies the will, and therefore satisfies life; but the attempt to rationalize it by means of dogmatic theology fails to satisfy the reason.[17]

On the other hand, recent sociologists and anthropologists of religion, with a broader view of our problems if less concerned to satisfy reason in every way, have found in Catholic realism a kind of earth religion preserved. One almost hears them murmuring prayers of thanks to Saint Pius X for preserving the stuff of Catholicism so that we, with our heightened sociological and anthropological awareness and methodologies, can admire and study it. Perhaps truth and balance lie somewhere in between, but the reader should find it no surprise that nineteenth-century Catholics were so committed to working out an adequate philosophy of religion. Neo-scholasticism[18] no doubt became the majority view because it seemed to promise, with its epistemological realism, a sure approach to the historical Redeemer, to the sacramental system, and to the papal and episcopal guardians of religious truth. It also upheld the spirituality and hence immortality of the soul. Unamuno unerringly hit a further facet of Catholicism in his remarks on the "bread of life." Traditional Catholicism, on earth, is but a means to an end; heaven is the goal, and without that goal Catholicism makes no sense at all—at least nineteenth-century Catholicism. One feels in reading nineteenth-century Catholic apologists that being outsiders to dominant public opinion did not bother them all that much, for they thought of heaven as their true home. In this they were doubtless aided by the widespread nineteenth-century fascination with death and dying.

Realism about the human soul, however, results in another constant characteristic of Catholicism: *synergism,* or the conviction that men and women have free wills and can, indeed must, cooperate with God in the work of their eternal salvation. The Brownson selection in this volume is a fine statement of this conviction. Another way of looking at Catholic synergism is to see it as rooted in the Catholic (Tridentine) dogma of Adam and Eve's fall. Whatever else the original pair may have lost, they did not lose free will, and hence did not lose the ability to cooperate freely with grace. As that genial defender of all things Catholic, G. K. Chesterton, wrote,

> The Fall is a view of life. It is not only the only enlightening, but the only encouraging view of life. It holds, as against the only real alternative philosophies, those of the Buddhist or the Pessimist or the Promethean, that we have misused a good world, and not merely been entrapped into a bad one. It refers evil back to a wrong use of the will, and thus declares that it can eventually be righted by the right use of the will. Every other creed except that one is some form of surrender to fate.[19]

Whether he knew it or not, Chesterton in 1930 was walking exactly in the footsteps of Möhler, who said that Luther's denial of free will made alternately Promethean or fatalistic idealists like Schleiermacher, as opposed to confessional Protestants, the only genuine disciples of Luther.[20] That would seem to be an overstatement, but it is undeniable that realism and synergism are constant and central traits to Catholicism.

It is in directing attention to these traits of Catholicism that we can see also the underlying difference between nineteenth-century Catholics and nineteenth-century Protestants. As is plain to anyone, some countries were culturally Catholic and some were Protestant; and some people, Catholics, said the pope was important, and others, Protestants, did not much care—unless, like W. E. Gladstone, they thought the pope might dispense the Catholics from civil obedience.[21] With all due respect to the social services provided throughout the nineteenth century by the Catholic religious orders, it nevertheless seems that the social problems faced by Catholics and Protestants, and the solutions offered by each, were not markedly different. Whether the ladle was Catholic or Protestant the soup was pretty much the same. At a deeper level, however, *we must attend to how Catholic realism attaches to history: what was once real is still real, what was once binding is still binding.* That is why, as Möhler saw clearly enough, a Catholic Schleiermacher is inconceivable—not to mention a Catholic Troeltsch. Or rather, a Catholic Troeltsch would have been a Catholic Modernist and would have been excommunicated right along with the rest by Pius X.[22] What really distinguishes nineteenth-century Catholics from their Protestant contemporaries is their conviction, sometimes maintained in agony, that they must carry their whole past along with them because it is all somehow pertinent. This conviction it is that gives Catholic apologetic writing the tone of seeking a restoration of the good old days, either a quite real restoration of throne and altar, as the ecclesiastical supporters of assorted Bourbons wanted, or a restoration of sensibilities, as Chesterton desired in this century.

It is true, of course, that Protestants were often readier—or freer—to accept changes in biblical scholarship than Catholics. But, I submit, the question of biblical interpretation should not be overemphasized. Nineteenth-century Catholics tended to see advanced Protestant positions on the Bible as a kind of halfway house between faith and agnosticism—or perhaps as the fate of those whose faith was wanting in correct dogmatic content. An editorial in the Paulist Fathers' *Catholic World* magazine in 1885, commenting on the American bishops' recent plenary council, states that

> ex-Protestants now far outnumber Protestants. We are fighting for the Bible itself with ex-Protestants; we are fighting for a trust in a future life with the children of the Pilgrim Fathers; we are especially fighting against the delusion of vast multitudes that the nobility of human nature is somehow debased by the simplicity of Christ's gospel; and these make up the big fight of the Catholic Church.

The editorial notes further that

> when the institutions of this nation are let do their work they unconsciously favor the triumph of Christianity, which in its concrete, organic existence is the Roman Catholic Church.

The editorialist praises the American bishops for their conviction that

> American political institutions are in advance of those of Europe in

helping a man to save his soul, and . . . promise a triumph for Catholicity more perfect than its victory in medieval times.[23]

The real problems are rationalism and political oppression. The real solution is realistic, synergistic, organic Catholicism. But even the image of triumph to come does not lead the writer to forget the thirteenth century.

We have seen how centralizing tendencies in the nineteenth-century Catholic church prepared the way for its twentieth-century form. We have also noted certain abiding characteristics of Catholicism, characteristics certainly discernible in its nineteenth-century form but not present in it in such a way as to suggest—without the intrusion of concerns from our time—that the nineteenth century offers a repertory of reforms to the twentieth. But it is possible to study nineteenth-century Catholic theology simply because it is humanly interesting. If what we have seen thus far could be summed up, if narrowly, in Pius IX's celebrated aphorism "*I* am tradition,"[24] the reflections to follow will, finally, allow free play to the romantic side of Catholicism. Consider the words of the "liberal"—and quite non-Catholic—poet and critic Matthew Arnold:

> I persist in thinking that the prevailing form for the Christianity of the future will be the form of Catholicism, but a Catholicism purged, opening itself to the light and air, having the consciousness of its own poetry, freed from sacerdotal despotism and freed from its pseudo-scientific apparatus of superannuated dogma.[25]

To be sure, if Arnold had been a Catholic he too would have been a Modernist; in fact his writings were to some extent influential on the Modernist Tyrrell.

Light a candle and bless yourself, if need be, but allow me a few lines on a Catholicism "having the consciousness of its own poetry." My evocation of the Modernist perspective[26] arises less from a concern to change the Catholic Church than from my eighteen years in the classroom, teaching the subject of this volume and related materials. In short, for the student, or teacher, who belongs to no particular religious tradition or who has but a hazy perception of his or her own tradition, the Modernist perspective is the only one in which the splendid theological literature of past eras can be seen to *live*. Continuing attention and cherishing is, I deeply believe, the tribute we owe to the love and care that a Möhler, a Newman, or a Scheeben lavished on his work. Whether provisional or permanent, adoption of a Modernist perspective is the only way many modern readers can approach and be touched and enriched by the great theological literature of the past.

A Catholicism having the consciousness of its own poetry is a Catholicism in which doctrine has been reconverted into myth—but myth, this time, that is *known to be myth*. This is the *consciousness* referred to. Some doctrines reconvert readily into myth, as for example, Jesus' institution of the eucharist. Others need a kind of two-stage conversion: first the doctrine must be viewed in terms of someone's acceptance of or witness to it, and then the story of that acceptance or witness must be held up as a paradigmatic story, or myth. There is no reason why a historical occurrence cannot in the retelling—or maybe even in itself— have this paradigmatic character. (In regard to the communion of saints, a nineteenth-century book title makes this point with beautiful simplicity: for children Bishop John Lancaster Spalding wrote a *History of the Church of God from the Creation to the Present Time*.[27] Medieval and renaissance saints are quite as much part of the story as Hebraic patriarchs and prophets.) Here the doctrine is viewed as the great mythic story, the story is seen to be lived by paradigmatic "heroes," and then one's own religious experience, one's own story, is viewed in terms of the great story of the religious community or tradition. In this case the individual's story becomes a kind of minor myth—or more exactly, model—for explaining his or her own existence.

Now suppose the individual is a writer of theological books. These books, if they are not merely technically proficient but also resonant in a literary sense—that is, if their subject matter is integrated with the personal quest of the writer and if that integration becomes visible in the writer's choice of vantage point and language—*such books, I would say, can be read as religious autobiography*. In short, Newman is the *protagonist* of, say, his *Grammar of Assent,* Möhler of his *Symbolik,* Scheeben of his *Mysterien des Christentums*. Readers have long sensed this about Newman. Möhler, unfortunately, is not well known in the English-speaking world, but the same can to a surprising degree be said of him. Scheeben is more the schoolmaster, but the mask slips occasionally, as when he calls his lifework a "science full of delights." In adopting the form of letters, Günther and Bautain were seemingly aiming in their work for the personal touch, and what might we say of the dramatic ending of Kenrick's Vatican Council speech? And then there is Chateaubriand the novelist, and so on, down to stuffy old Hermes, who is at least sincere. After all the apologists of all the faiths have had their say, there is really only one form of suasion in matters religious, or just as much, in matters literary: Try it, you'll like it. Having tried it, the reader may find that he or she likes reading theology as autobiography.

For the English-speaking reader, mention of the Modernist approach may well bring to mind the pragmatist William James.[28] But we can go a step further. Behind the Modernist approach as it has been applied here stands William James's younger brother Henry. I can think of no better example of how to understand the better sort of theological writer than how we view a major character in a Henry James novel. I have particularly in mind the point, toward the end of the story, where someone says to the character, "So there you are."[29] In other words, your living and striving within a certain set of conditions have inescapably produced, you being you, the insight, self-knowledge, and self-acceptance that you have. Similarly, for the thirteen writers included in this volume, nineteenth-century Catholicism was the self-imposed or at least willingly accepted theater, or novel setting, of their own development. Theirs the romance, theirs too the Rock. Just as we do not expect a Jamesian character to walk out of the novel's setting and away from his or her fate, so let us cherish these nineteenth-century Catholics, each in his place. To the degree that each plumbed the possibilities of that place he achieved such humanness as may appeal to us and enrich us in our place.

## NOTES

1. The best introduction to romanticism in religion I have seen is Bernard M. G. Reardon's *Religion in the Age of Romanticism: Studies in Early Nineteenth Century Thought* (New York and Cambridge: Cambridge Univ. Press, 1985), esp. vii–ix, 1–28. Pages 117–45 deal with German Catholic theology and include a good short summary of the difficult thought of Günther. It should be kept in mind—and Reardon, it seems, would agree—that guided experience in art history, especially the history of music, is a first-class way of learning what romanticism was and is. In my own case a first glimmering of this point occurred after I as a young organ student had played the second movement of Mendelssohn's second organ sonata rather badly. My teacher, René Dosogne, to whose memory this volume is dedicated, then played it properly, commenting, "*That* is romantic!" My lessons were held in a fine neo-Gothic church—Saint Ita's, Chicago—and as a young person I used to feel that music in this church manifested within it the same force that entered from the outside through the stained glass or at night somehow energized the stonework of the church. Later I played the music of, and became interested in the life of, Louis Vierne, organist of Notre Dame de Paris from 1900 till his death, while actually playing, in 1937. In his memoirs the (very late) romantic Vierne said of the organ of Notre Dame, "Il me sembla figurer la voix surnaturelle de la cathédrale, tant il se mariait avec la pierre. Il m'a ainsi donné, durant trente-sept années, l'impression quasi miraculeuse que, loin de jouer d'un instrument dans la cathédrale, je m'incorporais à elle; j'y ai connu le plus complet comme le plus grisant sentiment de domination, de possession totale, à quoi peut aspirer un artiste" (Bernard Gavoty, *Louis Vierne: La vie et l'oeuvre* [Paris, 1943], 276). See also *The American Organist* 14/11 (November 1980, an issue on Vierne), especially Scott

Cantrell, "Louis Vierne: His Life and Works," 42–49. Vierne's memoirs have
been translated by J. R. Crawford as *Mes Souvenirs, by Louis Vierne: An
Annotated Translation* (Ann Arbor, Mich.: UMI, 1973). I mention Vierne for
more than purely personal reasons. Studying Catholic *thought,* even in far larger
doses than possible in this anthology, should be complemented with reading
about Catholic *life,* above all in biographies and novels. Readers interested in
novels might well begin with the accounts of Irish clerical life, particularly *Luke
Delmege* (1901), by Canon P. A. Sheehan, or the account of Spanish town life in
*La Regenta* (1885), by Leopoldo Alas (trans. John Rutherford [Athens: Univ. of
Georgia Press, 1984]). There are significant qualitative differences between the
Catholicism of the so-called baby-boom and later generations and that of earlier
generations. Younger Catholics, even younger *conservative* Catholics engaging
in introspection, are not always aware that this is so—a deficiency that reading
biographies and novels can help overcome. With respect to the novel as histor-
ically illuminating, see the anthology *The Exiles of Erin: Nineteenth-Century
Irish-American Fiction,* ed. Charles Fanning (Notre Dame, Ind.: Univ. of Notre
Dame Press, 1987).
    2. C. S. Phillips, *The Church in France, 1848–1907* (London, 1936; New
York: Russell & Russell, 1967), 294ff. Regarding the effect of the condemnation
of Modernism, see Adrien Dansette, *Religious History of Modern France,* trans.
and abridg. John Dingle (New York: Herder & Herder, 1961), 309–14. See also
the discussion of Pius XII's encyclical *Humani Generis* (1950) in James M.
Connolly, *The Voices of France: A Survey of Contemporary Theology in France*
(New York: Macmillan, 1961), 173–215.
    3. See Stephen Neill, *Colonialism and Christian Missions* (New York:
McGraw-Hill, 1966). How often Catholics in all these places actually went to
church is quite another matter; the reader is warned against assuming that the
relatively high level of current Americans' involvement with organized religion is
to be found in other times and places.
    4. Adolf von Harnack, *History of Dogma,* trans. Neil Buchanan (reprint,
Gloucester, Mass.: Peter Smith, 1961), 7:80. Harnack seems to have got his *old
lion* from Madame de Staël; see her thoughtful discussion of Catholicism in *De
l'Allemagne* (London, 1813), part 4, chap. 4.
    5. Harnack, *Dogma* 7:110.
    6. Williston Walker et al., *A History of the Christian Church,* 4th ed. (New
York: Macmillan Co., 1985); and Paul Johnson, *A History of Christianity* (New
York: Atheneum, 1976).
    7. Edgar Hocedez, *Histoire de la théologie au XIXe siècle,* vol. 1 (Paris,
1948), 8.
    8. Ibid.
    9. Johann Joseph Ignaz von Döllinger (1799–1890) could not accept the
definition of papal infallibility; his commentary on Vatican I, published
pseudonymously as the work of Janus and Quirinus, is listed in the section of the
Bibliography on the First Vatican Council. See also Lord Acton's "The Munich
Congress," in *Essays on Church and State,* ed. Douglas Woodruff (London,
1952), 159–99; and Hugh MacDougall's *The Acton-Newman Relations: The
Dilemma of Christian Liberalism* (New York: Fordham Univ. Press, 1962), esp.
108–39.
    10. Feeling, thought, and language are too closely connected for the student

to overlook the fact that Newman is one of the two truly great theologians *to write in English*. The other is the Anglican Richard Hooker (ca. 1553–1600).

11. See Phillips, *Church in France, 1848–1907*, 259–89; Dansette, *Religious History*, 187–264. See also Malcolm O. Partin, *Waldeck-Rousseau, Combes, and the Church, 1899–1905; The Politics of Anti-Clericalism* (Durham, N.C.: Duke Univ. Press, 1969); John McManners, *Church and State in France, 1870–1940* (London, 1972); and Maurice Larkin, *Church and State after the Dreyfus Affair: The Separation Issue in France* (New York: Barnes & Noble, 1974). Students interested in Catholic social teaching might begin with Georges Goyau's *L'épanouissement social du credo* (Paris, 1931). Goyau also edited, in French translation, an anthology of selected writings by an extremely important figure, Wilhelm Emmanuel von Ketteler (1811–77), bishop of Mainz: *Ketteler* (Paris, 1907). There is a useful introduction on pp. ix–xlviii of that volume. See also *The Social Teachings of Wilhelm Emmanuel von Ketteler*, trans. Rupert J. Ederer (Washington, D.C.: Univ. Press of America, 1981). For the United States, see Aaron I. Abell, *American Catholics and Social Action* (Notre Dame, Ind.: Univ. of Notre Dame Press, 1963). See also below, selection 12, n. 21.

12. The painter and inventor of the telegraph was quite anti-Catholic. See Samuel F. B. Morse, "Professor in the University of the City of New York," ed., *Confessions of a French Catholic Priest, to Which Are Added Warnings to the People of the United States by the Same Author* (New York, 1837). The quotation is from the editor's introduction, p. x.

13. Concerning Lamennais, see C. S. Phillips, *Church in France, 1789–1848* (London, 1929; New York: Russell & Russell, 1967) 216–58; Dansette, *Religious History*, 207–26; Reardon, *Religion*, 176–206; and idem, *Liberalism and Tradition: Aspects of Catholic Thought in Nineteenth-Century France* (New York and Cambridge: Cambridge Univ. Press, 1975), 62–112. Catholics searching for forerunners of present-day social theory should, in fairness, bear in mind that conservatives like Chateaubriand and de Maistre, and Jaime Balmes and Juan Donoso Cortés, were in *their* day just as Catholic as Lamennais in the earlier part of his life. Concerning Balmes and Donoso Cortés, see the annotation appended to the Chateaubriand section of the Bibliography.

14. For a fine discussion of how the meaning of *ultramontanism* shifted in mid-century, see Phillips, *Church in France, 1848–1907*, 1–21.

15. In checking a footnote of Archbishop Kenrick's, I came across this interesting early-nineteenth-century view of Catholic church music:

> Sacred music in the modern Italian style is more pleasing; but it is little calculated to promote devotion, the only legitimate object of music composed for the church. *There* let that music, and that music only, be performed which is at once simple and solemn, which all can feel and in which most can join. Let it be strictly confined to pure melody; let the congregation be taught to sing it in exact unison and with subdued voices; let the accompaniment be full and chaste, never overwhelm the voice; and if it can be managed, in chanting the psalms, let the trebles and tenors sing alternately—in a word, let it be the Gregorian song. . . . And let it be accompanied by a Novello [Vincent, 1781–1861, organist of the Portuguese embassy chapel, London, and founder of the publishing firm]. A service thus performed will excite the finest feelings of piety, promote rational devotion, and in time equally satisfy the scientific and the unlearned. . . . If the evangelical sects gain so much, . . . is it not in some

measure owing the superior attraction of their music, and that a part of it is allowed to everyone who will bear a part in it? (Charles Butler, *Historical Memoirs of the English, Irish, and Scottish Catholics from the Reformation to the Present Time,* 3d ed. [London, 1822], 4:465–68) Butler's wish was granted, but only in part and toward the end of the century, with the revival of Gregorian chant by the Benedictines of Solesmes, the abbey founded by the liturgical reformer Dom Prosper Guéranger. Concerning Guéranger and other nineteenth-century liturgical reformers, see R. W. Franklin's articles in *Worship* 49 (1975): 318–28, 50 (1976): 146–62, 51 (1977): 378–99, 53 (1979): 12–39, and 59 (1985): 342–53. Franklin's article of 1985 is a response to Thomas F. O'Meara's "The Origins of the Liturgical Movement and German Romanticism," *Worship* 59 (1985): 326–42. The Gregorian reform never took hold as its proponents wished: on this and related matters in *American* Catholic church music, see Archbishop Rembert Weakland, O.S.B., "The Bishop and Music for Worship," *Worship* 57 (1983): 35–45. One of the brighter spots in American Catholic music was the founding of the now defunct Paulist Choristers by William J. Finn, C. S. P., first in Chicago in 1904 and then in New York in 1918. Finn in his autobiography locates the Choristers in the general Paulist apostolate of making Catholicism appealing to Protestants (*Sharps and Flats in Five Decades* [New York: Harper & Bros., 1947], 69–70, 85).

16. Rome has often been careless of its friends and defenders. I once had a student whose great-grandfather had been a papal zouave—for which service the family received a dispensation in perpetuity from fish on Friday. But in our century the rules on Friday abstinence changed.

17. Miguel de Unamuno, *Tragic Sense of Life,* trans. J. E. Crawford Flitch (reprint, New York: Dover Pubs., 1954), 66, 78. The original Spanish text was published in 1912.

18. In the Bibliography there is a separate section on neo-scholasticism and Thomism.

19. G. K. Chesterton, *The Thing: Why I Am a Catholic* (New York, 1930), 226. Catholic apologists directed their attention chiefly to rationalists and agnostics, in which pursuit exegetical ameliorations seem almost irrelevant. According to Chesterton, to raise objections against the doctrine of the Fall "by saying, 'Where is the Garden of Eden?' is like answering a philosophical Buddhist by saying, 'When were you last a donkey?' " For the philosophical Catholic, free will belongs to human nature, or essence, and therefore *cannot* be lost.

20. See Johann Adam Möhler, *Symbolik; oder, Darstellung der dogmatischen Gegensätze der Katholiken und Protestanten nach ihren öffentlichen Bekenntnisschriften,* ed. Josef Rupert Geiselmann, 2 vols. (Cologne: Hegner, 1960–61), 301–2.

21. Gladstone's objection and Cardinal Newman's response may be found in *Newman and Gladstone: The Vatican Decrees,* ed. Alvan S. Ryan (Notre Dame, Ind.: Univ. of Notre Dame Press, 1962).

22. The reader desirous of comparing the Protestant opposites of the Catholic positions in this volume can most usefully consult B. A. Gerrish's *The Old Protestantism and the New: Essays on the Reformation Heritage* (Chicago: Univ. of Chicago Press, 1982). The difference between the more progressive Catholics and the more progressive Protestants lies in the area of the development of doctrine, in that the Catholics while admitting developments insist that the past

retains its *prescriptive* force—in, that is, a much more *detailed* way than is the case among progressive Protestants.

23. *Catholic World,* February 1885, 714. I have taken the liberty of calling these remarks editorial, because the article from which they are taken ("The Catholic National Council," pp. 708–14) is unsigned. At this time Isaac Hecker was still serving as editor of the journal.

24. On the famous *I am,* see J. B. Bury, *History of the Papacy in the Nineteenth Century,* ed. R. H. Murray (London, 1930), 124; and A. B. Hasler, *How the Pope Became Infallible: Pius IX and the Politics of Persuasion,* trans. Peter Heinegg (New York: Doubleday & Co., 1981), 91–92, 120, 338–40. No matter what Pius IX actually said, the parallel with the Bourbons must be dismaying for Catholics minded to democratize, or "collegialize," the church. There can, it seems, be no *evolution* toward true sharing of power in the case of monarchy by divine right. If the ruler does not receive power from the ruled, neither can he give it to them. If they claim that it belongs to them by right they only invite trouble if they pretend to receive it from him. It may be possible, however, to analyze the modern growth of papal power in quite another way, namely, as a *response* to the population explosion beginning in the nineteenth century. Papal power grew at the expense of local elites, and one wonders if at least the *effect* of this growth was that the papacy helped fill the leadership vacuum afflicting "mass-man" and so deplored by José Ortega y Gasset in *The Revolt of the Masses* (New York: W. W. Norton & Co., 1932). But providing leadership for the masses is not always distinguishable from providing what the masses *want,* in this case, from what the papacy considers the great majority of its followers expect from it. In the latter hypothesis the democratization of the church has advanced rather more than many friends of the papacy would be willing to admit.

25. Matthew Arnold, "Irish Catholicism and British Liberalism," in *The Works of Matthew Arnold,* vol. 10, *Mixed Essays* (reprint, New York: AMS Press, 1970), 116. Arnold's understanding of Catholicism prefigures later social scientists' prizing it as "earth religion."

> Catholicism is that form of Christianity which is fullest of human accretions and superstitions, because it is the oldest, the largest, the most popular. (P. 111)

> But when [as Arnold hopes will be the case] Ultramontanism, sacerdotalism, and superstition are gone, Catholicism is not, as some may suppose, gone too. Neither is it left with nothing further but what it possesses in common with all forms of Christianity—the curative power of the word, character, and influence of Jesus. It is, indeed, left with this, which is the root of the matter, but it is left with a mighty power besides. It is left with the beauty, the richness, the poetry, the infinite charm for the imagination, of its own age-long growth, a growth [that is] unconscious, popular, profoundly rooted, all-enveloping. (P. 114)

The reader interested in speculating about the future of Catholicism may wish to compare this essay by Arnold with Andrew M. Greeley and Mary Greeley Durkin's *How to Save the Catholic Church* (New York: Viking Press, 1984). Greeley and Durkin would scarcely dispute Arnold's contention that higher education for the Irish promises benefits not only for the Irish but for too-

Puritan WASPS too! But Greeley and Durkin use the term *romantic* in, I believe, a misleading way; in the more usual sense of the term their sense of the Catholic church, and of how to save it, is altogether romantic.

26. I mean *the* Modernist perspective or approach in the sense of Pius X's encyclical *Pascendi Dominici,* esp. par. 12, where dogma is spoken of as *symbol.*

27. John Lancaster Spalding, *History of the Church of God from the Creation to the Present Time* (New York, 1884).

28. William James's pragmatism would seem to be a parallel phenomenon to, rather than a source of, Catholic Modernism. See James's own remarks in the preface to *Pragmatism,* in *William James: Writings, 1902–1910* (New York: Library of America, 1987), 481–82. Also of interest is Walter Marshall Horton's *The Philosophy of the Abbé Bautain* (New York, 1926), 199 n. 175, 289–93. Bernard M. G. Reardon (in his edited volume *Roman Catholic Modernism* [Stanford, Calif.: Stanford Univ. Press, 1970], 59 n. 2) notes that R. B. Braithwaite's *An Empiricist's View of the Nature of Religious Belief* (Cambridge: Cambridge Univ. Press, 1956) is a later example of the kind of pragmatist thinking engaged in by the Modernists.

29. In the preface to the New York edition of *The Ambassadors* Henry James writes of Lambert Strether,

> He has . . . missed too much, though perhaps after all constitutionally qualified for a better part, and he wakes up to it in conditions that press the spring of a terrible question. *Would* there yet perhaps be time for reparation?—reparation, that is, for the injury done his character; for the affront, he is quite ready to say, so stupidly put upon it and in which he has even himself had so clumsy a hand? The answer to which is that he now at all events *sees;* so that the business of my tale and the march of my action, not to say the precious moral of everything, is just my demonstration of this process of vision. (Henry James, *Literary Criticism: American and English Writers,* ed. Leon Edel and Mark Wilson [New York: Library of America, 1984], 1305).

# PART ONE

# The New
# Romantic Vision

# 1

# Christianity as Revealed

## François-René de Chateaubriand

On April 14, 1802, Chateaubriand's *Genius of Christianity* made its first appearance, and on the following April 18 Easter mass was reintroduced at Notre Dame in Paris. Both events, and the celebrity of the over-six-hundred-page book, may be taken as indicators that for many Frenchmen the revolution had gone too far. It was now necessary, while retaining the improvements brought by the tumultuous revolutionary years, to return to the sources of French life and of public order—to return, therefore, to Catholicism.

Viscount François-René de Chateaubriand (1768–1848) was a many-sided, complex man—traveler, author of real merit, diplomat, and man of the world generally (the steak was named for him). Born in Saint-Malo and educated in his native Brittany, he toured the United States in 1791—going as far as the Mississippi—and later the Near East. This was to develop background for his novels. He fought for the royalist cause on the eastern border of France and then spent a period of exile in England. After the Bourbon restoration he served as French ambassador in Berlin, London, and Rome, and in 1822–24 as foreign minister. The years after 1830 found him in the political opposition but also afforded him the opportunity to compose his autobiography, *Mémoires d'outre-tombe*. But it was the death of his mother and of one of his sisters that, together with political events, had turned his mind to religion around 1800, and to the production of *The Genius of Christianity*.

Though some have doubted both the sincerity and the cogency of Chateaubriand's defense of Catholic Christianity, the plan of his work is clear. Previous apologists, he writes, have started from the mission of Jesus Christ and then descended from one conclusion to another to establish the truths of faith. But this will no longer do: "This mode of reasoning, which might have suited the seventeenth century extremely well, when the groundwork was not contested, proved of no use in our days." The apologist of 1802 must move in the opposite direction, "must ascend from effect to cause—not prove that the Christian religion is excellent because it comes from God, but that it comes from God because it is excellent." In other words, this work is a romantic apologetic.

A romantic apologetic, then, will concentrate on the organic whole that is Western culture, arguing that this living totality could not have arisen and cannot happily continue without revealed Christianity as its animating principle. The twentieth-century reader may well wonder just what the probative force of this approach might be, particularly since our awareness of the interplay of religion and culture has been sharpened and our confidence in Western culture, if not shaken, at least rendered more modest. To understand Chateaubriand, we will need to grant him, provisionally, that some very important groundwork is not contested—the superiority of Western culture, especially in Catholic lands— and we will also need to accept, again provisionally, that an aesthetic mode of proof is useful in religious matters. What concerns Chateaubriand is the impression made by Christianity holistically presented. Logical cogency is important, but even more important is the impact of the great story on one's sensibilities, on one's life. And so, as one commentator on French musical romanticism has observed, Chateaubriand "made his pictures live vividly in the imagination; . . . he developed the grand orchestra of words as Berlioz later created the grand orchestra of sounds."

*The Genius* is divided into four parts. The first of these takes up the basic truths of Christianity: Trinity, Fall and redemption, virtue, sacraments and Scripture, and the philosophical questions of the existence of God and the immortality of the soul. The second and third are devoted to the influence of Christianity on the humanities, especially the fine arts. The fourth part discusses liturgical rites, the life of Christ our model, the secular clergy, the religious orders and their numerous forms of service (especially in the foreign missions), and the economic and political benefits of Christianity. The author concludes, "Christianity is a revealed religion."

## PART I, BOOK I

### 1. Introduction

Ever since Christianity was first published to the world it has been continually assailed by three kinds of enemies—heretics, sophists, and those apparently frivolous characters who destroy everything with the shafts of ridicule. Numerous apologists have given victorious answers to subtleties and falsehoods, but they have not been so successful against derision. St. Ignatius of Antioch, St. Irenaeus, Bishop of Lyons, Tertullian, in his *Prescriptions,* which Bossuet calls *divine,* combated the innovators of their time, whose extravagant expositions corrupted the simplicity of the faith.

Calumny was first repulsed by Quadratus and Aristides, philosophers of Athens. We know, however, nothing of their apologies for Christianity, except a fragment of the former, which Eusebius has preserved.[1] Both he and St. Jerome speak of the work of Aristides as a masterpiece of eloquence.

The Pagans accused the first Christians of atheism, incest, and certain abominable feasts, at which they were said to partake of the flesh of a newborn infant. After Quadratus and Aristides, St. Justin pleaded the cause of the Christians. His style is unadorned, and the circumstances attending his martyrdom prove that he shed his blood for religion with the same sincerity with which he had written in its defence. Athenagoras has shown more address in his apology, but he has neither the originality of Justin nor the impetuosity of the author of the *Apologetic.* Tertullian is the unrefined Bossuet of Africa. St. Theophilus, in his three books addressed to his friend Autolychus, displays imagination and learning; and the *Octavius* of Minucius Felix exhibits the pleasing picture of a Christian and two idolaters conversing on religion and the nature of God during a walk along the seashore.

Arnobius, the rhetorician, Lactantius, Eusebius, and St. Cyprian also defended Christianity, but their efforts were not so much directed to the display of its beauty as to the exposure of the absurdities of idolatry.

Origen combated the sophists and seems to have had the advantage over Celsus, his antagonist, in learning, argument, and style. The Greek

From *Génie du christianisme,* crit. ed. Louis Louvet, Chefs-d'oeuvre de la littérature (Paris: Garnier, n.d.), 5–23, 410–16, 505–6, 522–26, 534–37, 539–40. The translation is from *The Genius of Christianity,* trans. Charles I. White (Baltimore, 1856), 43–65, 526–33, 642–43, 664–68, 678–82, 684–85. The translation is based on the French edition of 1854.

of Origen is remarkably smooth; it is, however, interspersed with Hebrew and other foreign idioms, which is frequently the case with writers who are masters of various languages.

During the reign of the emperor Julian commenced a persecution, perhaps more dangerous than violence itself, which consisted in loading the Christians with disgrace and contempt. Julian began his hostility by plundering the churches; he then forbade the faithful to teach or to study the liberal arts and sciences. Sensible, however, of the important advantages of the institutions of Christianity, the emperor determined to establish hospitals and monasteries and, after the example of the gospel system, to combine morality with religion; he ordered a kind of sermons to be delivered in the Pagan temples.

The sophists by whom Julian was surrounded assailed the Christian religion with the utmost violence. The emperor himself did not disdain to combat those whom he styled contemptible *Galileans*. The work which he wrote has not reached us, but St. Cyril, Patriarch of Alexandria, quotes several passages of it in his refutation, which has been preserved. When Julian is serious St. Cyril proves too strong for him, but when the Emperor has recourse to irony the Patriarch loses his advantage. Julian's style is witty and animated; Cyril is sometimes passionate, obscure, and confused. From the time of Julian to that of Luther the Church, flourishing in full vigor, had no occasion for apologists; but when the western schism took place, with new enemies arose new defenders. It cannot be denied that at first the Protestants had the superiority, at least in regard to forms, as Montesquieu has remarked. Erasmus himself was weak when opposed to Luther, and Theodore Beza had a captivating manner of writing, in which his opponents were too often deficient.

When Bossuet at length entered the lists the victory remained not long undecided; the hydra of heresy was once more overthrown. His *Exposition de la Doctrine Catholique* and *Histoire des Variations* are two masterpieces which will descend to posterity.

It is natural for schism to lead to infidelity and for heresy to engender atheism. Bayle and Spinoza arose after Calvin, and they found in Clarke and Leibnitz men of sufficient talents to refute their sophistry. Abbadie wrote an apology for religion, remarkable for method and sound argument. Unfortunately his style is feeble, though his ideas are not destitute of brilliancy. "If the ancient philosophers," observes Abbadie, "adored the Virtues, their worship was only a beautiful species of idolatry."

While the Church was yet enjoying her triumph Voltaire renewed the persecution of Julian. He possessed the baneful art of making infidelity fashionable among a capricious but amiable people. Every species of self-love was pressed into this insensate league. Religion was attacked with every kind of weapon, from the pamphlet to the folio, from the epigram to the sophism. No sooner did a religious book appear than the author was overwhelmed with ridicule, while works which Voltaire was the first to laugh at among his friends were extolled to the skies. Such was his superiority over his disciples that sometimes he could not forbear diverting himself with their irreligious enthusiasm. Meanwhile the destructive system continued to spread throughout France. It was first adopted in those provincial academies, each of which was a focus of bad taste and faction. Women of fashion and grave philosophers alike read lectures on infidelity. It was at length concluded that Christianity was no better than a barbarous system and that its fall could not happen too soon for the liberty of mankind, the promotion of knowledge, the improvement of the arts, and the general comfort of life.

To say nothing of the abyss into which we were plunged by this aversion to the religion of the gospel, its immediate consequence was a return, more affected than sincere, to that mythology of Greece and Rome to which all the wonders of antiquity were ascribed. People were not ashamed to regret that worship which had transformed mankind into a herd of madmen, monsters of indecency, or ferocious beasts. This could not fail to inspire contempt for the writers of the age of Louis XIV, who, however, had reached the high perfection which distinguished them, only by being religious. If no one ventured to oppose them face to face, on account of their firmly established reputation, they were, nevertheless, attacked in a thousand indirect ways. It was asserted that they were unbelievers *in their hearts*, or at least, that they would have been much greater characters had they lived *in our times*. Every author blessed his good fortune for having been born in the glorious age of the Diderots and d'Alemberts, in that age when all the attainments of the human mind were ranged in alphabetical order in the *Encyclopédie*, that Babel of the sciences and of reason.

Men distinguished for their intelligence and learning endeavored to check this torrent, but their resistance was vain. Their voice was lost in the clamors of the crowd, and their victory was unknown to the frivolous people who directed public opinion in France, and upon whom, for that reason, it was highly necessary to make an impression.

Thus the fatality which had given a triumph to the sophists during the reign of Julian made them victorious in our times. The defenders of the Christians fell into an error which had before undone them: they did not perceive that the question was no longer to discuss this or that particular tenet, since the very foundation on which these tenets were built was rejected by their opponents. By starting from the mission of Jesus Christ and descending from one consequence to another they established the truths of faith on a solid basis, but this mode of reasoning, which might have suited the seventeenth century extremely well, when the groundwork was not contested, proved of no use in our days. It was necessary to pursue a contrary method, and to ascend from the effect to the cause: not to prove that *the Christian religion is excellent because it comes from God, but that it comes from God because it is excellent.*

They likewise committed another error in attaching importance to the serious refutation of the sophists, a class of men whom it is utterly impossible to convince, because they are always in the wrong. They overlooked the fact that these people are never in earnest in their pretended search after truth, that they esteem none but themselves, that they are not even attached to their own system except for the sake of the noise which it makes, and are ever ready to forsake it on the first change of public opinion.

For not having made this remark much time and trouble were thrown away by those who undertook the vindication of Christianity. Their object should have been to reconcile to religion not the sophists but those whom they were leading astray. They had been seduced by being told that Christianity was the offspring of barbarism, an enemy of the arts and sciences, of reason and refinement, a religion whose only tendency was to encourage bloodshed, to enslave mankind, to diminish their happiness, and to retard the progress of the human understanding.

It was therefore necessary to prove that, on the contrary, the Christian religion, of all the religions that ever existed, is the most humane, the most favorable to liberty and to the arts and sciences, that the modern world is indebted to it for every improvement, from agriculture to the abstract sciences—from the hospitals for the reception of the unfortunate to the temples reared by the Michelangelos and embellished by the Raphaels. It was necessary to prove that nothing is more divine than its morality—nothing more lovely and more sublime than its tenets, its doctrine, and its worship, that it encourages genius, corrects the taste, develops the virtuous passions, imparts energy to the ideas, presents noble images to the writer and perfect models to the artist, that there is no disgrace in being believers with Newton and Bossuet, with Pascal and Racine. In a word, it was necessary to summon all the charms of the imagination, and all the interests of the heart, to the assistance of that religion against which they had been set in array.

The reader may now have a clear view of the object of our work. All other kinds of apologies are exhausted, and perhaps they would be useless at the present day. Who would now sit down to read a work professedly theological? Possibly a few sincere Christians who are already convinced. But, it may be asked, may there not be some danger in considering religion in a merely human point of view? Why so? Does our religion shrink from the light? Surely one great proof of its divine origin is that it will bear the test of the fullest and severest scrutiny of reason. Would you have us always open to the reproach of enveloping our tenets in sacred obscurity, lest their falsehood should be detected? Will Christianity be the less true for appearing the more beautiful? Let us banish our weak apprehensions; let us not, by an excess of religion, leave religion to perish. We no longer live in those times when you might say, "Believe without inquiring." People *will* inquire in spite of us, and our timid silence, in heightening the triumph of the infidel, will diminish the number of believers.

It is time that the world should know to what all those charges of absurdity, vulgarity, and meanness that are daily alleged against Christianity may be reduced. It is time to demonstrate, that, instead of debasing the ideas, it encourages the soul to take the most daring flights and is capable of enchanting the imagination as divinely as the deities of Homer and Virgil. Our arguments will at least have this advantage, that they will be intelligible to the world at large, and will require nothing but common sense to determine their weight and strength. In works of this kind authors neglect, perhaps rather too much, to speak the language of their readers. It is necessary to be a scholar with a scholar, and a poet with a poet. The Almighty does not forbid us to tread the flowery path if it serves to lead the wanderer once more to him, nor is it always by the steep and rugged mountain that the lost sheep finds its way back to the fold.

We think that this mode of considering Christianity displays associations of ideas which are but imperfectly known. Sublime in the antiquity of its recollections, which go back to the creation of the world, ineffable in its mysteries, adorable in its sacraments, interesting in its history, celestial in its morality, rich and attractive in its ceremonial, it is fraught with every species of beauty. Would you follow it in poetry? Tasso, Milton, Corneille, Racine, and Voltaire will depict to you its miraculous effects. In the belles-lettres, in eloquence, history, and philosophy, what have not Bossuet, Fénelon, Massillon, Bourdaloue, Bacon, Pascal, Euler, Newton, and Leibnitz produced by its divine inspiration! In the arts, what masterpieces! If you examine it in its worship, what ideas are suggested by its antique Gothic churches, its admirable prayers, its impressive ceremonies! Among its clergy, behold all those scholars who have handed down to you the languages and the works of Greece and Rome, all those anchorets of Thebais, all those [who provided] asylums for the unfortunate, all those missionaries to China, to Canada, to Paraguay, not forgetting the military orders whence chivalry derived its origin. Everything has been engaged in our cause—the manners of our ancestors, the pictures of days of yore, poetry, even romances themselves. We have called smiles from the cradle, and tears from the tomb. Sometimes, with the Maronite monk, we dwell on the summits of Carmel and Lebanon; at others we watch with the Daughter of Charity at the bedside of the sick. Here two American lovers summon us into the recesses of their deserts;[2] there we listen to the sighs of the virgin in the solitude of the cloister. Homer takes his place by Milton, and Virgil beside Tasso; the ruins of Athens and of Memphis form contrasts with the ruins of Christian monuments, and the tombs of Ossian with our rural churchyards. At St. Denis we visit the ashes of kings, and when our subject requires us to treat of the existence of God we seek our proofs in the wonders of Nature alone. In short, we endeavor to strike the heart of the infidel in every possible way, but we dare not flatter ourselves that we possess the miraculous rod of religion which caused living streams to burst from the flinty rock.

Four parts, each divided into six books, compose the whole of our work. The *first* treats of dogma and doctrine. The *second* and *third* comprehend the poetic of Christianity, or its connection with poetry, literature, and the arts. The *fourth* embraces its worship—that is to say, whatever relates to the ceremonies of the Church, and to the clergy, both secular and regular.

We have frequently compared the precepts, doctrines, and worship of other religions with those of Christianity, and to gratify all classes of readers we have also occasionally touched upon the historical and mystical part of the subject. Having thus stated the general plan of the work, we shall now enter upon that portion of it which treats of *Dogma and Doctrine,* and as a preliminary step to the consideration of the Christian mysteries, we shall institute an inquiry into the nature of mysterious things in general.

## 2. Of the Nature of Mysteries

There is nothing beautiful, pleasing, or grand in life but that which is more or less mysterious. The most wonderful sentiments are those which produce impressions difficult to be explained. Modesty, chaste love, and virtuous friendship are full of secrets. It would seem that half a word is sufficient for the mutual understanding of hearts that love, and that they are, as it were, disclosed to each other's view. Is not innocence, also, which is nothing but a holy ignorance, the most ineffable of mysteries? If infancy is so happy it is owing to the absence of knowledge, and if old age is so wretched it is because it knows everything; but fortunately for the latter, when the mysteries of life are at an end those of death commence.

What we say here of the sentiments may be said also of the virtues: the most angelic are those which, emanating immediately from God, such as charity, studiously conceal themselves, like their source, from mortal view.

If we pass to the qualities of the mind we shall find that the pleasures of the understanding are in like manner secrets. Mystery is of a nature so divine that the early inhabitants of Asia conversed only by symbols. What science do we continually apply, if not that which always leaves something to be conjectured, and which sets before our eyes an unbounded prospect? If we wander in the desert a kind of instinct impels us to avoid the plains, where we can embrace every object at a single glance; we repair to those forests, the cradle of religion—those forests whose shades, whose sounds, and whose silence are full of wonders—those solitudes where the first fathers of the Church were fed by the raven and the bee and where those holy men tasted such inexpressible delights as to exclaim, "Enough, O Lord! I will be overpowered if thou dost not moderate thy divine communications." We do not pause at the foot of a modern monument, but if on a desert island in the midst of the wide ocean we come all at once to a statue of bronze whose extended arm points to the regions of the setting sun and whose base covered with hieroglyphics attests the united ravages of the billows and of time, what a fertile source of meditation is here opened to the traveller! There is nothing in the universe but what is hidden, but what is unknown. Is not man himself an inexplicable mystery? Whence proceeds that flash of lightning which we call existence, and in what night is it about to be extinguished? The Almighty has stationed Birth and Death, under the form of veiled phantoms, at the two extremities of our career; the one produces the incomprehensible moment of life, which the other uses every exertion to destroy.

Considering, then, the natural propensity of man to the mysterious, it cannot appear surprising that the religions of all nations should have had their impenetrable secrets. The Selli studied the miraculous words of the doves of Dodona;[3] India, Persia, Ethiopia, Scythia, the Gauls, and the Scandinavians had their caverns, their holy mountains, their sacred oaks, where the Brahmins, the Magi, the Gymnosophists, or the Druids proclaimed the inexplicable oracle of the gods.

Heaven forbid that we should have any intention to compare these mysteries with those of the true religion, or the inscrutable decrees of the Sovereign of the Universe with the changing ambiguities of gods, "the work of human hands."[4] We merely wished to remark that there is no religion without *mysteries;* these, with *sacrifices,* constitute the essential part of worship. God himself is the great secret of Nature. The Divinity was represented veiled in Egypt, and the sphinx was seated upon the threshold of the temples.

### 3. Of the Christian Mysteries: The Trinity

We perceive at the first glance that in regard to mysteries the Christian religion has a great advantage over the religions of antiquity. The mysteries of the latter bore no relation to man and afforded, at the utmost, but a subject of reflection to the philosopher or of song to the poet. Our mysteries, on the contrary, speak directly to the heart; they comprehend the secrets of our existence. The question here is not about a futile arrangement of numbers but concerning the salvation and felicity of the human race. Is it possible for man, whom daily experience so fully convinces of his ignorance and frailty, to reject the mysteries of Jesus Christ? They are the mysteries of the unfortunate!

The Trinity, which is the first mystery presented by the Christian faith, opens an immense field for philosophic study, whether we consider it in the attributes of God or examine the vestiges of this dogma, which was formerly diffused throughout the East. It is a pitiful mode of reasoning to reject whatever we cannot comprehend. It would be easy to prove, beginning even with the most simple things in life, that we know absolutely nothing; shall we, then, pretend to penetrate into the depths of divine Wisdom?

The Trinity was probably known to the Egyptians. The Greek inscription on the great obelisk in the *Circus Major,* at Rome, was to this effect: Μέγας θεὸς, *The Mighty God;* θεογένητος, *the Begotten of God;* Παμφεγγὴς, *the All-Resplendent* (Apollo, the Spirit).

Heraclides of Pontus, and Porphyry, record a celebrated oracle of Serapis:

Πρῶτα θεὸς, μετέπειτα λόγος καὶ πνεῦμα σὺν αὐτοῖς.
Σύμφυτα δὴ τρία πάντα, καὶ εἰς ἐν ἰόντα.

"*In the beginning was God, then the Word and the Spirit; all three produced together, and uniting in one.*"

The Magi had a sort of Trinity, in their Metris, Oromasis, and Araminis, or Mitra, Oramases, and Arimane.

Plato seems to allude to this incomprehensible dogma in several of his works. "Not only is it alleged," says Dacier, "that he had a knowledge of the *Word*, the eternal Son of God, but it is also asserted that he was acquainted with the Holy Ghost and thus had some idea of the Most Holy Trinity; for he writes as follows to the younger Dionysius:

"'I must give Archedemus an explanation respecting what is infinitely more important and more divine, and what you are extremely anxious to know, since you have sent him to me for the express purpose; for from what he has told me, you are of opinion that I have not sufficiently explained what I think of the nature of the first principle. I am obliged to write to you in enigmas, that if my letter should be intercepted either by land or sea those who read may not be able to understand it. All things are around their king; they exist for him, and he alone is the cause of good things—second for such as are second, and third for those that are third.'5

"In the *Epinomis,* and elsewhere, he lays down as principles the first good, the word or the understanding, and the soul. The first good is God; the word, or the understanding, is the Son of this first good, by whom he was begotten like to himself; and the soul, which is the middle term between the Father and the Son, is the Holy Ghost."6

Plato had borrowed this doctrine of the Trinity from Timaeus the Locrian, who had received it from the Italian school. Marsilius Ficinus, in one of his remarks on Plato, shows, after Jamblichus, Porphyry, Plato, and Maximus of Tyre, that the Pythagoreans were acquainted with the excellence of the number three. Pythagoras intimates it in these words: Προτίμα τὸ σχῆμα, χαὶ βῆμα χαὶ Τριώβολον; "Honor chiefly the habit, the judgment-seat, and the triobolus [three oboli]."

The doctrine of the Trinity is known in the East Indies and in Tibet. "On this subject," says Father Calmette, "the most remarkable and surprising thing that I have met with is a passage in one of their books entitled *Lamaastambam.* It begins thus: 'The Lord, the good, the great God, in his mouth is the Word.' The term which they employ personifies the Word. It then treats of the Holy Ghost under the appellation of the *Wind, or Perfect Spirit,* and concludes with the Creation, which it attributes to one single God."7

"What I have learned," observes the same missionary in another place, "respecting the religion of Tibet, is as follows: They call God *Konciosa* and seem to have some idea of the adorable Trinity, for sometimes they term him *Koncikocick,* the one God, and at others *Koncioksum,* which is equivalent to the Triune God. They make use of a kind of chaplet, over which they pronounce the words *om, ha, hum.* When you ask what these mean they reply that the first signifies intelligence, or arm, that is to say, power, that the second is the word, that the third is the heart, or love, and that these three words together signify God."[8]

The English missionaries to Otaheite have found some notion of the Trinity among the natives of that island.[9]

Nature herself seems to furnish a kind of physical proof of the Trinity, which is the archetype of the universe, or if you wish, its divine framework. May not the external and material world bear some impress of that invisible and spiritual arch which sustains it, according to Plato's idea, who represented corporeal things as the shadows of the thoughts of God? The number three is the term by excellence in nature. It is not a product itself, but it produces all other fractions, which led Pythagoras to call it the motherless number.[10]

Some obscure tradition of the Trinity may be discovered even in the fables of polytheism. The Graces took it for their number; it existed in Tartarus both for the life and death of man and for the infliction of celestial vengeance; finally, three brother gods[11] possessed among them the complete dominion of the universe.

The philosophers divided the *moral* man into three parts, and the Fathers imagined that they discovered the image of the spiritual Trinity in the human soul.

"If we impose silence on our senses," says the great Bossuet, "and retire for a short time into the recesses of our soul, that is to say, into that part where the voice of truth is heard, we shall there perceive a sort of image of the Trinity whom we adore. Thought, which we feel produced as the offspring of our mind, as the son of our understanding, gives us some idea of the Son of God, conceived from all eternity in the intelligence of the celestial Father. For this reason this Son of God assumes the name of the Word, to intimate that he is produced in the bosom of the Father, not as bodies are generated, but as the inward voice that is heard within our souls there arises when we contemplate truth.

"But the fecundity of the mind does not stop at this inward voice, this intellectual thought, this image of the truth that is formed within us. We love both this inward voice and the intelligence which gives it birth; and while we love them, we feel within us something which is not less precious to us than intelligence and thought, which is the fruit of both, which unites them and unites with them, and forms with them but one and the same existence.

"Thus, as far as there can be any resemblance between God and man, is produced in God the eternal Love which springs from the Father who thinks, and from the Son who is his thought, to constitute with him and his thought one and the same nature, equally happy and equally perfect."[12]

What a beautiful commentary is this on that passage of Genesis: *"Let us make man!"*[13]

Tertullian, in his *Apology,* thus expresses himself on this great mystery of our religion: "God created the world by his *word,* his *reason,* and his *power.* You philosophers admit that the *Logos,* the word and reason, is the Creator of the universe. The Christians merely add that the proper substance of the *word* and *reason*—that substance by which God produced all things—is *spirit;* that this word must have been pronounced by God; that having been pronounced, it was generated by him; that consequently it is the *Son* of God, and *God* by reason of the unity of substance. If the sun shoots forth a ray its substance is not separated but extended. Thus the Word is *spirit* of a spirit, and *God* of God, like a light kindled at another light. Thus whatever proceeds from God is *God,* and the two, with their spirit, form but one, differing in properties, not in number; in order, not in nature, the Son having sprung from his principle without being separated from it. Now this ray of the Divinity descended into the womb of a virgin, invested itself with flesh, and became man united with God. This flesh, supported by the spirit, was nourished; it grew, spoke, taught, acted; it was Christ."[14]

This proof of the Trinity may be comprehended by persons of the simplest capacity. It must be recollected that Tertullian was addressing men who persecuted Christ, and whom nothing would have more highly gratified than the means of attacking the doctrine, and even the persons, of his defenders. We shall pursue these proofs no farther but leave them to those who have studied the principles of the Italic sect of philosophers and the higher department of Christian theology.

As to the images that bring under our feeble senses the most sublime mystery of religion, it is difficult to conceive how the awful triangular fire, resting on a cloud, is unbecoming the dignity of poetry. Is Christianity less impressive than the heathen mythology, when it represents to us the Father under the form of an old man, the majestic ancestor of ages, or as a brilliant effusion of light? Is there not something wonderful in the contemplation of the Holy Spirit, the sublime Spirit of Jehovah, under the emblem of gentleness, love, and innocence? Doth God decree the propagation of his word? The Spirit then ceases to be that Dove which overshadowed mankind with the wings of peace; he becomes a visible word, a tongue of fire which speaks all the languages of the earth and whose eloquence creates or overthrows empires.

To delineate the divine Son, we need only borrow the words of the apostle who beheld him in his glorified state. He was seated on a throne, says St. John in the Apocalypse; his face shone like the sun in his strength and his feet like fine brass melted in a furnace. His eyes were as a flame of fire, and out of his mouth went a sharp two-edged sword. In his right hand he held seven stars and in his left a book sealed with seven seals; his voice was as the sound of many waters. The seven spirits of God burned before him like seven lamps, and he went forth from his throne attended by lightnings, and voices, and thunders.

### 4. Of the Redemption

As the Trinity comprehends secrets of the metaphysical kind, so the redemption contains the wonders of man and the inexplicable history of his destination and his heart. Were we to pause a little in our meditations, with what profound astonishment would we contemplate those two great mysteries which conceal in their shades the primary intentions of God and the system of the universe! The Trinity, too stupendous for our feeble comprehension, confounds our thoughts, and we shrink back overpowered by its glory. But the affecting mystery of the redemption, in filling our eyes with tears, prevents them from being too much dazzled and allows us to fix them at least for a moment upon the cross.

We behold, in the first place, springing from this mystery, the doctrine of original sin, which explains the whole nature of man. Unless we admit this truth, known by tradition to all nations, we become involved in impenetrable darkness. Without original sin how shall we account for the vicious propensity of our nature continually combated by a secret voice which whispers that we were formed for virtue? Without a primitive fall how shall we explain the aptitude of man for affliction—that sweat which fertilizes the rugged soil, the tears, the sorrows, the misfortunes of the righteous, the triumphs, the unpunished success, of the wicked? It was because they were unacquainted with this degeneracy that the philosophers of antiquity fell into such strange errors and invented the notion of reminiscence. To be convinced of the fatal truth whence springs the mystery of redemption we need no other proof than the malediction pronounced against Eve, a malediction which is daily accomplished before our eyes. How significant are the pangs, and at the same time the joys, of a mother! What mysterious intimations of man and his twofold destiny, predicted at once by the pains and pleasures of childbirth! We cannot mistake the views of the Most High when we behold the two great ends of man in the labor of his mother, and we are compelled to recognise a God even in a malediction.

After all, we daily see the son punished for the father and the crime of a villain recoiling upon a virtuous descendant, which proves but too clearly the doctrine of original sin. But a God of clemency and indulgence, knowing that we should all have perished in consequence of this fall, has interposed to save us. Frail and guilty mortals as we all are, let us ask, not our understandings, but our hearts, how a God could die for man. If this perfect model of a dutiful son, if this pattern of faithful friends, if that agony in Gethsemane, that bitter cup, that bloody sweat, that tenderness of soul, that sublimity of mind, that cross, that veil rent in twain, that rock cleft asunder, that darkness of nature—in a word, if that God, expiring at length for sinners, can neither enrapture our heart nor inflame our understanding, it is greatly to be feared that our works will never exhibit, like those of the poet, the "brilliant wonders" which attract a high and just admiration.

"Images," it may perhaps be urged, "are not reasons; and we live in an enlightened age, which admits nothing without proof."

That we live in an enlightened age has been doubted by some, but we would not be surprised if we were met with the foregoing objection. When Christianity was attacked by serious arguments, they were answered by an Origen, a Clarke, a Bossuet. Closely pressed by these formidable champions, their adversaries endeavored to extricate themselves by reproaching religion with those very metaphysical disputes in which they would involve us. They alleged, like Arius, Celsus, and Porphyry, that Christianity is but a tissue of subtleties, offering nothing to the imagination and the heart, and adopted only by *madmen* and *simpletons*. But if anyone comes forward, and in reply to these reproaches endeavors to show that the religion of the gospel is the religion of the soul, fraught with sensibility, its foes immediately exclaim, "Well, and what does that prove, except that you are more or less skilful in drawing a picture?" Thus, when you attempt to work upon the feelings they require axioms and corollaries. If, on the other hand, you begin to reason they then want nothing but sentiments and images. It is difficult to close with such versatile enemies, who are never to be found at the post where they challenge you to fight them. We shall hazard a few words on the subject of the redemption to show that the theology of the Christian religion is not so absurd as some have affected to consider it.

A universal tradition teaches us that man was created in a more perfect state than that in which he at present exists, and that there has been a fall. This tradition is confirmed by the opinion of philosophers in every age and country, who have never been able to reconcile their ideas on the subject of moral man without supposing a primitive state of perfection from which human nature afterward fell by its own fault.

If man was created he was created for some end: now, having been created perfect, the end for which he was destined could not be otherwise than perfect.

But has the final cause of man been changed by his fall? No, since man has not been created anew nor the human race exterminated to make room for another.

Man, therefore, though he has become mortal and imperfect through his disobedience, is still destined to an immortal and perfect end. But how shall he attain this end in his present state of imperfection? This he can no longer accomplish by his own energy, for the same reason that a sick man is incapable of raising himself to that elevation of ideas which is attainable by a person in health. There is, therefore, a disproportion between the power and the weight to be raised by that power; here we already perceive the necessity of succor, or of a redemption.

"This kind of reasoning," it may be said, "will apply to the first man; but as for us, we are capable of attaining the ends of our existence. What injustice and absurdity, to imagine that we should all be punished for the fault of our first parent!" Without undertaking to decide in this place whether God is right or wrong in making us sureties for one another, all that we know, and all that it is necessary for us to know at present, is that such a law exists. We know that the innocent son universally suffers the punishment due to the guilty father, that this law is so interwoven in the principles of things as to hold good even in the physical order of the universe. When an infant comes into the world diseased from head to foot from its father's excesses, why do you not complain of the injustice of nature? What has this little innocent done that it should endure the punishment of another's vices? Well, the diseases of the soul are perpetuated like those of the body, and man is punished in his remotest posterity for the fault which introduced into his nature the first leaven of sin.

The fall, then, being attested by general tradition and by the transmission or generation of evil, both moral and physical, and on the other hand, the ends for which man was designed being now as perfect as before his disobedience, notwithstanding his own degeneracy, it follows that a redemption, or any expedient whatever to enable man to fulfil those ends, is a natural consequence of the state into which human nature has fallen.

The necessity of redemption being once admitted, let us seek the order in which it may be found. This order may be considered either in man or above man.

First, in man. The supposition of a redemption implies that the price must be at least equivalent to the thing to be redeemed. Now how is it to be imagined that imperfect and mortal man could have offered himself in order to regain a perfect and immortal end? How could man, partaking himself of the primeval sin, have made satisfaction as well for the portion of guilt which belonged to himself as for that which attached to the rest of the human family? Would not such self-devotion have required a love and virtue superior to his nature? Heaven seems purposely to have suffered four thousand years to elapse from the fall to the redemption to allow men time to judge of themselves how very inadequate their degraded virtues were for such a sacrifice.

We have no alternative, then, but the second supposition, namely, that the redemption could have proceeded only from a being superior to man. Let us examine if it could have been accomplished by any of the intermediate beings between him and God.

It was a beautiful idea of Milton[15] to represent the Almighty announcing the fall to the astonished heavens, and asking if any of the celestial powers was willing to devote himself for the salvation of mankind. All the divine hierarchy was mute, and among so many seraphim, thrones, dominations, angels, and archangels none had the courage to make so great a sacrifice. Nothing can be more strictly true in theology than this idea of the poet's. What, indeed, could have inspired the angels with that unbounded love for man which the mystery of the cross supposes? Moreover, how could the most exalted of created spirits have possessed strength sufficient for the stupendous task? No angelic substance could, from the weakness of its nature, have taken upon itself those sufferings which, in the language of Massillon, accumulated upon the head of Christ all the physical torments that might be supposed to attend the punishment of all the sins committed since the beginning of time, and all the moral anguish, all the remorse, which sinners must have experienced for crimes committed. If the Son of Man himself found the cup bitter how could an angel have raised it to his lips? Oh, no; he never could have drunk it to the dregs, and the sacrifice could not have been consummated.

We could not, then, have any other redeemer than one of the three persons existing from all eternity and among these three persons of the Godhead it is obvious that the Son alone, from his very nature, was to accomplish the great work of salvation. Love which binds together all the parts of the universe, the Mean which unites the extremes, Vivifying Principle of nature, he alone was capable of reconciling God with man. This second Adam came—man according to the flesh by his birth of Mary, a man of sanctity by his gospel, a man divine by his union with the Godhead. He was born of a virgin, that he might be free from original sin and a victim without spot and without blemish. He received life in a stable, in the lowest of human conditions, because we had fallen through pride. Here commences the depth of the mystery; man feels an awful emotion, and the scene closes.

Thus the end for which we were destined before the disobedience of our first parents is still pointed out to us, but the way to secure it is no longer the same. Adam in a state of innocence would have reached it by flowery paths; Adam in his fallen condition must cross precipices to attain it. Nature has undergone a change since the fall of our first parents, and redemption was designed, not to produce a new creation, but to purchase final salvation for the old. Everything, therefore, has remained degenerate with man; and this sovereign of the universe who, created immortal, was destined to be exalted, without any change of existence, to the felicity of the celestial powers, cannot now enjoy the presence of God till, in the language of St. Chrysostom, he has passed through the *deserts of the tomb*. His soul has been rescued from final destruction by the redemption, but his body, combining with the frailty natural to matter the weakness consequent on sin, undergoes the primitive sentence in its utmost extent: he falls, he sinks, he passes into dissolution. Thus God, after the fall of our first parents, yielding to the entreaties of his Son, and unwilling to destroy the whole of his work, invented death, as a demi-annihilation, to fill the sinner with horror of that complete dissolution to which, but for the wonders of celestial love, he would have been inevitably doomed.

We venture to presume that if there be any thing clear in metaphysics, it is this chain of reasoning. There is here no wresting of words; there are no divisions and subdivisions, no obscure or barbarous terms. Christianity is not made up of such things as the sarcasms of infidelity would fain have us imagine. To the poor in spirit the gospel has been preached, and by the poor in spirit it has been heard: it is the plainest book that exists. Its doctrine has not its seat in the head but in the heart; it teaches not the art of disputation but the way to lead a virtuous life. Nevertheless, it is not without its secrets. What is truly ineffable in the Scripture is the continual mixture of the profoundest mysteries and the utmost simplicity—characters whence spring the pathetic and the sublime. We should no longer be surprised, then, that the work of Jesus Christ speaks so eloquently. Such, moreover, are the truths of our religion, notwithstanding their freedom from scientific parade, that the admission of one single point immediately compels you to admit all the rest. Nay, more: if you hope to escape by denying the principle—as for instance, original sin—you will soon, driven from consequence to consequence, be obliged to precipitate yourself into the abyss of atheism. The moment you acknowledge a God, the Christian religion presents itself, in spite of you, with all its doctrines, as Clarke and Pascal have observed. This, in our opinion, is one of the strongest evidences in favor of Christianity.

In short, we must not be astonished if he who causes millions of worlds to roll without confusion over our heads has infused such harmony into the principles of a religion instituted by himself; we need not be astonished at his making the charms and the glories of its mysteries revolve in the circle of the most convincing logic, as he commands those planets to revolve in their orbits to bring us flowers and storms in their respective seasons. We can scarcely conceive the reason of the aversion shown by the present age for Christianity. If it be true, as some philosophers have thought, that some religion or other is necessary for mankind, what system would you adopt instead of the faith of our forefathers? Long shall we remember the days when men of blood pretended to erect altars to the *Virtues* on the ruins of Christianity.[16] With one hand they reared scaffolds; with the other on the fronts of our temples they inscribed *Eternity* to God and *Death* to man; and those temples, where once was found that God who is acknowledged by the whole universe, and where devotion to Mary consoled so many afflicted hearts—those temples were dedicated to *Truth,* which no man knows, and to *Reason,* which never dried a tear.

## PART IV, BOOK III

### 1. Of Jesus Christ and His Life

About the time of the appearance of the Redeemer of mankind upon earth, the nations were in expectation of some extraordinary personage. "An ancient and constant opinion," says Suetonius, "was current all over the East, that persons coming from Judea should obtain universal empire."[17] Tacitus relates the same fact nearly in the same words. According to this great historian, "most of the Jews were convinced, agreeably to a prediction preserved in the ancient books of their priests, that about this time (the time of Vespasian) the East would prevail, and that some native of Judea should obtain the empire of the world."[18] Lastly, Josephus, speaking of the destruction of Jerusalem, informs us that the Jews were chiefly instigated to revolt against the Romans by an obscure prophecy, which foretold that about this period "a man would arise among them and subdue the universe."[19] The New Testament also exhibits traces of this hope shed abroad in Israel. The multitudes who thronged to the desert asked John the Baptist whether he was the great Messiah, the Christ of God, so long expected; and the disciples of Emmaus were disappointed to find that their Master was not he "that should have redeemed Israel."[20] The seventy weeks of Daniel, or the four hundred and ninety years from the rebuilding of the temple, were then accomplished. Finally, Origen, after repeating all these traditions of the Jews, adds that "a great number of them acknowledged Jesus Christ as the deliverer promised by the prophets."[21]

Heaven meanwhile prepares the way for the Son of man. States long disunited in manners, government, and language entertained hereditary enmities; but the clamor of arms suddenly ceases, and the nations, either allied or vanquished, become identified with the people of Rome.

On the one hand, religion and morals have reached that degree of corruption which of necessity produces changes; on the other, the tenets of the unity of God and the immortality of the soul begin to be diffused. Thus the ways are prepared on all sides for the new doctrine which a universal language will serve to propagate. The vast Roman empire is composed of nations, some barbarous, others civilized, but all excessively miserable. For the former, the simplicity of Christ, for the latter, his moral virtues, for all, mercy and charity are means of salvation contrived by heaven itself. So efficacious are these means that only two centuries after the advent of the Messiah, Tertullian thus addressed the judges of Rome: "We are but of yesterday, and yet we fill every place— your cities, your islands, your fortresses, your camps, your colonies, your tribes, your decuries, your councils, the palace, the senate, the forum; we leave you nothing but your temples."[22]

With the grandeur of natural preparations is combined the splendor of miracles; the oracles of truth which had been long silent in Jerusalem recover their voice, and the false sibyls become mute. A new star appears in the East; Gabriel descends to the Virgin Mary, and a chorus of blessed spirits sings at night from on high, *Glory to God! peace to men of good will!* A rumor rapidly spreads that the Saviour has come into the world; he is not born in purple but in the humble abode of indigence; he has not been announced to the great and the mighty but angels have proclaimed the tidings to men of low estate; he has not assembled the opulent but the needy round his cradle, and by this first act of his life declared himself in preference the God of the suffering and the poor.

Let us here pause to make one reflection. We have seen, from the earliest ages, kings, heroes, and illustrious men become the gods of nations. But here the reputed son of a carpenter in an obscure corner of Judea is a pattern of sorrows and of indigence; he undergoes the ignominy of a public execution; he selects his disciples from among the lowest of the people; he preaches naught but sacrifices, naught but the renunciation of earthly pomp, pleasure, and power; he prefers the slave to the master, the poor to the rich, the leper to the healthy man; all that mourn, all that are afflicted, all that are forsaken by the world are his delight, but power, wealth, and prosperity are incessantly threatened by him. He overthrows the prevalent notions of morality, institutes new relations among men, a new law of nations, a new public faith. Thus does he establish his divinity, triumph over the religion of the Caesars, seat himself on the throne, and at length subdue the earth. No! if the whole world were to raise its voice against Jesus Christ, if all the powers of philosophy were to combine against its doctrines, never shall we be persuaded that a religion erected on such a foundation is a religion of human origin. He who could bring the world to revere a cross, he who held up suffering humanity and persecuted virtue as an object of veneration to mankind—he, we insist, can be no other than a God.

Jesus Christ appears among men full of grace and truth; the authority and the mildness of his precepts are irresistible. He comes to be the most unhappy of mortals, and all his wonders are wrought for the wretched. "His miracles," says Bossuet, "have a much stronger character of beneficence than of power." In order to inculcate his doctrines, he chooses the apologue or parable, which is easily impressed on the minds of the people. While walking in the fields he gives his divine lessons. When surveying the flowers that adorn the meadow, he exhorts his disciples to put their trust in Providence, who supports the feeble plants and feeds the birds of the air; when he beholds the fruits of the earth, he teaches them to judge of men by their works; an infant is brought to him, and he recommends innocence; being among shepherds, he gives himself the appellation of the *good shepherd* and represents himself as bringing back the lost sheep to the fold. In spring he takes his seat upon a mountain and draws from the surrounding objects instruction for the multitude sitting at his feet. From the very sight of this multitude, composed of the poor and the unfortunate, he deduces his beatitudes: *Blessed are they that mourn, blessed are they that hunger and thirst,* etc. Such as observe his precepts and those who slight them are compared to two men who build houses, the one upon a rock, the other upon sand. . . . When he asks some water of the Samaritan woman he expounds to her his heavenly doctrine under the beautiful image of a well of living water.

The bitterest enemies of Jesus Christ never dared to attack his character. Celsus, Julian, and Volusian[23] admit his miracles, and Porphyry relates that the very oracles of the Pagans styled him a man illustrious for his piety.[24] Tiberius would have placed him in the rank of the gods,[25] and according to Lampridius, Adrian erected temples to him, and Alexander Severus venerated him among holy men and placed his image between those of Orpheus and Abraham.[26] Pliny has borne an illustrious testimony to the innocence of the primitive Christians, who closely followed the example of the Redeemer. There are no philosophers of antiquity but have been reproached with some vices: the very patriarchs had their foibles. Christ alone is without blemish: he is the most brilliant copy of that supreme beauty which is seated upon the throne of heaven. Pure and sanctified as the tabernacle of the Lord, breathing naught but the love of God and men, infinitely superior by the elevation of his soul to the vain glory of the world, he prosecuted amid sufferings of every kind the great business of our salvation, constraining men by the ascendency of his virtues to embrace his doctrine and to imitate a life which they were compelled to admire.

His character was amiable, open, and tender, and his charity unbounded. The evangelist gives us a complete and admirable idea of it in these few words: *He went about doing good.* His resignation to the will of God is conspicuous in every moment of his life; he loved and felt the sentiment of friendship; the man whom he raised from the tomb, Lazarus, was his friend; it was for the noblest sentiment of life that he performed the greatest of his miracles. In him the love of country may find a model: "Jerusalem, Jerusalem," he exclaimed, at the idea of the judgments which threatened that guilty city, "how often would I have gathered thy children together, even as a hen gathereth her chickens under her wings, and ye would not!" Casting his sorrowful eyes from the top of a hill over this city doomed for her crimes to a signal destruction, he was unable to restrain his tears: *He beheld the city,* says the evangelist, *and wept over it.* His tolerance was not less remarkable. When his disciples begged him to command fire to come down from heaven on a village of Samaria which had denied him hospitality, he replied, with indignation, *You know not of what spirit you are.*

Had the Son of man descended from his celestial abode in all his power it would certainly have been very easy to practise so many virtues, to endure so many afflictions; but herein lies the glory of the mystery: Christ was the man of sorrows, and acquainted with griefs; his heart melted like that of a merely human creature, and he never manifested any sign of anger except against insensibility and obduracy of soul. *Love one another,* was his incessant exhortation. *Father,* he exclaimed, writhing under the torments inflicted by his executioners, *forgive them, for they know not what they do.* When on the point of quitting his beloved disciples he was all at once dissolved in tears; he experienced all the terrors of death, all the anguish of the cross; the blood-sweat trickled down his divine cheeks; he complained that his Father had forsaken him. *Father,* said he, *if it be possible, let this chalice pass from me; nevertheless, not as I will, but as thou wilt.* Then it was that that expression, fraught with all the sublimity of grief, fell from his lips: *My soul is sorrowful, even unto death.* Ah! if the purest morality and the most feeling heart, if a life passed in combating error and soothing the sorrows of mankind, be attributes of divinity, who can deny that of Jesus Christ? A pattern of every virtue, Friendship beholds him reclining on the bosom of St. John or bequeathing his mother to his care; Charity admires him in the judgment of the adulteress; Pity everywhere finds him blessing the tears of the unfortunate; his innocence and his tenderness are displayed in his love of children; the energy of his soul shines conspicuous amid the torments of the cross; and his last sigh is a sigh of mercy.

## 2. The Hierarchy

Christ, having left his last instructions to his disciples, ascended from Mount Thabor into heaven. From that moment the Church subsisted in the apostles; it was established at the same time among the Jews and among the Gentiles. St. Peter by one single sermon converted five thousand persons at Jerusalem, and St. Paul received his mission to the pagan nations. The prince of the apostles soon laid in the capital of the Roman empire the foundations of the ecclesiastical power. The first Caesars yet reigned, and already the obscure priest who was destined to displace them from the capitol went to and fro among the crowd at the foot of their throne. The hierarchy began: Peter was succeeded by Linus, and Linus by Clement and that illustrious chain of pontiffs, heirs of the apostolic authority, which has been unbroken for more than eighteen hundred years and carries us back to Christ himself.

With the episcopal dignity we see the two other grand divisions of the hierarchy—the priesthood and the diaconate—established from the very beginning. St. Ignatius exhorts the Magnesians "to act in unity with their bishop, who fills the place of Jesus Christ; their priests, who represent the apostles; and their deacons, who are charged with the service of the altars."[27] Pius, Clement of Alexandria, Origen, and Tertullian confirm these degrees.[28]

Though no mention is made of metropolitans or archbishops before the Council of Nicaea, yet that council speaks of this ecclesiastical dignity as having been long established.[29] Athanasius[30] and Augustin[31] mention instances of it prior to the date of that assembly. As early as the second century Lyons is termed in civil writings a metropolitan city; and Irenaeus, who was its bishop, governed the whole Gallican *Church* ($\pi\alpha\rho o\chi\iota o\nu$).[32] . . . The title of cardinal was at first given indiscriminately to the highest dignitaries of the Church. As these heads of the clergy were in general men distinguished for their learning and virtues the Popes consulted them in important matters. They became by degrees the permanent council of the Holy See, and the right of electing the sovereign pontiff was vested in them when the communion of believers grew too numerous to be assembled together.

The same causes that had placed cardinals near the Popes also gave canons to the bishops. These were a certain number of priests who composed the episcopal court. The business of the diocese increasing, the members of the council were obliged to divide the duties among them. Some were called vicars and others vicars-general, according to the extent of their charge. The whole council assumed the name of *chapter,* and the members who composed it that of *canons,* that is, canonical administrators.

Common priests, and even laymen appointed by the bishops to superintend a religious community, were the source of the order of abbots. We shall presently see how serviceable the abbeys proved to letters, to agriculture, and in general, to the civilization of Europe.[33]

Parishes were formed at the period when the principal orders of the clergy became subdivided. The bishoprics being too extensive to allow the priests of the mother Church to extend their spiritual and temporal aid to the extremities of the diocese, churches were erected in the country. The ministers attached to these rural temples took, in the course of time, the name of curates, from the Latin *cura,* which signifies *care, fatigue.* . . .


BOOK 6


6. The Popes and Their Court

. . . Christian Rome has been to the modern what pagan Rome was to the ancient world, the common centre of union. This capital of nations fulfils all the conditions of its destiny and seems in reality to be the *eternal city.* There may, perhaps, come a time when it will be universally admitted that the pontifical power is a magnificent institution. The spiritual father, placed amid the nations, binds together all the different parts of Christendom. What a venerable character is a pope truly animated with the apostolic spirit! The general shepherd of the flock, he either keeps it within the bounds of duty or defends it against oppression. His dominions, sufficiently extensive to make him independent, too small to give room for any apprehension from his political rank, leave him the power of opinion alone—an admirable power, when it embraces in its empire no other works than those of peace, charity, and beneficence.

The transient mischief which some bad popes occasioned disappeared with them, but we still daily feel the influence of the immense and inestimable benefits for which the whole world is indebted to the court of Rome. That court has almost always proved itself superior to the age. It had ideas of legislation and civil administration, was acquainted with the fine arts and the sciences, and possessed refinement when all around was involved in the darkness of the Gothic institutions. Nor did it keep the light exclusively to itself but shed it abroad upon all. It broke down the barriers which prejudice erects between nations; it studied to soften our manners, to withdraw us from our ignorance, to wean us from our rude or ferocious customs. In the time of our ancestors the popes were missionaries of the arts sent among barbarians, legislators among savages. "Only the reign of Charlemagne," says Voltaire, "had a tincture of politeness, which was probably the consequence of his visit to Rome."

It is, therefore, generally admitted that to the Holy See Europe owes her civilization, part of her best laws, and almost all her arts and sciences. The sovereign pontiffs are now about to seek other means of being useful to mankind; a new career awaits them, and we have a presentiment that they will pursue it with glory. Rome has returned to that evangelical poverty which constituted all her wealth in days of yore.[34] By a remarkable similarity there are now Gentiles to be converted, nations to be restored to harmony, animosities to be extinguished, tears to be wiped away, and wounds which require all the balm of religion to be healed. If Rome is thoroughly sensible of her situation, never had she before her greater hopes and more brilliant destinies. We say *hopes,* for we reckon tribulations among the objects desired by the Church of Christ. The degenerate world requires a second preaching of the gospel; Christianity, in renewed vigor, is rising victorious over the most tremendous assault that the infernal powers ever made upon her. Who knows if what we have taken for the fall of the Church be not her reestablishment? She was declining in the enjoyment of luxury and repose; she forgot the cross: the cross has again appeared, and she will be saved.

## 12. General Recapitulation

It is not without a certain degree of fear that we approach the conclusion of our work. The serious reflections which induced us to undertake it, the hazardous ambition which has led us to decide, as far as lay in our power, the question respecting Christianity—all these considerations alarm us. It is difficult to discover how far it is pleasing to the Almighty that men should presume to take into their feeble hands the vindication of his eternity, should make themselves advocates of the Creator at the tribunal of the creature, and attempt to defend by human arguments those counsels which gave birth to the universe. Not without extreme diffidence, therefore, convinced as we are of the incompetency of our talents, do we here present the general recapitulation of this work.[35]

Every religion has its mysteries. All nature is a secret.

The Christian mysteries are the most sublime that can be; they are the archetypes of the system of man and of the world.

The sacraments are moral laws, and present pictures of a highly poetical character.

Faith is a force, charity a love, hope complete happiness, or as religion expresses it, a complete virtue.

The laws of God constitute the most perfect code of natural justice.

The fall of our first parents is a universal tradition.

A new proof of it may be found in the constitution of the moral man, which is contrary to the general constitution of beings.

The prohibition to touch the fruit of knowledge was a sublime command, and the only one worthy of the Almighty.

All the arguments which pretend to demonstrate the antiquity of the earth may be contested.

The doctrine of the existence of a God is demonstrated by the wonders of the universe. A design of Providence is evident in the instincts of animals and in the beauty of nature.

Morality of itself proves the immortality of the soul. Man feels a desire of happiness and is the only creature who cannot attain it; there is consequently a felicity beyond the present life, for we cannot wish for what does not exist.

The system of atheism is founded solely on exceptions. It is not the body that acts upon the soul, but the soul that acts upon the body. Man is not subject to the general laws of matter; he diminishes where the animal increases.

Atheism can benefit no class of people: neither the unfortunate, whom it bereaves of hope, nor the prosperous, whose joys it renders insipid, nor the soldier, of whom it makes a coward, nor the woman, whose beauty and sensibility it mars, nor the mother, who has a son to lose, nor the rulers of men, who have no surer pledge of the fidelity of their subjects than religion.

The punishments and rewards which Christianity holds out in another life are consistent with reason and the nature of the soul.

In literature characters appear more interesting and the passions more energetic under the Christian dispensation than they were under polytheism. The latter exhibited no dramatic feature, no struggles between natural desire and virtue.

Mythology contracted nature, and for this reason the ancients had no descriptive poetry. Christianity restores to the wilderness both its pictures and its solitudes.

The Christian marvellous may sustain a comparison with the marvellous of fable. The ancients founded their poetry on Homer while the Christians found theirs on the Bible, and the beauties of the Bible surpass the beauties of Homer.

To Christianity the fine arts owe their revival and their perfection.

In philosophy it is not hostile to any natural truth. If it has sometimes opposed the sciences, it followed the spirit of the age and the opinions of the greatest legislators of antiquity.

In history we should have been inferior to the ancients but for the new character of images, reflections, and thoughts to which Christianity has given birth. Modern eloquence furnishes the same observation.

The relics of the fine arts, the solitude of monasteries, the charms of ruins, the pleasing superstitions of the common people, and the harmonies of the heart, religion, and the desert lead to the examination of the Christian worship.

This worship everywhere exhibits a union of pomp and majesty with a moral design and with a prayer either affecting or sublime. Religion gives life and animation to the sepulchre. From the laborer who reposes in a rural cemetry to the king who is interred at St. Denis, the grave of the Christian is full of poetry. Job and David, reclining upon the Christian tomb, sing in their turn the sleep of death by which man awakes to eternity.

We have seen how much the world is indebted to the clergy and to the institutions and spirit of Christianity. . . . It is no exaggeration to assert that, whatever distress or suffering we may think of, religion has in all probability anticipated us and provided a remedy for it. From as accurate a calculation as we were able to make, we have obtained the following results:

There are computed to be on the surface of Christian Europe about four thousand three hundred towns and villages. Of these four thousand three hundred towns and villages, three thousand two hundred ninety-four are of the first, second, third, and fourth rank. Allowing one hospital to each of these three thousand two hundred ninety-four places (which is far below the truth), you will have three thousand two hundred ninety-four hospitals, almost all founded by the spirit of Christianity, endowed by the Church, and attended by religious orders. Supposing that, upon an average, each of these hospitals contains one hundred beds, or if you please, fifty beds for two patients each, you will find that religion, exclusively of the immense number of poor which she supports, has afforded daily relief and subsistence for more than a thousand years to about three hundred and twenty-nine thousand four hundred persons.

On summing up the colleges and universities, we find nearly the same results; and we may safely assert that they afford instruction to at least three hundred thousand youths in the different states of Europe.

In this statement we have not included either the Christian hospitals and colleges in the other three quarters of the globe, or the female youth educated by nuns.

To these results must be added the catalogue of the celebrated men produced by the Church, who form nearly two-thirds of the distinguished characters of modern times. We must repeat, as we have shown, that to the Church we owe the revival of the arts and sciences and of letters, that to her are due most of the great modern discoveries, as gunpowder, clocks, the mariner's compass, and in government, the representative system, that agriculture and commerce, and the laws and political science, are under innumerable obligations to her, that her missions introduced the arts and sciences among civilized nations and laws among savage tribes, that her institution of chivalry powerfully contributed to save Europe from an invasion of new barbarians, that to her mankind is indebted for

the worship of one only God,

the more firm establishment of the belief in the existence of that Supreme Being,

a clearer idea of the immortality of the soul, and also of a future state of rewards and punishments,

a more enlarged and active humanity,

a perfect virtue, which alone is equivalent to all the others—Charity,

a political law and the law of nations, unknown to the ancients, and above all, the abolition of slavery.

Who is there but must be convinced of the beauty and the grandeur of Christianity? Who but must be overwhelmed with this stupendous mass of benefits?


## 13. Conclusion

. . . Jesus Christ may therefore with strict truth be denominated, in a material sense, that Saviour of the World which he is in a spiritual sense. His career on earth was, even humanly speaking, the most important event that ever occurred among men, since the regeneration of society commenced only with the proclamation of the gospel. The precise time of his advent is truly remarkable. A little earlier, his morality would not have been absolutely necessary, for the nations were still upheld by their ancient laws; a little later, that divine Messiah would have appeared after the general wreck of society. We boast of our philosophy at the present day, but most assuredly the levity with which we treat the institutions of Christianity is anything but philosophical. The gospel has changed mankind in every respect and enabled it to take an immense step toward perfection. If you consider it as a grand religious institution which has regenerated the human race then all the petty objections, all the cavils of impiety, fall to the ground. It is certain that the pagan nations were in a kind of moral infancy in comparison to what we are at the present day. A few striking acts of justice exhibited by a few of the ancients are not sufficient to shake this truth or to change the general aspect of the case.

Christianity has unquestionably shed a new light upon mankind. It is the religion that is adapted to a nation matured by time. It is, if we may venture to use the expression, the religion congenial to the present age of the world, as the reign of types and emblems was suited to the cradle of Israel. In heaven it has placed one only God; on earth it has abolished slavery. On the other hand, if you consider its mysteries (as we have done) as the archetype of the laws of nature, you will find nothing in them revolting to a great mind. The truths of Christianity, so far from requiring the submission of reason, command, on the contrary, the most sublime exercise of that faculty.

This remark is so just, and Christianity, which has been characterized as the religion of barbarians, is so truly the religion of philosophers, that Plato may be said to have almost anticipated it. Not only the morality but also the doctrine of the disciple of Socrates bears a striking resemblance to that of the gospel. Dacier, his translator, sums them up in the following manner:

"Plato proves that the *Word* arranged this universe and rendered it visible, that the knowledge of this Word leads to a happy life here below and procures felicity after death, that the soul is immortal, that the dead will rise again, that there will be a last judgment of the righteous and the wicked, where each will appear only with his virtues or his vices, which will be the cause of everlasting happiness or misery.

Finally, says the learned translator, Plato had so grand and so true a conception of supreme justice, and was so thoroughly acquainted with the depravity of men that, according to him, if a man supremely just were to appear upon earth, he would be imprisoned, calumniated, scourged, and at length *crucified*, by those who, though fraught with injustice, would nevertheless pass for righteous.[36]

The detractors of Christianity place themselves in a false position, which it is scarcely possible for them not to perceive. If they assert that this religion originated among the Goths and Vandals it is an easy matter to prove that the schools of Greece had very clear notions of the Christian tenets. If they maintain, on the contrary, that the doctrine of the gospel is but the *philosophical* teaching of the ancients, why then do our *philosophers* reject it? Even they who discover in Christianity nothing more than ancient allegories of the heavens, the planets, and the signs of the zodiac by no means divest that religion of all its grandeur. It would still appear profound and magnificent in its mysteries, ancient and sacred in its traditions, which in this way would be traceable to the infancy of the world. How extraordinary that all the researches of infidels cannot discover in Christianity anything stamped with the character of littleness or mediocrity!

With respect to the *morality* of the gospel, its beauty is universally admitted: the more it is known and practiced, the more will the eyes of men be opened to their real happiness and their true interest. Political science is extremely circumscribed. The highest degree of perfection which it can attain is the representative system, the offspring, as we have shown, of Christianity. But a religion whose precepts form a code of morality and virtue is an institution capable of supplying every want and of becoming, in the hands of saints and sages, a universal means of felicity. The time may perhaps come when the mere form of government, excepting despotism, will be a matter of indifference among men, who will attach themselves more particularly to those simple, moral, and religious laws which constitute the permanent basis of society and of all good government.

Those who reason about the excellence of antiquity and would fain persuade us to revive its institutions forget that social order is not, neither can it be, what it formerly was. In the absence of a great moral power a great coercive power is at least necessary among men. In the ancient republics the greater part of the population, as is well known, were slaves; the man who cultivated the earth belonged to another man: there were *people,* but there were no *nations.*

Polytheism, which is defective in every respect as a religious system, might therefore have been adapted to that imperfect state of society, because each master was a kind of absolute magistrate, whose rigid despotism kept the slave within the bounds of duty and compensated by chains for the deficiency of the moral religious force. Paganism, not possessing sufficient excellence to render the poor man virtuous, was obliged to let him be treated as a malefactor.

But in the present order of things, how could you restrain an immense multitude of free peasants, far removed from the vigilance of the magistrate? How could you prevent the crimes of an independent populace, congregated in the suburbs of an extensive capital, if they did not believe in a religion which enjoins the practice of duty and virtue upon all the conditions of life? Destroy the influence of the gospel and you must give to every village its police, its prisons, its executioners. If, by an impossibility, the impure altars of paganism were ever reestablished among modern nations, if in a society where slavery is abolished the worship of *Mercury the robber* and *Venus the prostitute* were to be introduced, there would soon be a total extinction of the human race.

Here lies the error of those who commend polytheism for having separated the moral from the religious force and at the same time censure Christianity for having adopted a contrary system. They perceive not that paganism, having to deal with an immense nation of slaves, was consequently afraid of enlightening the human race, that it gave every encouragement to the sensual part of man and entirely neglected the cultivation of the soul. Christianity, on the contrary, meditating the destruction of slavery, held up to man the dignity of his nature and inculcated the precepts of reason and virtue. It may be affirmed that the doctrine of the gospel is the doctrine of a free people from this single circumstance: that it combines morality with religion.

It is high time to be alarmed at the state in which we have been living for some years past. Think of the generation now springing up in our towns and provinces, of all those children who, born during the revolution, have never heard anything of God, nor of the immortality of their souls, nor of the punishments or rewards that await them in a future life: think what may one day become of such a generation if a remedy be not speedily applied to the evil. The most alarming symptoms already manifest themselves: we see the age of innocence sullied with many crimes. Let philosophy, which after all cannot penetrate among the poor, be content to dwell in the mansions of the rich and leave the people in general to the care of religion; or rather, let philosophy, with a more enlightened zeal and with a spirit more worthy of her name, remove those barriers which she proposed to place between man and his Creator. . . .

We are convinced that Christianity will rise triumphant from the dreadful trial by which it has just been purified. What gives us this assurance is that it stands the test of reason perfectly, and the more we examine it the more we discover its profound truth. Its mysteries explain man and nature; its works corroborate its precepts; its charity in a thousand forms has replaced the cruelty of the ancients. Without losing anything of the pomp of antiquity its ceremonies give greater satisfaction to the heart and the imagination. We are indebted to it for everything—letters, sciences, agriculture, and the fine arts. It connects morality with religion, and man with God; Jesus Christ, the saviour of moral man, is also the saviour of physical man. His coming may be considered as an advent the most important and most felicitous, designed to counterbalance the deluge of barbarism and the total corruption of manners. Did we even reject the supernatural evidences of Christianity, there would still remain in its sublime morality, in the immensity of its benefits, and in the beauty of its worship sufficient proof of its being the most divine and the purest religion ever practised by men.

"With those who have an aversion for religion," says Pascal, "you must begin with demonstrating that it is not contradictory to reason; next show that it is venerable, and inspire them with respect for it; afterward exhibit it in an amiable light, and excite a wish that it were true; then let it appear by incontestable proofs that it is true; and lastly, prove its antiquity and holiness by its grandeur and sublimity."[37]

Such is the plan which that great man marked out, and which we have endeavored to pursue. Though we have not employed the arguments usually advanced by the apologists of Christianity we have arrived by a different chain of reasoning at the same conclusion, which we present as the result of this work.

Christianity is perfect; men are imperfect.

Now a perfect consequence cannot spring from an imperfect principle.

Christianity, therefore, is not the work of men.

If Christianity is not the work of men it can have come from none but God.

If it came from God men cannot have acquired a knowledge of it but by revelation.

Therefore Christianity is a revealed religion.

## NOTES

1. Eusebius *Ecclesiastical History* 4.3; Jerome *Epistle* 80. (The music historian quoted in the introduction to this selection is Arthur Ware Locke [*Music and the Romantic Movement in France* (London, 1920), 13]—ED.)

2. The author alludes to the beautiful and pathetic tale of *Atala; or, The Love and Constancy of Two Savages in the Desert*, which was at first introduced into the present work but was afterwards detached from it.—TRANS.

3. They were an ancient people of Epirus and lived near Dodona. At that place there was a celebrated temple of Jupiter. The oracles were said to be delivered from it by doves endowed with a human voice. Herodotus relates that a priestess was brought hither from Egypt by the Phoenicians; so the story of the doves might arise from the ambiguity of the Greek πελεια, which signifies *dove* in the general language, but in the dialect of Epirus . . . *an aged woman.*—TRANS.

4. Wisd. of Sol. 13:10.

5. This passage of Plato, which the author could not verify, from its having been incorrectly quoted by Dacier, may be found in *Plato Serrani* 1:312, letter the second to Dionysius. The letter is supposed to be genuine.—TRANS. (This is the first of many instances where a nineteenth-century writer gives, by twentieth-century standards, an incomplete citation. Here the second translation of Plato cited is *Platonis Opera Quae Exstant Omnia ex Nova Joannis Serrani Interpretatione Perpetuis Ejusdem Notis Illustrata,* ed. Henri Estienne, 3 vols. [Paris, 1578]. The first translation of Plato referred to is André Dacier's *Les oeuvres de Platon,* published with the translator's commentary in Paris in 1699 but also published in several later editions.—ED.)

6. *Oeuvres de Platon,* trans. Dacier, 1:194.

7. Jean Calmette, S.J., *Lettres édifiantes* 14:9. (Regarding Calmette, whose letters form part of the large literature of Jesuit missionaries' reports to their superiors in the sixteenth to eighteenth centuries, see the listings in *The British Library: General Catalogue of Printed Books to 1971* [London, 1980], 51:224. I have found that travelers' tales from the sixteenth through the early twentieth centuries have become "collectibles," and at serious shows such as the annual New York Antiquarian Book Fair they abound—at very high prices. Thus much of this material ends up in private hands.—ED.)

8. Calmette, *Lettres* 12:437.

9. "The three deities which they hold supreme are—1. *Tane te Medooa,* the Father; 2. *Oromattow,* God in the Son; 3. *Taroa,* the Bird, the Spirit" (*Appendix to the Missionary Voyage,* 333).—TRANS. (The reference is apparently to William Wilson's *A Missionary Voyage to the Southern Pacific Ocean, . . . in the Years 1796–98, in the Ship "Duff," . . . with an Appendix, including Details . . . of the Natural and Civil State of Otaheite* [London, 1799]. Otaheite is Tahiti. A more modern account of such matters may be found in Robert W. Williamson's *Religious and Cosmic Beliefs of Central Polynesia,* 2 vols. [Cambridge, 1933]; and his *Religion and Social Organization in Central Polynesia* [Cambridge, 1937]. Cp. Hegel's similar use of missionaries' reports in his lectures on the philosophy of religion. Today we might find that Chateaubriand and Hegel were too quick to draw conclusions, but it is fascinating to observe how these writers, in the infancy of what we have since termed the "history of religions," thought that "pagan" religions must have *something* to do with Christianity. Unlike Hegel, Chateaubriand had at least gone to the wilds of North America and met some Native Americans.—ED.)

10. Hierocles *Commentary on Pythagoras.* (See Noël Aujoulat, *Le néo-*

*platonisme alexandrin: Hiéroclès d'Alexandrie,* Philosophia Antiqua 45 [Leiden: E. J. Brill, 1986]—ED.) The 3, a simple number in itself, is the only one composed of simples [and the only one] that gives a simple number when decomposed. We can form no complex number, the 2 excepted, without the 3. The formations of the 3 are beautiful, and embrace that powerful unity which is the first link in the chain of numbers and is everywhere exhibited in the universe. The ancients very frequently applied numbers in a metaphysical sense, and we should not be too hasty in condemning it as folly in Pythagoras, Plato, and the Egyptian priests from whom they derived this science. (Cp. Chateaubriand, here, with Günther, later in this volume. It cannot be stressed too greatly how important to the romantics were the organicity and the constancy in pattern of the universe.—ED.)

11. I.e., Jupiter, Neptune, and Pluto.—TRANS.
12. Jacques-Bénigne Bossuet, *Discourse on Universal History,* trans. Elborg Forster (Chicago: Univ. of Chicago Press, 1976), 191.—ED.
13. Gen. 1:26.
14. Tertullian *Apology* 21. (In the passage on the Apocalypse that follows, Chateaubriand refers to chaps. 1 and 4.—ED.)
15. John Milton, *Paradise Lost,* book 3, lines 213–26.
16. The author alludes to the disastrous tyranny exercised by Robespierre over the deluded French people.—TRANS.
17. "Vespasian" (X), chap. 4, in *The Twelve Caesars.*
18. Tacitus *Histories* 5.13.
19. Josephus *War of the Jews* 6.5.4. [The prophecy concerned the term] αμφιβολος, applicable to several persons, and therefore referred by the Latin historians to Vespasian.
20. Luke 24:21.
21. Origen *Against Celsus.* (Chateaubriand does not further identify the quotation, which, it must be said, does not seem to agree with Origen's words in 2.1–3, 74–75.—ED.)
22. Tertullian *Apology* 37.
23. Origen *Against Celsus* 1.6; Cyril of Alexandria *Apology against Julian* 6; and Augustine *Letters* 132, 135, 137. (Regarding Cyril, see Johannes Quasten, *Patrology,* vol. 3 [Westminster, Md.: Newman Press, 1960], 129–30.—ED.)
24. Eusebius of Caesaria *Demonstratio Evangelica* 3.7.
25. Tertullian *Apology* 5.
26. Lampridius *Vita Alexandri Severi* 4, 31.
27. Ignatius *Letter to the Magnesians* 6.
28. Pius *Letter* 2; Clement of Alexandria *Stromata* 6.13; Origen *Homily II on Numbers;* Origen *Homily on the Canticle of Canticles;* Tertullian *On Monogamy* 2, Tertullian *On Flight* 41; and Tertullian *On Baptism* 17. (The letter of Pius [J. D. Mansi, . . . *Collectio* 1:675] is not considered authentic.—ED.)
29. Canon 6.
30. Athanasius *On the Opinion of Dionysius* 5.
31. Augustin, *Breviculus Collationis cum Donatistis,* 3d day, sec. 16.
32. Eusebius *Ecclesiastical History* 5.23. From *parochion* we have made *parish.*
33. Eusebius *Ecclesiastical History* 3:4–6. ED.
34. Chateaubriand alludes to Napoleon's treatment of Popes Pius VI and Pius VII.—ED.

35. The reader will understand that this summing-up refers in part to material not contained in the present volume.—ED.

36. André Dacier, *Discours sur Platon* [ = *Les oeuvres de Platon?*] 22.

37. A paraphrase of Blaise Pascal's *Pensées,* sec. 3, no. 187.—ED.

# 2

# Toward the
# Revision of the Present
# State of Theology

*Johann Sebastian Drey*

Johann Sebastian Drey, a theology teacher of considerable skill and influence, brings a certain precision to the broad romantic vision of Chateaubriand, which, however, he largely shares. He was born near Ellwangen in 1777. Ordained a priest in 1801, by 1812 he had become professor of apologetics, dogmatics, and the history of dogmatics on the theological faculty of Ellwangen. Since in Napoleon's restructuring of the German political order what became the kingdom of Württemberg acquired numerous Catholic subjects, the faculty that Drey had joined was in 1819 moved to the University of Tübingen for greater educational effectiveness and possibly also for closer supervision. (Ever since then, Tübingen has had both Catholic and Protestant theological faculties.) Drey thus became the founder of the "Tübingen school" of Catholic theologians, and also in 1819 he began what remains the oldest Catholic theological journal, the *Tübinger theologische Quartalschrift*. Drey continued teaching in Tübingen till 1846 and died there in 1853. He is chiefly remembered for his *Kurze Einleitung in das Stadium der Theologie* (1819) and his three-volume *Apologetik* (1838–47)—and for being the teacher of Möhler.

Chateaubriand was concerned that due attention be paid to Christian theology. Drey, on the other hand, senses that theology must be begun again. He compares the ruinous state of theology to the misfortunes that have befallen Germany in the earlier part of the Napoleonic period. Still, because old ways have been disrupted, Catholic theology has the chance to begin anew, and Drey finds much that is useful in Schleiermacher and, especially, Schelling to aid in this "revision." The reader may wish to compare Drey's remarks here with section 121 of Schleiermacher's *Christian Faith,* where the Holy Spirit, the inner spirit of the Christian church, and the national spirit are likened to one another. This comparison will, however, also suggest a crucial difference between Schleiermacher and Drey: Drey always insists on the transcendence of the divine influence on mankind that brings about—a most important concept for Drey— the kingdom.

A noteworthy characteristic of nineteenth-century romanticism was its enthusiasm for things medieval. An organic conception of human history made the Middle Ages not only relevant but archetypal, for according to many romantics like Drey, they were the last time in Western history that the organic nature of human community was lived to the full and rendered more or less fully self-conscious. A stunning manifestation of this nineteenth-century cherishing of the medieval is to be found in ecclesiastical architecture: original Gothic churches were restored, and the landscape was filled with new imitations, like New York's "new" Saint Patrick's. Likewise, for Drey, medieval theology "lived in the church, that is, in the contemplation of the [church as a] living organism developing out of the life principle dwelling within it." Earlier medieval theology thus becomes a theological model to which we must return, because it combines this sense of living corporate Christianity with great technical proficiency.

In tracing the course of theology from the later Middle Ages to 1812 Drey voices a theme that would become a commonplace of Catholic philosophy and theology through the nineteenth century and well into the twentieth. (What made the Modernists different is that they would not go along with this current.) This characteristic or current is the tendency to prize earlier medieval theology—down to Thomas Aquinas, or at the latest Duns Scotus—and to see the subsequent course of philosophy and theology as a progressive degeneration, down to Kant. To be sure, Drey and his Tübingen school are far from being neoscholastics. Their conception of a revision of theology consists of a synthesis of the best from the faith-filled Middle Ages with the best nineteenth-century ideas about human community and academic method.

In an estimate that will be powerfully developed by his pupil Möhler, Drey sees in Protestantism the apotheosis of the individual. Individual judgment applied to Scripture and church history leads, for Drey, to the fatuousness of trying to derive living communal religion from philology and empiricism. As so often happens with unskillful apologists, Catholics caught the disease they were trying to fight: it would seem that Drey has in mind apologetics in the manner of Hermes. Catholics must now make a new start, developing their medieval heritage for the present age.

. It should not surprise us if on closer examination we find a startling likeness of form between the political and the literary history of a people. For what is the scientific state of a nation but the highest expression of what lies in the nation, of what moves it, as its spiritual life? As the nation evidences its power in its warriors, its productive art in its artisans, and its justice in its lawgivers, so its characteristic mode of action is expressed in terms of public morality, and its characteristic mode of thought is expressed through the medium of its scholars, through the state of the sciences. The whole mass of a people never thinks or acts as such, but just as in a single man the functions of life as a whole are divided among certain organs, so in a people is life made manifest through eminent individuals.

Now if it is true of the sciences generally that their state in a people, their course, and their fate must run parallel with the rest of the history of the people, so that the history of literature can be interpreted in terms of this parallelism, and this parallelism in terms of the history of literature, so is it especially true of theology as the science that, to be sure, directly affects the whole mass of the nation just as little as any other science but that mediately, through its organs, affects the nation more universally and more intimately, perhaps, than all the rest of the sciences together. For theology is the science of the holiest and highest that mankind is susceptible of. As mankind understands the highest, so will it understand the common. If a nation understands it nobly, with reverence and love, so must the nation itself thereby be elevated, and so will it stand out in the history of peoples with a noble character and an awe-inspiring power. But if a nation understands the highest as common or mean, or understands it not at all, or even thrusts it away from itself, such a nation hastens toward impotence and dissolution—a point that even passing phenomena might demonstrate! He who cuts off the tree's roots makes it wither and fall, and no artificial hothouse care can prolong its existence.

It might, therefore, be possible, and perhaps also interesting, to consider the history of theology in our nation—for only our nation can properly be discussed here—as parallel with the rest of our nation's history, and from their juxtaposition come to an understanding of their interaction. Such a project, however, lies outside the scope of the pres-

"Revision des gegenwärtigen Zustandes der Thelogie," in *Geist des Christentums und des Katholizismus*, ed. Josef Rupert Geiselmann (Mainz: Matthias-Grünewald, 1940), 85–97. The translation is by Joseph Fitzer. (The essay originally appeared in *Archiv für die Pastoralkonferenzen in den Landkapiteln des Bistums Konstanz* 1 (1812): 3–26.)

ent essay. Instead, setting aside all other considerations, I will preface my statement on the revision of theology simply with a brief presentation of the varied and, for the most part, unhappy fate of theology, so as to point out how in the history of theology there gradually developed the weaknesses that prepared the dissolution of theology—as is analogously the case with the nation. Still, even though the present discussion concerns only theology, should the reader spontaneously discover divers correlations between theology and nation, so will my foregoing assertion about parallelism shine out all the more evidently to him.

Scarcely is the clamor over that was struck up for more than half a century concerning the old scholasticism. Nonetheless, theology must again and again turn back to scholasticism if it would describe its beginnings as a science. And what will people say if it is asserted that, in spite of all the clamor against it, never and nowhere has theology existed in such scientific form as in that so-called barbaric school? And yet it is not otherwise. That lively zeal for ever new presentations of the doctrines of Christianity not only singly but as a whole, that deep play of reflection and imagination, that boundless acumen for the finest distinction and separation of concepts, that creation of the most elaborate terminology for these numberless distinctions, that consistency in presentation—this vibrant philosophical life in an elite circle that bestowed on so many doctors such renowned honorific titles—when has the like since been seen? This exquisite game, this signal feat of the human spirit, has like an empty nutshell been thoughtlessly thrown away because, we are told, it contains nothing but words.

This last reproach would be difficult to answer if it were so unconditionally valid as people—if only, indeed, because of a new authority— have assumed. But is it really so valid? That game of words must be judged in terms of its own time if it is to be judged rightly. If this is done it will still ever appear to be a game, but a game that, like those of children, has life's earnestness and a real sense to it.

The age in which scholasticism was formed was the age of the most heartfelt religiosity. Christianity had taken for its own all the inclinations and capacities of the mind. It ruled as the very spirit of the time, and could so rule because it was the sole culture of a world that shortly before had been engulfed by still barbarous peoples but was now quietly possessed by them. Hence all its discoveries, arts, trades, and yes, even wars were permeated by a Christian religious spirit. Could the newly developing science have been inspired by another spirit? From Christianity alone could the new philosophy, and with it all culture, proceed. Philosophy, since the philosophy of the ancients was no more, had to be grounded by religion, not the other way round—religion by philosophy—as is the case in our time. And this religion was a given, a transmitted religion, not one produced artificially by demonstrations. It was a religion to which soul and feeling were attached—not understanding—because soul and feeling found it a mitigating, softening, quieting influence. But just as children objectify their feelings in the first games of their awakening intellectual activity, so the first thinkers of that time sought by concepts to hold fast and more closely to determine the inward contemplation of their faith. Thus all their philosophy and theology was a game of their awakening understanding, and they needed nothing more. For already and from another source were they convinced of the doctrines of Christianity. The game became important and interesting to them because it bore the imprint of their soul and feelings, and yet satisfied the understanding, which wanted to think. Of doubter and unbeliever there was none—against whom the new theology would be called to take the field.

It was in this way that the twofold character of medieval philosophy and theology initially came about. As proceeding by the impulse of living religious contemplation, they had to be, according to their inner essence, religious and Christian, but as the endeavor to develop externally this inner religious world, to set forth a copy of it in concept and word, they had to become dialectical. We already find them with this twofold character in the writings of the later church fathers, in the writings of the Venerable Bede, and still more definitely in the writings of the eleventh and twelfth centuries, those, for example, of John Scotus Erigena, Peter Damian, Lanfranc, Anselm, Bernard of Clairvaux, Bonaventure, Richard and Hugh of Saint Victor, and others. The spirit of all these writers is the mystical spirit, that is, the purely religious and Christian spirit that sees in what is temporal and finite an allegory and intimation of the divine, and just on that account is unable either to speak of a proper character and essence in these finite things or to inquire into their nature, inasmuch as it knows their nature more in terms of the eternal will and ordering of God than as parceled out in temporal appearances. But just by this detachment from the so-called real, the philosophizing spirit of the time could put itself to the test in the most manifold developments and stake out a wide field of abstractions and dialectical art. For when science has condescended to the empirical the concept clings to its object and to determinate form and can never again break free from them.

Meanwhile, it was easy to foresee that dialectics would not always remain in the service of mysticism but would separate itself from the mystical, would eventually come forward as the opponent of the mystical. For as the understanding outgrew the dominion of faith, so it naturally and necessarily became the enemy of the supersensible.

This separation actually ensued, and it took the form of the opposition of the nominalists and the realists, which parties under various names continued through the entire era of scholasticism, up to the complete dissolution of scholasticism. In vain did the church involve itself in the quarrel of the dialecticians, which seemed to threaten the doctrines of the Christian faith; in vain did the profound mystic and scholastic Peter Abelard force Roscelin and William of Champeaux, the heads of the parties, to limit their assertions. Aristotelian dialectics, spread abroad soon after by the Arabs, and purified of all mystical elements, withdrew within the confines of philosophy, in order now to have a freer hand and to avoid the appearance of deciding in matters of faith, which it left to theology. From now on theology remained separated from philosophy and henceforth shared the dialectical art with it.

This separation of the two elements of scholasticism had in more than one respect the most harmful results. Philosophical scholasticism, since it no longer lived in the contemplation of the divine and had just as little penetrated into a clear knowledge of the finite given in experience, now became an empty word game, without content and signification. Only the religious spirit of the age, being independent of the logical and dialectical direction of science, still held this slack formalism upright. Still, dialectics now began not infrequently to move into opposition to religious doctrine, as in the case of Amalric and of David of Dinant; and later on it played a notable role in the great religious dissensions. Theological scholasticism, however, which as such was not distinct from philosophical scholasticism and had at the same time also lost the mystical element, came in like manner to lose itself in a host of insignificant sophisms and thereby entangle itself all the more, since just these sophisms could be brought against theological assertions as objections. This scholasticism transformed itself into an eristic. It was in these times of division and separation that there first arose the foolish conceit of an essential and natural opposition between reason and revelation. Theology was thereby led to employ all the perverse means that have brought on its dissolution as a science. In the celebrated quarrel of the nominalists and the realists lay the proximate occasion thereto. This opposition of reason and revelation was, however, sanctioned by the method of Peter Lombard, which remained for centuries to come the model for theological scholastics. What Lombard did was this: after elaborating his proofs for theological theses, he always appended a few so-called objections from philosophy, which, where possible, he sought to refute on other philosophical grounds, or where he was unable to do so, by the authority of the church fathers. In this way he nourished and strengthened the faith—as if philosophy were striving against theology, and thus as if reason generally were striving against it. The harmful results of this erroneous method will presently be touched upon.

An equally necessary result of that separation of the mystical and the dialectical elements of scholasticism was this, that now mysticism itself rose up against the dominant philosophy and theology, disdaining both in like manner, and making both disdainful. Experiencing the essence of religion, mysticism necessarily found it inexcusable that one would call it human or divine wisdom to play with words whose proper sense and spirit had become unknown to the schools. And so mysticism itself, from which scholasticism had sprung, helped in the end to displace it. Everything now contributed to the dissolution of this old, honorable work of art from the time of the awakening of Christian culture.

This old theology had to undergo total dissolution when, with the end of the fifteenth century, an altogether new spirit began to stir among the European nations. That period of the Middle Ages must be considered the childhood of the modern world, for it resembled childhood in fullness of inner contemplation and experience, in innocence of concepts and morals, and in poverty in experience and cultural formation. But just for that reason it had to end and make way for a new era that characterized itself as a time of robust youth, striving for freedom and in general breaking through to life and the objective world. The awakening power of youth in this new world got its first impetus from the monuments of ancient Greek and Roman artistic sensibility and taste, which would ever thereafter remain the models for objective and real cultural formation. When in these monuments of art and science there was revealed a life so clear and sensible, so open and attractive, so infinitely rich in imagery and history, how could scholasticism, so rich in concepts but so poor in perceptions, still maintain itself and rule over the minds of men? The first, immediate result of this awakening of admiration for ancient culture was, to be sure, only that the better minds withdrew from scholasticism, rebelled against it. But another, far more detrimental result could not fail to appear.

This free and independent life brought division into the very halls of sacred science and into souls that were the dwelling of noble views. The misuse of authority, on which since the beginning of the human race all faith and all knowledge had been grounded—and on which they must necessarily be grounded, because the individual, with all his knowledge, embraces only a small part of space and time—the misuse of authority led youthfully tumultuous minds to reject all authority and to set in its place their own individual understanding. Thus the inconsistency of the scholastics, who in their conceit had equated the authority of an individual with the unobjectionable and esteemed authority of a universal tradition and of the great body of believers, was avenged by a like inconsistency on the part of the Reformers. All these events could not affect theology otherwise than to convulse it, and it was to be foreseen that theology would have to take on another form. With respect to externals this newer form did not as yet particularly distinguish itself from the older form, because the Reformers in theology had still received their first formation in the schools of scholasticism and for the most part were practiced in the arts of dialectics, and therefore readily developed their opinions in that form. Moreover, a new theology could not be created without a new philosophy, and this last was not yet at hand despite the many attempts made to provide it. The newer theology was, however, essentially different from the older in this wise, that, inasmuch as it meant to ground its assertions solely on its subjective knowledge, it had to seek out for this subjective knowledge an objective basis of another sort than such as had hitherto sufficed, and apparently found this most important objective basis in the holy Christian Scriptures, which were henceforth to become the sole basis of faith, the sole source of theological proofs.

Such a change of circumstances, however, prepared for theology its total collapse, since theology was made to depend upon a host of casual, profane, and empirical things quite alien to Christianity and the Christian faith, so that it could no longer lay claim to being a free, independently formed science. For if up to this point the theologian had lived in the church, that is, in the contemplation of the living organism developing out of the life principle dwelling within it, and his theology had been a self-animating, faithful copy of this organism, so now the reformer had to have recourse to other things. He left the living organism, because here and there abscesses had formed—which would either clear up of themselves or in due time be removed by surgery. But without the organism itself he could not and did not want to live. Thus he turned to a copy and description of this organism, which the historians of its youth had left behind, and believed that from this description, however fragmentarily it has come down to us, he could discern the nature and disposition of the organism better than from the anatomy of the body itself. Needless to say, if such a procedure was absurd in itself, to what consequences might it lead? Books written in ancient, dead languages—written by men some of whom were not writing in their native language, who therefore translated the spirit and flow of their original way of thinking and expressing themselves into scarcely learned foreign languages each of which, naturally, had its own manner of presentation, who wrote only on occasion, without the intention of giving an exhaustive, all-embracing presentation of the whole, who could describe this organic whole only to the extent that it had developed at that time, at a time when this whole had not yet attained a free and happy existence but rather still had to fight the long battle against heathen and Jew and decadent philosophy—these books were supposed to provide, after fifteen hundred years and for yet more millenniums of future peoples and races, under a wholly altered culture, just as clear, satisfying, and comprehensive a presentation of Christianity as they could in their own time, when moreover they were accompanied by oral commentary and by other, lost documents.

These highly incomplete and in no way satisfying accounts were now meant to foster the contemplation of pure Christianity and the scientific construction of the same by being handed over to the art and ability of the individual interpreter. It had to happen sooner or later that all theology was transformed into grammar and philology, and indeed, a philology that rummaged in words. Now it could no longer be living Christianity as it had developed in the course of time under the guidance of the divine Spirit and was embodied in the church that theology as a science and system was supposed to reproduce, "for that development had in the hands of men taken a rather perverse course, the body of the church was full of ulcers and pus, and the divine Spirit had watched over not the living body but the dead letter, so that the letter would not perish." It was this dead letter that science was supposed to enliven— this letter, which had so long been misunderstood, was supposed again to come to honor. But how would one help it thereto? All those great and marvelous powers that had once enlivened it and given it victory over the world, when the Spirit of God first spoke it through the mouths of simple men, all these marvelous powers were sleeping now when human wisdom wanted to master them. And since help did not come from above, one had to devise one's own means.

Now it came about that knowledge of those ancient languages, the art of research into and interpretation of ancient foreign customs and modes of expression, bold hypotheses, clever transference of the modern manner of thinking to that ancient period, the collecting of manuscripts, fragments, and variants, in short, the whole *apparatus eruditionis,* as torn apart and scattered as all the things in the world, now became the indispensable condition of a genuine theology. From these remains the rejuvenated phoenix was supposed to rise. Anyone who had appropriated something from this field of chance, down to the grammarian, could now surpass the most speculative of theologians.

Such a state of profanation, however, did not come about with the beginning of the Reformation. The better spirit of the Reformers held it off for a while. These men still retained an inheritance from their own and the foregoing times, which inheritance gave their efforts a religious coloring, and even success. It was mysticism, which precisely now, at the visible collapse of scholasticism, lifted up its head more victoriously than ever and made demands on men's spirits that could be satisfied by no profane science but only by a truly religious faith and life. Thus for these men it was not a question of the word itself for the sake of the mere word, but for the sake of faith and conscience; and they withdrew from the living body of the church because they thought that the living and life-giving word could no longer be heard there. Heresy proceeded not from irreligion but from error, and this error is one of the byways into which mysticism can go astray when pride overtakes it; that is, pride inclines mysticism to take its inner, subjective perceptions as objectively, universally valid, to oppose them to the universal faith. So long as this spirit, this religious earnestness, animated these theologians there was yet some transfer of it to degenerate theological science, and one could say of them that their heart was better than their subsequent reputation. This spirit lasted over a hundred years after the collapse of theology, and as long as the Catholics did not tire in opposing the Protestants in word and deed they forced the latter to maintain a more serious tone in theology.

Finally, however, the collapse had to become manifest. The empirical spirit in the sciences generally, the genuine product of the modern period, gained more ground everywhere and penetrated forcibly even into the field of theology, a science that, if any, must build on a higher ground than that of time and finitude. This empirical and sensuous spirit pushed aside mysticism, which is, after all, the very soul of Christianity. With the disappearance of mysticism there vanished also the exalted conception of Christianity as a great divine decree encompassing the whole history of mankind. Also lost was the concept of the church as the infinitely progressive realization of this decree, and there necessarily sprang up a view of Christianity that treated it as a contingent occurrence in human history, undertaking to explain it from similarly contingent causes. For only the contingent is welcome to empiricism, because the contingent sets something in its path for it to investigate, explain, and understand. Poking about is allowed here, for the contingent can have arisen from causes of different sorts—a probable procedure, because one cannot discover at once the right path; an inventing of hypotheses, because some explanation must after all be offered—and there is no easy end to this sort of rumination, because contingency extends as far and wide as the world.

Such an empirical outlook was gladly welcomed by a theology that, by reason of its primary and basic principle, had to rest on purely empirical data. It was eminently desirable to a system that had canceled the indivisible unity of Christianity and its history, set the early church in opposition to the later, and built its own defense on a past era and history. Now for the first time had Protestantism to grasp after all those expedients mentioned above, which had hitherto lain unused in it like a concealed store of arms and which, in its opinion, would surely give it a decided superiority over its opponents, who since they lived in an eternal present were unable to take any notice of the past. Now began explanation from contingencies, and it was not long before there were found in Christianity a great number of things that had in a chance way crept into it and that thus had to be banished as unessential and secondary. In this pursuit, Semler and Bahrdt[1] achieved great triumphs, and the attractiveness of these so easily won laurels set many others in action: in the field of theology it had never been so active and lively as now.

To this was added another circumstance. The same spirit that had drawn theology totally into the realm of empiricism had in the realm of philosophy a still more extensive field and held the upper hand over the misunderstood speculations that during this time had been ventured by a few acute philosophers. In this field, where there was no opposition to the empirical spirit from authority or history, empiricism necessarily soon reached its natural boundary: it ended in materialism and skepticism. Because there now remained nothing more for philosophy to do, out-of-work philosophers turned against religion and its defenders and bombarded them with the whole store of Voltaire's profound wit and Hume's melancholy doubts. The army of the theologians, though, already in a bad state for a long time, understood as little of the art of warfare as many another army and let itself be enticed by its enemies into a battlefield that could not have been more disadvantageous for it. It occurred to these theologians, namely, to attack naturalism on its own ground, on which Christianity can never be defended. They thought themselves strong enough, after abandoning everything miraculous, extraordinary, or divine—against which the naturalists greatly protested all the same—to achieve their purpose with a single natural miracle, the miracle of history, to which no one with sound eyes would be able to raise an objection. But the defenders of theology had forgotten that they themselves had annihilated history in the only sense that would be of use in refuting the naturalists, for they recognized in history not the work of eternal necessitation, which the religious man calls providence, but the work of subjective freedom, and therefore the work of chance, wafted together by the capricious dealings of individual men and nations. These Christian theologians were, according to their basic principles, themselves naturalists, except that they knew it not. There was thus no other possible result but that the naturalists would in the end win, and the theologians had to relinquish one (intrinsically) defensible position after another. They had to be satisfied whenever the naturalists would condescend to cry out a little less wildly about Christianity and grant that with all sorts of modifications it still had a certain usefulness for the common people. They consoled themselves over their loss by approximating the otherwise rigorous and serious study of theology to the easier and gamelike study of philology and antiquity—and this game playing with words, types of speech, and philological trifles became just as childish as had been the scholastics' game playing with concepts and distinctions. The most venerable science, the science of divine things, now sank more and more to being a profane science, and after the most unruly capricious play it ended with no one's knowing how well or badly off he was. The theologians had torn down their sole bulwark, the authority of a divine book.

It was necessary for me to speak so much about Protestant theology because about Catholic theology there is little to say. Single misfortunes it had in common with the former. Thus, for example, the mystical spirit vanished from it, too, and those who had sought to save it, such as a Fénelon or a Pascal,[2] were oppressed by the opposing party and silenced. This opposing party, which now monopolized theological discussion, however much it exerted itself for Catholicism, was nonetheless inspired by the Protestant spirit, and just like Protestants they clung to the letter, the letter of the Bible, the letter of tradition and history, the letter of the fathers and councils. They had so little knowledge of the advantages that the firm, consistent, organic form of Catholicism gave them against their opponents that they had to be made aware of them by Protestants. They were so little able to re-present in a scientific system the still-living whole that had been presented to their contemplation that their clumsy handling of the best of causes necessarily made the cause itself doubtful to their own brethren. They plodded along for such a long time in antiquated forms of presentation and proof that the proofs themselves were perforce distorted, because not a hint of any other necessity lay therein than that of an expressed but not understood (divine) authority.

While one Catholic theologian copied another, and few looked further around at what might possibly be going on in the realm of the other

sciences and in the altered manner of thinking of the time, they necessarily misunderstood the sciences and the time, and were in like manner
misunderstood. In the end, though, the spirit of the time penetrated the
well-guarded borders of even this theology, but only to bring along its
weaknesses. It now came about that the principles concerning the contingency of all things in Christianity dominated these theologians too,
with the result that they began to make a clean sweep. Much was given
up as decrepit and groundless, since they knew only the shell, so to
speak, and not the kernel—and granted, the shell had become old and
misshapen. No matter how much they hurried after the Protestants,
however, they still did not manage much progress in the philological arts.
But practical reason was more successful, because it was, well, practical,
and in addition easily understandable. One was now astonished at how
the fathers were able to be authentic Christians, since they were unaware
of practical Christianity or moral religion. People hastened everywhere
to prescribe this moral religion that had so opportunely appeared on the
scene to remedy the immorality of the time, and since the simplest
medicines are supposed to be the best, so must this one be given as pure
as possible, with no addition of the positive. Everything historical,
symbolic, or mystical one ought to push aside, because now a pure and
clear panacea had been found.

In this respect, it seems to me, the Catholics are going about things
more intelligently than the Protestants. The former now throw over-
board *brevi manu,* with only a categorical imperative as ballast, what the
others had anguished over carrying out through half a century of learned
folios.

## NOTES

1. Both Johann Salomo Semler (1725–91), professor at Halle from 1752, and
Karl Friedrich Bahrdt (1741–92), who was dismissed from a number of teaching
posts, stressed the role of reason in religion, but Bahrdt more than Semler, who
attacked him. Under the Prussian government's Edict of 1788, an attempt at
censorship, Bahrdt went to prison—ED.

2. Regarding Pascal and Fénelon, see the brief discussion in Fulbert Cayré's
*Patrologie et histoire de la théologie,* 2d ed., vol. 3 (Paris, 1950), 110–11, 187–89,
218–40. Drey's point here is that from Catholic officialdom and official theology
little inspiration and warmth were to be expected. In the *Einleitung* he noted that
"in the Church there must be an analogue with what in the State is called public
opinion," adding that "most of the proposals for improvements in liturgy and

ecclesiastical discipline that were actually introduced came, not from prelates, but from zealous and wise private persons." The translation is mine, from "J. S. Drey and the Search for a Catholic Philosophy of Religion," *Journal of Religion* 63 (1983): 244.—ED.

# 3

# Symbolics, the Eucharist, and the Church

*Johann Adam Möhler*

In the case of Möhler—if one has read enough of his work to form a serious opinion—there is a desire to repeat what Schumann wrote of Chopin: "Hats off, gentlemen—a genius!" Even crediting Drey's influence on him, Möhler defies explanation. He simply appears on the scene, takes in what is "in the air," and then works very hard. This is no doubt what the French religious journalist Georges Goyau meant when he called Möhler the "most self-taught theologian of modern times." From book to book, and from edition to edition of the *Symbolik* (Möhler died in 1838, while working on the fifth edition), he can be observed learning more and more of the lore of Catholicism and then recasting it in lucid prose—perhaps his early training in classical philology helped here— and recasting it as well in terms of German romantic sensibilities. In the recasting he himself appears in his books just enough to give them, in the manner described in the Introduction, not only theological but literary appeal.

Johann Adam Möhler was born in 1796 near Mergentheim, Württemberg. He studied for the priesthood at the Catholic theological faculty of Ellwangen and Tübingen. After ordination in 1820, and after holding lesser posts, he served from 1826 to 1835 as professor of church history at Tübingen. Of the books, some published posthumously, and the articles he produced he is particularly remembered for *Die Einheit in der Kirche*, or as the subtitle has it, the principle of Catholicism set forth in the spirit of the fathers of the first three centuries (1825), and for the *Symbolik* (first edition, 1832). It was the debate that the latter work aroused—particularly Möhler's extended exchange with Ferdinand Christian Baur of the Protestant faculty of Tübingen—that led to Möhler's departure for Munich. (See *Möhler and Baur in Controversy, 1832–1838,* by the editor of this volume [Tallahassee, Fla.: Scholars Press, 1974].) Möhler in the short period before his death served there also as professor of church history.

The Dublin lawyer, James Burton Robertson, who translated the *Symbolik* into English created some confusion by rendering the title *Symbolism*. This, Möhler's chief work, is concerned, as the subtitle makes clear, with the doctrinal differences between Catholics and Protestants as those are evidenced by their

74

principal confessional statements; the origin of the title lies in the Latin *symbolum,* "creed." Today we would call the work *Symbolics.* The modern reader, coming along after decades of the ecumenical movement, may well be astonished at the tone Möhler takes. Möhler's purpose is to define the place and the rights of Catholicism in a divided Germany. In so doing he delivers one of the most severe critiques of Protestantism ever. The actual plan of the work is stated in the introduction, given here. It is important to note that Möhler wishes his exposition to be holistic, organic, systematic. He finds the root error of the Reformers to be their estimate of Adam after the Fall. The Reformers said Adam's nature was changed. Catholicism—in Trent's decrees on original sin and justification—asserts that human nature or essence was not changed. Human beings are still capable of freely cooperating with divine grace and meriting heaven. Along the way to the heavenly goal Catholic humanity will be aided by the seven sacraments as Trent defined them. The *Symbolic* is thus a large-scale (over seven-hundred-page) presentation of Catholic synergism, a presentation characterized by romantic breadth of view, concern for systematic coherence, and literary grace. Fifty years after the work first appeared one commentator affirmed that "Möhler made it an honor again to be a Catholic."

Some theologians merit the distinction of having passages in their works become *loci classici* for certain doctrines. When, for example, one thinks of proofs for the existence of God one thinks of the five ways in the *Summa theologiae* of Thomas Aquinas. Möhler belongs to this exclusive club, on the strength of how he described the church and the sacraments. Möhler's treatment of these areas passed on into Pius XII's letters *Mystici Corporis* (1943) and *Mediator Dei* (1947), and from there into the constitutions of Vatican II on the church and on the liturgy. Möhler, it would seem, made romantic sensibilities a self-conscious and enduring ingredient of Catholicism. Obvious examples are his discussion of the Redeemer living in the church and operating there as the primary agent of biblical proclamation and sacramental transaction, and of the church as the continuation of the incarnation, so that "the visible Church . . . is the Son of God himself, everlastingly manifesting himself among men in a human form, perpetually renovated, eternally young."

In what is given here Möhler's extensive footnotes have been much curtailed. For the full footnotes the reader should consult Robertson's translation, or better, Geiselmann's critical edition.

## INTRODUCTION: NATURE, EXTENT, AND SOURCES OF SYMBOLISM

By Symbolism we understand the scientific exposition of the doctrinal differences among the various religious parties opposed to each other in consequence of the ecclesiastical revolution of the sixteenth century, as these doctrinal differences are evidenced by the public confessions or symbolical books of these parties. From this definition it follows:

First, that Symbolism has directly and immediately neither a polemical nor apologetical aim. It has only to give a statement, to furnish a solid and impartial account, of the differences which divide the abovementioned Christian communities. This exposition, doubtless, will indirectly assume partly a defensive, partly an offensive character, for the personal conviction of the writer will involuntarily appear, and be heard sometimes in the tone of adhesion and commendation, sometimes in the tone of reproof and contradiction. Still, the mere explanatory and narrative character of Symbolism is thereby as little impaired as that of the historical relation in which the historian conceals not his own personal opinion respecting the personages brought forward and the facts recounted. The claims of a deeper science, especially, cannot be satisfied unless the exposition occasionally assume in part a polemical, in part an apologetical, character. A bare narrative of facts, even when accompanied with the most impartial and most solid historical research, will not suffice; nay, the individual proportions of a system of doctrine must be set forth in their mutual concatenation and their organic connection. Here, it will be necessary to decompose a dogma into the elements out of which it has been formed and to reduce it to the ultimate principles whereby its author had been determined; there, it will be expedient to trace the manifold changes which have occurred in the dogma: but at all times must the parts of the system be viewed in their relation to the whole, and be referred to the fundamental and all-pervading idea. During this analytic process—without which a true, profound, and vivid apprehension of the essential nature of the different confessions is absolutely impossible—the relation of these to the gospel and to Christian reason must necessarily be brought out, and the conformity of the

From *Symbolik; oder, Darstellung der dogmatischen Gegensätze der Katholiken und Protestanten,* crit. ed. Josef Rupert Geiselmann, 2 vols. (Cologne: Hegner, 1960–61), 1:17–30, 352–76, 387–418, 427–32, 448–56. The translation is from *Symbolism; or Exposition of the Doctrinal Differences between Catholics and Protestants,* trans. James Burton Robertson, 2 vols. (London, 1843), 1:1–15, 333–53, 2:5–39, 49–54, 71–79.

one and the opposition of the other to universally acknowledged truths must follow as a matter of course. In this way, indeed, Symbolism becomes the most cogent apology, or allusive refutation, without designing to be, in itself, either the one or the other.

Secondly, in the definition we have given, the limits and extent of our course of Symbolism have been expressed. For, as they are only those ecclesiastical differences that sprang out of the convulsions of the sixteenth century that form the subject of our investigations, so all those religious communities that have arisen out of earlier exclusion or voluntary secession from the Church, even though they may have protracted their existence down to our times, will necessarily be excluded from the range of our enquiries. Hence the course of doctrinal disputes in the Oriental Church will not engage our attention. The religious ferment of the sixteenth century and the ecclesiastical controversies which it produced are of a totally different nature from the contest which divides the Western and Eastern Churches. The controversy agitated in the West regards exclusively Christian anthropology, for it will be shown that, whatever other things may be connected with this, they are all mere necessary deductions from the answer given to the anthropological question mooted by the Reformers. The controversy on the other hand agitated in the East has reference to Christology, for it would be strange indeed if the orthodox Greek Church, whose dispute with the Catholic regards no doctrine of faith, were alone to claim attention, while the Nestorians and the Monophysites, who are separated from Catholics, orthodox Greeks, and Protestants by real doctrinal differences, were to be excluded from the enquiry. But the special objects of our undertaking neither occasion nor justify so extended a discussion. An account of these doctrinal differences has, moreover, appeared to us uncalled for, since even the most abridged ecclesiastical history furnishes, respecting all these phenomena, more information than is requisite for practical purposes. In fact, no present interest conducts us to the Oriental Church and its various subdivisions, for although the ancient disagreement of these communities with the Catholic and Protestant Churches still continues, it is at present without real and vital influence.

On the other hand, the doctrinal peculiarities of the Lutheran and Reformed Churches, in opposition to the Catholic Church as well as to each other, must be set forth with the utmost precision and in every possible bearing, as must also be the positions of the Catholic Church against the negations of the two former. It might, indeed, appear proper to presuppose a general acquaintance with the Catholic dogmas as asserted and maintained against the Reformers, in the same way as Plank, in his *Comparative View of the Churches,* has presupposed the knowledge of the Lutheran system of doctrine.[1] But as the tenets of Protestants have sprung only out of opposition to Catholic doctrine they can be understood only in this opposition, and therefore the Catholic thesis must be paralleled with the Protestant antithesis and compared with it in all its bearings if the latter would be duly appreciated. On the other hand, the Catholic doctrine will then only appear in its true light when confronted with the Protestant. The present comparative view of the differences between the Christian confessions is besides, as indicated in the Preface, destined for Protestant readers also, but that these on an average possess more than a superficial acquaintance with Catholic doctrine we cannot here reasonably suppose.

The various sects which have grown out of the Protestant Church, like the Anabaptists or Mennonites, the Quakers, Methodists, and Sweden-borgians, could the less pass unnoticed by us as they only further developed the original Protestantism and have in part alone consistently carried out its principles and pushed them to the farthest length. Hence, although all these sects did not spring up in the sixteenth century, we still regard them as in their inward purport belonging to that age.

The Socinians and Arminians, also, will claim our attention. These appear, indeed, as the opposite extreme to primitive Protestantism. For while the latter sprang out of a strong but one-sided excitement of feelings, the former, as in the case of the Socinians, either originated in a one-sided direction of the understanding or, as in the case of the Armin-ians, terminated in such a course, completely rejecting the fundamental doctrines of the Reformation, so that in them one extreme was replaced by another, while Catholicism holds the just medium between the two. Whether, moreover, the Socinians are to be numbered among Protestant sects is a matter of dispute among the Protestants themselves. It is, however, really unquestionable that Socinianism ought not to be looked upon as an appendage to orthodox Protestantism, as was strongly pointed out by us when we just now called the Socinian conception of Christianity the precise opposite to the old Protestant view. But as the Protestants have not yet succeeded in dismissing the Rationalists from their community, . . . we do not see why they should now, at least, refuse admittance to the Socinians. Nay, every one who abandons the Catholic Church, who only ceases to be a Catholic, whatever in other respects may be the doctrines which he believes or refuses to believe, though his creed may stand ever so low beneath that of the Socinians, is sure to find the portals of the Protestant Church thrown open to him with joy. It would therefore not be praiseworthy on our parts if in the name of Protestants we were to exercise an act of intolerance and deny to the Socinians the gratification of seeing, in one writing at least, the object of their ancient desire attained. On the other hand, the doctrines of the Rationalists cannot be matter of investigation here, because they form no separate ecclesiastical community, and we should have to set forth only the views of a thousand different individuals, not the tenets of a church or sect. They have no symbol and therefore can claim no place in our Symbolism. . . .

Thirdly, the definition we have given establishes the limits within which the characterization of the different ecclesiastical communities that fall within the compass of the present work must be confined. Treating only of doctrinal differences, it is the object of the present work solely to unfold the distinctive articles of belief, and to exclude all liturgical and disciplinary matters and in general all the nonessential ecclesiastical and political points of difference. . . . In this respect, Symbolism is distinguished from the science of comparative liturgy, ecclesiastical statistics, etc. It is only in a few cases that an exception from this principle has appeared admissible.

Fourthly and lastly, the sources are here pointed out from which Symbolism must draw. It is evident that the public confessions, or symbols, of the ecclesiastical communities in question must, above all, be attended to, and hence hath the science itself derived its name. Other sources, meanwhile, which offer any desirable explanation or more accurate decisions in reference to the matters in hand must not be neglected. To liturgies, prayers, and hymns, also, which are publicly used and are recognized by authority Symbolism may accordingly appeal, for in these the public faith is expressed. In appealing to hymns, however, great prudence is necessary, as in these the feeling and the imagination exert a too exclusive sway and speak a peculiar language which has nothing in common with dogmatic precision. Hence even from the Lutheran church-songs, although they comprise much very serviceable to our purpose, and some peculiar Protestant doctrines are very accurately expressed in them, as also from Catholic lays, hymns, and the like, we have refrained from adducing any proofs.

That even those writings of the Reformers which have not obtained the character of public confessions must be of great importance to our inquiries into Symbolism must be perfectly clear. Reference must especially be made to these when the internal signification and the worth of Protestant dogmas is to be apprehended. In the same way, Catholic theologians of acknowledged orthodoxy and, above all, the history of the Council of Trent offer many satisfactory and fuller elucidations of particular decisions in the Catholic formularies. Yet the individual opinion of one or more teachers belonging to any confession must not be confounded with the doctrine of the confession itself, a principle which must be extended even to the Reformers, so that opinions which may be found in their writings but have not received any express public sanction must not be noted down as general Protestant tenets. Between the use, however, of Catholic writers and of the Reformers for the purpose of proof and illustration in this Symbolism a very observable difference exists. The importance of the matter will render deeper insight into this difference necessary. The relation, namely, wherein the Reformers stand to the religious belief of their followers is of a very peculiar nature, and totally different from that of Catholic teachers to Catholic doctrine. Luther, Zwingli, and Calvin are *the creators* of those religious opinions prevalent among their disciples, while no Catholic dogma can be referred to any theologian as its author. As in Luther the circle of doctrines which constitute the peculiar moral life of the Protestant communities was produced with the most independent originality, as all who stand to him in a spiritual relation, like children to their parents, and on that account bear his name draw from him their moral nurture and live on his fulness, so it is from him we must derive the most vivid, profound, and certain knowledge of his doctrines. The peculiar emotions of his spirit, out of which his system gradually arose, or which accompanied its rise, the higher views wherein often, though only in passing, he embraced all its details as well as traced the living germ out of which the whole had by degrees grown up, the rational construction of his doctrine by the exhibition of his feelings—all this is of high significancy to one who will obtain a genuine scientific apprehension of Protestantism as a doctrinal system and who will master its leading, fundamental principle. The Protestant articles of faith are so livingly interwoven with the nature of their original production in the mind of Luther and with the whole succession of views which filled his soul that it is utterly impossible to sever them. The dogma is equally subjective with the causes which cooperated in its production and has no other stay nor value than what they afford. Doubtless, as we have before said, we shall never ascribe to the Protestant party as such what has not been received into their symbolical writings. But although we must never abandon this principle, yet we cannot confine ourselves to it. For this religious party was generally satisfied with the results of that process of intellectual generation whereby its doctrines had been produced, and separating by degrees those results from their living and deepest root, it rendered them thereby for the most part unintelligible to science, as the bulk of mankind are almost always contented with broken, unsubstantial, and airy theories. But it is for science to restore the connection between cause and effect, between the basis and the superstructure of the edifice; and to discharge this task the writings of Luther and, in a relative degree, of the other Reformers are to be sedulously consulted.

It is otherwise with individual Catholic theologians. As they found the dogmas on which they enlarge, which they explain or illustrate, *already preexisting,* we must in their labours accurately discriminate between their special and peculiar opinions and the common doctrines declared by the Church and received from Christ and the apostles. As these doctrines existed *prior to* those opinions, so they can exist *after* them and can therefore be scientifically treated *without* them and quite *independently* of them. This distinction between individual opinion and common doctrine presupposes a very strongly constituted community, based at once on history, on life, on tradition, and is only possible in the Catholic Church. But as it is possible, so also it is necessary, for unity in its essence is not identity. In science as in life such scope is to be afforded to the free expansion of individual exertion as is compatible with the existence of the common weal, that is to say, so far as it is not in opposition to it nor threatens it with danger and destruction. According to these principles the Catholic Church ever acted, and by that standard we may estimate not only the oft-repeated charge that, amid all their vaunts of unity, Catholics ever had divisions and various disputes among themselves but also the Protestant habit of ascribing to the whole Church the opinions of one or more individuals. Thus, for instance, it would argue a very defective insight into the nature of Catholicism if any one were to give out as the doctrine of the Church Augustine's and Anselm's exposition of original sin, or the theory of the latter respecting the vicarious atonement of Christ, or Anton Günther's speculative enquiries on those dogmas. These are all very laudable and acute endeavours to apprehend, as a conception of reason, the revealed doctrine, which alone is binding upon all, but it is clear that it would be gross ignorance to confound them with the teaching of the Church itself. For a time even *a conception of a dogma,* or an opinion, may be tolerably general without, however, becoming an integral portion of a dogma, or a dogma itself. There are here eternally changing individual forms of an universal principle which may serve this or that person or a particular period for mastering that universal principle by way of reflection and speculation—forms which may possess more or less of truth but whereon the Church pronounces no judgment, for the data for such a decision are wanting in tradition, and she abandons them entirely to the award of theological criticism.

From what has been said it follows that such a distinction as we speak of between dogma and opinion must extremely difficult for Protestants.

As their whole original system is only an individuality exalted into a generality, as the way in which the Reformers conceived certain dogmas and personally thought and lived in them perfectly coincided, in their opinion, with those dogmas themselves, so their followers have inherited of them an irresistible propensity everywhere to identify the two things. In Luther it was the inordinate pretension of an individuality which wished to constitute itself the arbitrary centre round which all should gather—an individuality which exhibited itself as the universal man in whom everyone was to be reflected—in short, it was the formal usurpation of the place of Christ, who undoubtedly as individual represents also redeemed humanity—a prerogative which is absolutely proper to Him, and after Him to the universal Church, as supported by Him. In modern times, when the other opposite extreme to the original Reformation has in many tendencies found favour with the Protestants, not only are all the conceivable individualities and peculiarities which can attach themselves to dogma willingly tolerated but even all the peculiar Christian dogmas are considered only as doctrines which we must tolerate and leave to individuals who may need them for their own personal wants, so that, if Luther raised his own individuality to the dignity of a generality, the generality is now debased into a mere individuality, and thus the true relation of the one to the other can never be established. In the consistent progress of things everyone considered himself, in a wider circle, the representative of humanity, redeemed from error at least—as a sort of microcosmic Christ. But in order that this phenomenon might not appear too strange, for it is no easy matter to reconcile one Christ with the other, an expedient of compromise was discovered by leaving to each one his own—that is to say, by permitting him to be his own Redeemer and to represent himself, as also to consider the extreme points wherein all individuals concur, as representing redeemed humanity. The common property of Protestants could only now consist of some abstract formulas, which must be acceptable to very many non-Christians. As everyone wished to pass for a Christ, the true Christian, the real scandal to the world, necessarily vanished, for as each one redeemed himself there was no longer a common Redeemer.

To this we may add the following circumstances, whereby was formed that peculiar kind of individuality which the Protestants would fain confound with the universal principles of the Catholic Church. Protestantism arose partly out of the opposition to much that was undeniably bad and defective in the Church, and therein consists the good it has achieved, although this was by no means peculiar to it, since hostility to evil upon Church principles existed before it and has never ceased to exist beside it. Protestantism, too, sprang partly out of the struggle against peculiar scientific expositions of doctrine and against certain institutions in ecclesiastical life which we may comprehend under the expression of a mediaeval individuality, but a change in this respect was the object of many zealous churchmen since the latter half of the fourteenth century. As the contest grew in vehemence it came to pass, as passion views everything in a perverse light, that matters took such a shape in the eyes of the Reformers as if the whole preexisting Church *consisted* of those elements of evil, and of those individual peculiarities—as if both constituted the *essence* of the Church. This opinion having now been formed, the two things were further set forth in the strongest colours of exaggeration, for in this course of proceeding there was a manifest advantage, since with such weapons the Catholic Church was most easily combated. Accordingly, among the Reformers we very frequently find (if we except some rare but gratifying avowals in Luther's writings) not only the necessary distinction between the dogmas of the Church and the individual views or conceptions of particular writers and periods of time entirely overlooked but the latter so pointedly brought forward that the former not seldom sink totally into the background. The nature of the origin of any institution determines in general its duration. If, accordingly, Protestants would enter into the distinction in question, if, in their estimate of Catholicism, they would look only to what was universally received, what was laid down in her public formularies, and leave all the rest to history, then as their first rise would have been impossible, their separate existence even now would be essentially endangered. The complaint here adverted to, a complaint which has so often been made by Catholics, appears, therefore, to be so intimately interwoven with their whole opposition against Protestantism that it is only by the cessation of that opposition the complaint will ever be set aside.

Though from this it will be evident that in the course of our symbolical enquiries a use is to be made of the works of the Reformers which cannot be made of those of any Catholic writer, we must nevertheless now draw attention to some peculiar difficulties attending the use of Luther's and Melanchthon's writings. Luther is very variable in his assertions. He too often brings forward the very reverse of his own declarations and is in a surprising degree the sport of momentary impressions and transient moods of mind. He delights also in exaggerations, willingly runs into extremes, and likes what are called energetic expressions, in which oftentimes, when taken by themselves, his true meaning is certainly not easy to be discovered. The most advisable course under these circumstances is by a careful study of his writings to learn the keynote which pervades the whole: individual passages can in no case be considered as decisive in themselves, and a sort of average estimate, therefore, naturally recommends itself to our adoption. With Melanchthon we have fewer difficulties to encounter. He, indeed, is involved in contradictions of greater moment than Luther, but for that very reason he lightens for us the task of separating in his works the genuine Protestant elements from their opposites. In this respect his reforming career may be accurately divided into two distinct parts. In the first, being yet a young man, little familiar with theological studies and versed only in classical literature, he was by degrees so subjugated in religious matters by the personal influence of Luther as to embrace without any qualification his way of thinking; and it was in this period that the first edition of his most celebrated work, the *Loci Theologici*, appeared. When his ripening talents, his more extended theological learning, and a more enlarged experience of life had pointed out to him the abyss before which he had been conducted he receded by degrees but yet was never able to attain to a decided independence of mind, for in the flower of his years he had given himself up to foreign influences that confined and deadened his spirit. He now on one side vacillated without a compass between Catholicism and Lutheranism, on another side between Lutheranism and Calvinistic opinions. Hence, we have felt no difficulty in making use only of his above-mentioned work in the edition described, and in opposition to those who may be of another opinion we appeal to the controversies that have been agitated among the Lutherans respecting the *Corpus Philippicum* and to the final settlement of the question. In respect to Zwingli and Calvin there are no such difficulties, as the former for the most part has only an historical importance, and the latter is ever uniform with himself.

## 34. Doctrine of the Catholics on the Most Holy Sacrament of the Altar, and on the Mass

The mighty subject which is now about to engage our attention gave birth to the most important controversies between the Christian communions. All the other distinctive doctrines are here combined, though in a more eminent degree, for although, as has been clearly shown, in every point of difference the whole system of doctrine is mirrored forth, yet here this is more especially the case. On the view, too, which we take of this subject depends the fact whether the Church be destined to possess a true and vital worship or ought to be devoid of one.

According to the clear declarations of Christ and his apostles and the unanimous teaching of the Church, attested by the immediate followers of our Lord's disciples, Catholics firmly hold that in the sacrament of the altar Christ is truly present, and indeed in such a way that Almighty God, who was pleased at Cana, in Galilee, to convert water into wine, changes the inward substance of the consecrated bread and wine into the body and blood of Christ.

We therefore adore the Saviour mysteriously present in the sacrament,[2] rejoice in his exceeding condescending compassion, and express in canticles of praise and thanksgiving our pious emotions as far as the divinely enraptured soul of man can express them.

Out of this faith sprung the Mass, which, in its essential purport, is as old as the Church, and even in its more important forms can be *proved to have been already in existence* in the second and third centuries. But to unfold more clearly the Catholic doctrine on this point, it is necessary to anticipate somewhat of our reflections on the Church. The Church, considered in one point of view, is the living figure of Christ, manifesting himself and working through all ages, whose atoning and redeeming acts it, in consequence, eternally repeats and uninterruptedly continues. The Redeemer not merely lived eighteen hundred years ago, so that he hath since disappeared and we retain but an historical remembrance of him as of a deceased man, but he is, on the contrary, eternally living in his Church; and in the sacrament of the altar he hath manifested this in a sensible manner to creatures endowed with sense. He is, in the announcement of his word, the abiding teacher; in baptism he perpetually receives the children of men into his communion; in the tribunal of penance he pardons the contrite sinner, strengthens rising youth with the power of his spirit in confirmation, breathes into the bridegroom and the bride a higher conception of the nuptial relations, unites himself most intimately with all who sigh for eternal life under the forms of bread and wine, consoles the dying in extreme unction, and in holy orders institutes the organs whereby he worketh all this with never-tiring activity. If Christ, concealed under an earthly veil, unfolds to the end of time his whole course of actions begun on earth, he of necessity eternally offers himself to the Father as a victim for men; and the real permanent exposition hereof can never fail in the Church if the historical Christ is to celebrate in her his entire imperishable existence.[3]

The following may perhaps serve to explain the Catholic view on this subject, since it is matter of so much difficulty to Protestants to form a clear conception of this dogma.[4]

Christ, on the cross, has offered the sacrifice for our sins. But the incarnate son of God, who hath suffered, died, and risen again from the dead for our sins, being according to his own teaching present in the Eucharist, the Church from the beginning hath at His command (Luke 22:20) substituted the Christ mysteriously present and visible only to the spiritual eye of faith for the historical Christ, now inaccessible to the corporeal senses. The former is taken for the latter, because the latter is likewise the former—both are considered as one and the same; and the eucharistic Saviour, therefore, as the victim also for the sins of the world. And the more so as, when we wish to express ourselves accurately, the sacrifice of Christ on the cross is put only as a part for an organic whole. For his whole life on earth—his ministry and his sufferings, as well as his perpetual condescension to our infirmity in the Eucharist—constitute one great sacrificial act, one mighty action undertaken out of love for us, and expiatory of our sins, consisting indeed of various individual parts, yet so that none by itself is strictly speaking the sacrifice. In each particular part the whole recurs, yet without these parts the whole cannot be conceived. The will of Christ to manifest his gracious condescension to us in the Eucharist forms no less an integral part of his great work than all besides, and in a way so necessary indeed that, whilst we here find the whole scheme of Redemption reflected, without it the other parts would not have sufficed for our complete atonement. Who, in fact, would venture the assertion that the descent of the Son of God in the Eucharist belongs not to his general merits which are imputed to us? Hence the sacramental sacrifice is a true sacrifice—a sacrifice in the strict sense, yet so that it must in no wise be separated from the other things which Christ hath achieved for us, as the very consideration of the end of its institution will clearly show.[5] In this last portion (if we may so call it) of the great sacrifice for us all the other parts are to be present and applied to us: in this last part of the objective sacrifice the latter becomes subjective and appropriated to us. Christ on the cross is still an object strange to us: Christ in the Christian worship is our property, our victim. There he is the universal victim—here he is the victim for us in particular, and for every individual amongst us. There he was only the victim—here he is the victim acknowledged and revered. There the objective atonement was consummated—here the subjective atonement is partly fostered and promoted, partly expressed.

The Eucharistic sacrifice, in conformity to its declared ends, may be considered under a twofold point of view. The Church in general and every particular community within her being founded by the sacrifice of the son of God and by faith in the same and thus owing their existence to him, the Eucharistic sacrifice must, in the first place, be regarded as one of praise and thanksgiving. In other words, the Church declares that she is incapable of offering up her thanks to God in any other way than by giving him back who became the victim of the world, as if she were to say: "Thou didst, O Lord, for Christ's sake look down with graciousness and compassion upon us as *Thy children;* so vouchsafe that we with grateful hearts may revere Thee as *our Father* in Christ, thy Son, here present. We possess nought else that we can offer Thee save Christ; be graciously pleased to receive our sacrifice." While the community, in the person of the priest, performeth this it confesses perpetually what Christ became and still continues to be for its sake. It is not, however, the interior acts of thanksgiving, adoration, and gratitude which it offers up to God, but it is Christ himself present in the sacrament. These emotions of the soul are indeed excited, unfolded, kept up, and fostered by the presence and the self-sacrifice of the Saviour, but of themselves they are deemed unworthy to be presented to God. Christ, the victim in our worship, is the copious, inexhaustible source of the deepest devotion, but in order to be this, the presence of the Saviour, sacrificing himself for the sins of the world, is necessarily required—a presence to which, as to an outward object, the interior soul of man must attach itself and must unbosom all its feelings.

The community, however, continually professes itself a sinner, needing forgiveness and striving ever more and more to appropriate to itself the merits of Christ. Now the sacrifice appears propitiatory, and the Redeemer present enables us to be entirely his own children, or to become so in an ever-increasing degree. The present Saviour, in a voice audible to the spiritual-minded, incessantly addresses His Father above, "Be graciously pleased to behold in me the believing and repentant people," and then he crieth to his brethren below, "Come to me, all you that labour and are heavy laden, and I will refresh you: each one who returneth to me with all his heart shall find mercy, forgiveness of sins, and every grace." Hence in the liturgy of the Latin as well as of the Greek Church it is rightly said that it is Christ who, in the holy action, offers himself up to God as a sacrifice; he is at once the victim and the high priest. But we, recognising in the Eucharistic Christ that same Christ who out of love for us delivered himself unto death, even the death of the cross, exclaim at the elevation of the Host, wherever the Catholic Church extends, with that lively faith in his manifest mercy from which humility, confidence, love, and repentence spring, "O Jesus! for Thee I live; for Thee I die! O Jesus! Thine I am, living or dead."

It is now evident to all that the belief in the real presence of Christ in the Eucharist forms the basis of our whole conception of the mass. Without that presence the solemnity of the Lord's supper is a mere reminiscence of the sacrifice of Christ, exactly in the same way as the celebration by any society of the anniversary of some esteemed individual whose image it exhibits to view, or by some other symbol recalls to mind his beneficent actions. On the other hand, with faith in the real existence of Christ in the Eucharist the past becomes the present—all that Christ hath merited for us, and whereby he hath so merited it, is henceforth never separated from his person: He is present as that which he absolutely is, and in the whole extent of his actions, to wit, as the real victim. Hence the effects of this faith on the mind, the heart, and the will of man are quite other than if by the mere stretch of the human faculty of memory Christ be called back from the distance of eighteen hundred years. He himself manifests his love, his benevolence, his devotedness to us: He is ever in the midst of us, full of grace and truth.

Accordingly, the Catholic mass, considered as a sacrifice, is a solemnisation of the blessings imparted to humanity by God in Christ Jesus and is destined, by the offering up of Christ, partly to express in praise, thanksgiving, and adoration the joyous feelings of redemption on the part of the faithful, partly to make the merits of Christ the subject of their perpetual appropriation. It is also clear why this sacrifice is of personal utility to the believer, namely, because thereby pious sentiments, such as faith, hope, love, humility, contrition, obedience, and devotion to Christ, are excited, promoted, and cherished. The sacrifice presented to God, which as we have often said, is not separated from the work of Christ, merits internal grace for the culture of these sentiments, which are psychologically excited from without by faith in the present Saviour, whose entire actions and sufferings are brought before the mind. As according to Catholic doctrine forgiveness of sins cannot take place without sanctification, and a fitting state of the human soul is required for the reception of grace as well as an active concurrence towards the fructification of grace, the reflecting observer may already infer that it is not by a mere outward or bodily participation on the part of the community that the mass produces any vague indeterminate effects.

The sacrifice of the mass is likewise offered up for the living and the dead; that is to say, God is implored, for the sake of Christ's oblation, to grant to all those who are dear to us whatever may conduce to their salvation. With the mass, accordingly, the faithful join the prayer that the merits of Christ, which are considered as concentrated in the Eucharistic sacrifice, should be applied to all needing them and susceptible of them. To consider merely himself is a matter of impossibility to the Christian; how much less in so sacred a solemnity can he think only of himself and omit his supplication that the merits of Christ, which outweigh the sins of the whole world, may likewise be appropriated by all? The communion with the happy and perfect spirits in Christ is also renewed, for they are one with Christ, and his work cannot be contemplated without its effects. Lastly, all the concerns of inward and outward life—sad and joyful events, good and ill fortune—are brought in connection with this sacrifice; and at this commemoration in Christ, to whom we are indebted for the highest gifts, we pour out to God our thanksgivings and lamentations, and in Him and before Him we implore consolation, courage, and strength under sufferings, self-denial, clemency, and meekness in prosperity.

Hitherto, however, we have considered the mass merely as a sacrificial oblation, but this view by no means embraces its whole purport. The assembled congregation declares, from what we have stated, that *in itself, without Christ,* it discovers nothing—absolutely nothing—which can be agreeable to God: nay, nothing but what is inadequate, earthly, and sinful. Renouncing itself, it gives itself up to Christ full of confidence, hoping for his sake forgiveness of sins and eternal life, and every grace. In this act of self-renunciation and of entire self-abandonment to God in Christ the believer has, as it were, thrown off himself, excommunicated himself, if I may so speak, in his existence as separated from Christ, in order to live only by him and in him. Hence he is in a state to enter into the most intimate fellowship with Christ, to commune with him, and with his whole being to be entirely absorbed in him. For the unseemliness of the congregation no longer communicating every Sunday (as was the case in the primitive Church) and of the priest in the mass usually receiving alone the body of the Lord is not to be laid to the blame of the Church (for all the prayers in the holy sacrifice presuppose the sacramental communion of the entire congregation) but is to be ascribed solely to the tepidity of the greater part of the faithful. Yet are the latter earnestly exhorted to participate at least spiritually in the communion of the priest, and in this way to enter into the fellowship of Christ.[6]

Who will not call such a worship most Christian, most pious, and real—a worship wherein God is adored in spirit and truth? Indeed, how can a carnal-minded man, who will not believe in the incarnation of the Son of God—for the most powerful obstacle to this belief is in the fact that man clearly perceives he must be of a godly way of thinking so soon as he avows that God has become man—how can such a man look upon the mass as other than mere foolishness? The mass comprises an ever-recurring invitation to the confession of our sins, of our own weakness and helplessness. It is a living representation of the infinite love and compassion of God towards us, which He hath revealed and daily still reveals in the delivering up of His only-begotten Son, and therefore it contains the most urgent exhortation to endless thanksgiving, to effective mutual love, and to our heavenly glorification. Hence an adversary to such a worship must be one whose thoughts creep exclusively on the earth, or who of the whole act understands nought else but that the priest turns sometimes to the right, sometimes to the left, and is clothed in a motley-coloured garment. On the other hand, he who misapprehends the wants of man and the high objects of our Divine Redeemer in the establishment of the sacraments, he who, like the Manicheans, rejects the sacraments as coarse, sensual institutions and follows the track of a false spirituality, will regard the Catholic dogma as incomprehensible. In the opinion of such a man a worship is in the same degree spiritual as it is untrue. He lays before his God the lofty conceptions that have sprung out of the fulness of his intellectual powers, his holy feelings and inflexible resolves; these have no reference to the outward historical Christ but only to the ideal one, which is merged in the subjectivity of these feelings and ideas, while yet, by the fact of the external revelation of the Logos, internal worship must needs obtain a perpetual outward basis and, in truth, one representing the Word as delivered up to suffering, because it was under the form of a self-sacrifice for the sins of the world that this manifestation occurred. How, on the other hand, anyone who has once apprehended the full meaning of the incarnation of the Deity and who with joy confesses that his duty is the reverse (namely, to pass from seeming to real and divine existence) and has accordingly attained to the perception that the doctrine of a forgiveness of sins in Christ Jesus, of an exaltation of man unto God, and of a communication of divine life to him through our Lord must remain unprofitable until it be brought before us in concrete forms and be made to bear on our most individual relations—how anyone, I say, who clearly perceives all this can refuse to revere in the Catholic mass a divine institution I am utterly at a loss to conceive.

After this exposition we are probably now enabled to give a satisfactory solution to the chief objection which the Protestant communities have urged against the Catholic sacrifice of the mass. It is argued that by the mass the sacrifice of Christ on the cross is abolished, or that at any rate it receives a detriment, since the latter is considered as incomplete and needing a supplement. Now it is self-evident that the sacrifice of the mass, by keeping the oblation of Christ on the cross, or rather his whole ministry and sufferings, eternally present, presupposes the same and in its whole purport maintains the same; and so far from obliterating, it stamps them more vividly on the minds of men; and instead of supplying the bloody sacrifice of the cross with some hetergeneous element, it brings that sacrifice in its true integrity and original vitality to bear the most individual application and appropriation throughout all ages. It is one and the same undivided victim, one and the same High Priest, who on the mount of Calvary and on our altars hath offered himself up as an atonement for the sins of the world. But as this view is so obvious and as the Reformers nevertheless constantly repeated their objections, and impressed them so strongly on the minds of their followers that down to the present day they are repeated, something deeply rooted in the constitution of Protestantism itself seems to lurk under these objections and requires to be dragged to light. The decisive, conscious, undoubting faith that Christ before our eyes offers himself up for us to his eternal Father is quite calculated to produce an effect piercing into the inmost heart of man—far below the deepest roots of evil, so that sin in its inmost germ should be plucked from the will and the believer be unable to refuse to consecrate his life to God.[7] This ordinance of divine compassion necessarily leads, along with others, to the doctrine of internal justification as, on the other hand, the mass must be rejected with a sort of instinct wherever that doctrine is repudiated. If such great and living manifestations of the Redeemer's grace be unable thoroughly to purify the heart of man, if they be incapable of moving us to heartfelt gratitude and mutual love, to the most unreserved self-sacrifice and to the supplication that God would accept the oblation of ourselves, then we may with reason despair of our sanctification, and abandon ourselves to a mere *theory of imputation.* Now, perhaps, we may understand the full sense of the prayer which the Catholic at the elevation of the host utters to his Saviour: "To thee let my whole life be consecrated!"

Yet it ought not to be overlooked that the Reformers might be led into error through various, and some extremely scandalous abuses— especially an unspiritual, dry, mechanical performance and participation in this most mysterious function. Moreover, in default of historical learning, the high antiquity and apostolic origin of the holy sacrifice was unknown to them. If it cannot even be denied that their whole system, when regarded from one point of view, should have led them rather zealously to uphold than to disapprove of the sacrificial worship, yet they instinctively felt that in that worship there lay something infinitely more profound than all the doctrinal foundations of their own theological system, and accordingly they were driven by an unconscious impulse into a negative course.

There are now some particulars which remain to be considered. The doctrine of the change of bread and wine into the body and blood of Christ occupies an important place in the Catholic system of theology. Who doth not immediately think of that true, moral change which must take place in man so soon as he enters into communion with Christ, when the earthly man ceases, and the heavenly one begins, so that not we, but Christ liveth in us? In the Lord's supper Luther could not find Christ alone—bread and wine ever recurred to his mind because in the will of those regenerated in Christ he saw a permanent dualism, a perpetual co-existence of a spiritual and a carnal inclination, so that the latter, evil principle in man could never be truly converted into the former. Moreover, the doctrine of transubstantiation is the clearest representation of the objectivity of the food of the soul offered to us in the sacraments, and if we may dare to speak of the internal motions of the Divine economy, we should affirm that by this transubstantiation, wrought through a miracle of God's omnipotence, the strongest barrier is raised against any false subjective opinion. This doctrine, which most undoubtedly was at all times prevalent in the Church[8] though at one time more clearly, at another less clearly expressed according as occasion seemed to require, was in the Middle Ages laid down as a formal dogma, at a period when a false pantheistic mysticism, which we have elsewhere described, confounded the distinctions between the human and the divine and identified the Father with the world, the Son of God with the eternal idea of man and the Holy Ghost with religious feelings. Several Gnostic sects, and afterwards Amalrich of Chartres and David of Dinant, inculcated these errors. They regarded the historical revelation of God in Christ Jesus as a self-revelation of man and the sacraments were, therefore, in the eyes of these people nought else than what man chose of himself to attribute to them. Hence they rejected them as useless, and identifying with God the energies of the world, they conceived it singular that those powers which in themselves were thoroughly divine should receive from any external cause a divine nature or property. In this juncture of time it appeared necessary to point out more clearly than had been done at any previous period the primitive doctrine that had been handed down, and to set it in the strongest light with all the consequences deducible from it. The doctrine of a change *of substance* in created powers, to be applied as a divine and sanctifying nourishment of the spirit, most clearly established the opposition of Christianity to the fundamental tenet of these sects which took so much pleasure in the world as to confound it with the divinity, failing to observe that through the creative energy of the Redeemer only could a new world be called into existence and that, consequently, it was impossible for him to be engendered by the world. Moreover, out of the general movement of the age sprang a peculiar form of the most solemn adoration of the Eucharist (*festum corporis Christi*) so that it should be no longer possible to confound the internal acts of the human mind with the historical Christ, for by the very nature of the festival Christ was represented as *extraneous* to man and neither as one in himself with us nor as evolved out of us but as coming to us only from without.[9] In the doctrine of transubstantiation Christianity with its entire essence exhibits itself as an external, immediate divine revelation. At the period of the

Reformation, therefore, it was the more necessary to bring out this doctrine and the ecclesiastical rites connected with it in the most prominent form, as an empty, erroneous spiritualism was everywhere manifesting itself.

Lastly, in the Catholic Church the custom prevails of receiving communion only under one kind—a matter, as is evident, belonging to discipline and not to doctrine.[10] It is well known that this custom was not first established by an ecclesiastical law, but, on the contrary, it was in consequence of the general prevalence of the usage that this law was passed in approval of it. It is a matter of no less notoriety that the monasteries in whose centre this rite had its rise, and thence spread in ever wider circles, were led by a very nice sense of delicacy to impose on themselves this privation. A pious dread of desecrating, by spilling and the like, even in the most conscientious ministration, the form of the sublimest and the holiest whereof the participation can be vouchsafed to man was the feeling which swayed their minds. Some may hold this opinion for superstitious, and according as they see in the consecrated elements but mere material species the more easily will such an opinion occur to their minds. But the Catholic who even in this formality proves that it is not with him a mere matter of form when he abstains from the consecrated chalice and who, taught by examples in Scripture, or at any rate, by the authority of the primitive Church, thinks himself justified in so abstaining without becoming alienated from the spirit of Jesus Christ or losing any portion of his Eucharistic blessings—the Catholic, we say, rejoices that though in his Church there may be men of a perhaps exaggerated scrupulosity, yet none are found so carnal minded as to desire to drink in the communion not the holy blood but the mere wine and often, on that account, protest among other things against what they call a mutilation of the ordinance of Christ. We regret the more to be obliged to call the attention of our separated brethren to this abuse in their Church, as we must add that the number of those in their communion is not less considerable who forgo the the partaking of the sacred blood not from any spiritual dread of desecrating it by spilling but from a mere sensual feeling of disgust at the uncleanliness of those with whom they are to drink out of the same cup. When even the Zwinglians complain of this mutilation—they who have taken away the body with the blood of Christ and left in the room of them mere bread and mere wine—it is difficult not to think of that passage in Holy Writ wherein the Redeemer reproaches the Pharisees that they strain at gnats but swallow camels. However, we should rejoice if it were left free to each one to drink or not of the consecrated chalice; and this permission would be granted if with the same love and concord a universal desire were expressed for the use of the cup as, from the twelfth century, the contrary wish has been enounced.

36. Notion of the Church—Combination of Divine
    and Human Elements in Her—Infallibility
    of the Church

. . . By the Church on earth Catholics understand the visible community of believers founded by Christ, in which by means of an enduring apostleship, established by him and appointed to conduct all nations in the course of ages back to God, the works wrought by him during his earthly life for the redemption and sanctification of mankind are, under the guidance of his spirit, continued to the end of the world.

Thus, to *a visible society of men* is this great, important, and mysterious work entrusted. The ultimate reason of the visibility of the Church is to be found in the *incarnation* of the Divine Word. Had that Word descended into the hearts of men without taking the form of a servant, and accordingly without appearing in a corporeal shape, then only an internal, invisible Church would have been established. But since the Word became *flesh,* it expressed itself in an outward, perceptible, and human manner; it spoke as man to man, and suffered and worked after the fashion of men in order to win them to the kingdom of God, so that the means selected for the attainment of this object fully corresponded to the general method of instruction and education determined by the nature and the wants of man. This decided the nature of those means whereby the Son of God, even after He had withdrawn himself from the eyes of the world, wished still to work in the world and for the world. The Deity having manifested its action in Christ according to an *ordinary human fashion,* the form also in which His work was to be continued was thereby traced out. The preaching of his doctrine needed now a *visible, human* medium, and must be entrusted to visible envoys, teaching and instructing after the wonted method; men must speak to men, and hold intercourse with them in order to convey to them the word of God. And as in the world nothing can attain to greatness but in society, so Christ established a community; and his divine word, his living will, and the love emanating from him exerted an internal, binding power upon his followers, so that an inclination implanted by him in the hearts of believers corresponded to his outward institution. And thus a living, well-connected, visible association of the faithful sprang up, whereof it might be said—there they are, there is his Church, his institution, wherein he continueth to live, his spirit continueth to work, and the word uttered by him eternally resounds. Thus the visible

Church, from the point of view here taken, is the son of God himself, everlastingly manifesting himself among men in a human form, perpetually renovated and eternally young—the permanent incarnation of the same, as in Holy Writ even the faithful are called "the body of Christ." Hence it is evident that the Church, though composed of men, is yet not purely human. Nay, as in Christ the divinity and the humanity are to be clearly distinguished though both are bound in unity, so is he in undivided entireness perpetuated in the Church. The Church, his permanent manifestation, is at once divine and human—she is the union of both. He it is who, concealed under earthly and human forms, works in the Church, and this is wherefore she has a divine and a human part in an undivided mode, so that the divine cannot be separated from the human nor the human from the divine. Hence these two parts change their predicates. If the divine—the living Christ and his spirit—constitute undoubtedly that which is infallible and eternally inerrable in the Church, so also the human is infallible and inerrable in the same way, because the divine without the human has no existence for us; yet the human is not inerrable in itself but only as the organ and as the manifestation of the divine. Hence we are enabled to conceive *how* so great, important, and mysterious a charge *could* have been entrusted to men.

In and through the Church the redemption announced by Christ hath obtained, through the medium of his spirit, a reality, for in her his truths are believed and his institutions are observed, and thereby have become living. Accordingly we can say of the Church that she is the Christian religion in its objective form—its living exposition. Since the word of Christ (taken in its widest signification) found, together with his spirit, its way into a circle of men and was received by them it has taken shape, put on flesh and blood; and this shape is the Church, which accordingly is regarded by Catholics as the essential form of the Christian Religion itself. As the Redeemer by his word and his spirit founded a community wherein his word should ever be living, he entrusted the same to this society that it might be preserved and propagated. He deposited it in the Church that it might spring out of her ever the same and yet eternally new and young in energy, that it might grow up and spread on all sides. His word can never more be separated from the Church, nor the Church from his word. The more minute explanation how in the community established by Christ this word is maintained and propagated and each individual Christian can attain to the undoubted true possession of Christian doctrine is accordingly the first and most important matter to which we must direct attention. But as the Church is connected with the apostleship established by Christ and can by this only maintain itself, so this, in the second place, must come under consideration. But it is necessary to premise a closer examination of the leading propositions on which all others turn—a more detailed exposition of the ultimate reasons for that high reverence which Catholics pay to this Church.

### 37. More Detailed Exposition of the Catholic View of the Church

1. When the time appointed by Christ for the sending down of the Spirit was come, he communicated himself to the apostles and the other disciples, when gathered together in one place, and all of "one accord" (ὁμοθυμαδόν), they were longing for his coming. It was not while one here, the other there, abode in some hidden place: nay, they were expressly commanded[11] to wait for him while assembled in Jerusalem. At last the Holy Spirit that had been promised *appeared:* he took an outward shape—the form of fiery tongues—an image of his power that cleansed hearts from all wickedness and thereby united them in love. He wished not to come inwardly, as if he designed to uphold an invisible community; but in the same way as the Word was become *flesh,* so he came in a manner obvious to the senses and amid violent sensible commotions, like to "a rushing mighty wind." If individuals were filled with power from above in such a way that only inasfar as they constituted a *unity* could they become participators of the same, and if the hallowing of the spirit took place under sensible forms, so, according to the ordinance of the Lord for all times, the union of the interior man with Christ could take effect only under outward conditions and in communion with his disciples. *Under outward conditions:* for independently of outward instruction what are the sacraments but visible signs and testimonies of the invisible gifts connected with them? *In communion:* for no one by the act of baptism sanctifies himself; each one is, on the contrary, referred to those who already belong to the community. Nor is anyone but momentarily introduced into fellowship with the members of the Church—to remain only until, as one might imagine, the holy action should be consummated, for the fellowship is formed in order to be permanent and the communion begun in order to be continued to the end of life. Baptism is the *introduction* into the Church—the reception into the community of the faithful—and involves the duty as well as the right of sharing forever in her joys and her sorrows. Moreover, the administration of the sacraments, as well as the preaching of the word, was intrusted by the Lord to the apostolic college and to those commissioned by it, so that all believers, by means of this Apostolic College, are linked to the community and in a living manner connected with it. The

fellowship with Christ is accordingly the fellowship with his community—the internal union with him a communion with his Church. Both are inseparable, and Christ is in the Church and the Church in him.[12]

On this account, the Church, in the Catholic point of view, can as little fail in the pure preservation of the word, as in any other part of her task: she is infallible. As the individual worshipper of Christ is incorporated into the Church by indissoluble bonds, and is by the same conducted unto the Saviour and abideth in him only insofar as he abideth in the Church, his faith and his conduct are determined by the latter. He must bestow his whole confidence upon her, and she must therefore merit the same. Giving himself up to her guidance, he ought in consequence to be secured against delusion: she *must* be inerrable. To no individual considered as such doth infallibility belong, for the Catholic, as is clear from the preceding observations, regards the individual only as a member of the whole, as living and breathing in the Church. When his feelings, thoughts, and will are conformable to her spirit, then only can the individual attain to inerrability. Were the Church to conceive the relation of the individual to the whole in an opposite sense and consider him as personally infallible, then she would destroy the very notion of community, for communion can only be conceived as necessary when the true faith and pure and solid Christian life cannot be conceived in individualisation.

Hence it is with the profoundest love, reverence, and devotion [that] the Catholic embraces the Church. The very thought of resisting her, of setting himself up in opposition to her will, is one against which his inmost feelings revolt, to which his whole nature is abhorrent, and to bring about a schism—to destroy unity—is a crime before whose heinousness his bosom trembles and from which his soul recoils. On the other hand, the idea of community, in the first place, satisfies his feelings and his imagination and, in the second place, is equally agreeable to his reason, while in the third place the living appropriation of this idea by his will appears to him to concur with the highest religious and ethical duty of humanity. Let us now consider the first of these reasons. No more beautiful object presents itself to the imagination of the Catholic, none more agreeably captivates his feelings, than the image of the harmonious interworkings of countless spirits who, though scattered over the whole globe, endowed with freedom, and possessing the power to strike off into every deviation to the right or to the left, yet preserving still their various peculiarities, constitute one great brotherhood for the advancement of each other's spiritual existence—representing one idea, that of the reconciliation of men with God, who on that account have been reconciled with one another and are become one body.[13] If the state be such a wonderful work of art that we account it if not a pardonable, yet a conceivable, act for the ancients to have made it an object of divine worship and almost everywhere considered the duties of the citizen as the most important—if the state be something so sacred and venerable that the thought of the criminal who lays on it a destroying and desecrating hand fills us with detestation—what an object of admiration must the Church be, which with the tenderest bonds unites such an infinite variety of subjects, and this unimpeded by every obstacle, by rivers and mountains, deserts and seas, by languages, national manners, customs, and peculiarities of every kind, whose stubborn, unyielding nature defies the power of the mightiest conquerors? Her peace, which cometh down from Heaven, strikes deeper roots into the human breast than the spirit of earthly contention. Out of all nations, often so deeply divided by political interests and temporal considerations, the Church builds up the house of God, in which all join in one hymn of praise as in the temple of the harmless village all petty foes and adversaries gather round the one sanctuary with one mind. And as often here, on a small scale, the peace of God will bring about earthly peace, so there, on a larger scale, the same result will frequently ensue. But who can deem it a matter of astonishment that Catholics should be filled with joy and hope and, enraptured at the view of the beautiful construction of their Church, should contemplate with delight that grand corporation which they form, since the philosophers of art declare that the beautiful is only *truth manifested and embodied!* Christ, the eternal truth, hath built the Church; in the communion of the faithful, truth transformed by his spirit into love is become living among men: how could then the Church fail in the highest degree of beauty? Hence we can comprehend that indescribable joy which hath ever filled the Church when existing contests have been allayed and schisms have been terminated. In the primitive ages we may adduce the reunion of the Novatian communities with the Catholic Church, so movingly described by Dionysius of Alexandria and Cyprian of Carthage, the termination of the Meletian schism, and the rest. From a later period we may cite the event of the reunion of the Western and Eastern Churches which occurred at the Council of Florence. Pope Eugenius IV expresses the feelings which then overflowed all hearts when he says, "Rejoice, ye heavens, and exult, O earth: the wall of separation is pulled down which divided the Eastern and the Western Churches; peace and concord have returned; for Christ, the cornerstone, who out of two hath made one, unites with the strongest bands of love both walls and holds them together in the covenant of eternal unity: and so, after long and melancholy evils, after the dense, cloudy darkness of a protracted schism, the light of long-desired union beams once more upon all. Let our mother the Church rejoice, to whom it hath been granted to see her hitherto contending sons return to unity and peace: let her who during their division shed such bitter tears now thank Almighty God for their beautiful concord. All believers over the face of the earth, all who are called after Christ, may now congratulate their mother, the Catholic Church, and rejoice with her," etc.[14]

2. Yet it is not merely the imagination and the feelings of the Catholic which are contented by this idea of the Church, but his reason also is thereby satisfied—and indeed, because the idea which he has conceived of the Church alone corresponds to the notion of the Christian Church and to the end of revelation. It corresponds, in the first place, to the notion of the Christian Church, as is clear from what follows. Truth we cannot conceive other than as one, and the same holds good of Christian truth. The Son of God, our Redeemer, is a distinct being: he is what he is, and none other, eternally like unto himself, constantly one and the same. Not in vain do the Holy Scriptures connect all with *His Person:* the more they do this, the more important is it to conceive him exactly as he really was. Certain it is that every error in relation to his person exercises a more or less injurious influence on the piety and virtue of its professors, whereas a right knowledge of his person forms the surest and most solid basis of a holy and happy life. In like manner will the pure appropriation of *his work* by and in our souls produce the richest, most substantial, and fairest fruits, while any falsification of that work, in any one respect, is sure to be attended with injurious consequences to practical life. As Christ, therefore, is one, and his work is one in itself, as accordingly there is but one truth and truth only maketh free, so he can have willed but one Church, for the Church rests on the basis of belief in him and hath eternally to announce him and his work. On the other hand, the human mind is everywhere the same, and always and in all places is created for truth and the one truth. Its essential spiritual wants, amid all the changing relations of time and place, amid all the distinctions of culture and education, remain eternally the same: we are all sinners and stand in need of grace, and the faith which one has embraced in the filial simplicity of one's heart another cannot outgrow, though he be gifted with the subtlest intellect and possess all the accumulated wisdom which the genius of man in every zone and in every period of his history may have produced. Thus the oneness of the human spirit, as well as the oneness of truth, which is the food of spirits, justifies in the views of the reflecting Catholic *the notion* of the one visible Church.

But secondly, the end of revelation requires a Church as the Catholic conceives it, that is, a Church one and necessarily visible. The manifestation of the eternal Word in the flesh had the acknowledged end to enable man (who by his own resources was capable neither of obtaining, with full assurance, a true knowledge of God and of his own nature nor of mastering that knowledge even with the aid of old surviving traditions), to enable man, we say, to penetrate with undoubting certainty into religious truths. For those truths, as we stated above, will then only give a vigorous and lasting impulse to the will in an upward direction when they have first taken strong hold of the reason, whence they can exert their effects. The words of Archimedes, δόσ μοί ποῦ στῶ,[15] are here applicable, and in an especial degree. The divine truth, in one word, must be embodied in Christ Jesus and thereby be bodied forth in an outward and living phenomenon, and accordingly become a deciding authority, in order to seize deeply on the whole man and to put an end to pagan skepticism—that sinful uncertainty of the mind, which stands on as low a grade as ignorance.

But this object of the divine revelation in Christ Jesus would, according to the conviction of Catholics, either have wholly failed or in any case have been very imperfectly attained if this bodying forth of the divine truth had been only momentary and the personal manifestation of the Word had not had sufficient force to give to its sounds the highest degree of intensive movements and to impart to them the utmost efficacy, or in other words, to breathe into them the breath of life and call into existence a society which, in its turn, should be the living exposition of the truth and remain unto all times a derivative but adequate authority, that is, should represent Christ himself.

This sense Catholics give to the words of the Lord, "As the Father hath sent me, so I send you"; "whoso heareth me, heareth you"; "I shall remain with you all days, even to the consummation of the world"; "I will send the Spirit of truth, who will lead you into all truth." Man is so much a creature of sense that the interior world—the world of ideas—must be presented to him in the form of an image to enable him to obtain a consciousness or to gain a true and clear apprehension of it, and to hold by it firmly as the truth, and indeed, the image must be *permanent,* that being present to every individual through the whole course of human history it may constantly renew the prototype. Hence the authority of the Church is necessary if Christ is to be a true, determining authority for us. Christ wrought miracles, nay, his whole life was a miracle, not merely to establish the credibility of *his words* but also *immediately to represent and symbolise* the most exalted truths, to wit, God's omnipotence, wisdom, love, and justice, the immortality of man, and his worth in the eyes of God. If we adopt the idea of an invisible Church then neither the *incarnation* of the Son of God nor his *miracles* nor in general any outward, positive revelation can be conceived, because they comprise *authoritative proofs, outward visible manifestations* of eternal ideas, and accordingly they are by force of an internal necessity there gradually rejected where it is assumed that Christ has founded a mere invisible Church, since the members of such a Church need only invisible, internal proofs to obtain certitude. *On the other hand, the authority of the Church is the medium of all which in the Christian religion resteth on authority and is authority, that is to say, the Christian religion itself, so that Christ himself is only insofar an authority as the Church is an authority.*

We can never arrive at an external authority, like Christ, by *purely spiritual* means. The attempt would involve a contradiction which could only be disposed of in one of two ways: either we must renounce the idea that in Christ God manifested himself in history to the end that the conduct of mankind might be permanently determined by him, or we must learn the fact through a living, definite, and vouching fact. Thus authority must have authority for its medium. As Christ wished to be the adequate authority for all ages, he created by virtue of his power something homogeneous to it, and consequently something *attesting and representing* the same, eternally destined to bring his authority before all generations of men. He established a credible institution in order to render the true faith in himself perpetually possible. Immediately founded by him, its existence is the de facto proof of what he really was, and in the same way as in his life he made, if I may so speak, the higher truths accessible to the senses, so doth his Church, for she hath sprung immediately out of the vivid intuition of these symbolised truths. Thus as Christ in his life represented under a visible typical form the higher order of the world, so the Church doth in like manner, since what he designed in his representation hath through the Church and in the Church been *realised.* If the Church be not the authority representing Christ then all again relapses into darkness, uncertainty, doubt, distraction, unbelief, and superstition; *revelation becomes null and void, fails of its real purpose, and must henceforth be even called in question and finally denied.*

The truth which the Catholic here expresses can be in another way made evident by occurrences in everyday life and by great historical facts. The power of society in which man lives is so great that it ordinarily stamps its image on him who comes within its circle. Whether it serve truth or falsehood, whether it direct its efforts towards higher objects or follow ignoble pursuits, invariably will it be found to fashion the character of its members after its own model. Hence where skepticism has spread in a community and has impressed its image on its bosom it is a work of infinte difficulty for the individual to rise superior to its influence. Faith, on the other hand, when man sees it firmly established like a rock about him, and the community, which presents a great and lively image of attachment to the Redeemer and of happiness in him—the community, we say, whose imperishable existence is faith in him and accordingly himself—necessarily seize and fill up the whole mind of the individual. Accordingly, should the religious man not live in a community which hath the indestructible consciousness of possessing the truth and which hath the strongest internal and external grounds for that belief, such an individual would necessarily become a prey to the most distracting doubts, and his faith would either take no root or soon again wither.

Let us once more recur to the miracles in the history of the Christian religion but regard the subject from a different point. A certain view of divine things which has once obtained full consistency among any people, or any number of nations, takes so strong a hold on the individual man that without some higher extraneous interposition any *essential* change for the better, that is to say, any transition from falsehood to truth, is utterly impossible. Had Christ not wrought miracles, had the labours of the apostles not been accompanied with signs, had the Divine power to work such wonders not been transmitted to their disciples, never would the Gospel have overcome the heathenism of the Greek and Roman world. Error had usurped the rights which belong to truth alone, and man, who by his very nature is compelled to receive the worship of the social state in which he has been fixed as the true expression, the faithful image, of religious truth as it is in itself, needed, of course, extraordinary external proofs for the new order of things and indeed till such time as this order had been consolidated into a vast social organism. These high attestations in favour of truth appear most striking and most frequent in the life of the Redeemer himself, because the yet concentrated power of the old world was first to be burst asunder, and those who were destined to be the first fruits of the new kingdom of God were to be torn from its magic circle. In proportion as the boundaries of the Church were extended and the idea of redemption and the power of the cross were embodied in a more vigorous social form miracles declined, till at last they had completely fulfilled their destination and had caused the recognition of the authority that was to supply their place. In this authority, as we said above, they always continue their attestation, because that authority is their own production; and the Church is conscious of owing her very existence to those miracles and without them cannot at all conceive herself. Hence the fact, again, that together with the authority founded by these extraordinary works of God faith too in these works ever simultaneously disappears.

Hence what a whimsical—we cannot say wonderful—race are the idealists of our time! St. Paul, who had such a spiritual but at the same time ecclesiastical conception of all things, instituted so living a relation between his faith and the conviction of the Lord's resurrection that he expressly declared, "If Christ be not risen from the dead, then is our faith vain." And how was it otherwise possible, since in Christianity, which is a divine and positive revelation, the abstract idea and the historical fact, the internal and the external truth, are inseparably united? Our idealists and spiritualists have no need of miracles for the confirmation of their faith! *Yes, truly, for that faith is one of their own making, and not the faith in Christ;* and it would be indeed singular if God were to confirm a faith so fabricated by men. No less false and idle is that idealism which separates the authority of the Church from the authority of Christ. Even in this point of view the reverence which the Catholic bears for his Church is fully justified by reason. As from the beginning the abstract idea and the positive history, doctrine and fact, internal and external truth, inward and outward testimony were organically united, so must religion and Church be conjoined, and this for the reason *that God became man.* Could Satan succeed in annihilating the Christian Church, then the Christian religion would be at the same time annihilated and Christ himself would be vanquished by him.

3. The third point in which the Catholic finds his view of the Church so commendable is the influence which it has exerted on the cultivation and direction of the will, on the religious and moral amelioration of the whole man. We speak here no longer of the influence of a clear and firm belief of the truth on the will—a firmness of belief which only the recognition of an outward and permanent teaching authority can produce (of this we have already spoken)—but of a direction given to the will by a living membership with an all-embracing, religious society. An ancient philosopher has with reason defined man to be a social animal. However little the peculiarity of man's nature is here defined (for his peculiar kind of sociability is not pointed out), yet a deep trait of what determines the civilisation of man by means of man is in this definition undoubtedly indicated. It is only races which, groaning under the destiny of some heavy curse, have sunk into the savage state that become from the loss of their civilisation seclusive and with the most limited foresight fall back on their own resources, feel no want of an intercourse with other nations, or of an exchange of ideas, of which they possess nothing more, or of a communication of the products of their industry

and art, that have entirely disappeared. These productions, which are already in themselves symbols of the intellectual character of their authors, flow into foreign countries dressed, as it were, in the mental habits and characteristics of their home. Traces of the spirit of all the nations through which these productions pass are impressed upon them in their course, so that they always arrive at the place of their destination with a wealth of a far higher kind than that which they intrinsically possess. From all these currents of civilisation is the savage withdrawn, for because he is all-sufficient to himself is he a savage, and because he is a savage he suffices for himself. When the foreigner *(hostis)* was synonymous with the enemy, when one's country (Iran) included all that was absolutely good, and abroad (Turan) all that was absolutely evil, when the gods in the east and the west, in the land of the Colchians, the Cretans, and the Egyptians, rejoiced in the blood of foreigners, what a gloomy, ferocious existence must have circumscribed nations in this their seclusion and mutual independence! For the divinity of the nation was regaled with such blood only because the nation itself found therein a horrible gratification and made its own delight a standard for the joys of its deity. *The maintenance of intercourse and communion with foreigners and, accordingly, the voluntary establishment of relations of dependence on them* is thus an absolute condition to the general civilisation of man, so that the more this communion and mutual dependence is extended, that is to say, the more the notion of what is foreign disappears, the more is humanity exalted. With this general relation of dependence the dependence of man on the domestic relations of law and government keeps equal pace. The more polished and civilised the members of a state, the more are they bound together by wise ordinances, holy laws, venerable customs and manners, which wisely determine the mutual relations of rights and duties, so that, in fact, with every higher degree of internal freedom the outward bonds are proportionably straitened. On the other hand, the greater the state of barbarism, the greater is the external independence, so that the wildest savage is, in a material point of view, the most free.

What do these facts import but a wonderful, mysterious, inexplicable connection of the individual man with the human race, so that he comprehends himself better the more he seems to be absorbed in his kind and it is only in humanity that man is understood? Yet this internal emancipation by means of outward restraints of which we have hitherto spoken is not that which is the most interior, and serves only as a similitude or illustration of something higher. The true emancipation from low-mindedness and self-seeking is a problem which, as is avowed, religion alone can solve. In the same way as civilisation is determined by political life and by obedience to the institutions of the state, yea, even by the dependence, though naturally looser, on other nations, so is true religiousness promoted by subjection to the Church. For it is an incontrovertible maxim of experience that the individual who is unconnected with any ecclesiastical community has either no religion or a very meagre and scanty one, or is given up to a distempered fancy and a wild fanaticism, so that in none of the three cases can religion exert her blessed influences. On the other hand, the more stable the ecclesiastical community to which we belong, the more will the true, interior qualities of man expand and bloom forth in freedom, so that he who will lead a righteous life in the Catholic Church, whereof the very principle is the real unity and vital communion of all believers, he, we say, will attain to the highest degree of moral and religious perfection. It is no inane conception, no idle phantom, no illusion of a diseased mind which he embraces and to which he surrenders his obedience, but it is a reality, and a holy reality, wherein true faith, and love manifesting itself in deeds—coupled with *humility* and *self-denial* in the strongest and most comprehensive sense of the words—are nurtured. The more widely diffused the community to which the Catholic belongs, the more defined and the more manifold are the relations wherein he stands, the more multiplied the bonds wherewith he is encompassed. But as we said above, those very bonds which exhibit the reality of the community produce a result the very reverse of restraint and establish the internal freedom of man, or promote the purest *humanity;* for this expression may be used, since God became man. Without external bonds there is no true spiritual association, so that the idea of a mere invisible universal community to which we should belong is an idle, unprofitable phantom of the imagination and of distempered feelings destitute of all influence on mankind. In proportion only as a religious society approximates to the Catholic Church doth it exert a more efficacious influence on spiritual life. Here indeed we may observe, as shall be afterwards proved, that it is only according to Catholic principles a Church can be consistently formed, and where out of her pale anything of the kind exists the truth of what we assert is confirmed, to wit, that where a ray of true Christian light doth fall it will have the effect of binding and uniting, whereby all the doctrines tending to schism and division are, practically at least, refuted.

And what the Catholic, in the way described, feels and thinks, wishes and strives for he finds clearly laid down in Holy Writ. The divine Founder of the Church in the following important words enlarges, among other things, on the oneness and visibility of the community into which those who were to take his name were to be received: "And not for them only do I pray *but for them also who through their word shall believe in me,* that they all may be one, as thou Father in me, and I in thee, that they also may be one in us, *that the world may believe that thou hast sent me.* And the glory which thou has given me I have given to them, that they may be one as we also are one. I in them, and thou in me, that they may be made perfect in one, and the world may know that thou hast sent me, and hast loved them as thou hast also loved me."[16] What fulness of thoughts we find here! The Lord putteth up a prayer for the gift of unity and the union of all who shall believe, and for a unity, too, which finds its model only in the relation existing between the Father and the Son of Man. "*In us* shall they be one": that is to say, the unity of those believing in me is of so exalted a nature that it is only by the communication of a higher life, by a divine principle [that] it can be brought about, by the one faith, the same hope, and love, which are of divine institution. In the same way as the living foundation of this unity is divine, so shall it be attended with divine effects: by this unity the world shall recognise the heavenly mission of Christ. The unity must be a visible unity—obvious to the eyes, perceptible by the identity of doctrine, by the real mutual relations and communion of all the followers of Christ with each other, for otherwise the consequences adverted to could not be deduced from it. Thus the true vital communion of all attests the dignity of Christ, as every work vouches for its master. On the other hand, in the schisms and dissensions among believers, the dignity of Christ is lost sight of, strangers are brought not to the faith, and even those already believing are delivered up to doubt and unbelief.

In expressions a little altered but still more energetic the Saviour now repeats the same prayer, whose mighty themes are the conditions of the prosperity, the growth, and the duration of God's kingdom upon earth. He saith: "The glory which thou hast given me I have given to them, that they may be one as we are one. I in them, and thou in me, that they may be made perfect in one." Or in other words, he would say: The glorious destination, the mission which as the Son of Man I received from thee for the glorification of thy name to the end that I might enter into the inmost fellowship with thee (I in thee), I have transferred to them also, that I might contract the most living fellowship with them in order that they might thereby attain unto perfect unity. "And that the world may know that thou hast sent me, and hast loved them as thou hast also loved me": that is to say, their oneness in all things—a oneness not to be brought about by human powers—oneness in belief, thought, and will; and every effort shall be to unbelievers a sign that I have worked according to thy commission and with divine plenipotence, and that the believers are thy chosen people, to whom out of love thou hast revealed thyself, as out of love thou hast constituted me thine envoy. So speaketh the Lord himself.

Paul the apostle is admirable when in simple words he expounds the relation betwen the law and grace, between the works of the law and faith, when he instructs us respecting the series of divine revelations and the education of the human race by God, and respecting the laws which govern the world's history. But his philosophy, if I may be allowed so to speak, his philosophy on man's social relations generally and on his ecclesiastical ones in particular is in depth and majestic simplicity inferior to none of his other expositions. Our reason feels itself irresistibly compelled to accede to his judgments, whether he enlarge in general on the infirmity of the individual man and the absolute necessity of aiding it by attachment to a community, or whether he point to the limited powers of individual reason and show how they are dilated and improved, preserved, and rescued from destruction by means of society, or whether he remind us of the one spirit that should pervade all diversities or of the diversities that are permitted in the one spirit or, lastly, represent the idea which he spiritually contemplates under the image of the relations of the members of the body.[17] And how doth not our bosom swell when he calls the attention of his readers to the living foundation out of which the new community that had appeared in the world and was destined to unite all nations had arisen. It is at times as if we felt the infinite power stirring within us which gave existence to that society. In Christ national distinctions, in a religious point of view, are obliterated.[18] The enmities of people he hath destroyed—he is become our peace, and by "breaking down the middle wall of partition" hath made one out of two. All men in a like degree have in him access to God, but as in Christ they all become one, so they are united with each other in one body and one spirit. All invites to this unity, the one Lord, the one baptism, the one faith, the one God and father of all. The oneness of faith and of the knowledge of the Son of God is at once the reality and the supreme ideal which should be aimed at; and without this unity, in which the individual is strong, he is given up to every wind of doctrine and to the craftiness of men.[19]

These and similar passages are the foundations whereon the Catholic theory of the Church has been constructed. Hence flowed the inspired eloquence of Cyprian; hence Augustine drew his reflections on the Church, which in depth of feeling and vigour of thought contain by far the most splendid things that since the time of the apostles have been written on this subject. Hence, too, in later times came the glow that warmed the iron bosoms of the chilly north and melted them into a heat whereby all the gold and silver of our modern European civilisation were by degrees purified from dross.

To the Catholic it appears the most trivial proceeding when such pictures of the Church as we have attempted to trace are ridiculed as ideal representations which have never had in past nor ever will have in all future times a perfectly corresponding reality. In fact little is told him but what he already knows, to wit, that the idea is not the vulgar reality, and vice versa; but he knows, likewise, that where there is no fundamental idea to any reality there is as little truth as where no reality corresponds to the idea. He feels convinced that if, in the above-mentioned manner, the doctrine of his Church is to be seriously assailed the gospel itself would be open to the same attacks, for one might say "All is indeed excellent and wonderful which is there prescribed touching the pious sentiments and holiness of conduct which *should* distinguish Christians, but do these sentiments and this conduct *really* distinguish them? This is the question at issue." Everything must live according to an ideal to which the vulgar reality is not equal, for how else could it be vulgar? The words of the Lord "Be ye perfect, as your heavenly Father is perfect" will not therefore be vain, because no man is like to God. No, woe to him who shall reject the ideal because he finds it not perfectly represented among men.

Even the fact that at all times, from our Lord and his apostles (in the midst of whom a Judas was found) downwards, there has been much evil in the Church, nay, that the evil seemed at times to exceed the good, cannot impair the reverence of Catholics for their Church. The Church, as the institution of Christ, hath never erred, hath never become wicked, and never loses its energy, which is constantly evinced though the proof may not always be so obvious to the eye. To exhibit the kingdom of God on earth, *and also to train mankind for the same,* she has had to deal with men who were all born sinners and were taken from a more or less corrupt mass. Thus she can never work out of the sphere of evil, nay, her destination requires her to enter into the very midst of evil and to put her renovating power continually to the test. The Catholic Church has, moreover, experienced a long and often arduous history; she has passed through periods of time wherein all the elements of life were unbound and in wild uproar seemed arrayed one against the other. The anterior civilisation and the social institutions under which Christianity had hitherto flourished were really destroyed by savage and semibarbarous hordes, and they were not civilised Greeks and Romans but wild, untamed natures who now entered into the Church, which henceforth assumed quite another form. As her priests and bishops fall not from the skies, as she must take them out of the description of men that the age

can furnish, she could indeed for a succession of centuries boast of no
Clement of Alexandria, no Origen, no Cyprian, no Basil and Gregory of
Nazianzen, no Hilary, Jerome, and Augustine, who were trained up in
all the art and science of ancient Greece and Rome before they became
priests or anywise attached themselves to the Church. And yet it is
impossible to estimate the great and splendid things which the Church
achieved in those troublous times! Upon the foundation of the same
doctrine which in more flourishing ages had been developed into a
systematic form universally received the Church displayed her educating
power. Nay, all the fulness of energy which Christianity had manifested
in the first centuries it now again unfolded, though in quite another
form, for the matter to be wrought was totally different. Under such
circumstances there sprang up from the twelfth century a variety of
sects, born of yesterday, without any historical ancestry, consisting of a
small number of elect to whom was vouchsafed the privilege of dreaming
a Church and who ventured to urge against the existing Church that had
passed through so many storms and revolutions the reproach that *she*
had failed to fulfil her destination; and with the learning which they had
received from the Church they resisted her on account of the ignorance
to be found within her. Had these creations of fancy and egotism, which
they are certainly to be considered, even if we should not deny the better
elements they contained, borne the burden of ages imposed on the
Catholic Church, they would in the first moment have sunk back into the
original nothingness from which they had emerged. Doubtless, examples enough can be alleged of priests, bishops, and popes who in the
most unconscionable and unjustifiable manner have failed to discharge
their duty when it was quite in their power to bring about a reform of
morals, or who by their own scandalous conduct and lives have extinguished the still glimmering torch which they ought to have kindled.
Hell hath swallowed them up. Avowals of this kind Catholics must not
shrink from and never have shrunk from; it would be even idle to
attempt to elude them, for the Protestants themselves furnish an irrefragable proof of the state of manifold neglect into which the people had
fallen during the fifteenth century. Never would a system of doctrine like
theirs have sprung up, still less have obtained such wide diffusion, had
individual teachers and priests been faithful to the duties of their calling.
Truly, the ignorance could not have been slight on which a system of
faith like that of the Reformers was imposed as worthy of acceptance,
and thus Protestants may learn to estimate the magnitude of the evil
which then oppressed the Church by the magnitude of the errors into
which they themselves have fallen. This is the point at which Catholics
and Protestants will in great multitudes one day meet and stretch a

friendly hand one to the other. Both, conscious of guilt, must exclaim, "We all have erred—it is the Church only which cannot err. We all have sinned—the Church only is spotless on earth." This open confession of mutual guilt will be followed by the festival of reconciliation. Meanwhile we still smart under the inexpressible pain of the wound which was then inflicted—a pain which can be alleviated only by the consciousness that the wound has become an issue through which all the impurities have flowed off that men had introduced into the wide compass of the dominions of the Church, for she herself is ever pure and eternally undefiled.

In thus stating the view which Catholics take of their Church, without pretending to any completeness of detail, we think we have duly prepared our readers for understanding the following section.

38. The Church as Teacher and
    Instructress—Tradition—The Church as
    Judge in Matters of Faith

The main question which we have now to answer is this: how doth man attain to possession of the true doctrine of Christ, or to express ourselves in a more general and at once more accurate manner, how doth man obtain a clear knowledge of the institute of salvation proffered in Christ Jesus? The Protestant says, by searching Holy Writ, which is infallible; the Catholic, on the other hand, replies, by the Church, in which alone man arrives at the true understanding of Holy Writ. In a more minute exposition of his views the Catholic continues: doubtless the Sacred Scriptures contain *divine* communications, and consequently, the pure truth; whether they contain *all* the truths which in a religious and ecclesiastical point of view are necessary or at least very useful to be known is a question which does not yet come under consideration. Thus the scripture is God's unerring word, but however the predicate of inerrability may belong *to it, we ourselves* are not exempt from error; nay, we only become so when we have unerringly received the word, which is in *itself* inerrable. In this reception of the word human activity, which is fallible, has necessarily a part. But in order that in this transit of the divine contents of the Sacred Scriptures into possession of the human intellect no gross illusion or general misrepresentation may occur, it is taught that the Divine Spirit to which are entrusted the guidance and vivification of the Church becomes, in its union with the human spirit in the Church, a peculiarly Christian tact, a deep sure-guiding feeling which, as it abideth in truth, leads also into all truth. By a confiding attachment to the perpetuated Apostleship, by education in the Church, by hearing, learning, and living within her pale, by the reception of the higher principle which renders her eternally fruitful, a deep interior sense is formed that alone is fitted for the perception and acceptance of the written Word, because it entirely coincides with the sense in which the Sacred Scriptures themselves were composed. If with such a sense acquired in the Church the sacred volume be perused, then its general essential import is conveyed unaltered to the reader's mind. Nay, when instruction through the apostleship, and the ecclesiastical education in the way described, takes place in the individual the Sacred Scriptures are not even necessary for our acquisition of their general contents.[20]

This is the ordinary and regular course. But errors and misunderstandings, more or less culpable, will never fail to occur; and as in the times of the apostles the word of God was combated out of the word of God, so this combat hath been renewed at all times. What, under such circumstances, is the course to be pursued? How is the Divine Word to be secured against the erroneous conceptions that have arisen? The general sense decides against particular opinion—the judgment of the Church against that of the individual: *the Church interprets the Sacred Scriptures.* The Church is the body of the Lord: it is, in its universality, his visible form—his permanent, ever-renovated, humanity—his eternal revelation. He dwells in the community; all his promises, all his gifts are bequeathed to the community—but to no individual, as such, since the time of the apostles. This general sense, this ecclesiastical consciousness, is tradition, in the subjective sense of the word.[21] What then is tradition? The peculiar Christian sense existing in the Church and transmitted by ecclesiastical education; yet this sense is not to be conceived as detached from its subject matter—nay, it is formed in and by this matter, so it may be called a full sense. Tradition is the living word, perpetuated in the hearts of believers. To this sense, as the general sense, the interpretation of Holy Writ is entrusted. The declaration which it pronounces on any controverted subject is the judgment of the Church, and therefore the Church is judge in matters of faith *(judex controversiarum).* Tradition, in the objective sense, is the general faith of the Church through all ages, manifested by outward historical testimonies; in this sense tradition is usually termed the *norma*—the standard of Scriptural interpretation—the rule of faith.

Moreover, the Divine Founder of our Church, when he constituted the community of believers as his permanent organ, had recourse to no other law than that which prevails in every department of human life. Each nation is endowed with a peculiar character, stamped on the deepest, most hidden parts of its being, which distinguishes it from all other nations and manifests its peculiarity in public and domestic life, in art and science, in short, in every relation. It is, as it were, the tutelary genius, the guiding spirit transmitted from its progenitors, the vivifying breath of the whole community; and indeed, the nations anterior to Christianity personified this their peculiar character, revered it as their national divinity, deduced from it their civil and religious laws and customs, and placed all things under its protection.

In every general act of a people the national spirit is infallibly expressed; and should contests, should selfish factions occur, the element destructive to the vital principle of the whole will most certainly be detected in them, and the commotion excited by an alien spirit either miscarries or is expelled as long as the community preserves its own self-consciousness, as long as its peculiar genius yet lives and works within it. . . .

According to this type hath the infallibility of the Church also, in its interpretation of the Divine Word, been formed, and by this standard we are to judge it. All the developments of its dogmas and its morality, which can be considered as resulting from formal acts of the whole body, are to be revered as the sentences of Christ himself, and in these his spirit ever recurs. . . .

### 40. Formal Distinction between Scriptural and Ecclesiastical Doctrine[22]

If we have hitherto shown that, conformably to the principles of Catholics, the doctrine of Scripture is one and the same with the doctrine of the Church, since the Church hath to interpret the Scripture and in this interpretation cannot err, so this unity applies to the substance only and not to the form. In respect to the latter, a diversity is found inherent in the very essence and object of the Church, so that indeed if the divine truth must be preserved and propagated by human organs the diversity we speak of could not possibly be avoided, as will appear from the following observations. The conduct of the Redeemer in the announcement of his word was corresponded to by that of the Apostles, and the Word became immediately in them faith—a human possession—and after his ascension existed for the world in no other form than in this faith of the Lord's disciples, whose kernel in Peter he therefore called the rock, whereon his Church was in such a way to be built that the powers of hell should never prevail against it. But after the Divine Word had become human faith it must be subject to all mere human destinies. It must be constantly received by all the energies of the human mind and imbibed by the same. The preservation and communication of the Word were in like manner attached to a human method. Even with the

Evangelists, who only wished to recount what Christ had spoken, wrought, and suffered, the Divine Word appears subject to the law here described, a law which manifests itself in the choice and arrangement of the matter, as well as in the special plan which each proposed to himself and in the general conception and execution of his task.

But the Divine Word became still more subject to this law when the Apostles were fulfilling their mission—executing the divine charge which they had received—for various questions of dispute arose the settlement whereof could not be avoided, and on that account claimed human reflection and required the formation of notions, judgments, and conclusions, things which were not possible to be effected without tasking the reason and the understanding. The application of the energies of the human mind to the subject matter received from the Lord necessarily caused the Divine Word, on the one hand, to be analysed and, on the other hand, to be reduced to certain leading points, and [caused] the multiplicity of objects to be contemplated in their mutual bearings and resolved into a higher unity, whereby the human mind obtained on these matters greater clearness and definiteness of conception. For everything that the human mind hath received from an external source and which is destined to become its property wherein it must find itself perfectly at home must be first reproduced by that mind itself. The original doctrine as the human mind had variously elaborated it exhibited itself in a much altered form: it remained the original and yet did not; it was the same in substance and yet differed as to form. In this process of the development of the Divine Word during the apostolic age we may exalt as high and extend as wide as we please the divine guidance given to the disciples of Christ; yet certainly, without human cooperation, without the peculiar activity of man, it did not advance of itself. As in the good work of the Christian free will and grace pervade each other, and one and the same undivided deed is at once divine and human, so we find this to be the case here.

The same could not fail to hold good even after the death of the apostles, even after the Gospels and the Epistles had been written and whatever else we include in the canon of the New Testament had been already in the hands of the faithful. When in the manner described the Church explains and secures the original doctrine of faith against misrepresentations the apostolic expression is necessarily changed for another, which is the most fitted alike clearly to set forth and reject the particular error of the time. As little as the apostles themselves in the course of their polemics could retain the form wherein the Saviour expounded his divine doctrine, so little was the Church enabled to adhere to the same. If the evangelical doctrine be assailed by a definite theological system and by a terminology peculiar to itself, the false notions cannot by any means be repelled in a clear, distinct, evident, and intelligible manner unless the Church have regard to the form of the error and exhibit its thesis in a shape qualified by the garb wherein the adverse doctrine is invested, and thus render itself intelligible to all contemporaries. The origin of the Nicene formula furnishes the best solution to this question. This form is in itself the human, the temporal, the perishable element and might be exchanged for a hundred others. Accordingly, tradition often hands down to later generations the original deposit in another form, because that deposit hath been entrusted to the care of men, whose conduct must be guided by the circumstances wherein they are placed.

Lastly, in the same manner as in the Apostolic writings the truths of salvation are laid open with greater clearness and in all their mutual organic connection, so in the doctrine of the Church the doctrine of Scripture is ever progressively unfolded to our view. Dull, therefore, as it is to find any other than a mere *formal* distinction between the doctrine of Christ and that of his apostles, no less senseless is it to discover any other difference between the primitive and the later tradition of the Church. The blame of this formal difference arises from overlooking the fact that Christ was a God-man and wished to continue working in a manner conformable to his twofold nature.

Moreover, the deeper insight of the human mind into the divine revelations in Christ seems determined by the struggles of error against Christian truth. It is to the unenlightened zeal of the Jewish Christians for the law [that] we owe the expositions of Paul touching faith and the power of the Gospel, and to the schisms in Corinth we are indebted for his explanation of principles in respect to the Church. The Gnostic and Manichean errors led to a clearer insight into the character of evil, destitute of and opposed to all existence as it is, as well as to a maturer knowledge of the value of God's *original* creation (nature and freedom) and its relation to the *new* creation in Christ Jesus. Out of the Pelagian contest arose a fuller and more conscious recognition of human infirmity in the sphere of true virtue, and so have matters gone on down to our days. It would be ridiculous on the part of Catholics to deny as a foolish boast of Protestants (should the latter be inclined to claim any merit in the case) that the former had gained much from the controversy with them. By the fall of the Protestants the Catholics necessarily rose, and from the obscurity which overclouded the minds of the reformers a new light was cast upon the truth; and such indeed had ever been the case in all earlier schisms in the Church. Assuredly, in Christian knowledge we stand one degree higher than the period prior to the Reformation, and all the dogmas that were called in question received such an elucidation and confirmation that it would require no very diligent or long-continued comparison between the modern theological works and those written prior to the Council of Trent to see the important difference which, in this respect, exists between the two epochs.

The fact that the deeper consciousness of Christian truth (in itself eternally one and unchangeable) is the result of contest and struggle, and consequently a matter of history, is of too much importance not to detain our attention for some moments. It explains the necessity of a living, visible authority which in every dispute can with certainty discern the truth and separate it from error. Otherwise we should have *only* the variable—the disputed—and at last Nihilism itself. Hence it happens (and this we may venture to premise) that where Holy Writ, without Tradition and the authority of the Church, is declared to be the sole source and rule for the knowledge of Gospel truth, all more precise explanations and developments of Christian dogmas are willingly left in utter ignorance, nay, are even absolutely rejected. Guided by this principle, men can find no rational object to connect with the history of believing intelligence in the Christian Church, and must necessarily evince hostility towards everything of this tendency which hath occurred in the Church. Or, when they lose all confidence and all hope of freeing themselves from the turmoil of opinions and of seeing a bright, steady light arise out of the dark chaos, they cast in their despair upon the Bible the whole mass of opinions that ages have thrown up, and of that which is boldly assert it could not have been otherwise, consequently exists of necessity, and is inherent in the very essence of Christianity. They do not see that with that complaisance to acknowledge every variety of opinion which in the course of time may have gradually been founded on Scripture a destructive principle for the solution of all the enigmas of Christian history is laid down—to wit, the principle that its object is to show that the Scripture, as it includes *every* sense, hath consequently none. . . .

### 43. The Hierarchy

It now remains for us to make a few remarks on the Hierarchy. The primary view of the Church as a divine and human institution is here evinced in a very striking form. Accordingly, for the exercise of public functions in the Church, for the discharge of the office of teaching and the administration of the sacraments, a divine internal calling and a higher qualification are, above all things, required. But as the divine, invisible nature of the Church is connected with a human, visible form, so the calling from above must necessarily be here below first discerned and then acknowledged, and the heavenly qualification must appear attached to an act obvious to the senses and executed in the visible Church. Or in other words, the authorisation for the public exercise of ecclesiastical functions is imparted by a sacrament—an outward act to be performed by men according to the commission of Christ, and which partly denotes, partly conveys, an inward and divine grace.[23] The introduction into an invisible Church requires only a spiritual baptism; the continuance in the same needs only an internal nourishment, we cannot say with the body of Christ (because "body" already reminds us of an *outward* origin of the Church), but with the logos of God. An invisible Church needs only an inward purely spiritual sacrifice and a universal priesthood.[24] But it is otherwise with a visible Church. *This* requires that the baptism of fire and of the Spirit should be likewise a baptism of water, and that the nurture of the soul which Christ imparts should be visibly represented by a bodily food. In the very idea of such a Church an external sacrifice also is necessarily involved. The same observation will apply to priestly orders: the internal and outward consecration go together; the heavenly and the earthly unction become one and the same. As the preservation of the doctrines and institutions of Christ hath been intrusted to the Church, so it is impossible for her to revere as a priest every individual who declares he hath been inwardly consecrated to the priesthood. On the contrary, as he must previously be carefully and strictly bred up, and instructed in the divine dogmas of the Church, in order to contribute towards their further propagation, so he receives through the Church, through her external consecration, the inward consecration from God, or in other words, he receives, through the imposition of the hands of *the bishops,* the Holy Ghost. The visibility and the stability of the Church connected therewith require, accordingly, an ecclesiastical ordination, originating with Christ the fountainhead and perpetuated in uninterrupted succession, so that as the apostles were sent forth by the Saviour, they in their turn instituted bishops, and these appointed their successors, and so on down to our own days. By this episcopal succession beginning from our Saviour and continued on without interruption we can especially recognise, as by an outward mark, which is the true Church founded by him.[25]

The episcopate, the continuation of the apostleship, is accordingly revered as a Divine institution, and not less so, and even on that very account, the Pope, who is the centre of unity and the head of the episcopate. If the episcopate is to form a corporation, outwardly as well as inwardly bound together, in order to unite all believers into one harmonious life, which the Catholic Church so urgently requires, it stands in need of a centre whereby all may be held together and firmly connected. What a helpless, shapeless mass, incapable of all combined action, would the Catholic Church have been, spread as she is over all the kingdoms of the earth, over all parts of the world, had she been possessed of no head, no supreme bishop, revered by all. She would, of necessity, have been split into an incalculable number of particular Churches devoid of all consistence had not a strong, mighty bond united all, had not the successor of Peter firmly held them together. Had not the universal Church possessed a head instituted by Christ and had not this head *by acknowledged rights and obligations* been enabled to exert an influence over each of its parts, those parts, abandoned to themselves, would soon have taken a course of development contrary to each other and absolutely determined by local relations—a course which would have led to the dissolution of the whole body. No one can be so weak-minded as not to perceive that then the whole authority of the Church in matters of faith would have vanished, since the several Churches opposed to each other could not attest one and the same thing, nay, must stand in mutual contradiction. Without a visible head the whole view which the Catholic Church takes of herself as a visible society representing the place of Christ would have been lost, or rather, never would have occurred to her. In a visible Church a visible head is necessarily included. The following instances may serve to evince more clearly the truth of what is here asserted. If in the appointment of bishops to their particular districts the universal Church exerted no decisive influence, did not possess, for example, the right of confirmation, then views inimical to the interests of the Church would infallibly raise to the episcopal dignity men who in a short time would venture to destroy, or at least permit the destruction of, the common faith. The same would be the result if the universal Church did not enjoy the right of deprivation in case the pastor of a particular church did not fulfil his essential duties or even acted in open violation of them. But what could the universal Church accomplish without her organ, or the organ itself, if no one were bound to obey it? Yet it is, of course, to be understood that the rights of the head of the Church are restricted to purely ecclesiastical concerns, and if in the course of the Middle Ages this was otherwise the causes of this occurrence are to be sought for in the peculiar circumstances and necessities of that period. With the visibility of the Church, with the visible, regular, and established reciprocal intercourse of the faithful, with the internal necessity of their very existence to be members of one body, a visible head with essential and inalienable rights was accordingly ordained. In addition to his essential ecclesiastical rights, whose limits may be found traced out in the canonists, the Pope, according to the different degrees of civilisation in particular ages and among particular nations, acquired the so-called nonessential rights, admitting of various changes, so that his power appears sometimes more extended, sometimes more contracted. Moreover, it is well known that partly in consequence of the revolutions of time and of disorders in the Church, partly through the internal development of opposite ideas, two systems became prevalent, the episcopal and the papal system, the latter whereof, without questioning the divine institution of bishops, exalted more particularly the central power, while the former, without denying the divine establishment of the Primacy, sought to draw authority more particularly towards the circumference.[26] As each system acknowledged the essence of the other to be divine, they constituted an opposition very beneficial to ecclesiastical life, so that, by their counteraction, the peculiar free development of the several parts was on the one hand preserved, and the union of these in one living, indivisible whole was on the other maintained.

The dogmatic decrees of the episcopate, united with the general head and centre—are infallible; for it represents the universal Church, and one doctrine of faith falsely explained by it would render the whole a prey to error. Hence as the institution which Christ hath established for the preservation and the explanation of his doctrines is subject, in this its function, to no error, so the organ through which the Church speaks is also exempt from error.

The Metropolitans (archbishops) and patriarchs are not in themselves essential intermediate grades between the Bishops and the Pope; yet has their jurisdiction, the limits whereof have been determined by general councils, proved very useful for maintaining a closer connection and a more immediate superintendence over the bishops subject to their authority.

The priests (taking the word in a more limited sense) are, as it were, a multiplication of the bishops; and as they acknowledge themselves his assistants they revere in him the visible fountain of their jurisdiction, their head and their centre. In this way, the whole body is bound and jointed together in a living organism; and as the tree, the deeper and wider it striketh its roots into the earth, the more goodly a summit of intertwining boughs and branches it beareth aloft unto the sky, it is so with the congregation of the Lord. For the more closely the community of believers is established with him and is enrooted in him as the all-fruitful soil, the more vigorous and imposing is its outward manifestation.

As to the remaining nonsacerdotal orders, the deacons were instituted by the apostles and, as their representatives, were charged more immediately with the affairs of administration not immediately connected with the apostolic calling. The subdeaconship and the four so-called minor orders are restricted to a circle of subordinate yet indispensable ministrations and in former times formed altogether (including the deaconship) a practical school wherein the training for higher ecclesiastical functions was acquired and a test of qualification for their discharge was afforded. . . . In the ancient Church the pastors as well as believers were formed in and by the immediate experience of life, as the inferior ministers constantly surrounded the bishop or priest and, attending him in all his sacred functions, imbibed the spirit which animated him and qualified themselves to become one day his successors. But they rose only slowly and by degrees, and every new ordination was but the recompense of services faithfully performed and a period of probation for a still more important trust. At present these orders, from the subdeaconship downwards, are preserved but as ancient customs, for the educational system of modern times bears an essentially different character and follows a decidedly theoretical course. Hence the duties which the inferior members of the clergy once performed are now nearly everywhere discharged by laymen, such as acolytes, sacristans, and the like.

## NOTES

1. Gottlieb Jakob Planck (1751–1833). Another, much more significant model for Möhler's *Symbolik* was the *Christliche Symbolik* by Philipp Marheineke (1780–1846), in the words of the subtitle, a "historicocritical and dogmatic-comparative presentation of the Catholic, Reformed, and Socinian doctrinal concept" (3 vols., 1810–13). Planck taught at Göttingen; Marheineke studied at Göttingen and subsequently (from 1811) taught at Berlin.—ED.
2. Council of Trent, session 13, chaps. 4, 5.
3. Council of Trent, session 22, chaps. 1, 2.
4. See appendix B [not given here].
5. Möhler refers to a twelfth-century Greek text that he discussed in *Tübinger theologische Quartalschrift*, 1833:1, 173.—ED.
6. Council of Trent, session 13, chap. 8.
7. In Luther's *The Babylonian Captivity of the Church*. (See *Luther's Works*, vol. 36 [Philadelphia: Fortress Press, 1959], 41—ED.) Luther still expresses the glorious reminiscences of his Catholic education, which however became always feebler till at last they were totally extinguished. . . . Luther says, "We should meditate [on the promises of Christ during mass], ponder [these words], exercise and nourish our faith in them, make it grow and add to its strength, by daily commemoration of it." This is indeed true, but, to overlook every other consideration, such an idealism would render the sacraments utterly unnecessary and

*public* worship useless, since something external *must* always form the foundation of the latter.

8. Möhler here gives long quotations from the liturgy of Saint Chrysostom,
from that of the Alexandrine church, and from the "so-called universal canon of
the Ethiopians." Here we are brought up against the fundamental unsatisfac-
toriness of this or any anthology. By making drastic cuts in Möhler's footnotes it
is possible to offer the beginning student a taste of how Möhler wrote; but the
more advanced student—who has, of course, learned German—should study
Möhler's own integral text, to see what he knew (from the state of patristics at
the time) and how he used it. The effect produced by dropping notes reminds
the editor of a distinguished dogmatics professor whose lectures he attended in
the twilight of that worthy man's career: "Gentlemen," said the professor one
day, "my theological synthesis is as firm as ever even if I can't remember what it's
based on."—ED.

9. That it was not in the Middle Ages, as a frivolous ignorance has often
asserted, that the adoration of the Eucharist first arose numberless authorities
can prove. For example, [passing] over the much more ancient testimonies of
Origen, [Möhler quotes again from the liturgy of Saint Chrysostom].

10. Council of Trent, session 21, canons 1–4; and session 22, decree on the
use of the chalice.

11. Acts 1:4.

12. Eph. 5:29–33.

13. Eph. 4:11–16.

14. Jean Hardouin, *Acta conciliorum* (Paris, 1714–15), 9:985. Eugenius
spoke in the same strain when he informed the Christian princes and universities
of the reconciliation in question (fol. 1000). At the same time the Armenians
and Jacobins, as the documents style them, meaning the Copts and Jacobites,
renounced their errors and united with the Latins (fol. 1015–25).

15. "Give me a fulcrum on which to rest [and I will move the earth]."

16. John 17:20–24.

17. 1 Corinthians 12.

18. Eph. 4:16; 11:15.

19. Eph. 4:14.

20. See Irenaeus *Against Heresies* 3.3.2, where we can see how ancient the
doctrine given above is.

21. See Eusebius *Ecclesiastical History* 5.28; and Vincent of Lerins *Com-
monitorium* 2. See also Council of Trent, session 13, chap. 1; and session 4,
decree on Scripture.

22. See Henry Tristram, "J. A. Moehler et J. H. Newman: La pensée allemande et la renaissance catholique en Angleterre," *Revue des sciences philosophiques et théologiques* 27 (1938): 184–204. Tristram concludes that Newman
arrived at his view of the development of doctrine independently, not because of
reading Möhler. The fact that Newman (b. 1801) lived so long may cause the
modern reader to forget that he really belonged to the same generation as
Möhler (b. 1796), who died relatively young.—ED.

23. Council of Trent, session 23, chap. 3.

24. Council of Trent, session 23, chap. 1. . . . In an invisible church only the
invisible forgiveness of sins and confession before God are necessary, but it is
otherwise in the visible church.

25. See Irenaeus *Against Heresies* 3.3, 4.43. See also Tertullian *On Prescrip-*

*tion* 32. For the definition of papal power given by the Council of Florence, see Hardouin, *Acta conciliorum* 9:423. (This is the passage quoted by Vatican I, in this anthology sec. 1835.—ED.)

26. The most general maxims of the episcopal system are comprised in the Synods of Constance (1414) and of Basel (1431). (The "episcopal system" is usually called "conciliarism."—ED.) They assert the pope is *subject* to a general council lawfully convoked, representing the Church militant—a one-sided principle which, when carried out to its legitimate consequences, threatened the Church with annihilation. This coarse opinion must now be considered as obsolete. For these two councils, see Hardouin, *Acta conciliorum* 8:252, 1121. (The second volume of Geiselmann's critical edition of the *Symbolik* is entirely composed of commentary; regarding this section on the hierarchy, see Geiselmann's remarks on the evolution of the text itself through the five editions [pp. 259–61] and on the evolution of Möhler's views [pp. 626ff., esp. pp. 672–98; see also pp. 754–56]. With time and study Möhler gave inceasing emphasis to the visible hierarchy generally, and to the power of the pope in it.—ED.)

# PART TWO

# Philosophies of
# Religion

# 4

# Criteria for Determining the Authenticity of Alleged Revelations

*Georg Hermes*

In many religious traditions doing philosophy is a luxury, a luxury that, preoccupied with being saved, people may or may not get around to. This is not so in Catholicism, or at least, to speak more accurately, it was not so in nineteenth-century Catholicism. Nineteenth-century Catholics whose education had progressed beyond the primitive or the primary considered certain philosophical tasks to be religiously necessary. Why was this so, and what sort of philosophy did they produce?

Catholics engaged in philosophy for the same reason that they built cathedrals, composed polyphonic masses, and in their more sanguine moments, allowed dancing on the village green. Catholicism is optimistic about humankind, about the products of the human psyche. If God is really going to save humankind, then integral salvation demands that all dimensions of the human be valued, held available for the touch of grace. So just as Catholic-Tridentine humanity synergistically cooperates with God in the bringing forth of good works, so also will its faith be a rational service. If reason did not prepare the way for faith a kind of violence would be done to the maturely human.

Philosophical reason, then, has two tasks here. The first is to stabilize, mentally, the conditions under which revelation can occur. Catholic metaphysics must show that there is a God and that the human being—destined for the supernatural vision of God in heaven—is rational, has a spiritual soul, and is immortal. The second task of reason is to work out an epistemology applicable to historical events, a bridging philosophy between the mind's quest for truth and the alleged proclamation of revealed truths by historical prophets, a prelude to the assent not only that revelation *can* occur but that in a particular case it actually *has* occurred.

From the beginning of the nineteenth century the chief obstacle Catholic philosophers encountered was the work of Kant. (The reader would do well to ponder Kant's manner of dismissing, and then reestablishing, the affirmation of God and immortality; Kant's *Religion within the Limits of Reason Alone* is also highly pertinent here.) One way of dealing with Kant is, while criticizing him, partially to adapt his work to Catholic use; this is what Hermes attempts. Another way of dealing with Kant is to employ the kind of metaphysical judo usually associated with Hegel, to assert that the thinking mind is not the puzzle but the solution, the key to all that is; this extrapolation of the analyzed mind is modified for Catholic use by Günther. Yet another approach to Kant is to admit that he was mostly on the right track, not to attempt to Catholicize him, and so to say, putting all one's chips on the second task of philosophy as sketched above, to assert that revelation in history is the proper preparation for yet more revelation in history. This third way is attempted by Bautain. Whatever his faults, Bautain does at least see that the only way to get around Kant is to avoid heavy reliance on conceptual reason and to rely instead on human experience. Newman emphasizes that the experience best relied on is the individual's own; schematically, though not in terms of actual medieval research or master-disciple relationships, Newman prepares the way for the flowering of neo-Thomism that occurred after the end of the period covered by this volume, above all, the work of Etienne Gilson and Jacques Maritain (see Bibliography). In due course we will take up Newman's blending of empiricism and a moderate employment of "reasoning."

But first Hermes. Georg Hermes was born in 1775 in Dreierwalde, Westphalia, and died in Bonn in 1831. Ordained a priest in 1799, he became professor of dogmatics at Münster in 1807 and held the same position in Bonn from 1819. He exercised widespread influence as a teacher, and his work in the classroom is at least partially summed up in his magnum opus, the *Einleitung in die christkatholische Theologie,* from which part 1, section 85, here follows. Part 1 of this large work is a philosophical introduction to Catholic Christian theology. Part 2 is historical, but only a part of it was ever published; Hermes died before completing it. Fortunately for him, perhaps, he also died before Pope Gregory XVI (reigned 1831–46) condemned his work. (Herman Schwedt argues that this judgment in 1835–36 was arrived at in a thoroughly unprofessional manner: see his *Das römische Urteil über Georg Hermes* [Rome: Herder & Herder, 1980].) For good measure the fathers of Vatican I condemned again what they thought Hermes meant. What especially troubled them was Hermes's apparent subordination of faith to ethics.

The twentieth-century reader will also wonder at Hermes's very considerable confidence in historical records and traditions. More is at stake here, however, than a certain naiveté on the part of Hermes. There is an abiding problem: if the historical record is uncertain, is faith in a particular "divine legate" thereby rendered whimsical, and if it is not uncertain, does it then suffice of itself, rendering faith unnecessary? In reference to what was above termed the second task of Catholic philosophy, Hermes at least tries to work out a way in which in the absence of completely convincing historical data a faith assent to revelation would be a reasonable act. Also to Hermes's credit is his attempting to describe the psychological process of someone's coming to such a faith assent. Perhaps what Hermes says is not all that can be said of the process of conversion, but one must take due care not to mix up what is sayable from one vantage point with what is sayable only from another. Traditional dogmatics may insist on the supernatural origin of the act of faith, but from within that act the person does not in some way see God giving him or her faith.

The foregoing, first chapter of this Investigation[1] has shown that theoretical reason cannot necessitate our acknowledgment that an alleged supernatural, divine revelation really is what it purports to be. Only practical reason can do that. Belief in the authenticity of such a revelation—which is what is under consideration here—can therefore be furnished a necessary ground, or firm support, not from some point of theoretical knowledge but from duty. Hence the sole, all-inclusive condition for acknowledging the authenticity of a revelation alleged to have been supernaturally given by God, or rather, for belief in its authenticity, must consist of a thorough demonstration of the duty or, what comes to the same, of the moral necessity, of accepting this revelation as supernaturally originating from God. The thorough demonstration of this duty is thus the sole condition for this belief with respect to both the proximate and the remote subject of the revelation, that is to say, in the case of an immediate as well as a mediate revelation.[2] . . . Our objective, in this Investigation, requires that the conditions be laid down according to which we can decide, in regard to each particular revelatory fact [*Offenbarungs-Factum*] alleged to be such, whether this revelatory fact must be believed in as authentically originating from God. Our objective therefore requires the conditions under which the duty of belief is clearly seen to be present and without which that duty cannot be made evident. . . .

These more closely determined conditions were also set forth in the foregoing first chapter. . . . From the demonstration given there it becomes evident that there is a duty to accept an alleged revelation that is of, first, supernatural, and then, divine origin, for certitude concerning the supernatural origin of a revelation is totally useless for our purpose if we are not also completely certain of its divine origin. Hence in a particular case we should always inquire whether there is an evident duty to assume a divine origin, in which case a supernatural origin follows as a matter of course.[3] . . . Note, however, that with respect to the more remote subject of revelation everything—the knowledge of the revealed doctrine along with the proofs of its supernatural origin—depends on the history of the revelatory fact. Thus, before considering all other conditions for the authenticity of a mediate revelation one must attend to this point: under what condition can it become a duty to

From *Einleitung in die christkatholische Theologie: Erster Theil, Philosophische Einleitung* (Münster, 1819; Frankfurt am Main: Minerva, 1967), 604–17, 579–82. The translation is by Joseph Fitzer.

127

believe what is put forward as the history of this revelation? . . . In the following discussion I will be chiefly concerned with mediate revelation; where immediate revelation forms an exception I will make a special comment to that effect.

[The conditions for acknowledging the authenticity of a revelation will be stated as *if*-clauses.] The single most general such condition is this: *If it can be fully demonstrated that it is a duty to accept the alleged supernatural revelation by God as, in fact, a revelation supernaturally originating from God.*

The more determinate general conditions, or the conditions of the most general condition just given, may be stated as follows:

1. *If what is presented as the history, oral or written, of the revelatory fact in question meets the general criterion for obligatory assent (here, for the commanded belief in history).*[4] [This condition does not, obviously, apply to immediate revelation.]

2. *If the alleged revelation is a religious or moral doctrine.* Unless the revealed doctrine has this character one cannot on the basis of its content, and hence in no way at all, draw any conclusion about the morality of its originator; and thus the primary basis is then lacking for a proof of its divine origin.[5] It is to be noted that something is elevated to certitude here which people commonly believe but which is still doubted by many: that only religious and moral doctrine is a possible object of supernatural divine revelation—not because God cannot impart something else but because man cannot prove anything else to be imparted by him.

3. *If the alleged revelation perfectly agrees in all its doctrines with moral reason, in such a way that it cooperates with the will and assists it to fulfill the demands of moral reason.* This condition is essential for proving that the originator of the revelation is a morally good being and that he, in the end, is God himself. But one must distinguish this condition from the following, negative condition to which, to make the difference more apparent and so to avoid confusion, I now pass.

4. *If no contradiction can be discovered between the alleged revelation and the doctrines of theoretical and practical reason.* This condition prohibits there being an *objective* contradiction between the revelation and theoretical and practical reason. The foregoing, third condition called for agreement between the revelation and practical (or moral) reason *in subjective matters.* This is the great difference between the two. The basis of the demand made in this fourth condition is apparent: God, who is the highest reason, cannot contradict himself in his natural and supernatural manifestations, and cannot demand the impossible, namely, that the directress which he first gave to man, reason, would

through any assumption cancel herself out. On the same grounds God cannot through a later supernatural revelation contradict an earlier one or, if one and the same revelation contains several doctrines, contradict one by another. Furthermore, when the alleged revelation evidently contains no such contradiction, it is nevertheless not requisite that he who believes must also grasp the objective agreement in it. Such a requirement could be based only on the false position refuted above,[6] that supernatural revelation cannot go beyond reason—whereof the opposite is self-evident—and that one supernatural revelation cannot go beyond another.

5. *If the alleged revelation is offered, either explicitly or implicitly, as divine teaching, or doctrine.* Here the greatest possible emphasis must be given to the theoretical demonstration, given above,[7] that the supernatural being who reveals must be morally good and devoted to God, and therefore not lie. Such emphasis is necessary in order that there be made evident a duty to accept the revelation as originating from God. Here also it first becomes fully possible to demonstrate, as a presupposition of the first [more determinate] condition given above, that it is a duty to believe in the history of this revelation.[8]

6. *If the alleged revelation teaches natural duties, either exclusively or in connection with other duties.* It is at this point that it becomes fully possible to see how in regard to the content of the revealed doctrine it can be a duty to accept the revelation as a rule of life, and with that in mind, as divine. For reason directly commands, everywhere, only the fulfillment of natural duties; the cases wherein these bind should be known, and to that end theoretically doubtful knowledge should be accepted as true. But reason cannot command one to seek and accept other duties beyond natural ones.[9]

7. *If men need, for certain and undoubted knowledge of their natural duties, extraneous teaching—and such is the case with the incomparably greater number of men—and if this need is wholly or partially met by the alleged revelation.* As soon as this condition is taken together with the foregoing one, reason expresses the duty of accepting the revelation in question as a teaching truly coming from God—but still only for those in need of instruction. He, however, who does not consider himself in need of instruction must nonetheless accept this revelation as a doctrine given by God, if not, now, as compelled to do so by a command of moral reason, even through the reflection of theoretical reason.[10]

Where these conditions are fulfilled the acceptance of the divine origin of an alleged revelation is morally necessary as soon as its supernatural origin is accepted. (This has been made evident partly through the passage referred to in the first chapter, partly through what has been said here.) Consideration must now be given to the condition under which the supernatural origin of an alleged revelation must be accepted with moral necessity.

8. *If the supernatural origin of the alleged revelation has been confirmed by miracles performed in public or at least in the presence of several persons.*[11] This public character of the miracles is required in order that a duty of believing the historical account be demonstrable where this history reports to us the extraordinary facts that, according to our criterion, we are compelled to accept as true miracles. Indeed, all established miracles of this kind are already suitable for directly proving the divine origin of the doctrine, because according to the fifth condition above, the doctrine must in the nature of the case be presented as divine if no separately adduced explanation alters matters. Nevertheless, the miracles demonstrate only that there is a supernatural origin for the doctrine, since not a divine but only a supernatural power need be assumed as the cause of them. But because at least a supernatural power is active in them, so is the doctrine confirmed by the miracles thus shown to be the teaching of a supernatural being, and thus its supernatural origin can no longer be subjected to any doubt. That, now, the revealing supernatural being is morally good and works in the service of God, or even is God himself, and hence that its teaching is a doctrine originating from God, which is what the revealing being asserts of itself and its teaching—all this can and must be accepted with moral necessity under the above conditions for the sake of the doctrine itself. But in order that this moral necessitation not be canceled by the miracles themselves there must yet be in regard to the miracles the following negative conditions:

9. *The miracles worked in confirmation of the doctrine may not be unworthy of God in any respect, not, therefore,* (a) *in regard to their proximate goal, nor* (b) *in regard to their object* [Gegenstand], *nor* (c) *in regard to the manner in which they are performed or in which they are employed for the confirmation of the doctrine.* For God can never act in a manner unworthy of himself either where he himself acts or where he acts through a representative; where this were the case it could no longer be assumed that God, or someone on God's commission, were acting and teaching. All necessity for accepting the alleged revelation as originating from God would then be canceled. If these conditions are customarily stated positively, namely, "The miracles must be worthy in respect to God," they have the same significance for our goal (to demonstrate the divine origin of an alleged revelation) as when they are stated negatively. But considered in itself, the positive expression is incorrect, first, because the character of the miracles, according to their

nature, can have only a negative influence on the acceptance of the doctrine that they prove,[12] and then also because the existence of the conditions thus becomes unknowable, for man cannot determine what is worthy of God but can only show that something cannot be demonstrated to be unworthy of God. In order to determine that something is worthy of God a positive agreement of the same with the divine attributes would have to be known; this, however, is impossible. Because we think the divine attributes only by means of the analogous concepts of our similarly named attributes, and can thus, at most, know a positive agreement only with these last, it is apparent that one would reason incorrectly if from agreement with the analogue of the divine attributes one were to conclude to agreement with the divine attributes—if, that is, because something is entirely worthy of the analogue of God one were to consider it to be worthy of God too. But to be unable to show that something is unworthy of God it suffices simply that one be unable to show that it conflicts with the analogue of the divine attributes, our similarly named positive human attributes. If, however, something were in conflict with these, that is, were already unworthy of these, it would have to be considered all the more unworthy of the divine attributes, since we found throughout the treatise on God's attributes[13] that these attributes, insofar as they are in God, must be qualified as more perfect than the merely human. To all this we now add the last negative condition for mediate revelation:

10. *That the man who as the first proclaimer of the alleged revelation claims to be sent to other men and who presents miracles as proof of his mission and doctrine—the first [or immediate] subject of revelation—not comport himself in this presentation of doctrine in a manner unworthy of God or make use of a means unworthy of God in such wise as he would appear, according to the ninth condition, unworthy of the miracle working of God.* The basis of this condition is the same as for the ninth. But that this emissary from God must also, as is customarily added, live holily himself, in accord with this sacred teaching, does not appear to me to be demonstrable, for in his private life he represents not God but himself. To be sure, in the opposite case God's choice would be quite incomprehensible, especially since this circumstance would for some—though without adequate grounds—impede the acceptance of the revelation, but we do not comprehend all the ways of God. Still, let us rejoice that this reproach does not affect our revelation—even if it can be made in reference to others. Let us rejoice too that with respect to those alleged revelations appearing on earth from time to time to which this reproach can be made, it is insignificant compared with the other reasons for rejecting those alleged revelations.

Everything has now been considered that can in any sense pertain to the revelatory fact, and with respect to each element of it the requisite negative conditions have been given. No other negative conditions can therefore be demanded beyond those stated.

*Note.* If someone thinks that after all these conditions it has become impossible for God through supernatural revelation to reform the human race from a state of crudeness and ignorance—because an already very significant formation, especially of moral sentiment and of the power of the will for good, is required to enable man to authenticate a revelation as divine—and that therefore supernatural revelation by God to men has through these conditions been explained to be impossible just where it was most necessary, such a person should well reflect that here all the conditions had to be stated to which a supernatural revelation must correspond *if it is intended for all men of all times,* including a time in which men stand at the highest point of culture. It is not thereby being said that those to whom a certain revelation was first given, and who in many ways, perhaps, were not so advanced in their formation, had to have each of these conditions in mind when they accepted the divine origin of that revelation. Each man convinces himself in his own way and makes use of whatever in the grounds for conviction presented to him corresponds to his capacity. What remains lies unused until someone comes along who needs it too. If it be inferred from this that such uneducated men could be easily led astray through a supposed divine revelation, this would be undeniable if God did not otherwise protect them by his extraordinary care from apparent but inauthentic divine revelations that they could not verify for themselves. On the other hand, it would be inappropriate for anyone to rely on this protective care of God if he himself did not, to proceed the more securely, use all that lay in his power. With respect to revelations that were not intended for all men of all times, it could not be found contradictory if God had provided them with only such grounds of proof of their divine origin as were required and useful for the men to whom they were given.

*The criterion for faith in history.* [14] Because all historical certitude is by nature moral certitude—since, theoretically, any history is doubtful—and because the object in question seems sometimes in many ways and sometimes in no way to be connected with morality, in order not to waver with uncertainty between affirmation and negation, . . . we must above all grasp in a definite manner the general relationship of historical certitude to the fulfillment of duty. . . . Historical certitude is a result of the command to believe in history. Practical reason demands that in general we call to our aid the knowledge and experience of our ancestors where our own insight, along with such insight of our contemporaries as is commended to us, might not, perhaps, make a sure and perfect fulfillment of our duties possible. Practical reason consequently commands us to believe in history, for the knowledge and experience of our ancestors are the subject matter of history and are knowable from it alone. In order, therefore, to assure ourselves all the more of the fulfillment of duty, and all the more certainly to exclude all omissions (arising from limited knowledge), and for no other reason, we ought to believe history. . . . The relationship of this faith, or historical certitude, to the fulfillment of duty is apparent.

Now if anyone before us, be he more or less distant from us, claimed himself to be supernaturally instructed by God as regards the most sure and perfect way in which men can fulfill their duty, and if this claim cannot be shown to be false by reason of the intrinsic content of the alleged instruction, then we have the duty when we hear this claim, and according to the above command to "make use also of others' knowledge and experience from the past to make the fulfillment of duty surer and more perfect," to investigate this knowledge and experience, and to that end, to believe history. We are so commanded, provided that, in some other way, regarding our knowledge of duties and of how perfectly to fulfill them, we have not already attained to the highest level of perfection and surety and become so certain of our high state that we see all confirmation of our knowledge, even if it comes from God, as quite indubitably superfluous for us—an exception that does not occur even with the greatest philosophers. All our investigation of this claim—after the fact of its occurrence has become certain—must, however, be directed to the proofs for belief in the divine origin of this instruction that are supposed to have been given to or through the claimant (the first subject of this revelation), for as already shown, we cannot believe such an assertion on the word of the claimant. In the report of these proofs we should thus believe history—on the condition, of course, that the history we have of these proofs meets the criterion cited above[15] as the general criterion regarding the duty of making this act of faith. . . .

If we are to believe history and if the aforementioned criterion makes it clear what history, then the inner possibility of historical certitude about this object lacks nothing more. It is a question here solely of the *inner* possibility of this certitude.[16] Whether it is also *externally* possible, or what is fundamentally the same, whether it can be attained in reality, cannot be inquired into until a *particular* alleged revelation comes to be investigated. In the *Positive Introduction* such will be the case with respect to Christianity. I will then show that the history of Christian doctrine as well as of the external proofs of its divine origin joined to its impartation through Jesus is precisely the most credible of all histories. For the sake of clarity, nonetheless, it must still expressly be noted that the aforementioned criterion cannot be used for the history of these proofs if the proofs handed on are not external events, . . . and if they have not taken place before several witnesses (at the origin or the subsequent proclamation of the doctrine). For without this publicity everything would in the end rest on the assertion of the first subject alone, and thus there would yet remain more or less ground for the suspicion of credulity, fanatical exaggeration, and even intentional falsification. According to that criterion, such grounds must be excluded as much as possible in a historical report if reason is to command faith in it.


## NOTES

1. Sec. 85, which is reproduced here, forms part of chap. 2 of the third "Investigation."—ED.
2. The proximate (or immediate) subject (or recipient) is a religious seer or prophet; the remote (or mediate) subjects are his disciples, for as many centuries as the religion stemming from this seer or prophet lasts. Hermes is formulating categories in which to discuss Jesus and the church.—ED.
3. See secs. 78, 79, 81 (part 2), and 82.
4. See sec. 41. (The criterion for faith in history is quoted below, pp. 132–34.—ED.) The basis of this condition is apparent from sec. 81 (part 1), where it was demonstrated that under this condition but not without it there is an evident duty to believe this history because of the doctrine reported in it—if, of course, the doctrine reported and the proofs given for it have the character described in sec. 81 (part 1) and *required by the conditions given here.*
5. See sec. 79.
6. Ibid.
7. Ibid.
8. See sec. 81 (part 1).
9. See sec. 79.
10. Ibid.
11. The criterion of true miracles is given in sec. 81 (part 2).
12. See sec. 82.
13. See sec. 73 (part 3). In the case of mediate revelation only external miracles are *a priori* conceivable as rationally allowable means of proof (sec. 81). In the case of immediate revelation, however, a supernatural elevation of the natural human power of knowing in the subject of revelation can take the place of external miracles and make them superfluous.
14. Excerpted from sec. 81, pp. 579–82.—ED.
15. The criterion in question is found in sec. 41, pp. 239–40: "We are always, but on no other grounds than these, obliged to accept as true a theoretically

doubtful piece of knowledge on assent to which there depends the possibility of fulfilling a certain and unconditioned general duty, knowledge, namely, concerning the actual presence of an instance of duty. We are so obliged if the grounds for doubting the truth of this knowledge all arise out of the general circumstances that must be present for the general duty in question to bind us and thus make an instance of this duty actually arise and if the particular circumstances that individualize the instance at hand add no new grounds for doubt."—ED.

16. By *inner possibility* Hermes apparently means the absence of internal contradiction in the notion of historical certitude arising from belief in a historical account. But where Hermes saw no internal contradiction others very well might see it.—ED.

# 5

# A Letter on
# Human Knowledge
# and the Divine Trinity

*Anton Günther*

Anton Günther was born in Lindenau, Bohemia, in 1783. After studies in Prague he was ordained a priest in 1821. Declining offers of academic posts, he lived from 1824 as a private scholar in Vienna, where he died in 1863. Despite the efforts of Günther's friends and admirers, Pius IX (reigned 1846–78) condemned his works in 1857. Günther piously accepted this judgment and remained—unlike Lamennais, for example—a loyal Catholic.

Readers unskilled in philosophy may wish to pass over this selection, the most difficult one in the volume. The reader who plunges into it may, however, begin to suspect that its difficulty lies more in its language than in the ideas behind the language. A writer employing the German Idealist Grand Manner may strike the English-language reader—in an uncharitable moment, of course—as resembling the Wizard of Oz: behind the puffs of smoke and the flashing lights there is something less awe inspiring. (Germans, too, sometimes feel this way: see n. 3 to this selection.) At any rate, the reader who is skilled, curious, and charitable may be aided in understanding this and similar texts by these two thoughts: (1) Philosophers like Günther feel that the more usual, straightforward language of philosophy has been spoiled by Wolffians and Kantians, and that to go beyond these philosophers a new language is necessary. (2) Philosophers of this kind are attempting to describe a situation in which elements of human mental life participate in transcendental elements of being, but in which these transcendental elements, in us and beyond us, are never available for separate, restricted examination. It is as if one knew, somehow, that ordinary sunlight contains the color violet, and one wanted to talk about violet without, however, being able to isolate it with a prism. In fairness one must allow that discussion of philosophical participation is never without problems: witness how participation in the thought of Thomas Aquinas, despite the good intentions of nineteenth-century neo-scholastics, was not handled well until well into the twentieth century.

Günther casts his apologetic in the form of imaginary letters. It is important to bear in mind that the following selection really is apologetic in intent:

136

Günther is trying to make the Trinity, the fundamental doctrine of Christianity, acceptable to the contemporary mind, and his way of doing this is in some respects evocative of Anselm. Or more exactly, it is a mirror reversal of Anselm: here, what is understood is more likely to be accepted. In the estimate of Pius IX and his advisers, however, Günther went too far. In the Roman view the Trinity is a strict mystery: its very existence can be known only by revelation. Its inner nature, or the internal necessity of what it is, will never be known by the human intellect at all: to understand God that well one would have to be God. Perhaps Günther fell into an illusion not uncommon in the pious mind: to have become so at home with the truths of faith as to fancy that they are comprehensible and that one comprehends them.

What Günther is about in the following letter will be clearer if we extract from it five statements. To begin with, there is a continuity of pattern or articulation in being, or at all levels of being. This is akin, using the example above, to my being convinced that violet is violet both right at the sun and in my back yard. Günther writes, (1) "So long as you have not grasped God as triune in his eternal self-consciousness, so also will you not grasp relative being [that is, creatures] in terms of God." Now this same thought can be stated in reverse: (2) "It is the moments of self-consciousness that, in their not absolute but modified transferral to the so-called concept of the Absolute, constitute the triune God." Combining both terms of the comparison, (3) "In God and in the creature self-consciousness is an essential form, in the former, of absolute being, in the latter, of relative being, with only the difference . . . that in the former the elements of the form (the moments in the self-activation of the principle) are not mere phenomena (or appearances) but real moments (noumena, or substances)." Now just this continuity of pattern, says Günther, is what Paul teaches in Rom. 1:19; and moreover, (4) "Paul . . . before his calling . . . may have set before his profoundly insightful soul the thought of the universe as a primordial manifestation of the Deity in its Trinity." That is to say, the knowledge of the Trinity is an attainment possible for natural reason unaided by faith. In other words, (5) "The decrees of God, so long as they perdure in God," remain hidden; "but when those ideas stand realized before us, as does the created world, . . . they are a heavenly sign to our earth."

What in the introduction to the selection from Hermes were called the two tasks of philosophy are here accomplished in one stroke. Metaphysics there must yet be, but there is no longer any thought of its preparing the mind for revelation; it *is* revelation. In addition, one need no longer be concerned to develop criteria for dealing with alleged revelatory moments in the historical process, for metaphysics is in principle possible at any time and place. But the nineteenth-century Catholic church was not ready to collapse the distinction between nature and grace, or to proclaim that faith as a means of knowledge was no longer necessary for the educated Christian.

My dear Thomas Wendeling,

I could be indignant that, this year at least, you mean to excuse yourself from the praiseworthy old custom of eating the Easter lamb with your uncle in Kirchfels.[1] And on top of that you still want me to boil and decorate Easter eggs for your pleasure, for if you are to break them open on the feast of the Resurrection they must be prepared in good time. Such a request scarcely deserves consideration.

Be that as it may, you also asked me in your last letter if I would extend my hand to you to help you *rise up.* Of course I will, but have you been laid in the *tomb* yet, and before that, hung on the *cross*?

Do you not know what Schelling says in his memorable treatise on human freedom: that *nothing is the cross of the understanding?*—that is, the nothing out of which, by the power of God, the world is said to arise, or, what his predecessors and contemporaries had already said: that no one has yet brought forth an intelligent word about creation from nothing?

What this proposition means, in other words, is that creation systems are a blot on speculation.

On the other hand, I have by no means forgotten, nor could I forget, what you so rightly wrote in an earlier letter: "As firm as the earth under my feet is the proposition *'If God creates, he does not thereby posit his own being, for his is an uncreated being.'* " But, the objection did not occur to you that the act of positing can also be called an act of creating, in which case the Second and Third Persons of the godhead, without further ado, would presumably have to be creatures.

I do not as yet have any direct proof that you have understood and taken to heart what I had set before you as the reverse of that proposition, namely, that the positing of another, nondivine substance stands to the idea of God not only in no contradiction but in the most beautiful harmony, since the being that is by and of itself trinitarian can reveal itself externally (*ad extra,* as the old theology expressed it) only in this manner, in this its character: that it posits beings that are another, something essentially distinct from it.

Nevertheless, why should I not let your request serve me as an indirect proof that you have nothing to object to my assertion? You will

---

Letter 11 of *Vorschule der speculativen Theologie des positiven Christenthums,* 1st sec., 2d ed. in *Gesammelte Schriften: Neue Ausgabe in 9 Bänden* (Vienna, 1882; Frankfurt am Main; Minerva, 1968), 1:100–122. The first edition of the *Vorschule* appeared in 1827. The translation is by Joseph Fitzer.

also call to mind how I told you that the riddle of the Sphinx—the dualism of the substances in creaturely being, together with their synthesis—can be fully solved only from the nature of God and its all-round comprehension.

[*The relationship of human thought and the Trinity.*] It is precisely in the all-round evaluation of the otherwise correctly grasped idea of God that our thinkers commonly fail; and quite to the point here is what Lessing says somewhere so appropriately: most men believe that they have attained the goal of their reflection just where they should have started thinking.[2]

It certainly belongs to the very gratifying phenomena of our time that in its speculation it does not want to hear any more about an impersonal, unselfconscious God. Where today would anyone still suggest in public, with Fichte, that "to attribute consciousness and personality to God means to make him a finite being, for consciousness and the higher level of the same, personality, are bound up with limitation and finitude." In Fichte's opinion, then, *clever words,* not only about creation from nothing, but even about the personality and Trinity of God, are something scandalous. Or consider what Schelling writes in the preface to his *System of Transcendental Idealism:* "That which would be viewed as the ultimate ground of the harmony between subjective and objective must indeed be thought as an absolute identity; to present it, however, as a substantial and personal being would be no better than to posit it as a bare abstraction."

In short, on the one hand, speculative reason cannot let go the idea of a God who from eternity determines himself to absolute reflection, that is, to absolute self-contemplation; and still, on the other hand, where do you find a system of philosophy that discusses a God that is conscious of himself as triune in himself, quite before the creation of the world? Indeed, when such matters are discussed, as we have just seen from the fragment quoted, does not the Trinity first come about through creation, as God's falling out from himself, and his restoration in world history to his prior condition? Furthermore, is God's consciousness before the world comes into being another in God, as in man, who as creature, is not the creator? Or is it something nobler in God, which self-consciousness (or simple personality) in the human race is not? But now hear, my dear Tom, if you have ears to hear: so long as you have not grasped God as triune in his eternal self-consciousness, so also will you not grasp relative being, in the antithesis and synthesis of its substances, in terms of God.

The speculative spirit of the age strikes me as suffering from a kind of lockjaw when, on the one hand, with what it so beautifully knows about the nature of the higher and lower consciousness in man, and on the other, with antipathy against impersonality[3] in the Absolute, it still does not know what to make of the eternally self-conscious God as a God at once tripersonal and one—and arrogantly leaves this theme either to the old scholasticism and its mad urge for metaphysics or to the so-called positivism of modern theology. The latter is dimwitted enough not to perceive in the Christian doctrine of the Trinity the remnants of ancient polytheism, and hence proceeds to find hints of ancient polytheism in the writers of the Old Testament.

But speculation also has a positive basis: its only true foundation is the facts of the life of the spirit [Geisteslebens]. For this reason it is especially the moments of self-consciousness that, in their not absolute but modified transferral to the so-called concept of the Absolute, constitute the triune God. This is the stand I take in this letter, which however consists as little in a complete theory of consciousness as in one of the Trinity, for only to already received results in the former area do I appeal in the latter. And so to the matter at hand.

[Human knowing.] It is a question, among other things, of proceeding from a definition with which you are acquainted: consciousness is an essential form of being.[4] The elements of this form, furthermore, are the two moments of the distinction of the representer and the represented, and of the representation as the unity and likeness of the first two. Self-consciousness in this form is termed a higher level of consciousness, since in it spirit makes itself (not another, outside it) the object of inner representation.

The spirit itself, however, is both activity and the ground of activity (substance and accident = noumenon and phenomenon), and on this basis is then established the division of self-consciousness into the pure and the empirical, of which the former is expressed in the proposition "I am," and the latter in the proposition "I am active (thinking, feeling, or willing)." Further, as you know, all appearances in the spirit [or representations in the mind] are only the product of its basic powers [Grundkräfte] in their reciprocal penetration, sometimes with the preponderance of one power, sometimes of another.

Now the spirit is supposed to be able to make, directly, only the appearances of its essence [Wesen] the object of its inner vision, not however its essence itself, which it characterizes by the word I. The spirit's essence itself is only indirectly, or mediately, viewed and presupposed, but it must be presupposed and anticipated as long as appearances are spoken of as what are posited, as what cannot posit themselves, or as what must necessarily proceed as determined from an original undetermined.[5] In short, the I as substance never as such becomes the object of a so-called immediate representation—but it must be held fast as something behind all appearances which through the basic powers mediates itself to revelation and appearance and which thus, as something given but still unmediated (and only as unmediated) forms the basis of all mediation. This mediate understanding of the unmediated ground of all inner appearances does not thereby militate against certitude in knowledge of the ground, for this mediate understanding in no way makes the so-called unmediated uncertain and unsure, not even if the ground is found to be presupposed and indeed, later, posited.

To be sure, to know oneself as an act of thought (with being as its content) certainly occurs; but being as such is not in that act in which it (as something thought, or emerging in consciousness) is translated from an original indeterminacy into determinateness under the name *I*. As the ground of this limitedness of the spirit in its externally mediated (and to that end purely mediate) self-contemplation there cannot easily be put forward anything other than the conditionedness of the spirit itself, which is likewise an undeniable fact of consciousness. What does not simply *be* (or what is not per se) does not through itself come to self-revelation or to the externalization of its powers.

Under this law of conditioned existence, then, stands the human spirit, which, as is so frequently repeated, is called into the light of self-consciousness only by a spirit that has already advanced to self-consciousness—in no way, therefore, through the mere operation of external nature, which does not understand its being.

Further, what is enabled to externalize its power only by another outside it can, for this reason, first and immediately bring to representation only its appearance—and only as a result of this (mediately) bring its essence to representation, as the ground of that appearance, always mediated only through that appearance. One has recourse here to a likeness: just as the physical eye never sees itself but only through itself sees all other things, so does reason act as the eye of the spirit. But this comparison limps. In the first place, the physical eye is not there to become objective to itself as such, that is, to perceive itself, but is there for all that exists in addition to it. In it nature indeed maintains her subjectivity, but only to look upon herself as appearing object. Thus the eye belongs to nature as much as the visible object, along with light, the rapport between both. In this mutual relation is also completed the coming to itself of nature-substance, which has in this relation its insurmountable boundary in the animal realm, below man.

[*God's knowing.*] But if this limitation of spirit lies in the conditionedness of its nature, it must, however, fall away in an Unconditioned.

If God is, as being-through-itself, for that reason also knowledge-through-itself, that is absolute self-consciousness, so will the character of this absolute self-knowledge consist in precisely this: that it makes its absolute being as such immediately (without mediation from the out-side) the object of its contemplation. *Inner* mediation, however, is not excluded. This inner mediation proceeds simply from being, and consists of the opposition in which being enters into relation with itself.

This modification of the concept of consciousness in its transference from creaturely to divine being anyone will willingly grant. But what immediately follows from this is not clear to many; and it is not clear, I might add, not because it is in and for itself obscure but because a strong light only blinds, not enlightens, the unpracticed eye.

From these reflections follows the thought that God, when he comprehends himself immediately in his substantiality (that is, becomes conscious of himself), posits his own essence in opposition to himself, that is, posits himself again. In other words, only in this way does it become thinkable for us that God makes himself in his essentiality the object of immediate contemplation, namely, if he really opposes himself in himself as substance or duplicates himself in himself by emanation. So also can the human spirit raise its thinking activity (its thinking itself as being) to an object of reflection, not by some sort of bypassing of thought but through a second, similarly living thought. This thought of thought is no mere silhouette of thought but light from light, life from life.

Now what is true of the *object* in the self-consciousness of God (which in its likeness to the divine *subject* is, just like it, absolute substance) is true also (according to the aforementioned received axioms about the nature of consciousness) of the second moment of self-objectification, which in addition to the subject and object posits a *third* element in the absolute self-consciousness. It is, like the two previous moments, absolute substance, which proceeding from subject and object attests to the simultaneous positing of the two members in opposition, that is, of these in their perfection and completion.

Thus in God and in the creature self-consciousness is an essential form, in the former, of absolute being, in the latter, of relative being, with only the difference (which is determined by the quality of being) that in the former the elements of the form (the moments in the self-activation of the principle) are not mere phenomena (or appearances) but real moments (noumena, or substances). In other words, since all self-consciousness is a conviction about being [*Überzeugung vom Seyn*],[6] so can this conviction arise only out of a prior generation; but in the creature this generation is the primordial appearance of substance in the differentiating moments of receptivity and reaction (as stimulated by some external influence). Self-consciousness in the creature is the relating back of both by the principle unto itself, as the causal bearer of both, and vice versa. In the divine self-consciousness the principle moves to itself as such in the opposition and thus has its conviction in a moment in which those two members again find themselves undivided and identical, because it has proceeded from both as third principle alongside both. We can thus describe this act of conviction as an intensification of either relative or absolute being.

This process of conviction, or intensification (also called the self-objectification of the principle), is perfected in two moments with three factors. The first moment of the opposition already presupposes the principle as the first factor, which precisely through the relationship to it of that which is opposed attains subjecthood, as the exclusive causality of that which is opposed. Both factors, however, witness their mutual substantial likeness in a second moment of opposition, a twofold emanation that posits a third factor, in which the total identity of being of both (their simultaneous positing in opposition) brings itself to objective, real contemplation. As this third factor is related to itself as the positing of both, so in like manner is it related to both as its twofold cause.

A counterpart to this is found in natural life, where the sexual factors, in their unlikeness, produce an offspring that objectifies that unlikeness precisely in one-sided sexuality, that is, neither in sexlessness nor in bisexuality. On the other hand, the unsexual *spirit* finds its objectivity in the twofoldness and unlikeness of the moments of differentiation (passivity and activity, which it relates to itself precisely as causal principle and hence wins as subject). The spirit must presuppose itself as the undivided and simple but also undetermined principle of that divided objectivity (also its determinateness) and must recognize the identity of principle and subject in terms of substance.[7]

So much, then, for the triune or tripersonal God in and through the immediate consciousness of himself, the consciousness of being through and from itself. In this connection you must not forget what I said to you at the very beginning, that you must not expect from me today either a perfected theory of consciousness or a complete doctrine of the Trinity. I have here provisionally concerned myself only with this: whether what is known up to the present, even if incompletely, from psychologies (which are rarely complete doctrines of the soul, let alone the spirit) can usefully show you, first, that one must be silent about the self-consciousness and personality of the Absolute if one does not want to know anything about the triune God as presented by positive Christianity[8], and, second, that God does not need to create the world in order to arrive at self-manifestation and self-knowledge. For the immediate (mediated through itself) contemplation of himself as absolute principle coincides with the real opposition and simultaneous positing by means of emanation. If, however, God creates, he does not posit his essence, for his essence is not created but simply is what it is.

[*Creation.*] Now if God is manifest to himself before and without any creation there unavoidably arises the question, *Why has God still created?* In my reply to this question I trust you will find the key to relative being, to its puzzling dualism of substantiality in the realms of nature and spirit as well as to the synthesis of that antithesis in the world of man.

If before all creation God is manifest to himself, so the secondary manifestation of God cannot, to begin with, have any other goal but this, that God become manifest to other beings [Wesen] outside him. (Note well, though, that I said, "to begin with," that is, in relation to us as rational beings.) This manifestation to others entails the positing of these other beings; that is, creation and external manifestation stand to each other in the relation of means and end, and condition each other. This manifestation, however, is at once identical with the division between that which manifests itself as object and the subject of the manifestation, to which the manifestation is supposed to occur. To be sure, this division is on God's part, like all distinctions, an affirmation in negation and a negation in affirmation.

Such a division comes into being only through creation, through the positing of a substance that is not the absolute substance, for only in such do affirmation and negation meet. This same distinction, finally, as an act proceeding from God, must be perfect, complete.

This distinction and manifestation *ad extra* will be complete only when it is the real reflex of [God's] self-manifestation *ad intra*, that is, when the three moments of the latter (which are there identical with God's absolute self-consciousness) are again found in the former.[9] You will be startled, but take your time. I will extend my hand to you as you wished, in this wise: I want to direct your attention to facts that the inquiring mind is aware of but does not always sufficiently consider. If God himself has set the limits of human confusion, it should not surprise you that these limits are everywhere encountered.

Among other things, then, what necessitates the thinking spirit to recognize itself as changeless in the changeable? The mere succession of appearances would not suffice for an answer, I think, if the manifoldness of appearances could not be reduced to the opposition of so-called powers, which for just this reason are called basic powers, since one can never be derived from its opposite. (It is rather that from both in their reciprocity can all other manifestations in the life of spirit be developed.) Just this opposition of the so-called basic powers necessitates the spirit to pass beyond this opposition and seek itself as the common ultimate ground of both. This ground, in opposition to them, it designates *being* [*Seyn*], and since it itself is this being as being-in-act [*der Seyende*] it designates this being *I*. In this being, accordingly, inhere those so-called basic powers of receptivity and spontaneity as primordial ways of manifesting and being.

We must follow the same procedure in regard to the external appearances of nature. So long as we are necessitated by the power of our self-consciousness not to view natural appearances as (arbitrary or nonarbitrary) products of our own spirit, we are also necessitated to look for their ultimate ground not in ourselves but outside ourselves, in nature. And so we claim for nature its own principle along with the basic powers of this principle, contraction and expansion, as primordial ways of manifestation (from which first so-called *matter* and then the great field of natural appearances in all three realms can be grasped).[10] In this way, then, the opposition of powers as the proximate ground for appearances necessitates us, throughout relative being, to go beyond this opposition to attain the ultimate ground in a unity (which ground could then not improperly be termed a relative absolute).

But it is not enough that we are necessitated to claim for nature its own (independent) principle. We must also establish this principle in essential difference from the spirit of man as principle, and indeed, by the same right as that by which nature will have its own principle recognized by us. Nature as a whole is homogeneously formed and ordered. Now, just as thousands of years ago, its organisms exist. To an influence exerted upon it there corresponds an equally determinate counterinfluence as a reaction; never does one basic power deny another its operation. Not so is the sphere of spirit.

Attention is indeed called to the spontaneous power in man by what the receptive power each time brings to it, but the spontaneous power must not be thought to correspond to the receptive power too closely. To explain, the spontaneous, or active, power must indeed externalize itself—as so prompted by receptivity for both other and its own being—but this necessary reaction can also be a resistance to what the receptive powers present.

Even in those activities of the spirit that appear to go on of themselves and without the spirit we see by careful observation that there is at work a principle of which we find no living trace outside the circle of human activity. It has not infrequently been asserted that every conceptualization in man is, as a process of desensualization, as a lifting up over the power and influence of sense, an indicator of the superiority of spirit over nature—even though this process, by each formal conceptualization, stands only in the service of nature, so as to assist it in its striving toward internalization.[11] In short, the principle of external appearance stands in essential qualitative distinction from that of inwardness. We thus call spirit *free*, nature *necessary*. And thus as little as man can treat natural phenomena as externalizations of the power of his being, or conversely, treat his own activities as appearances of nature, just as little can he consistently transpose both the principle of nature and his spirit as principle into forms of activity or ways of appearance of another, third substance.

If he did this, it would happen at the cost not only of his substantiality but also of his personality (I-ness), in which the former, precisely as such, thinks itself (that is, knows)—an advantageous characteristic which he shares with no individuality found in the life of nature, however excellent.

Still, if the dualism of substantiality in relative being is preserved, this opposition of substances drives us beyond the opposition to a substantial principle of both, and it is a question now of the correct determination of this principle. No doubt the opposedness of the substances of created being would allow us without further ado to explain the absolute ground of both as the synthesis of both were that synthesis not already given to us in relative being, in human nature, as a combination of spirit and nature. Note that we could not characterize the ground as the indifference of freedom and necessity without canceling the substantiality of both areas of relative being and by so doing making it again a mere accident.

If the absolute ground is not indifference and not the synthesis of the opposites, so it must be beyond both, neither of the two—and consequently a third substance, to which is related all other substantiality not as accident and modification but as [the result of] free positing, that is, as creature in essential distinction from creator. The necessary presupposition of this distinction is that God distinguish himself from those beings [*Wesen*] to which, as distinct from himself, he will manifest himself. So much then, provisionally, for the solution of the puzzle.[12]

[*Conclusion.*] As you see, in the investigation of the *relation* between relative and absolute (which, however indistinct, is certainly an element of your self-consciousness), you can either ascend from relative being [*Seyn*] or, conversely (presupposing God as absolute consciousness), descend from the Absolute to the reconstruction of relative being. You are always necessitated to "state" God as a third substance, which in this divine substantiality can no more be spirit than nature as long as both are held to be creaturely life principles. Moreover, it is self-evident that man can nonetheless call God *spirit,* partly because God can be brought under one concept with created spirit (insofar as God and spirit have it in common that, in opposition to nature, they are not material), partly because God and spirit are included in the concept *self-conscious beings.* In the former case the concept *spirit* appears as purely negatively, in the latter case as purely positively, determined, but still only in formal, that is, purely logical relation, a relation that does not entitle one to treat the relationship between spirit and God as if it had metaphysical value.

As I conclude this letter I want to direct your attention to a uniquely characteristic moment of the separateness of the Absolute, or rather, of the incommensurability of God with the created world (in substantial relation). It consists in this, that essence [*Wesen*] and form in the Absolute Being [*Seyn*] and essence and form in relative being stand to each other in exactly inverse relation.

God is unity according to his essence, threeness according to his essential form. The created world, however, the totality of the relative, is triplicity in substantiality, namely, spirit, nature, and humanity, and unity in form or accident; for each principle in the three realms of the universe comes to self-manifestation through the dualism of basic powers and their reciprocity—even if the result thereof, thought, consciousness, is each time something else, like being [*Seyn*] itself.

One could thus say without exaggeration, *the creation is God inverted, the counterpoint of God,* and thus even not-God, because otherwise God through an inner self-contradiction would have to invert his own essence. Such a contradiction is unthinkable, and hence impossible. Correctly appropriated, this inversion of form and essence means that the creature, by reason of its total essential distinction from the creator, yet recognizes and prizes itself as a work of God. It discovers traces of its high birth, gladly acknowledges itself the image of God. For even if the creature as such does not have in common with God the essence of God, so in the distinction of essence it still has form (the *modus existendi*) in common with him. The creature has form in common with God insofar as this is possible, in the sense that form, as manifestation of essence, must also co-manifest distinction in essence. And this we find, no matter whether we conceive of the world as a totality or as composed of individuals.

If we view the world in terms of the individuals that compose it we find that each substance is a principle of life and as such is the ultimate ground of a certain sum of appearances, that is, a relative absolute with a relative universe. Hence each subject attains its self-manifestation, or becomes knowing being [*Seyn*]—or what comes to the same, each principle becomes subjective-objective in its own way, which way each time forms a formal trinity, as a form of life of the same principle.

As a totality, however, creaturely being [*Seyn*] stands before us as a triad of substances in which man, as it were, the spirit of the universe, presupposes spirit and nature as an antithesis, and to that extent proceeds from both as synthesis. Dear Tom, has it not struck you how in Rom. 1:19 we read,

> For what can be known about God is plain to [the heathen]. Ever since the creation of the world his invisible nature, namely, his eternal power and deity, has been clearly perceived in the things that have been made. So they are without excuse; for although they knew God they did not honor him as God or give thanks to him, but they became futile in their thinking and their senseless minds were darkened. Claiming to be wise, they became fools.[13]

And if this passage has struck you, why then? Perhaps because Paul, who before his calling was so little a common fisherman as a common thinker, may have set before his profoundly insightful soul the thought of the universe *as a primordial manifestation of the Deity in its Trinity*—just as he already accepted the idea of the resurrection of all flesh when he was a Pharisee. Be that as it may, you owe it to this passage, and especially to certain words in it, if from today on you owe something to your uncle. Before all, praise God, who gave such power to unlock mystery, even in the realm of science, to those men whom he chose as vessels to bear his name to the heathen, the name unique and exalted above all names. And now would I close, but it occurs to me that a point I have made in my letter might trouble both your enjoyment [of Easter] and your understanding.

I have spoken in the conclusion of this letter of the unity of the divine essence, but also, earlier, of the real objectification of the one essence both in the Second and in the Third Person, and consequently of a threeness, or tripled existence, of one and the same divine substance. On the one hand, this apparent contradiction might prove a difficulty to your understanding, just as on the other the thought of tritheism might cause you concern about the orthodoxy of your uncle. He, however, is neither a tritheist nor a Christian polytheist who holds fast to the one divine substance posited twice according to two moments of objectification in absolute self-consciousness. Otherwise Augustine and Leibnitz would also have to be considered tritheists.

You will recall a marginal note in the theology of Leibnitz that gives as much trouble to translators and commentators as to readers. It runs, "Sunt ergo tres substantiae singulares, relatio una absoluta, quae illas complectitur."[14] I must admit that when I encountered these lines in the text of the Leibnitzian theology, I at first found them shocking. Now, however, they are very dear and agreeable to me, especially because they shed light on a passage in the *De Trinitate* of Saint Augustine. In book 7 of that treatise Augustine raises this question among others: why do we not say there are three gods, just as we say there are three divine persons? He finds the reason in a pedagogical maxim of the church, which, impelled by necessity, introduced this manner of speaking and holds fast to it. The passage reads,

> When human feebleness sought to express in words the doctrine about the Lord God its creator, to which it held fast according to its capacity, in the inner recesses of the mind, whether by its pious faith or by any reflections of its own, it feared to say three essences, lest a diversity of any kind should be understood in that highest equality. But on the other hand it could not say that they were not three somethings [*tria quaedam*], since by denying this Sabellius fell into heresy.[15]

With this opinion of Augustine there later agreed many and great theologians, from Peter Lombard to Thomas Aquinas. Thomas, however, would not agree to Augustine's assertion that to the concept of personality as such there belongs also the concept of substance and essence only, apparently, on this superficial ground, that to do so would give heretics a means to slander Catholic doctrine as heathen. Noteworthy in this connection is a passage in the dogmatics of the learned Petavius, who means to hold out a helping hand to the great Thomas, this in reference to Augustine's main argument for the above-mentioned assertion of the threeness of substances in the Deity. Augustine had written, "If *to be* is said of [God] in respect to himself, but *person* relatively, . . . what then? Shall we call the Father the person of the Son, . . . or the Son the person of the Father?"[16]

To this Petavius now offhandedly replies,[17] Augustine has forgotten that the term *person* is only improperly used of God, since it is properly and originally valid only of creatures; in regard to creatures personality is predicated not merely with relative but with absolute validity; but such is by no means the case when the term *person* is transferred to God.

Now who has seen more correctly, Augustine in the sixth [*sic*] century or Petavius in the eighteenth [*sic*]? And of the pair, who should have been able to see farther? To stand on someone else's shoulders is a good idea if you want to see farther than another, but the important thing is still always natural sharpness of vision, and this Augustine possessed to a rare degree. Could not, indeed, should not, Petavius also have said that the thoughts *being* and *substance* are also only improperly employed in reference to God?

Augustine, however, found the image of God's Trinity in the inner being of man: that man *is*, that he *knows* his being, and that he *loves* this being and knowing. [18] Others after him found it much more agreeable to seek the likeness of God in man exclusively in the so-called powers of the soul, without reference to their principle. But here the question arises, Who stood nearer the truth? These and similar questions should make you aware of the great task of theologians in our time, which consists of this, to transform the old cross of the understanding from a pillory to a sign of honor for the free spirit. This free spirit possesses equally from God's grace its authority and its autonomy in the fathoming of the given.

You will surely forgive me if I speak again of the great apostle, who said, "The Spirit searches everything, even the depths of God. For what person knows a man's thoughts except the spirit of the man which is in him? So also no one comprehends the thoughts of God except the Spirit of God."[19] That is to say, he presented to his time the relationship of philosophy, as a profane science, to theology—or even that of speculative to merely positive theology—more correctly and more lovingly than many a *doctor theologicus* in our speculative century. To this latter type the spirit of man appears to be nothing better at the present moment than a bearer of forms, to which material must be given exclusively from the outside. But fear not for orthodoxy—your uncle's, I mean—for he believes that the decrees of God, so long as they abide in God as ideas, can certainly not be known or guessed at by the spirit of man. But *when those ideas stand realized before us, as does the created world* and on it *the cross*, they are like a heavenly sign to our earth.

Written on Good Friday.

Peregrinus,
Pastor at Kirchfels

## NOTES

1. Father Peregrinus ("pilgrim") is writing to Wendeling (*wenden*, "to change") from Kirchfels ("church rock").—ED.
2. "It is infinitely difficult to know where and when one should rest; a thousand to one, the goal of their reflection is the place where they get tired of reflecting."
3. What Günther apparently means is that contemporary thinkers really would prefer to speak of the Absolute in personal terms if they could only find a philosophically acceptable way of doing so. For consolation, the English-speaking reader should be aware that contemporary *Germans* on occasion found the

German Idealists' language perplexing. A charming illustration of this is the story of Goethe's bringing Hegel, his guest, to the dinner table, where the latter held forth at great length in abstruse formulas. Goethe's daughter-in-law Ottilie did not know who the guest was and later asked, adding that he must be either inspired or insane. Not at all, said Goethe with an ironic smile, "Just the most famous modern philosopher" (*Gedenkausgabe der Werke, Briefe und Gespräche*, ed. Ernst Beutler [Zurich, 1949], 23:517–18).—ED.

4. *Bewusstseyn ist eine wesentliche Form des Seyns.* In other words, consciousness, the prime characteristic of the essence of man, is a mode of being. By *its* essence consciousness necessarily *is* being. The analysis of consciousness is the starting point of the human *Geist*—mind and/or spirit—in the doing of philosophy.—ED.

5. The expressions used to describe our understanding—or cognitively laying hold of—the ground are, as is well known, different with different psychologists. Some say the I is inferred; others, induced. The former expression would seem to be the more apt were it not so easily confused with logical inference, which is not at all the same as this living, ontological inference. The real ground [*Realgrund, Ur-Sache*] is inferred [*entschlossen*] insofar as it has disjunctively manifested [*ausgeschlossen*] itself in its external manifestation. (Regarding the term *appearance*, appearances or mental phenomena [as opposed to phenomena in the external world of nature] are *accidents*, of which the inquiring mind seeks the substance.—ED.)

6. By *Überzeugung* Günther apparently wishes to emphasize the actual knowing of being, the assurance that one is knowing being, as opposed to a purely formal consideration of the process by which spirit knows being—though, of course, this process is being-in-act, too. For spirit, the act of being/knowing is simpler than any formula of words used to describe it.—ED.

7. In other words, the spirit can think of itself in different ways. "That which underlies" something else—appearances or powers or operations—is spoken of as substance (*Substanz*). The reader will note that the underlying human I is spoken of as essence (*Wesen*) to distinguish it from "nonessential" appearances, and as being (*Seyn*) to indicate that it is the ground (*Grund*) of its basic powers (*Grundkräfte*). But *essence* can also mean *nature*, in the sense of what something is, or even *possessor of a nature*.—ED.

8. *Positive* here means *historical*, in the sense of the history of the church as the scene of various doctrinal developments.—ED.

9. In my book *Thomas à Scrupulis*, I have discussed this motivation of creation (which is based on the idea of God as love, in the sense of a moral attribute). . . . See also my books *Die Just-Milieux in der deutschen Philosophie* and *Euristheus und Heracles.*

10. A bit of early-nineteenth-century philosophy of science makes its appearance here, which the reader can safely ignore. The three realms are given below, p. 147, as spirit, nature, and humanity.—ED.

11. Günther's point is that there is a reciprocity between human beings and the infrahuman world of nature. The infrahuman can receive an internal dimension, that of being-as-knowing, by reason of its inclusion in the human composite nature-plus-spirit. Thus humankind "serve" the infrahuman.—ED.

12. The puzzle is that to which attention is drawn above, p. 144: that of the "puzzling" division of the created world into nature and spirit. Why the division? Apparently so that it could be resolved in humankind. But if one asks why

creation *at all*, then the answer is presumably that appended by Günther in n. 9. If God does not create by necessity of his nature, then he must do it out of love.—ED.

13. RSV.—ED.

14. One hopes that the following would merit Günther's approval: "There are three unique substances, [but] one absolute relation that embraces them." But what is an "absolute relation"? One might suppose it to be (*a*) a relationship within ultimate being, not between the ultimate and lesser beings, and (*b*) a relationship involving the totality of the being(s) so related, as in the relationship of the Father and the Word/Son in John. Günther's point is that ultimate being is always and irreducibly threefold.—ED.

15. From Augustine's *The Trinity*, trans. Stephen McKenna, C.SS.R., Fathers of the Church 45 (Washington, D.C.: Catholic Univ. of America Press, 1963), 7.4.9, p. 233.—ED.

16. Ibid., 7.6.11, p. 236; italics added. Günther mixes quotation and paraphrase, it seems. In the passage cited, Augustine observes that a term predicated relatively, indicating a relation to others—e.g., *friend*—can be used interchangeably for all those so related.—ED.

17. Denys Petau (1583–1652), *de Trinitate*, book 4, chap. 12.

18. *Augustine City of God* 11.26.

19. Given here in full is the text that Günther apparently paraphrases: 1 Cor. 2:11 (RSV).—ED.

# 6

# A Letter on
# How God's Existence
# Cannot Be Proved

*Louis Bautain*

Unlike Günther's Thomas Wendeling, the recipient of this letter, Adeodatus, was a real person, although, mercifully, he was not really called Adeodatus. He was Théodore Ratisbonne, one of a group of three young Jews whom Bautain converted to Christianity in the period after 1822 when, having lost a government teaching post, he gave private lessons in philosophy and theology. Apparently position papers from those lessons formed the basis of the *Philosophy of Christianity,* of 1835. (See W. M. Horton, *The Philosophy of the Abbé Bautain* [New York: New York Univ. Press, 1926], 81.)

Louis Bautain was born in Paris in 1796 and died there in 1867. A disciple of Victor Cousin, he became professor of philosophy in Strasbourg in 1817. In 1819 he underwent a philosophical and religious conversion, influenced by reading Kant and von Baader. After Bautain lost his teaching post—allegedly for teaching skepticism, which undermines religion and morals, but also perhaps because of his political views—he studied medicine and, without studying theology in the usual courses, was ordained a priest and made cathedral preacher. Between 1834 and 1840 he ran into difficulty with two different bishops of Strasbourg over his philosophical views, and he had to sign a succession of articles attesting his orthodoxy. In 1843 he was able to resume teaching philosophy and psychology; in 1850 he became vicar general of the archdiocese of Paris, and from 1853 to 1862 taught moral theology at the Sorbonne.

In the selection given here, Bautain emphatically asserts that the only way the human mind can know God is by faith. "God in his divine essence, in the purity and simplicity of his Being, is inaccessible to created intelligence, absolutely incomprehensible to man." The human mind is limited to finite realities. Even the much celebrated common sense of humankind cannot logically affirm God, for any God so affirmed would simply be an idol, a logical entity. (The reader should be aware that *common sense* here does not have its usual conversational meaning but refers to a philosophical position first developed in Scotland in the later eighteenth century and subsequently taken up in France; see Frederick Copleston, S.J., *A History of Philosophy,* vol. 5 [Westminster, Md.: Newman

Press, 1959], chap. 18.) The only course is to open oneself to the "higher light that illuminates and fecundates the mind; and thus the reason of the first man had to be stimulated by a higher speech in order to begin to be active." After Adam's fall it is even more necessary to depend on the "light deposited in sacred speech, transmitted by preaching, and accepted by hearing and the faith of the heart," by the "divine grace that attracts man" to accept "the Mosaic word, the prophetic word, the evangelical word." If for Günther philosophy looked as if it might take the place of revelation, here revelation takes the place of at least the higher reaches of philosophy.

At the insistence of Pope Gregory XVI and of Bishop Raess, Bautain signed these articles in 1840 (the translation being from *The Church Teaches: Documents of the Church in English Translation,* ed. J. F. Clarkson, et al. [Rockford, Ill.: TAN Books, 1973], 12–13):

1. The reasoning process can prove with certitude the existence of God and the infiniteness of his perfections. Faith, a heavenly gift, is posterior to revelation; hence faith cannot be employed against an atheist to prove the existence of God.

2. The divine origin of the Mosaic revelation is proved with certitude both by the oral and the written traditions of the Jewish religion and by those of the Christian religion.

3. The proof based on the miracles of Jesus Christ, sensible and striking for the eyewitnesses, has by no means lost its force and clarity for subsequent generations. We find this proof with all its certitude [contained] in the authenticity of the New Testament and in the written and oral traditions of all Christians [that is, the New Testament and these traditions can be shown to be credible]. By this twofold tradition we must point out the proof for the divine origin of revelation to those who either reject it or who have not yet accepted it but are seeking it.

4. We have no right to demand that the unbeliever admit the resurrection of our divine Savior before we have proposed to him arguments that are certain. These arguments are deduced by a reasoning process from the aforesaid tradition.

5. In these various questions reason precedes faith and must lead us to it.

6. Even though reason was rendered weak and clouded by original sin, it still has a sufficiently clear power of perception to lead us with certitude to the knowledge of the existence of God and to the revelation given to the Jews through Moses and to the Christians through our adorable God-man.

It is fascinating to watch how elements of Christianity combine and recombine. Here we have what reads like biblical fundamentalism (nineteenth-century Catholics commonly held views that today we would consider fundamentalist) joined to a neo-scholastic position on the existence of God. If it is correct to say that nineteenth-century scholastics often had a rather shaky grasp of the actual principles of the great medievals, we might want to say as well that Bautain had the better of the argument and was unjustly put upon.

The fact remains, however, that proving the existence of God, more or less following the famous five ways of Thomas Aquinas, is an integral part of Catholic teaching. As suggested, however, Thomas had to wait till well into the twentieth century to have his proofs for God recast in modern terms that are in any way persuasive. (The reader should by all means look at Etienne Gilson's *Being and Some Philosophers* and *Elements of Christian Philosophy,* and Jacques Maritain's *Approaches to God;* additional works by these and like-minded writers are listed under "Neo-Scholasticism and Thomism" in the Bibliography.) It is characteristic of these later expositors of Thomism that actual existence be considered a veritable predicate of God and the world, but a predicate that is philosophically usable in a way that other predicates are not. Much is made of (intuitive) wonder that the world actually exists, when it is possible that it might not have. (That is, existence is a predicate that *might* not be applicable to it.) Some readers will find these old-new arguments persuasive, some will not; it should be remembered, however, that showing there is a God was for the educated nineteenth-century Catholic the narrow gate through which alone the Catholic faith could be reached. In a public letter to Bautain, Möhler, sympathizing with Bautain's dislike for "external" proofs, nonetheless advised him to submit; for "to have to prove [God's] existence is the sign that God's image in us is unutterably darkened, but still to be able to prove it is the sign that this image is not altogether extinguished" (*Gesammelte Schriften und Aufsätze* 2:154).

## The Master to Adeodatus

Here, my dear Adeodatus, is a first letter in response to the grave questions you posed at the beginning of our correspondence. These questions, at once philosophical and theological, bear on the first of all truths, on the fundamental dogma of the Christian faith, that of God in his ineffable Trinity. Permit me, then, to urge you to read these pages with all the recollection, calm, attention, and reverence that are due to the object of which they treat.

You ask whether the Christian recognizes but one God and whether he understands the name *God* to designate infinitely simple and pure Being. Here we must first agree on the sense that you attach to the term *recognize,* for no amount of precision is too great when metaphysical truths are in question. If, then, you mean by this term the act of the intelligence by which it adheres to the word that announces to it the truth of Being, to the word that reveals Being, my reply will be fully affirmative. Yes, the Christian, like the faithful Israelite, believes in one God, the omnipotent Father, the Creator of heaven and earth and of all things visible and invisible; he believes in the infinitely pure and simple Being, absolutely one; and not only does he believe *that* there is a God but he believes *in* God: he adores only the one God. But if you were to take the term *recognize* in its ordinary, literal sense—as meaning not the simple act of the will adhering to the word but the functioning of the mind actively reflecting in itself and thinking either the image of an object that it has seen or the name of a notion or idea that it has heard spoken of—then my reply would be negative, because the Christian who believes in one God believes also, with the whole church, that this one God is known in his absolute unity only to himself, that God in his divine essence, in the purity and simplicity of his Being, is inaccessible to created intelligence, absolutely incomprehensible to man. The Christian believes that God, the principle of all that exists, is the unfathomable abyss, the devouring fire, the jealous God whom no creature can approach, whom no intelligence can contemplate, and of whom no one can form either an idea or an image. The Christian assents to the word that affirms to him the existence of Being, but convinced that he can know of the Being of beings only what this word teaches him of that Being, he most assuredly does not seek to acquire intuitive evidence, or speculative or reflective knowledge, of the properties of infinite Being.

Letter 14 of *Philosophie du christianisme* (Paris, 1835; Frankfurt am Main: Minerva, 1967 [2 vols.]), 1:183–203. The translation is by Joseph Fitzer.

He is profoundly convinced that he can know God only in his substantial manifestation: in a word, the Christian believes that *no one knows the Father except the Son, and him to whom the Son wills to reveal him.* This point is of great importance not only in Christian doctrine but also in all metaphysical and psychological doctrine. It will thus be of use to pause here a moment.

Man, in his present state, is incapable of elevating himself by his own effort to the scientific knowledge of any principle whatever.[1] As an intelligent creature, placed as it were at the center of the physical realm, he sees what he can attain by his gaze. His line of sight measures the heavens and the stars. He perceives the forms that exist around him in space. He sees sensible existences. He conceives images or types of them. He distinguishes them, knows them such as they appear to him, and recognizes them such as he has seen, perceived, conceived, and known them. But his gaze does not penetrate into the interior of these forms; by no means does he know the principle of existences or the life that animates them. All the distinctions and abstractions, all the eliminations and inductions that he can produce in his mind will never unveil for him the ground [*fond*] of these forms. He cannot see the principle of any creature. He cannot abstract being from existence, nor existence from being. He does not possess the objectivity of such being as is outside him.

Furthermore, he does not know the being that sustains his own form. You cannot, indeed, see yourself in your bearing, your physiognomy, and your movements; you see neither your visage nor your eye. If you stand before a mirror the light that surrounds you and that you reflect into the mirror from all points on the surface of your body retraces your image there by reflecting it there. This image is reproduced in your eye; you see a factitious representation, a copy of a copy of the exterior of your person. Never will the mirror show you the original, much less what is the ground of that original. If you say to me that it is not in directing his gaze outward but rather in recollecting himself, in returning into himself, in shutting himself up in his inmost heart that man learns to know himself, I reply that such a procedure is, in effect, the means to acquire knowledge not of his being nor of his ground but of his manner of being, of his internal modifications. It must still come about—and this is a necessary condition—that a mirror akin to his spiritual nature be presented to him, and that intelligible light illumine it. In vain would you exert every effort at recollecting yourself, retiring within yourself and concentrating on yourself in order to see your ego. This ego, all by itself, can never become the object of itself; never can man arrive at the immediate and intuitive evidence of the being that sees and admires, that loves, contemplates, reflects, and thinks in him—any more than the organic eye can become the object of its own vision, see itself actually seeing, or contemplate itself in the very act of sight. The visual ray is projected forward; the eye certainly does not see backward. If you close your eye you deprive it of the light that is its element; you remove the indispensable means of vision. If you insist on keeping it closed, as you are able, you run the risk of paralyzing it; and it is the same with the eye of your soul—of which the material organ is only the external minister for perceiving physical light and the objects illuminated by it.

But if no intelligent creature has ever had or can ever have evidence of its subjective principle, how could its gaze ever attain to the principle of this principle? If man can see his form only in an image, in a factitious, lifeless representation, if he cannot concentrate hard enough or elevate himself high enough to grasp being in himself, the human ego, how, by what power, by what faculty would he arrive at the immediate evidence of the divine Being? And if he cannot contemplate him who dwells in inaccessible light, if he cannot see being, how will he conceive by himself a pure, true, and adequate idea of Being? And if, on the other hand, the scientific knowledge of God and of his own nature constitutes his dignity and happiness, if he is man only in virtue of the sacred character that renders him capable of that science, and if he cannot in his present state grasp the objective principle by means of vision, is it not necessary that he receive it by word and by means of hearing? For what would science be without principle and without idea? And what word could give man the principle, the idea, and the science of God, if not the word of God?

I insist on this point, my dear Adeodatus, in the desire and hope of sparing you much fatigue of mind and many dangers and detours while showing you at the outset the sole font from which you can safely draw the principle of the science, the true knowledge, of the true God. It is a wondrous, if deplorable, thing to see man, tormented as he is by the need to know and ever thirsty for science, traversing the world to find it, knocking on every door to ask for it, always hoping to receive it, or exhausting himself in vain efforts to create it in himself, when the treasure that includes all truth is in his hand. No, friend, it is not in natural phenomena, in the objects of a world that is only a perishable figure, that you will find the immutable and eternal principle. It will not be your reason that will establish in a peremptory manner the unity of this principle, for reason everywhere finds evil alongside good. It is not the dictates of the *common sense* that will give you conviction and certitude about things metaphysical. Science needs an objective princi-ple, and I affirm to you with the deepest conviction that for man as he is this principle is to be found in the books of divine revelation and nowhere else. The subjective principle of science is in your soul, in your intelligence, and not in your reason; and the authority that guarantees to you the truth of the principle and of the doctrine that flows from it is in the church, where individual reason is Christianized, where the common sense is universalized by faith.

People speak much today of the common sense. They make an imposing authority of it; they present it to us as the source of certitude, without clearly telling us whence this marvelous sense comes to us or what it is. It was worth the trouble, though, to seek out its foundation and to ascertain its nature and power, for people go so far as to subordinate to it the ancient and sacred authority of the church; and it is supposed to be it, the common sense, that is to impose faith on me! The sense termed *common,* since it is to be found in every human individual, is only the capacity to comprehend the truth of Being, the sense of the Word, when Word and Being are proclaimed to us. It is the comprehensive form of speech, it is understanding, or if you will, it is our natural reason, at first excited by the sight of natural phenomena, then developed, formed, determined, and exercised by the speech of our fellow man. It is not only the sight of the spectacle of nature that forms the common sense in man (a person born deaf sees this spectacle and comprehends nothing of it), it is the action of living speech that renders us rational, thinking and speaking. The sudden impression of an object can indeed occasion a spontaneous movement of joy or fear, provoke in the soul admiration or aversion, but speech must come to man to reveal him to himself, to give him the consciousness of that which he sees, the name of that which he senses, the knowledge of himself and his state. The consciousness that distinguishes the non-ego from the ego and the reason that concerns itself with the relationship of speech to phenomena develop only in virtue of the speech that is addressed to man, and of which he forms a conception of the spirit or sense. This law is general for all the children of Adam; I will even affirm that it is the law of every created intelligence. It is always a higher light that illuminates and fecundates the mind; and thus the reason of the first man, like that of all his descendants, had to be stimulated by a higher speech in order to begin to be active. But who could address the first speech to the created intelligence, to the reason of the first man, if not the Creator of man? What could creative and legislative speech put in the human mind, if not the Truth of the Word, the substantial Truth? What could the result in him of this speech be, if not self-consciousness at the same time as consciousness of the Being who had addressed this speech to him—the consciousness of the existence of God and of his relationship with man, and that of man's own existence and of his relationship with God, the consciousness of the authority of the Being speaking and of the necessary subordination of the being listening? Here is the foundation of the common sense, truly common to all men, since it is the essential characteristic of humanity. This is by no means a being of reason, an abstract or imaginary form, a contingent modification of the mind; moreover, it is by no means a general or collective unity existing outside the individual and necessarily acting as an authority for him. It is in each the capacity for knowledge and science; it is the mother idea, conceiving the truth of Being, of the Word, and the reality of existences at all levels. I say *mother idea,* because this common or general idea awaits excitation, fecundation, to develop into a living form; and it is here that the idea, the same in all men with respect to the ground, becomes diverse in form and dignity according to the influences that each man undergoes, according to the speech that he hears and receives.

This influence proceeds from a higher agent, and this agent-fecundator of the idea, of the understanding, or of our common sense is the light that presents itself to man in three forms: the physical, the rational, and the metaphysical. Light at the lowest level, or the physical light reflected by natural objects and perceived by the organic eye, forms the natural common sense by giving us the knowledge of these objects.[2] The rational light reflected by the mind, transmitted by speech and received by hearing, forms the rational common sense, or reason, by giving us the knowledge of language, that of human thoughts and deeds; and the intellectual or metaphysical light deposited in sacred speech, transmitted by preaching and accepted by hearing and by the faith of the heart, forms the religious or metaphysical common sense by nourishing faith and then by giving us the knowledge of eternal truths. If the fecundating action of intelligible light did not come to your mind, the common sense would in you remain sterile as regards intelligible truths; just as it would remain empty of rational knowledge if human speech were lacking to you, just as it would remain dead as regards natural things if you had been deprived of sense organs. The result of this is that the common sense, wholly common as it fundamentally is, is, however, different in individual men, more or less developed, more or less noble and pure in each because, as natural common sense, it is modified by place and circumstance, by the character of external nature, by climate, etc.; and the rational common sense, though more general and more elevated, is still variable and uncertain like the thought and speech of man, like the instruction and education he receives. The common sense is formed in this case by natural influences that pertain to space and time and do not teach it anything of what might exist beyond. But note, this is all that rational sense, or reason, can grasp, conclude, and affirm about this subject; that is, if there exist, as we are told, a world superior to that which we inhabit, there has to have been an envoy from this world to proclaim its existence to us and to inform us about the relationship in which we stand to it; if there be supernatural truths there has to have been supernatural speech, akin to those truths, in order to teach them to us; and if we are interested in knowing that speech, insofar as it is not addressed immediately to us, it is necessary that it be transmitted to us by a succession and guaranteed by a visible and permanent authority— an authority instituted by this speech itself—which it is necessary to believe. All the reasoning in the world cannot take the place of this speech, any more than I can create it or give it to myself. The common sense of all men taken together can no more guarantee its truth to me than prove it illusory; and thus no one has the right either to impose it upon me with authority or oppose it to my faith. Rational authority, whether individual or general, can talk sense to natural good sense, extend it, fortify it, perfect it, but it cannot speak the speech of science and intelligence in its own name. Worthy of respect in the government of the things of earth, it is inadmissible for those of heaven. It can lead one to the gate of the sanctuary, but it cannot open the gate, cannot introduce one there, still less teach there. It is divine grace that attracts man; it is divine speech that proclaims to him the mystery of God and eternity, that gives him the key to metaphysical science; and it is the church that teaches him how to use it. There is the authority that has a right to the homage of heart and mind, to the free submission of man, to whom it promises science at the same time as it commands faith.

Before men tried to erect the common sense into a sovereign authority, they had conceded to individual reason a power that it never has had and never will have, that of elevating itself, by itself and by natural light, to certitude of the existence of the true God, the one God. Nature, so they said, proclaims the power and wisdom of its maker. Very well. But what it is important for man to know is not only the author of nature, the great architect, the soul of the world, etc., but above all, his own author, his God, the God of man; and nature is silent on this point. It leaves man confused with all purely natural products. Besides, nature is finite, limited, and one cannot conclude from a finite work to the infinity of the worker. Reason, it is said, can elevate itself by induction from effect to cause. So be it. But between finite effects and an infinite cause, between contingent and temporary existences and absolute and eternal Being, there is an abyss that reason will never cross. If in the first place it admits a first cause, I ask from where it has taken the notion of this cause and how it establishes its priority. It has been unable to find it in nature, since nature displays to us only phenomena, effects, results—only, as they say, secondary causes. It cannot find it in itself, obtain it by induction or deduction, because induction, no matter how far you push it, will never establish the absolute priority of a principle, and deduction supposes the principle and does not prove it. Then again, there remains the great question of the origin of evil, the stumbling block in this path that terminates in Manicheism, as we shall see presently.

I have already said this, it seems to me, to your friend, and there is nothing wrong in repeating it. The prejudice that accords reason the power of establishing by itself or proving by arguments the truth of the existence of the one God tends to do nothing less than propagate among us the crime of idolatry; and there, my dear Adeodatus, is the danger I felt obliged to point out to you. It is not animals, fantastic images, idols of stone, wood, or metal that civilized man adores. It is no longer to material idolatry but to rational idolatry that the enemy of truth leads astray the most developed minds. Reason, proud of its self-attributed power of establishing the truth of God, deifies without scruple the conceptions of natural sense. It believes with confidence in a being that it has laboriously abstracted from the forms of nature and which is only a logical entity. It creates for itself a dynamic God, a supreme being, to whom it lends a power according to its own measure, a wisdom according to its views, and a justice according to its interest; and it is the more satisfied with itself and attached to its philosophical idol the more it has troubled to rough out its idol, disengage it from matter, and form it into a notion. One thus makes for oneself the image of a wholly natural, wholly rational divinity; one honors it in one's own way, defends it with all one's power—and the true God, the *one* God, is then for the majority of our modern sages what it was eighteen hundred years ago for the sages of Athens, the unknown God! The Eternal has said to you through Moses, "It is I who am the Lord your God. You will not have any other gods before my face; you will not make any image, any representation, of infinite Being." But if the Decalogue forbids you to acknowledge any other god save him whom it proclaims, if it forbids you to make any material image of the Deity and to adore the work of your hands, it also forbids you, beyond question, to form a spiritual image, an abstract notion, of Deity, to adore the work of your mind, for the sculptured idol, after all, is only the realization of the imagined idol, the external figure of what has been inwardly elaborated and constructed.

Moses and the prophets tell you that Jehovah is *He who is,* that he is the creator, the legislator, the conserver of man and the universe. The gospel tells us that God is love, light and life, Father, Son and Spirit, and that man can and ought to participate in the divine life, light, and love.

If in our present state we had been able by the sole strength of our mind and by using our natural lights to elevate ourselves to these pure and sublime ideas, revelation would not have been necessary. If after the fall of the first man and in the total ignorance of the true God into which the greater part of his descendants had fallen no one could any longer awaken in himself the sense of truth, recall the memory of God, give to himself the reminiscence of the idea of God, or acquire certitude of the existence of the one true God, if for this effect was required a resounding divine action, a solemn manifestation, an immediate revelation made to the people most capable of receiving it, it is clear that to participate in this immense benefit it is necessary to have recourse to the Mosaic word, the prophetic word, the evangelical word; it is necessary to listen to the church, which is the depository of this word and which has received the authority to teach it. Certitude of the existence of God presupposes the idea of God, and that idea can be obtained not by speculation, by abstraction, but only by faith in God, which is born of hearing and word. All the best arguments of reason in favor of this certitude never have more than a negative value; they serve only to combat the sophisms of unbelieving reason, to reverse or to fend off the obstacles that hinder the approach of light and one's acceptance of the divine word. When the obstacles have been destroyed the combat ceases, and it is then necessary that the word of God be exposed in all its purity, in all its simplicity, and that learned and ignorant alike receive it with the candor of a child, for it is only this word that has the power to engender faith in our soul, to awaken the idea of God in our mind, to fecundate that idea, and to raise it to the level of science.

Here then, my dear Adeodatus, is Christian belief relative to your first question: the Christian believes in one God alone; he adores only this sole God.

He believes that the pure idea of Deity is innate in man, simply because man is man, the image of his divine maker, but that this idea was tarnished and, so to say, extinguished in the first man as a result of his perversion, that is was effaced more and more from the minds of his descendants, and that there was then an epoch in the life of humanity wherein, with the exception of a few just men, all men fell into ignorance of the true God.

He believes that the Eternal One spoke to Moses, and through Moses to the children of Israel, to awaken in them that precious idea and to lead them back to faith in the one God.

He believes that faith in the Mosaic revelation is the condition of acquiring the idea and the knowledge of the oneness of God, that faith in the evangelical word is the condition of obtaining the idea of, and the knowledge of the existence of, the divine Trinity, and that it is only by faith in these two revelations that man can elevate himself to the scientific knowledge of God, of himself, and of the universe.

The Christian receives and admits these two revelations as divine but general gifts. He regards faith in these two revelations as a divine but special gift, and he recognizes in the deeper knowledge, in the intuitive evidence, of revealed truths a particular grace bestowed on frank and free adherence to the sacred word and the actualization of this word in life by works.

Here, to back up what I have just told you, are the words of a famous pope, Leo the Great:[3]

> The essence of the good consists in recognizing our need of grace. Not to accept grace in all its plenitude as grace is to deny it. Just as he who holds to a private opinion contrary to the catholic faith finds himself by this restriction excluded from the number of the faithful, placed outside the communion of the saints, so is he excluded from grace who restrains its action in his soul or who denies something of its plenitude, as if man had need of grace in one moment and not in another, as if there were a time, a single instant, when it was not a misfortune for him to be deprived of the assistance of the Holy Spirit. By his divine essence, of course, this Spirit is present everywhere, embraces and fills all things; and yet we say that he withdraws from those who do not allow themselves to be governed by him. If, then, man deprives himself of divine assistance, if in refusing it or ignoring it he concludes from the privation he undergoes as a result of his refusal that grace is not granted to anyone, if in his aberration he goes so far as to rejoice over this abandonment by or absence of grace as if it were praiseworthy for him to be able to operate and act without the aid of the Holy Spirit, then he becomes complacent in his power and works, he appropriates to himself the good he believes he has done without God, and he elevates himself in his pride above God. It is necessary to recognize both our need of grace and the fact that grace is truly offered to us; it is necessary to admit the gift of God in all its plenitude, and even that is already a grace. This is why the apostle says to the Corinthians, "We have received not the spirit of the world, but the Spirit which is from God, that we might understand the gifts bestowed on us by God."[4] If, then, someone fancies that he has some good of which God is not the author and giver (and is not the greatest of all goods the knowledge of the true God?) and if he claims to have it of himself, he proves that he does not have the Spirit of God but the spirit of the world and that he is inflated with those doctrines of the wisdom of the age of which the Lord has said, "I will destroy the wisdom of the wise and reject the learning of the learned. What have the wise become, the doctors of the law, the scrutinizers of the world, the curious minds of the sciences of the age? Has not God convicted of folly the wisdom of this world? For many have known what can be discovered of God in the laws and products of nature, God himself having made them know, and they have not glorified him as God, they have not rendered thanks for the gift that he has made them, but have gone astray in their

vain reasoning, and their senseless heart has been filled with darkness. They have become fools in believing and proclaiming themselves to be wise."[5] Behold where the pride of human science leads and what all those merit who, having been protected by grace and having some knowledge of the truth, attribute this knowledge to their own wisdom and boast of the power of their natural reason as if they had arrived at that precious knowledge not by a gratuitous gift of God, by pure grace, but by the efforts of their own minds.

It is true that the elements of this world and all creatures render visible to us by their forms what is invisible in God. Nature is like an open book that speaks constantly of its author and witnesses in a living manner in favor of the doctrine of the Scriptures. This is much for the external senses, for the natural man, and is little for the heart, for the spiritual man; and if the supreme Cultivator of our souls does not come and with his power bless the seed and make it sprout it will not take root and bear fruit. Whether, therefore, you consider the world and its creatures to discover traces there of the power of its maker, or whether you meditate on the text of our holy books, or consult the science of the doctors, it is ever necessary to render bold homage to this truth: "Neither he who plants nor he who waters is anything, but only God who gives the growth."[6]

Note, again a remarkable word of Saint Chrysostom, as he explains to the faithful of Constantinople this text of Saint Paul to the Romans:[7]

It is through Jesus Christ that we have received grace and apostleship to bring about the obedience of faith for the sake of his name among all the nations.

The orator draws attention to the fact that Paul, speaking of the faith of the nations, does not say,

to bring about reasoning, or the fashioning of arguments or syllogisms, but to bring about obedience. God has not sent us, he says, to engage in disputation or the reasoning of philosophy, but to give men the deposit of truth that has been confided to us.

It is this method of simple exposition that we shall follow, my dear Adeodatus, all the while seeking to reply to your doubts and to shed light on such difficulties as may arise in your mind.

## NOTES

1. In the thirteenth letter of *Philosophie du christianisme* (Paris, 1835; Frankfurt am Main: Minerva, 1967 [2 vols.]), 1:172–73, Bautain compares Kant to Socrates as a modern critic of metaphysical sophistry but a critic whose work is supportive of true religion. On p. 174, Kant's work is associated with 1 Cor. 2:14;

Bautain says, "L'homme animal de S. Paul est le même que l'animal raisonnable d'Aristote."—ED.

2. Bautain's language does not seem quite consistent here. His meaning seems to be that "whatever we get" from our visual experience is a necessary basis for the functioning of the *sens commun* in the full sense of the term.—ED.

3. Leo the Great *Letter to Demetrias* 7. (This document is commonly regarded as spurious. The translation here is from Bautain's French text.—ED.)

4. 1 Cor. 2:12.

5. Bautain cites Rom. 1:3, 19; the customary Catholic interpretation of v. 19 is that it is the Scripture text most clearly *opposed* to the views Bautain advances in the fourteenth letter.—ED.

6. 1 Cor. 3:17.

7. Chrysostom *Sermon* 2 on Rom. 1:5. (Translated from Bautain's French text.—ED.)

# 7

# Implicit and Explicit Reason

*John Henry Newman*

People whose interest in religion includes some historical awareness usually know that Newman was a great Victorian religious figure and that he produced a large number of beautifully written sermons and lectures. On the other hand, the present writer has in the Introduction affirmed his considered judgment that Möhler, Scheeben, and Newman are the three greatest Catholic theologians of the nineteenth century. In what, then, does Newman's not personal or purely literary but truly theological greatness consist? Some additional if perforce too brief remarks are in order.

John Henry Newman (born, London, 1801; died, Birmingham, 1890) lived long and wrote prodigiously: the London edition of his collected works (1878–1921) numbers forty volumes, and there are thirty-one more volumes of letters and diaries. After studies at Oxford, then positions at Oxford's Oriel College as fellow and tutor, he served as vicar of the university church from 1833 to 1843. His study of the fathers went hand in hand with personal religious development from an evangelical approach to the Church of England, to Anglo-Catholicism: he was among the founders of the Oxford Movement. His growing awareness of what he came to consider the untenable position of Anglicanism in relation to the universal church led him to join the Roman church in 1845. In Rome, in 1846–47, he prepared for Roman Catholic ordination to the priesthood, also joining the community founded by Saint Philip Neri, the Oratorians. Back in England, he founded the Oratorian house in Birmingham. The middle period of this long life was difficult; he was often mistrusted, and projects in which he was interested—such as the founding of a Catholic university in Dublin—came to nought. A public attack on the authenticity of his conversion did, however, provide him, in 1864, the occasion for writing the subsequently much acclaimed autobiography, *Apologia pro Vita Sua*. He did not attend the Vatican Council, but in his *Letter to the Duke of Norfolk* he presented a loyal, carefully nuanced defense of its teaching on infallibility. Some recognition finally came after the death of Pius IX; in 1879, Leo XIII made him a cardinal.

Newman's reputation as a technical theologian rests especially, in this writer's estimate, on three books and on a way of approaching religion that runs through all his works. The three books are *An Essay on the Development of Christian Doctrine* (1845), which attempts to account for the obvious difference between patristic and nineteenth-century Catholicism; *The Idea of a University* (1852), which sets forth the relationship of theology to other learned disciplines; and above all, *An Essay in Aid of a Grammar of Assent* (1870), Newman's mature apologetics, which deals with what have here been termed the two tasks of philosophy in regard to revelation. Since these three books are not difficult to obtain, the present anthology includes a selection from what may be considered a foreshadowing of the *Grammar,* the *Oxford University Sermons* of 1843. These sermons, which Newman republished as a Roman Catholic, are a fine example of "Newman's way," which amounts to a great sensitivity to, and power of describing, the states of soul of the Christian. Newman's empiricism, however, is joined to and placed in the service of a really quite traditional Catholic orthodoxy, even though his Catholic contemporaries were often unable to see this. Sometimes those who *now* celebrate Newman's power as a religious writer forget that he really did join the Roman Catholic church in 1845!

The sermon given here, then, stands in sharp contrast to the articles that Louis Bautain had to sign. "True faith," for Newman, "admits, but does not require, the exercise of what is commonly understood by Reason." Reason is the "faculty of gaining knowledge without direct perception, or of ascertaining one thing by means of another." Reason may be considered implicit or explicit, depending on whether a man does not or does reflect on his human reasonable acts: "How a man reasons is as much a mystery as how he remembers. . . . All men have a reason, but not all men can give a reason."

Now faith is a reasonable process, but apologetics, or the arranging of evidences, can be misleading, "for no analysis is subtle and delicate enough to represent adequately the state of mind under which we believe, or the subjects of belief, as they are presented to our thoughts." What happens in apologetics is that "defenders of Christianity naturally select as reasons for belief, not the highest, truest, the most sacred, the most intimately persuasive, but such as best admit of being exhibited in argument." Newman concludes by praying that he and his hearers will be "drawn heavenward by [Christ's] wonder-working grace."

A word of special thanks is due to Father Basil Lynch, of the Birmingham Oratory, for an act of uncommon kindness. Some thirty years ago—the details of the conversation are forgotten—he invited some American college-student visitors to see Newman's rooms, providing a running commentary during our stay upstairs. I particularly remember his holding a large round, flat box. Opening it, he said simply, "Here is Newman's red hat." Profoundly moving was the contrast between the hat, and what it stood for, and the gray morning light falling into the spareness of Newman's bedroom-study. I date my interest in nineteenth-century theology from that moment.

## Implicit and Explicit Reason

> Sanctify the Lord God in your hearts; and be ready always to give an answer to every man that asketh you a reason of the hope that is in you, with meekness and fear. (1 Peter 3:15)

St. Peter's faith was one of his characteristic graces. It was ardent, keen, watchful, and prompt. It dispensed with argument, calculation, deliberation, and delay, whenever it heard the voice of its Lord and Saviour: and it heard that voice even when its accents were low, or when it was unaided by the testimony of the other senses. When Christ appeared walking on the sea, and said, "It is I," Peter answered Him, and said, "Lord, if it be Thou, bid me come unto Thee on the water." When Christ asked His disciples who He was, "Simon Peter answered and said," as we read in the Gospel for this day, "Thou art the Christ, the Son of the Living God," and obtained our Lord's blessing for such clear and ready Faith. At another time, when Christ asked the Twelve whether they would leave Him as others did, St. Peter said, "Lord, to whom shall we go? Thou hast the words of eternal life; and we believe and are sure that Thou art the Christ, the Son of the Living God." And after the Resurrection, when he heard from St. John that it was Christ who stood on the shore, he sprang out of the boat in which he was fishing, and cast himself into the sea, in his impatience to come near Him. Other instances of his faith might be mentioned. If ever Faith forgot self, and was occupied with its Great Object, it was the faith of Peter. If in any one Faith appears in contrast with what we commonly understand by Reason, and with Evidence, it so appears in the instance of Peter. When he reasoned, it was at times when Faith was lacking. "When he saw the wind boisterous, he was afraid"; and Christ in consequence called him, "Thou of little faith." When He had asked, "Who touched Me?" Peter and others reasoned, "Master," said they, "the multitude throng Thee, and press Thee, and sayest Thou, Who touched Me?" And in like manner, when Christ said that he should one day follow Him in the way of suffering, "Peter said unto Him, Lord, *why* cannot I follow Thee now?"—and we know how his faith gave way soon afterwards.

2. Faith and Reason, then, stand in strong contrast in the history of Peter: yet it is Peter, and he not the fisherman of Galilee, but the inspired Apostle, who in the text gives us a precept which implies, in order to its due fulfilment, a careful exercise of our Reason, an exercise

---

Sermon 13 of *Fifteen Sermons Preached before the University of Oxford,* 3d ed. (London: Rivingtons, 1872), 251–77. Preached on Saint Peter's Day, 1840.

both upon Faith, considered as an act or habit of mind, and upon the Object of it. We are not only to "sanctify the Lord God in our hearts," not only to prepare a shrine within us in which our Saviour Christ may dwell, and where we may worship Him; but we are so to understand what we do, so to master our thoughts and feelings, so to recognize what we believe, and how we believe, so to trace out our ideas and impressions, and to contemplate the issue of them, that we may be "ready *always* to give an answer to *every* man that asketh us an account of the hope that is in us." In these words, I conceive, we have a clear warrant, or rather an injunction, to cast our religion into the form of Creed and Evidences.

3. It would seem, then, that though Faith is the characteristic of the Gospel, and Faith is the simple lifting of the mind to the Unseen God, without conscious reasoning or formal argument, still the mind may be allowably, nay, religiously engaged, in reflecting upon its own Faith; investigating the grounds and the Object of it, bringing it out into words, whether to defend, or recommend, or teach it to others. And St. Peter himself, in spite of his ardour and earnestness, gives us in his own case some indications of such an exercise of mind. When he said, "Thou art the Christ, the Son of the Living God," he cast his faith, in a measure, into a dogmatic form: and when he said, "To whom shall we go? Thou hast the words of eternal life," he gave "an account of the hope that was in him," or grounded his faith upon Evidence.

4. Nothing would be more theoretical and unreal than to suppose that true Faith cannot exist except when moulded upon a Creed, and based upon Evidence; yet nothing would indicate a more shallow philosophy than to say that it ought carefully to be disjoined from dogmatic and argumentative statements. To assert the latter is to discard the science of theology from the service of Religion; to assert the former, is to maintain that every child, every peasant, must be a theologian. Faith cannot exist without grounds or without an object; but it does not follow that all who have faith should recognize, and be able to state what they believe, and why. Nor, on the other hand, because it is not identical with its grounds, and its object, does it therefore cease to be true Faith, on its recognizing them. In proportion as the mind reflects upon itself, it will be able "to give an account" of what it believes and hopes; as far as it has not thus reflected, it will not be able. Such knowledge cannot be wrong, yet cannot be necessary, as long as reflection is at once a natural faculty of our souls, yet not an initial faculty. Scripture gives instances of Faith in each of these states, when attended by a conscious exercise of Reason, and when not. When Nicodemus said, "No man can do these miracles that Thou doest, except God be with him," he investigated. When the

Scribe said, "There is One God, and there is none other but He; and to love Him with all the heart . . . is more than all whole burnt offerings and sacrifices," his belief was dogmatical. On the other hand, when the cripple at Lystra believed, on St. Paul's preaching, or the man at the Beautiful gate believed in the Name of Christ, their faith was independent not of objects or grounds (for that is impossible), but of perceptible, recognized, producible objects and grounds: they believed, they could not say what or why. True Faith, then, admits, but does not require, the exercise of what is commonly understood by Reason.

5. I hope it will not seem any want of reverence towards a great Apostle, who reigns with Christ in heaven, if, instead of selecting one of the many lessons to which his history calls our attention, or of the points of doctrine in it which might so profitably be enlarged upon, I employ his Day to continue a subject to which I have already devoted such opportunities of speaking from this place, as have from time to time occurred, though it be but incidentally connected with him. Such a continuation of subject has some sanction in the character of our first Lessons for Holy days, which, for the most part, instead of being appropriate to the particular Festivals on which they are appointed, are portions of a course, and connected with those which are assigned to others. And I will add that, if there is a question, the intrusion of which may be excused in the present age, and to which the mind is naturally led on the Days commemorative of the first Founders of the Church, it is the relation of Faith to Reason under the Gospel; and the means whereby, and the grounds whereon, and the subjects wherein, the mind is bound to believe and acquiesce, in matters of religion.

6. In the Epistle for this Day we have an account of St. Peter, when awakened by the Angel, obeying him implicitly, yet not understanding, while he obeyed. He girt himself, and bound on his sandals, and cast his garment about him, and "went out and followed him"; yet "wist not that it was true which was done by the Angel, but thought he saw a vision." Afterwards, when he "was come to himself, he said, Now I know of a surety, that the Lord hath sent His Angel, and hath delivered me." First he acted spontaneously, then he contemplated his own acts. This may be taken as an illustration of the difference between the more simple faculties and operations of the mind, and that process of analyzing and describing them, which takes place upon reflection. We not only feel, and think, and reason, but we know that we feel, and think, and reason; not only know, but can inspect and ascertain our thoughts, feelings, and reasonings: not only ascertain, but describe. Children, for a time, do not realize even their material frames, or (as I may say) count their limbs; but, as the mind opens, and is cultivated, they turn their attention to soul

as well as body; they contemplate all they are, and all they do; they are no longer beings of impulse, instinct, conscience, imagination, habit, or reason, merely; but they are able to reflect upon their own mind as if it were some external object; they reason upon their reasonings. This is the point on which I shall now enlarge.

7. Reason, according to the simplest view of it, is the faculty of gaining knowledge without direct perception, or of ascertaining one thing by means of another. In this way it is able, from small beginnings, to create to itself a world of ideas, which do or do not correspond to the things themselves for which they stand, or are true or not, according as it is exercised soundly or otherwise. One fact may suffice for a whole theory; one principle may create and sustain a system; one minute token is a clue to a large discovery. The mind ranges to and fro, and spreads out, and advances forward with a quickness which has become a proverb, and a subtlety and versatility which baffle investigation. It passes on from point to point, gaining one by some indication; another on a probability; then availing itself of an association; then falling back on some received law; next seizing on testimony; then committing itself to some popular impression, or some inward instinct, or some obscure memory; and thus it makes progress not unlike a clamberer on a steep cliff, who, by quick eye, prompt hand, and firm foot, ascends how he knows not himself, by personal endowments and by practice, rather than by rule, leaving no track behind him, and unable to teach another. It is not too much to say that the stepping by which great geniuses scale the mountains of truth is as unsafe and precarious to men in general, as the ascent of a skilful mountaineer up a literal crag. It is a way which they alone can take; and its justification lies in their success. And such mainly is the way in which all men, gifted or not gifted, commonly reason—not by rule, but by an inward faculty.

8. Reasoning, then, or the exercise of Reason, is a living spontaneous energy within us, not an art. But when the mind reflects upon itself, it begins to be dissatisfied with the absence of order and method in the exercise, and attempts to analyze the various processes which take place during it, to refer one to another, and to discover the main principles on which they are conducted, as it might contemplate and investigate its faculty of memory or imagination. The boldest, simplest, and most comprehensive theory which has been invented for the analysis of the reasoning process, is the well-known science for which we are indebted to Aristotle, and which is framed upon the principle that every act of reasoning is exercised upon neither more nor less than three terms. Short of this, we have many general words in familiar use to designate particular methods of thought, according to which the mind reasons

(that is, proceeds from truth to truth), or to designate particular states of mind which influence its reasonings. Such methods are antecedent probability, analogy, parallel cases, testimony, and circumstantial evidence; and such states of mind are prejudice, deference to authority, party spirit, attachment to such and such principles, and the like. In like manner we distribute the Evidences of Religion into External and Internal; into a priori and a posteriori; into Evidences of Natural Religion and of Revealed; and so on. Again, we speak of proving doctrines either from the nature of the case, or from Scripture, or from history; and of teaching them in a dogmatic, or a polemical, or a hortatory way. In these and other ways we instance the reflective power of the human mind, contemplating and scrutinizing its own acts.

9. Here, then, are two processes, distinct from each other—the original process of reasoning, and next, the process of investigating our reasonings. All men reason, for to reason is nothing more than to gain truth from former truth, without the intervention of sense, to which brutes are limited; but all men do not reflect upon their own reasonings, much less reflect truly and accurately, so as to do justice to their own meaning; but only in proportion to their abilities and attainments. In other words, all men have a reason, but not all men can give a reason. We may denote, then, these two exercises of mind as reasoning and arguing, or as conscious and unconscious reasoning, or as Implicit Reason and Explicit Reason. And to the latter belong the words, science, method, development, analysis, criticism, proof, system, principles, rules, laws, and others of a like nature.

10. That these two exercises are not to be confounded together would seem too plain for remark, except that they have been confounded. Clearness in argument certainly is not indispensable to reasoning well. Accuracy in stating doctrines or principles is not essential to feeling and acting upon them. The exercise of analysis is not necessary to the integrity of the process analyzed. The process of reasoning is complete in itself, and independent. The analysis is but an account of it; it does not make the conclusion correct; it does not make the inference rational. It does not cause a given individual to reason better. It does but give him a sustained consciousness, for good or for evil, that he is reasoning. How a man reasons is as much a mystery as how he remembers. He remembers better and worse on different subject-matters, and he reasons better and worse. Some men's reason becomes genius in particular subjects, and is less than ordinary in others. The gift or talent of reasoning may be distinct in different subjects, though the process of reasoning is the same. Now a good arguer or clear speaker is but one who excels in analyzing or expressing a process of reason, taken as his

subject-matter. He traces out the connexion of facts, detects principles, applies them, supplies deficiencies, till he has reduced the whole into order. But his talent of reasoning, or the gift of reason as possessed by him, may be confined to such an exercise, and he may be as little expert in other exercises, as a mathematician need be an experimentalist; as little creative of the reasoning itself which he analyzes, as a critic need possess the gift of writing poems.

11. But if reasoning and arguing be thus distinct, what is to be thought of assertions such as the following? Certainly, to say the least, they are very inaccurately worded, and may lead, as they have led, to great error.

12. Tillotson,[1] for instance, says: "Nothing ought to be received as a divine doctrine and revelation, *without good evidence* that it is so: that is, without some *argument* sufficient to *satisfy* a prudent and considerate man."[2] Again: "Faith . . . is an assent of the mind to something as revealed by God: now all assent must be *grounded upon evidence;* that is, no man can believe any thing, unless he have, or think he hath, some *reason* to do so. For to be confident of a thing without reason is not faith, but a presumptuous persuasion and obstinacy of mind."[3] Such assertions either have an untrue meaning, or are unequal to the inferences which the writers proceed to draw from them.

13. In like manner Paley and others[4] argue that miracles are not improbable unless a Revelation is improbable, on the ground that there is no other conceivable way of ascertaining a Revelation; that is, they would imply the necessity of a conscious investigation and verification of its claims, or the possession of grounds which are satisfactory in argument; whereas considerations which seem weak and insufficient in an explicit form may lead, and justly lead, us by an implicit process to a reception of Christianity; just as a peasant may from the look of the sky foretell tomorrow's weather, on grounds which, as far as they are producible, an exact logician would not scruple to pronounce inaccurate and inconsequent. "In what way," he asks, "can a Revelation be made," that is, as the context shows, be ascertained, "but by miracles? In none which we are able to conceive."

14. Again: another writer says, "There are but two ways by which God could reveal His will to mankind; either by an immediate influence on the mind of every individual of every age, or by selecting some particular persons to be His instruments . . . and for this purpose vested by Him with such powers as *might carry the strongest evidence* that they were really divine teachers."[5] On the other hand, Bishop Butler tells us that it is impossible to decide what evidence will be afforded of a Revelation, supposing it made; and certainly it might have been given

without any supernatural display at all, being left (as it is in a manner even now) to be received or rejected by each man according as his heart sympathized in it, that is, on the influence of reasons, which, though practically persuasive, are weak when set forth as the argumentative grounds of conviction.

15. Faith, then, though in all cases a reasonable process, is not necessarily founded on investigation, argument, or proof; these processes being but the explicit form which the reasoning takes in the case of particular minds. Nay, so far from it, that the opposite opinion has, with much more plausibility, been advanced, viz. that Faith is not even compatible with these processes. Such an opinion, indeed, cannot be maintained, particularly considering the light which Scripture casts upon the subject, as in the text; but it may easily take possession of serious minds. When they witness the strife and division to which argument and controversy minister, the proud self-confidence which is fostered by strength of the reasoning powers, the laxity of opinion which often accompanies the study of the Evidences, the coldness, the formality, the secular and carnal spirit which is compatible with an exact adherence to dogmatic formularies; and on the other hand, when they recollect that Scripture represents religion as a divine life, seated in the affections and manifested in spiritual graces, no wonder that they are tempted to rescue Faith from all connexion with faculties and habits which may exist in perfection without Faith, and which too often usurp from Faith its own province, and profess to be a substitute for it. I repeat, such a persuasion is extreme, and will not maintain itself, and cannot be acted on, for any long time; it being as paradoxical to prohibit religious inquiry and inference, as to make it imperative. Yet we should not dismiss the notice of it, on many accounts, without doing justice to it; and therefore I propose now, before considering[6] some of the uses of our critical and analytical powers, in the province of Religion, to state certain of the inconveniences and defects; an undertaking which will fully occupy what remains of our time this morning.

16. Inquiry and argument may be employed, first, in ascertaining the divine origin of Religion, Natural and Revealed; next, in interpreting Scripture; and thirdly, in determining points of Faith and Morals; that is, in the Evidences, Biblical Exposition, and Dogmatic Theology. In all three departments there is, first of all, an exercise of implicit reason, which is in its degree common to all men; for all men gain a certain impression, right or wrong, from what comes before them, for or against Christianity, for or against certain interpretations of Scripture, for or against certain doctrines. This impression, made upon their minds, whether by the claim itself of Revealed Religion, or by its documents, or

by its teaching, it is the object of science to analyze, verify, methodize, and exhibit. We believe certain things, on certain grounds, through certain informants; and the analysis of these three, the why, the how, and the what, seems pretty nearly to constitute the science of divinity.

17. (1.) By the Evidences of Religion I mean the systematic analysis of all the grounds on which we believe Christianity to be true. I say "all," because the word Evidence is often restricted to denote only such arguments as arise out of the thing itself which is to be proved; or, to speak more definitely, facts and circumstances which presuppose the point under inquiry as a condition of their existence, and which are weaker or stronger arguments, according as that point approaches more or less closely to be a necessary condition of them. Thus blood on the clothes is an evidence of a murderer, just so far as a deed of violence is necessary to the fact of the stains, or alone accounts for them. Such are the Evidences as drawn out by Paley and other writers; and though only a secondary part, they are popularly considered the whole of the Evidences, because they can be exhibited and studied with far greater ease than antecedent considerations, presumptions, and analogies, which, vague and abstruse as they are, still are more truly the grounds on which religious men receive the Gospel; but on this subject something has been said on a former occasion.

18. (2.) Under the science of Interpretation is of course included all inquiry into its principles; the question of mystical interpretation, the theory of the double sense, the doctrine of types, the phraseology of prophecy, the drift and aim of the several books of Scripture; the dates when, the places where, and persons by and to whom they were written; the comparison and adjustment of book with book; the uses of the Old Testament; the relevancy of the Law to Christians and its relation to the Gospel; and the historical fulfilment of prophecy. And previous to such inquiries are others still more necessary, such as the study of the original languages in which the sacred Volume is written.

19. (3.) Under Dogmatic Theology must be included, not only doctrine, such as that of the Blessed Trinity, or the theory of Sacramental Influence, or the settlement of the Rule of Faith, but questions of morals and discipline also.

20. Now, in considering the imperfections and defects incident to such scientific exercises, we must carefully exempt from our remarks all instances of them which have been vouchsafed to us from above, and therefore have a divine sanction; and that such instances do exist, is the most direct and satisfactory answer to any doubts which religious persons may entertain, of the lawfulness of employing science in the province of Faith at all. Of such analyses and determinations as are

certainly from man, we are at liberty to dispute both the truth and the utility: but what God has done is perfect, that is, perfect according to its subject-matter. Whether in the department of evidence, Scripture interpretation, or dogmatic teaching, what He has spoken must be received, not criticized—and in saying this, I have not to assign the limits or the channels of God's communications. Whether He speaks only by Scripture, or by private and personal suggestion, or by the first ages, or by Tradition, or by the Church collective, or by the Church in Council, or by the Chair of Saint Peter, are questions about which Christians may differ without interfering with the principle itself, that what God has given is true, and what He has not given may, if so be, be not true. What He has not given by His appointed methods, whatever they be, may be venerable for its antiquity, or authoritative as held by good men, or safer to hold as held by many, or necessary to hold because it has been subscribed, or persuasive from its probability, or expedient from its good effects; but after all, except that all good things are from God, it is, as far as we know, a human statement, and is open to criticism, because the work of man. To such human inferences and propositions I confine myself in the remarks that follow.

21. Now the great practical evil of method and form in matters of religion—nay, in all moral matters—is obviously this: their promising more than they can effect. At best the science of divinity is very imperfect and inaccurate, yet the very name of science is a profession of accuracy. Other and more familiar objections readily occur; such as its leading to familiarity with sacred things, and consequent irreverence; its fostering formality; its substituting a sort of religious philosophy and literature for worship and practice; its weakening the springs of action by inquiring into them; its stimulating to controversy and strife; its substituting, in matters of duty, positive rules which need explanation for an instinctive feeling which commands the mind; its leading the mind to mistake system for truth, and to suppose that an hypothesis is real because it is consistent: but all such objections, though important, rather lead us to a cautious use of science than to a distrust of it in religious matters. But its insufficiency in so high a province is an evil which attaches to it from first to last, an inherent evil which there are no means of remedying, and which, perhaps, lies at the root of those other evils which I have just been enumerating. To this evil I shall now direct my attention, having already incidentally referred to it in some of the foregoing remarks.

22. No analysis is subtle and delicate enough to represent adequately the state of mind under which we believe, or the subjects of belief, as they are presented to our thoughts. The end proposed is that of delineat-

ing, or, as it were, painting what the mind sees and feels: now let us consider what it is to portray duly in form and colour things material, and we shall surely understand the difficulty, or rather the impossibility, of representing the outline and character, the hues and shades, in which any intellectual view really exists in the mind, or of giving it that substance and that exactness in detail in which consists its likeness to the original, or of sufficiently marking those minute differences which attach to the same general state of mind or tone of thought as found in this or that individual respectively. It is probable that a given opinion, as held by several individuals, even when of the most congenial views, is as distinct from itself as are their faces. Now how minute is the defect in imitation which hinders the likeness of a portrait from being successful! how easy is it to recognize who is intended by it, without allowing that really he is represented! Is it not hopeless, then, to expect that the most diligent and anxious investigation can end in more than in giving some very rude description of the living mind, and its feelings, thoughts, and reasonings? And if it be difficult to analyze fully any state, or frame, or opinion of our own minds, is it a less difficulty to delineate, as Theology professes to do, the works, dealings, providences, attributes, or nature of Almighty God?

23. In this point of view we may, without irreverence, speak even of the words of inspired Scripture as imperfect and defective; and though they are not subjects for our judgment (God forbid), yet they will for that very reason serve to enforce and explain better what I would say, and how far the objection goes. Inspiration is defective, not in itself, but in consequence of the medium it uses and the beings it addresses. It uses human language, and it addresses man; and neither can man compass, nor can his hundred tongues utter, the mysteries of the spiritual world, and God's appointments in this. This vast and intricate scene of things cannot be generalized or represented through or to the mind of man; and inspiration, in undertaking to do so, necessarily lowers what is divine to raise what is human. What, for instance, is the mention made in Scripture of the laws of God's government, of His providences, counsels, designs, anger, and repentance, but a gracious mode (the more gracious because necessarily imperfect) of making man contemplate what is far beyond him?[7] Who shall give method to what is infinitely complex, and measure to the unfathomable? We are as worms in an abyss of divine works; myriads upon myriads of years would it take, were our hearts ever so religious, and our intellects ever so apprehensive, to receive from without the just impression of those works as they really are, and as experience would convey them to us: sooner, then, than we should know nothing, Almighty God has condescended to

speak to us so far as human thought and language will admit, by approximations, in order to give us practical rules for our own conduct amid His infinite and eternal operations.

24. And herein consists one great blessing of the Gospel Covenant, that in Christ's death on the Cross, and in other parts of that all-gracious Economy, are concentrated, as it were, and so presented to us those attributes and works which fill eternity. And with a like graciousness we are also told, in human language, things concerning God Himself, concerning His Son and His Spirit, and concerning His Son's incarnation, and the union of two natures in His One Person—truths which even a peasant holds implicitly, but which Almighty God, whether by His Apostles, or by His Church after them, has vouchsafed to bring together and methodize, and to commit to the keeping of science.

25. Now all such statements are likely at first to strike coldly or harshly upon religious ears, when taken by themselves, for this reason if for no other—that they express heavenly things under earthly images, which are infinitely below the reality. This applies especially to the doctrine of the Eternal Sonship of our Lord and Saviour, as all know who have turned their minds to the controversies on the subject.

26. Again, it may so happen, that statements are only possible in the case of certain aspects of a doctrine, and that these seem inconsistent with each other, or mysteries, when contrasted together, apart from what lies between them; just as if one were shown the picture of a little child and an old man, and were told that they represented the same person—a statement which would be incomprehensible to beings who were unacquainted with the natural changes which take place, in the course of years, in the human frame.

27. Or doctrinal statements may be introduced, not so much for their own sake, as because many consequences flow from them, and therefore a great variety of errors may, by means of them, be prevented. Such is the doctrine that our Saviour's personality is in His Godhead, not in His manhood; that He has taken the manhood into God. It is evident that such statements, being made for the sake of something beyond, when viewed apart from their end, or in themselves, are abrupt, and may offend hearers.

28. Again, so it is, however it be explained, that frequently we do not recognize our sensations and ideas, when put into words ever so carefully. The representation seems out of shape and strange, and startles us, even though we know not how to find fault with it. This applies, at least in the case of some persons, to portions of the received theological analysis of the impression made upon the mind by the Scripture notices concerning Christ and the Holy Spirit. In like manner, such phrases as

"good works are a condition of eternal life," or "the salvation of the regenerate ultimately depends upon themselves," though unexceptionable, are of a nature to offend certain minds.

29. This difficulty of analyzing our more recondite feelings happily and convincingly, has a most important influence upon the science of the Evidences. Defenders of Christianity naturally select as reasons for belief, not the highest, the truest, the most sacred, the most intimately persuasive, but such as best admit of being exhibited in argument; and these are commonly not the real reasons in the case of religious men.

30. Nay, they are led for the same reason, to select such arguments as all will allow; that is, such as depend on principles which are a common measure for all minds. A science certainly is, in its very nature, public property; when, then, the grounds of Faith take the shape of a book of Evidences, nothing properly can be assumed but what men in general will grant as true; that is, nothing but what is on a level with all minds, good and bad, rude and refined.

31. Again, as to the difficulty of detecting and expressing the real reasons on which we believe, let this be considered—how very differently an argument strikes the mind at one time and another, according to its particular state, or the accident of the moment. At one time it is weak and unmeaning—at another, it is nothing short of demonstration. We take up a book at one time, and see nothing in it; at another, it is full of weighty remarks and precious thoughts. Sometimes a statement is axiomatic, sometimes we are at a loss to see what can be said for it. Such, for instance, are the following, many like which are found in controversy—that true saints cannot but persevere to the end; or that the influences of the Spirit cannot but be effectual; or that there must be an infallible Head of the Church on earth; or that the Roman Church, extending into all lands, is the Catholic Church; or that a Church, which is Catholic abroad, cannot be schismatical in England; or that, if our Lord is the Son of God, He must be God; or that a Revelation is probable; or that, if God is All-powerful, He must be also All-good. Who shall analyze the assemblage of opinions in this or that mind, which occasions it almost instinctively to reject or to accept each of these and similar positions? Far be it from me to seem to insinuate that they are *but* opinions, neither true nor false, and approving themselves or not, according to the humour or prejudice of the individual: so far from it, that I would maintain that the recondite reasons which lead each person to take or decline them, are just the most important portion of the considerations on which his conviction depends; and I say so, by way of showing that the science of controversy, or again the science of Evidences, has done very little, since it cannot analyze and exhibit these

momentous reasons; nay, so far has done worse than little, in that it professes to have done much, and leads the student to mistake what are but secondary points in debate, as if they were the most essential.

32. It often happens, for the same reason, that controversialists or philosophers are spoken of by this or that person as unequal, sometimes profound, sometimes weak. Such cases of inequality, of course, do occur; but we should be sure, when tempted so to speak, that the fault is not with ourselves, who have not entered into an author's meaning, or analyzed the implicit reasonings along which his mind proceeds in those parts of his writings which we not merely dissent from (for that we have a right to do), but criticize as inconsecutive.

33. These remarks apply especially to the proofs commonly brought, whether for the truth of Christianity, or for certain doctrines from texts of Scripture. Such alleged proofs are commonly strong or slight, not in themselves, but according to the circumstances under which the doctrine professes to come to us, which they are brought to prove; and they will have a great or small effect upon our minds, according as we admit those circumstances or not. Now, the admission of those circumstances involves a variety of antecedent views, presumptions, implications, associations, and the like, many of which it is very difficult to detect and analyze. One person, for instance, is convinced by Paley's argument from the Miracles, another is not; and why? Because the former admits that there is a God, that He governs the world, that He wishes the salvation of man, that the light of nature is not sufficient for man, that there is no other way of introducing a Revelation but miracles, and that men, who were neither enthusiasts nor impostors, could not have acted as the Apostles did, unless they had seen the miracles which they attested; the other denies some one, or more, of these statements, or does not feel the force of some other principle more recondite and latent still than any of these, which is nevertheless necessary to the validity of the argument.

34. Further, let it be considered, that, even as regards what are commonly called Evidences, that is, arguments a posteriori, conviction for the most part follows, not upon any one great and decisive proof or token of the point in debate, but upon a number of very minute circumstances together, which the mind is quite unable to count up and methodize in an argumentative form. Let a person only call to mind the clear impression he has about matters of every day's occurrence, that this man is bent on a certain object, or that that man was displeased, or another suspicious; or that one is happy and another unhappy; and how much depends in such impressions on manner, voice, accent, words uttered, silence instead of words, and all the many subtle symptoms which are

felt by the mind, but cannot be contemplated; and let him consider how very poor an account he is able to give of his impression, if he avows it, and is called upon to justify it. This, indeed, is meant by what is called moral proof, in opposition to legal. We speak of an accused person being guilty without any doubt, even though the evidences of his guilt are none of them broad and definite enough in themselves to admit of being forced upon the notice of those who will not exert themselves to see them.

35. Now, should the proof of Christianity, or the Scripture proof of its doctrines, be of this subtle nature, of course it cannot be exhibited to advantage in argument: and even if it be not such, but contain strong and almost legal evidences, still there will always be a temptation in the case of writers on Evidence, or on the Scripture proof of doctrine, to over-state and exaggerate, or to systematize in excess; as if they were making a case in a court of law, rather than simply and severely analyzing, as far as is possible, certain existing reasons why the Gospel is true, or why it should be considered of a certain doctrinal character. It is hardly too much to say, that almost all reasons formally adduced in moral inquiries, are rather specimens and symbols of the real grounds, than those grounds themselves. They do but approximate to a representation of the general character of the proof which the writer wishes to convey to another's mind. They cannot, like mathematical proof, be passively followed with an attention confined to what is stated, and with the admission of nothing but what is urged. Rather, they are hints towards, and samples of, the true reasoning, and demand an active, ready, candid, and docile mind, which can throw itself into what is said, neglect verbal difficulties, and pursue and carry out principles. This is the true office of a writer, to excite and direct trains of thought; and this, on the other hand, is the too common practice of readers, to expect every thing to be done for them, to refuse to think, to criticize the letter, instead of reaching forwards towards the sense, and to account every argument as unsound which is illogically worded.

36. Here is the fertile source of controversy, which may undoubtedly be prolonged without limit by those who desire it, while words are incomplete exponents of ideas, and complex reasons demand study, and involve prolixity. They, then, who wish to shorten the dispute, and to silence a captious opponent, look out for some strong and manifest argument which may be stated tersely, handled conveniently, and urged rhetorically; some one reason, which bears with it a show of vigour and plausibility, or a profession of clearness, simplicity, or originality, and may be easily reduced to mood and figure. Hence the stress often laid upon particular texts, as if decisive of the matter in hand: hence one

disputant dismisses all parts of the Bible which relate to the Law, another finds the high doctrines of Christianity revealed in the Book of Genesis, another rejects certain portions of the inspired volume, as the Epistle of St. James, another gives up the Apocrypha, another rests the defence of Revelation on Miracles only, or the Internal Evidence only, another sweeps away all Christian teaching but Scripture—one and all from impatience at being allotted, in the particular case, an evidence which does little more than create an impression on the mind; from dislike of an evidence, varied, minute, complicated, and a desire of something producible, striking, and decisive.

37. Lastly, since a test is in its very nature of a negative character, and since argumentative forms are mainly a test of reasoning, so far they will be but critical, not creative. They will be useful in raising objections, and in ministering to scepticism; they will pull down, and will not be able to build up.

38. I have been engaged in proving the following points: that the reasonings and opinions which are involved in the act of Faith are latent and implicit; that the mind reflecting on itself is able to bring them out into some definite and methodical form; that Faith, however, is complete without this reflective faculty, which, in matter of fact, often does interfere with it, and must be used cautiously.

39. I am quite aware that I have said nothing but what must have often passed through the minds of others; and it may be asked whether it is worth while so diligently to traverse old ground. Yet perhaps it is never without its use to bring together in one view, and steadily contemplate truths, which one by one may be familiar notwithstanding.

40. May we be in the number of those who, with the Blessed Apostle whom we this day commemorate, employ all the powers of their minds to the service of their Lord and Saviour, who are drawn heavenward by His wonder-working grace, whose hearts are filled with His love, who reason in His fear, who seek Him in the way of His commandments, and who thereby believe on Him to the saving of their souls!


### NOTES

1. Of course the statements of these various authors are true and important in their own place and from their own point of view.

2. John Tillotson, *Sermons* 2:260. (Tillotson's sermons were published in a number of editions, and I have yet to see the source from which Newman quotes in this and in the following note. Newman, however, was *not* using the edition

edited by Ralph Barker and published in 1696–1704 or the edition of 1757.—
ED.)

3. Ibid. 4:42.

4. William Paley, *A View of the Evidences of Christianity,* 4th ed. in 2 vols. (London, 1795), 3. See also Hugh Farmer, *A Dissertation on Miracles,* 3d ed. (London, 1810), 326–27.

5. John Douglas, *The Criterion, or Rules by Which the True Miracles Recorded in the New Testament Are Distinguished from the Miracles of Pagans and Papists* (London, 1807), 37–38.

6. See Sermons 14 and 15 [of Newman's *Oxford University Sermons*].

7. See [Newman's] *History of the Arians,* 3d ed. (London, 1871), 77.

# PART THREE

# The Church as
# Bearer of Revelation

# 8

# The Role of the Pope

*Joseph de Maistre*

In nature, organic life produces the organs needed for survival and growth. It is no different, according to a romantic world view, in human affairs. Societies produce the organs of governance that they require. Thus, as we have seen, Möhler observed that in differing circumstances the church required differing degrees of overt "centeredness" and so conceded the papacy more or less authority. Or to put the matter a somewhat different way, romantic theology begins as, and largely remains, what twentieth-century commentators have termed theological anthropology. And the intrinsic goodness and good destiny of the whole of humankind is considered prior to the consideration of the parts.

Suppose, however—and this is equally a nineteenth-century estimate of humankind—suppose the parts are considered before the whole. Suppose that these parts, if not utterly corrupt, are far from perfect and not such as to incline one to optimism if their future is left to their own devices—that in terms of the proverbial glass of water, they are not half-full but half-empty. In short, consider humanity less in terms of Adam's hope than of Adam's fall. Would it not then make sense for a provident God to ordain one organ of the human whole, one body of men, or even one man, to lead the rest to safety? For many nineteenth-century Catholics this is the role of the papacy, of Peter who would care for the faith of his brethren, of the Rock against which hell would not prevail.

It is true, of course, that in its actual determination of the role of the papacy the First Vatican Council limited itself to citing scriptural and other historical precedents, not philosophical ones. Still, it is legitimate to inquire what philosophy of man led at least some of the conservatives at the council to push for the dogmas of papal primacy and infallibility. (*Primacy* refers to the universal jurisdiction of the pope; *infallibility* refers to the absence of error in at least some of the exercises of that jurisdiction.) There is no better philosophically conservative advocate for the papacy than de Maistre.

Count Joseph de Maistre was born in 1753 at Chambéry, in Savoy, which then formed part of the kingdom of Sardinia. After legal studies he became a civil servant, then a member of the Sardinian senate, and then, from 1802 to 1817,

Sardinian ambassador to St. Petersburg. While there he wrote *Du pape* (Lyon, 1819) and its sequel, *De l'église gallicane dans son rapport avec le souverain pontife* (Paris, 1821), along with other works of a more purely political character. He died in Turin in 1821.

Given here, from *Du pape,* are book 1, chapters 1–5, the greater part of chapter 15, and chapters 18 and 19. (Book 2 of this work deals with the relationship of the papacy to temporal sovereignties, book 3 with its relationship to "civilization and the happiness of peoples," and book 4 with its relationship to the schismatic churches.) For de Maistre, then, "theological truths are no other than general truths manifested and divinized within the sphere of religion, in such a manner that it is impossible to attack one without attacking a law of the world." Thus the church is infallible because it is a sovereignty. In this respect the church is no different from any other sovereignty, "for every government is absolute, and from the moment it can be resisted, under pretext of error or injustice, it no longer exists." Were the church without a central governing power it would be without unity, that is, there would be a church in name only. Furthermore, the best form for this central authority to take is, as Bellarmine argues, quite simply the best form of government: monarchy tempered with aristocracy.

As de Maistre develops his argument, however, we discover that aristocracy is not allowed to do much tempering. The bishops, one would think, are the aristocracy of the church, but de Maistre is no defender either of ecumenical councils (he doubted that after Trent another would be needed) or of quasi-national aggregates of bishops (as had risen to prominence in France, Germany, and Austria, concerning which the reader should look into Gallicanism, Febronianism, and Josephism). Groupings of bishops, according to our author, cannot in any way constitute a higher tribunal than the papacy, because they are not universal, not in constant session, or as is plain, just too hard to assemble as needed.

The twentieth-century reader who has grown up with the spectacle of an enormously powerful papacy should be warned that it was not ever thus. The papal-monarchy conception of the church, it can be argued, is to a significant degree a nineteenth-century development; like preachers fulminating against sin—fulminating without the sinning is senseless—de Maistre is concerned to uphold papal claims that had, to many, become somewhat doubtful by 1819. The idea that gathered bishops are in some way superior to the pope—or to give the idea its broadest name, *conciliarism*—has had a long history in the church, reaching back in developed theoretical form to the fourteenth century. In a more moderate form the questions raised by the conciliarists are alive today, for as some commentators on Vatican II have asserted, the most serious unfinished business left from that council is the determination of what the bishops' "collegiality" really means.

To round out his argument, de Maistre notes that *in fact* the popes have never erred in the highest exercise of the papal office. He thus takes up the two most celebrated cases of alleged papal error, both involving patristic-period christological heresies (the popes in question being Liberius, who reigned in 352–56, and Honorius I, 625–38). Certainly it is a formidable task to show that the popes have never erred in making purportedly infallible statements, but two factors are worthy of consideration: (1) The popes do have an extraordinary record of doctrinal accuracy, and thus it makes sense "not to admit anomalies before having endeavored to bend those phenomena to the general rule." (2) In cases where a pope might have erred he at such a time "no longer taught as the master and teacher of all the faithful, [and] is not acknowledged by us to be infallible." In the quotation incorporated into this second point de Maistre is quoting the editor of the great collection of conciliar documents, J. D. Mansi; and Mansi, in what might at first seem a bizarre statement, is simply reiterating an observation of late medieval canonists that a heretical pope would, by being heretical, cease to be pope. Jurisdiction crowned with infallibility is thus not to be feared, for that infallibility is limited in advance by the boundaries of the Catholic faith, and God will surely keep his church from losing the faith. So "infallibility is on the one hand humanly supposed, and on the other divinely promised."

## 1. Infallibility

What has not been said about infallibility in a theological point of view! It would be difficult to add new arguments to those which the defenders of this high prerogative have already accumulated, in order to support it by undoubted authorities and to disencumber it of the misrepresentations with which it has pleased the enemies of Christianity and of unity to surround it in the hope of rendering it odious at least, if it was by no means possible to do worse.

But I am not aware it has been sufficiently remarked, with regard to this great question as well as so many others, that theological truths are no other than general truths manifested and divinized within the sphere of religion in such manner that it is impossible to attack one without attacking a law of the world.

*Infallibility* in the spiritual order of things, and *sovereignty* in the temporal order, are two words perfectly synonymous. The one and the other denote that high power which rules over all other powers—from which they all derive their authority—which governs, and is not governed—which judges, and is not judged.

When we say that *the Church is infallible,* we do not ask for her, it is quite essential to be observed, any particular privilege; we only require that she possess the right common to all possible sovereignties, which all necessarily act as if infallible. For every government is absolute; and from the moment it can be resisted under pretext of error or injustice, it no longer exists.

Sovereignty, indeed, has different forms. It speaks not the same language at Constantinople as at London, but once it has spoken in the one place and the other after the fashion peculiar to each, the *bill* and the *fefta* are alike without appeal.

The case is the same in regard to the Church. In one way or another, it must be governed, like any other association whatsover; otherwise there would be no aggregation, no wholeness, no unity. It is the nature of this Government, therefore, to be infallible—that is to say, absolute—else it would no longer govern.

In the judiciary order, which is nothing else than a portion of the Government, is it not obvious that we must acknowledge a power which judges and is not judged, and that for no other reason than that it

From *Du pape,* ed. Jacques Lovie and Joannès Chetail (Geneva: Droz, 1966). This edition is based on the second edition (1821). The translation is from *The Pope,* trans. Aeneas McD. Dawson (London, 1850), 1–24, 77–95, 101–8.

pronounces in the name of the supreme power of which it is considered the organ and the voice? Let us view it as we will, let us give to this high power whatever name we please, there must always be one to whom it never can be said, "You have erred." As a matter of course, the party condemned is always displeased with the sentence and never doubts of the injustice of the tribunal. But disinterested policy, which looks from a higher point of view, makes no account of these vain complaints. It knows there are limits beyond which none must proceed—that interminable trials, appeals without end, and the uncertain tenure of properties are, if it may be so expressed, more unjust than injustice.

The question, then, is to know where resides sovereignty in the Church? For once it is recognized, there is no longer room to appeal from its decisions.

Now if there be anything evident to reason as well as to faith, it is that the universal Church is a monarchy. The very idea of *universality* supposes this form of Government, the absolute necessity of which rests on the twofold ground of the number of subjects and the geographical extent of the empire. So all Catholic writers worthy of the name agree unanimously that the rule of the Church is monarchical but sufficiently tempered with aristocracy to be the best and the most perfect of governments.[1]

Bellarmine so understands it, and he admits with perfect candour that mixed monarchical government is better than pure monarchy.[2]

It may be remarked that in no age of Christianity has this monarchical form been contested or undervalued except by the factious whom it embarrassed.

The rebels of the sixteenth century attributed sovereignty to *the Church*—that is, to the people. The eighteenth century did only transfer these maxims to politics; the system and the theory are the same, even to their remotest consequences. *What difference is there between the Church of God, guided solely by His word, and the great republic, one and indivisible, governed solely by the laws and by the deputies of the sovereign people?* None. It is the same folly renewed only at a different time and under another name.

What is a republic once it has exceeded certain dimensions? It is a country, more or less extensive, commanded by a certain number of men, who call themselves *the republic*. But the government is always *one,* for there is not, nay, there cannot be, a dispersed republic. Thus, in the time of the Roman republic, the republican sovereignty was in the *Forum,* and the subject countries—that is to say, about two-thirds of the known world—were a monarchy, of which the *Forum* was the absolute and merciless sovereign. Remove this state of rule, and there remains no longer any tie or common government, and all unity disappears.

Very little to the purpose, then, have the Presbyterian Churches pretended to make us accept, by dint of talking, as a possible hypothesis, the republican form, which by no means belongs to them except in a divided and particular sense, viz., that each country has its Church, which is republican; but there is not, and there cannot be, *a Christian republican Church:* so that the Presbyterian form destroys that article of the Apostles' Creed which, nevertheless, the ministers of this persuasion are obliged to pronounce at least every Sunday: "I believe in the One, Holy, Catholic and Apostolic Church." For as soon as there is no longer a centre or common government there can be no unity, nor consequently a *universal* or *Catholic Church,* since there is no individual Church which, under this supposition, has even the constitutional means of knowing that it is in religious communion with other Churches.

To maintain that a number of independent Churches form *one universal* Church is to maintain in other words that all the political governments of Europe constitute only *one universal* government. These two ideas are identical. There is no room for cavil.

If anyone thought of proposing a *kingdom of France without a King of France, an empire of Russia without an Emperor of Russia,* he would justly be considered out of his mind; it would nevertheless be exactly the same idea as that of a *universal Church* without a chief.

It would be superfluous to speak of an aristocracy, for there never having been in the Church a body that pretended to rule it under any form, whether elective or hereditary, it follows that its Government is necessarily monarchical, every other form being rigorously excluded.

Monarchical government once established, infallibility becomes a necessary consequence of *supremacy*—or rather, it is absolutely the same thing under a different name. But although this identity be evident, never have men seen or been willing to see that the whole question depends on this truth; and this truth depending, in its turn, on the very nature of things, it by no means requires to be supported by theology— so that, in speaking of unity as necessary, error (supposing it possible) could not be opposed to the Sovereign Pontiff any more than it can be in opposition to temporal Sovereigns, who have never pretended to infallibility. It is, in reality, absolutely the same thing in practice not to be liable to error and to be above being accused of it. Thus, even though it should be agreed that no Divine promise has been made to the Pope, he would not be less infallible, or considered such, as the highest tribunal, for every judgment from which there can be no appeal is and ought to be held just in every human association, under all imaginable forms of government; and every sound statesman will understand me when I say that the question is not only to know whether the Sovereign Pontiff *is,* but also whether he ought to be, infallible.

He who should have the right to say to the Pope that he is wrong would also, on the same ground, be entitled to disobey him—which would entirely do away with supremacy (or infallibility); and this fundamental idea is so striking that one of the most learned Protestant authors of our age[3] has written a dissertation to prove that *the appeal from the Pope to a future council* destroys *visible unity.* Nothing can be more true, for from a habitual and indispensable government there can be no appeal, under pain of the dissolution of the body governed, to a power that only exists occasionally.

Behold then, on the one hand, Mosheim, who demonstrates by irrefragable proofs that appeal to a future council destroys *the visible unity of the Church*—that is to say, Catholicity in the first place, and shortly afterwards Christianity itself—and on the other hand, Fleury, who enumerating the *liberties* of his Church says, *We believe that it is permitted to appeal from the Pope to a future council, notwithstanding the bulls of Pius II and Julius II which have forbidden it.*[4]

It is, indeed, strange that those Gallican doctors should be ignominiously compelled, through the excess of their national prejudices, to see themselves refuted at last by Protestant Theologians. Would that such a spectacle had been only once presented!

The innovators Mosheim had in view maintained "that the Pope has a right only to preside over councils, and that the government of the Church is aristocratic." *But,* says Fleury, *this opinion is condemned at Rome and in France.*

This opinion, therefore, has all the conditions necessary to make it be condemned. But if the government of the Church is not aristocratic, it follows that it must be monarchical, and if monarchical, as it certainly and invincibly is, what authority shall receive an appeal from its decisions?

Endeavour to divide the Christian world into patriarchates, as the schismatical Churches of the East would have it; each patriarch, in this supposition, would have the same privileges which we here attribute to the Pope, and in like manner none could appeal from his decisions, for there must always be a limit which cannot be overstepped. The sovereignty would be divided but would always exist; it would only be necessary to make a change in the Creed and say, *I believe in divided and independent Churches.*

To this monstrous idea we should find ourselves driven, but it would ere long be improved upon by temporal princes, who making very little account of this vain patriarchal division would establish the independence of their particular churches and disencumber themselves of the patriarch, as has happened in Russia, so that instead of one infallibility, rejected as too sublime a privilege, we should have as many as it would suit policy to create by the division of states. Religious sovereignty, fallen in the first instance from the Pope to patriarchs, would descend afterwards from them to synods, and all would end by Anglican supremacy and pure Protestantism, an inevitable state of things, which can only be more or less delayed or avowed wherever the Pope reigns not. Once admit appeal from his decrees, and there is no longer government, unity, or a visible Church.

Because of not having understood these obvious principles have theologians of the first order, such as Bossuet and Fleury, for instance, missed the idea of infallibility, so as to entitle the good sense of laymen to smile as they read them.

The first tells us quite seriously that *the doctrine of infallibility was first broached at the Council of Florence,*[5] and Fleury still more precisely names the Dominican Cajetan as the author of this doctrine under the pontificate of Julius II.

It cannot be comprehended how men, otherwise so distinguished, have been able to confound two ideas so different as those of *believing* and *maintaining* a dogma.

Wrangling is no attribute of the Catholic Church; she believes without discussion, for *faith* is a *belief through charity,* and charity argues not.

The Catholic knows that he cannot be deceived; he knows, moreover, that if he could be led into error there would no longer be revealed truth nor assurance for man in this world, since *every divinely instituted society supposes infallibility,* as Mallebranche has admirably remarked.

The Catholic faith has no need, therefore (and this is its principal characteristic, which has not been sufficiently remarked), to return upon itself, to interrogate itself with regard to its belief, and to ask itself why it believes; it is not possessed with that disputative restlessness by which sects are agitated. Doubt engenders books: why, then, should she write, who never doubts?

But a stranger though she be to all idea of contention, if any dogma comes to be disputed she moves from her proper state; she seeks the grounds of the dogma called in question; she interrogates antiquity; she creates words especially, of which her good faith had no need but which are become necessary to characterize the dogma and raise between the innovators and her children an everlasting barrier.

I must humbly beg pardon of the illustrious Bossuet; but when he tells us that the doctrine of infallibility was introduced in the fourteenth

century, he appears to draw near to those men whom he has so much
and so well combated. Did not Protestants say, also, that the doctrine of
*transubstantiation* was not more ancient than the name? And did not the
Arians argue, in the same fashion, against *consubstantiality*? Bossuet,
may I be permitted to say it, without disrespect to so great a man, was
evidently in the wrong on this important point. We must guard against
taking a word for the thing expressed, and the commencement of an
error for that of a dogma. The truth is precisely the contrary of what
Fleury teaches: for it was about the time he assigns that men began not
*to believe,* but *to discuss, infallibility.*[6] The disputes raised on the supremacy of the Pope caused the question to be more narrowly inquired
into, and the defenders of truth called this supremacy *infallibility,* in
order to distinguish it from every other kind of sovereignty; but there is
nothing new in the Church, and never will it believe what it has not
always believed. Would Bossuet prove to us the novelty of this doctrine,
let him assign a period in the history of the Church when the dogmatical
decisions of the Holy See were not laws; let him blot out all the writings
in which he has maintained the contrary with overwhelming logic,
immense erudition, and unrivalled eloquence; above all, let him point
out the tribunal which examined these decisions and reformed them.

If, moreover, he grants, proves, demonstrates *that the dogmatical
decrees of the Sovereign Pontiffs have always been held law in the Church,*
let him say as he pleases *that the doctrine of infallibility is new:* what can
it matter?

## 2. Councils

Vainly, in order to preserve unity and a visible tribunal, would recourse
be had to councils, the nature and rights of which it is essential we
should examine. Let us begin by an observation which admits not of the
least doubt, viz., *that a periodical or intermittent sovereignty is a contradiction in terms;* for sovereignty must always live, always watch, always
act. *There is no medium for it between life and death.*

Now, councils being occasional powers in the Church, and not only so
but extremely rare and purely accidental, without any periodical and
legal return, the government of the Church could not belong to them.

Councils, besides, decide nothing without appeal unless they be
general, and such councils are attended with so much inconvenience that
it cannot have entered into the designs of Providence to confide to them
the government of the Church.

In the first ages of Christianity councils were much more easily
assembled, because the Church was much less numerous and because

the united powers accumulated on the heads of the emperors enabled them to call together a sufficiently great number of bishops to make at once such an impression as that nothing more was required than the assent of the rest. And, nevertheless, what pains did it not cost—what difficulty was there not in assembling them!

But, in modern times, since the civilized world has been cut up into so many sovereignties and immensely extended by our adventurous navigators, an œcumenical council has become an impossibility. Five or six years would not suffice merely to convoke all the bishops and to establish legal proof of their convocation.

I am almost convinced that if ever a general council of the Church could appear necessary, which is far, I think, from being probable, it would be determined according to the prevailing ideas of the age, which always exercise a certain influence in affairs, to hold a representative assembly. It being morally, physically, and geographically impossible to assemble all the bishops, why should not each Catholic province send deputies to the states-general of the monarchy? The *commons* never having been called thereto, and the aristocracy being now both too numerous and too widely disseminated to appear in person, what better idea could be fallen upon than a representation of the Episcopacy? It would in reality be nothing else than a form already recognized but only extended, for in all councils the proxies of the absent have been always received.

In whatever way these holy assemblies be convoked and constituted, the Inspired Writings are far from offering, in support of the authority of councils, any passage comparable to that which establishes the authority and prerogatives of the Sovereign Pontiff. There is nothing so clear, nothing so magnificent, as the promises contained in this latter text, but if I am told, for instance, *as often as two or three are gathered together in my name I shall be in the midst of them,* I will ask what these words mean, and it will be very difficult to make me see in them any other thing than what I already see, namely, that *God will deign to lend a more particularly merciful ear to every assembly of men gathered together to pray.*

Other passages would present other difficulties; but I pretend not to raise the least doubt in regard to the *infallibility* of a general council; this only I say, that it holds this high privilege of its chief, to whom the promises have been made. We know well that *the gates of hell shall not prevail against the Church.* But why? Because of Peter, on whom she is built. Remove this foundation, how should she be infallible, since she would no longer exist? *To be anything whatever* it is necessary, if I mistake not, *to be.*

Let us never forget that no promise was ever made to the Church apart from its head; and reason alone would show this, since the Church, like every other moral body, being incapable of existence without unity, the promises can only have been made to unity, which disappears with the Sovereign Pontiff.

### 3. Definition and Authority of Councils

Thus œcumenical councils are nothing else than *the parliament or states-general of the Church, assembled by the authority and under the presidency of the Sovereign.*

Wherever there is a Sovereign, and in the Catholic economy his existence is undeniable, there can be no legitimate national assemblies without him. No sooner is his veto pronounced than the assembly is dissolved or its co-legislative power suspended; if it resists, there is revolution.

This very simple and undoubted truth, which never can be shaken, shows in its full light the extreme absurdity of the question so much discussed: *whether the Pope be above the council, or the council above the Pope?* For it is the same as to inquire, in other words, *whether the Pope be above the Pope, or the council above the council?*

I firmly believe, with Leibnitz, *that God has hitherto preserved the truly ecumenical councils from all error contrary to sound doctrine.*[7] I believe, moreover, that He will always so preserve them, but, since there can be no œcumenical council without the Pope, what signifies the question *whether it be above or inferior to the Pope?*

Is the king of Great Britain superior to the parliament, or is the parliament above the king? Neither way; but the king and the parliament, united, constitute the legislature or the sovereignty; but there is not an inhabitant of the three kingdoms who would not rather have his country governed by a king without a parliament than by a parliament without a king.

The question, therefore, is precisely what in English is called *nonsense.*[8]

Although I do not by any means think of disputing the high prerogative of general councils, I do not the less understand the immense inconvenience of those great assemblies and the abuse to which they were subjected in the first ages of the Church. The Grecian emperors, whose theological dynasty is one of the great scandals of history, were always ready to convoke councils, and when they absolutely willed it, there was no help but consent, for the Church ought not to refuse to sovereignty which obstinately insists anything that only occasions inconvenience. Modern incredulity has often been pleased to point out the influence exercised by princes over councils, in order to make us despise those assemblies, or to separate them from the authority of the Pope. It has been answered thousands of times in regard to both of these false conclusions, but let it say what it will on this subject, nothing is more indifferent to the Catholic church, which ought not to be, and cannot be, governed by councils. The emperors in the first ages of the Church had only to will it in order to call together a council, and they willed it but too often. The bishops, on their side, became accustomed to look upon those assemblies as a permanent tribunal, always open to zeal and to doubt; hence the frequent mention they make of them in their writings and the extreme importance they attached to them. But if they had beheld other times, if they had reflected on the dimensions of the globe, and if they had foreseen what was destined to happen one day in the world, they would have well understood that an accidental tribunal, depending on the caprice of princes and on meetings exceedingly rare and difficult, could not have been chosen to govern the eternal and universal Church.

When, therefore, Bossuet inquires—with that tone of superiority less unpardonable, to be sure, in him than any other man—"why so many councils, if the decision of the Popes always sufficed to the Church?" Cardinal Orsi makes an admirable reply: "Ask not us, ask not the Popes Damasus, Celestine, Agatho, Adrian, Leo, who have condemned all heresies from Arius to Eutyches, with the consent of the Church, or of an immense majority, and who never imagined that œcumenical councils were necessary to repress them. Inquire of the Greek emperors, who absolutely willed there should be councils, who convoked them, who exacted the assent of the Popes, and excited so much useless disturbance in the Church."[9]

To the Sovereign Pontiff alone belongs essentially the right of convoking general councils, which does not exclude the moderate and legitimate influence of sovereigns. He alone is judge of the circumstances which require this extreme remedy. Those who pretended to assign this power to temporal authority quite overlooked the strange paralogism into which they fell. They suppose a universal and (what is more) an everlasting monarchy; they go back, without reflecting, to those times when all the mitres in the world could be called together by one sceptre only, or by two. "The Emperor alone," says Fleury, "was able to convoke general councils, because he alone could command the bishops to undertake extraordinary journeys. He, for the most part, defrayed the expenses of them, and indicated the place they were to be held in. . . .

The Popes confined themselves to asking for these assemblies, . . . and they often asked without obtaining."[10]

Well! here is another proof that the Church cannot be governed by general councils—God, the author of nature and of the Church, not having been able to put the laws of his Church in contradiction with those of nature.

Political sovereignty being essentially neither indivisible nor perpetual, if we refuse to the Pope the right of convoking general councils, to whom shall we grant it? Would his most Christian Majesty summon the bishops of England, or his Britannic Majesty those of France? See how these vain talkers have abused history! and, worse still! behold them combating the very nature of things, which absolutely requires, independently of all theological views, that an œcumenical council cannot be otherwise convoked than by an œcumenical power.

But how could men, subject to a power—and subject they are, since it convokes them—be superior to that power, although separated from it? The mere uttering of this proposition demonstrates its absurdity.

It may be said, nevertheless, and quite truly in one sense, *that a general council is above the Pope;* for as there could be no council of this nature without the Pope, if it be said that the Pope and the whole Episcopacy are above the Pope—or in other words, that the Pope *alone* cannot revise a dogma decided by himself and the bishops assembled in general council—the Pope and sound sense alike admit the proposition.

But that the bishops, separated from the Pope and in opposition to him, are above him is what cannot but be looked upon, even in the least unfavourable view, as extravagant.

And the first supposition, even if not rigidly restricted to dogma, no longer satisfies good faith, and allows a crowd of difficulties to remain. *Where is sovereignty in the long intervals between ecumenical councils? Why should not the Pope have power to abrogate or change what he might have done in council, provided there be not question of dogmas, and if circumstances imperiously require it?* If the wants of the Church called for one of those great measures which admit of no delay, as we have seen twice over in the course of the French Revolution,[11] what should be done? Supposing the judgments of the Pope can only be reformed by a general council, who will summon together the council? If the Pope refuses, who will oblige him? And, in the meantime, how will the Church be governed, etc., etc.?

All these considerations recall us to the decision of sound sense, dictated by the clearest analogy, *that the Bull of the Pope,* speaking alone from his chair, differs only from canons pronounced in general council—

as, for instance, an ordinance of the *Marine,* or of the *Waters and Forests,* differed in regard to the French people from one of Blois or of Orleans.

The Pope, in order to dissolve the council, inasfar as it is a council, has only to leave the room, saying, "I am no longer of it." From that moment it is no longer anything but *an assembly,* and an unlawful one if it persists. I never could understand the French when they affirm that the decrees of a general council have the force of law independently of the acceptation or confirmation of the Sovereign Pontiff.[12]

If they mean to say that the decrees of the council having been made under the presidency and with the approbation of the Pope or his legates, the Bull of approbation or confirmation which concludes the acts is no longer anything else than a matter of form, we can understand them (still, however, as cavillers); if they would say anything beyond this they are no longer to be borne with.

But it will be said, perhaps, as is the fashion with modern wranglers, if the Pope became heretical, mad, an enemy of the rights of the Church, etc., where would be the remedy?

I answer, in the first place, that the men who, in our days, delight in such suppositions—although, during eighteen hundred and thirty-six years, none of them have ever been realized—are either exceedingly simple or culpably blind.

In the second place, and under all imaginable suppositions, I ask in my turn: What would be done if the king of Great Britain were so far indisposed as to be no longer able to perform his functions? What has been done in the case[13] would be done again, or perhaps something else, but would it follow, by any chance, that the parliament was above the king, or that it could be convoked by others than the king, etc. etc., etc.?

The more attentively we examine the subject, the more we shall be convinced that, *notwithstanding* the councils, and *by virtue* even of the councils, without the Papal monarchy the Church no longer exists.

We may satisfy ourselves as to this by a very simple hypothesis. It is sufficient to suppose that the separated Eastern Church (all the dogmas of which were then attacked as well as our own) had been assembled in œcumenical council at Constantinople, at Smyrna, or elsewhere, in order to pronounce anathema against the recent errors, whilst we were assembled at Trent for the same purpose: where would the Church have been? Remove the Pope and no answer can be given.

And if the Indies, Africa, and America—which I shall suppose to be likewise peopled with Christians of the same description—had adopted the same measure, the difficulty becomes greater, confusion increases, and the Church disappears.

Let it be observed, moreover, that the œcumenical character in regard to councils does not arise from the number of bishops which compose them; it is sufficient that all be convoked: then come who will. There were one hundred and eighty bishops at Constantinople in 381, there were a thousand at Rome in 1139, and ninety-five only in the same city in 1512, including the cardinals. Nevertheless, all these are general councils: a clear proof that councils derive their power only from their chief, for if councils had inherent and independent authority, the numbers constituting them could not be indifferent—all the more that in this case the acceptation of the Church is no longer necessary and that decrees once pronounced are irrevocable. We have seen the number of voters decrease as far as eighty, but as there are neither canons nor customs which assign limits to the number, I am quite at liberty to diminish it to fifty and even as low as ten, and what man, let him be but moderately reasonable, will be made to believe that so small a number of bishops has a right to command the Pope and the Church?

This is not all. If, on occasion of any urgent want of the Church, the same zeal which animated of old the Emperor Sigismund took possession at the same time of several princes and that each one of them at the same time called together a council, where would be the œcumenical council and infallibility?[14]

The state of temporal affairs will present farther analogies.

## 4. Analogies Derived from Temporal Power

Suppose that, during an *interregnum,* there being no king of France or the succession doubtful, the states-general were divided in opinion, and shortly afterwards literally separated, so as that there should be states-general at Paris and others at Lyons or elsewhere: *where would be the kingdom of France?* This is the same question as the preceding: *where would the Church be?* And, in either case, no answer can be given until the Pope or the king pronounce, *"It is here."* Remove the *Queen bee,* you will still have bees in abundance, but a hive never.

In order to escape the comparison of national assemblies, which is so urgent, so luminous, so decisive, our modern cavillers have objected that *there is no parity between the councils of the Church and the states-general, because the latter possessed only the right of representation.* What sophistry! what dishonesty! How can they fail to see that there is question here of states-general such as the argument requires? I enter not, therefore, into the inquiry whether they had a right to co-legislative power; I suppose them possessed of this privilege: and what is wanting in the comparison? Are not the œcumenical councils ecclesiastical states-general, and are not the states-general political œcumenical councils? Are they not co-legislative, according to our supposition, until they separate, without being so a moment after? Do not their power, their validity, their moral and legislative existence depend on the sovereign who presides over them? Do they not become seditious, *separate,* and consequently null the moment they act without him? And as soon as they are dispersed, does not the fulness of legislative power devolve on the person of the sovereign?

Does the ordinance of Blois, of Moulins, or of Orleans, impair in the least that of the *Marine,* the *Woods and Waters,* etc.?

If there be any difference between the states and general councils, it is wholly to the advantage of the former; for there may be states-general, in the *literal sense of the term,* because they relate only to one empire and because all the provinces of that empire are represented in them, whilst a general council, *in the literal sense of the term,* is absolutely impossible, considering the great number of sovereignties and the dimensions of the terrestrial globe, the superficies of which is well known to be equal to four great circles, each three thousand leagues in diameter.

If it were remarked that as the states-general are not permanent, can only be convoked by a superior, can only decide in accordance with him, and cease to exist at the last session, there necessarily results from this (without taking anything else into consideration) that they are not co-legislative in the full force of the term, I should have very little difficulty in replying to this objection, for it would not be less certain that the states-general may be absolutely useless during the time they are assembled and that all the while the sovereign legislator acts in concert with them.

I should be entitled, nevertheless, to speak as unfavourably of councils as Gregory Nazianzen has done: "I never saw," said this great and holy personage, "a council assembled without danger and inconvenience. . . . To speak truly, I must say that I avoid, as much as I can, assemblies of priests and bishops; I never saw so much as one concluded in a happy and agreeable manner, and which did not tend rather to increase evils than to remove them."[15]

But I will not urge this argument; all the more, that the holy doctor whose words I have just quoted has, if I mistake not, explained his meaning. Councils may be useful. They would exist by natural if not by ecclesiastical right, there being nothing so natural, in theory particu-

larly, as that every human association should assemble as it best may—
that is, by its representatives, under the presidency of a chief—in order
to make laws and watch over the interests of the community. I by no
means contest this point; I only say that an intermittent representative
body (if, especially, it be casual and not periodical) is by the very nature
of things always and everywhere unfit to govern, and that during its
sessions, even, it has no existence and legitimacy except through its
chief.

Let us transfer to England the political schism I have just supposed in
France. Let the parliament be divided: where will be the true one? With
the king. But if it were doubtful who should be king, there would no
longer be *a parliament,* but only *assemblies* endeavouring to find a king,
and if they could not agree, there would be war and anarchy. Let us
make a supposition still more to the point and admit only an assembly:
never will it be *parliament* until it has found the king, but it will exercise
lawfully all the powers necessary to attain this great end, for those
powers, simply because they are necessary, are founded on natural right.
As it is impossible for a nation to be literally assembled, it must act
through its representatives. At all periods of anarchy a certain number
of men will seize on power for the purpose of establishing order in some
way, and if this assembly, retaining the ancient name and forms, enjoyed
moreover the consent of the nation, manifested at least by its silence, it
would possess all the legitimacy such unfortunate circumstances admit
of.

But if the monarchy, instead of being hereditary, were elective and if
there were several competitors elected by different parties, the assembly
ought either to declare who should be king if it discovered in favour of
one of them obvious grounds of preference, or if it saw no such decisive
grounds, set them all aside and elect another.

But here would be the limits of its power. If it assumed the liberty of
making other laws the king, immediately after his accession, would have
a right to reject them, for the words *anarchy* and *laws* exclude one
another, and everything done in the former state can only have a momentary value, arising merely from circumstances.

If the king found several things done in a parliamentary manner—
that is, according to the principles of the constitution—he could give the
royal sanction to these various dispositions, which would become laws
binding even on the king—who is, and on that account particularly, the
*image of God upon earth,* for according to the beautiful thought of
Seneca, "God obeys laws, but it was He who made them."

And in this sense the law might be said to be *above the king,* as a
general council is *above the Pope,* that is to say, that neither the king nor

the Sovereign Pontiff can recall what has been done in a parliamentary manner and by a council—in other words, by themselves *in parliament* and *in council*—which far from weakening the idea of monarchy, completes it, on the contrary, and carries it to its highest degree of perfection by excluding all accessory notion of despotism or of inconstancy.

Hume has made a brutal remark on the Council of Trent, which it is worth while, nevertheless, to take into consideration: "It is the only general council which has been held in an age truly learned and inquisitive. No one need expect to see another general council till the decay of learning and the progress of ignorance shall again fit mankind for these great impostures."[16]

If you take from this passage the insulting and scurrilous tone from which heresy is never free,[17] there remains a good deal that is true: the more enlightened the world becomes, the less will a general council be thought of. There have just been twenty-one the whole time since the origin of Christianity, which would give about one general council to each period of eighty years, but we see that for two centuries and a half religion has done very well without them, and I do not believe that any one thinks of them, notwithstanding the extraordinary wants of the Church, for which the Pope will provide much better than a general council if men only understand how to make use of his power.

The world is become too great for general councils, which seem only to have been intended for the youth of Christianity.

## 5. Digression on What Is Called the Youth of Nations

But this word *youth* reminds me of what ought to be observed here: that this expression, and some others of the same kind, relate to the whole duration of a body or an individual. If I picture to myself, for instance, the Roman republic, which lasted five hundred years, I know what these expressions mean: *the youth, or the earliest years, of the Roman republic;* and if there be question of a man who is to live about eighty years, I shall be guided in this case also by the total duration, and it is obvious that if man lived a thousand years, he would be young at two hundred. What, then, is the youth of a religion that is destined to last as long as the world? There is much said about the *first ages of Christianity.* In truth, I know not what assurance we have that they are past. Whatever may be the case, there cannot be a more fallacious argument than that which would recall us to the first ages without knowing what is said.

It would be better to say, perhaps, that in one sense the Church never grows old. The Christian religion is the only institution which knows no decay, because it alone is Divine. As to externals, practices, ceremonies, it makes allowance more or less for human variations. But in things essential it is always the same—"its years shall not fail." Thus, rather than overthrow the laws of the human race, it will allow itself to be obscured by the barbarism of the middle ages, but it produces, nevertheless, in those times, a multitude of superior men, who from it alone derive their superiority. It renews itself afterwards together with mankind, accompanies them, perfects them in their various relations—differing thus, and that in a striking manner, from all human institutions and empires, even, which have their infancy, their manhood, their old age, and their end.

Without urging these observations, let us not speak so much (now that the world is grown so great) of the *first ages,* or of *œcumenical councils;* particularly let us avoid dwelling on the *first ages* as if time had any hold on the Church. The wounds inflicted on her proceed only from our vices; centuries, as they glide past, can only promote her improvement.

I shall not conclude this chapter without declaring anew, in express terms, my perfect orthodoxy on the subject of general councils. It is quite possible, no doubt, that certain circumstances may render them necessary, and I am far from denying, for instance, that the Council of Trent accomplished things which it alone could accomplish. But never will the Sovereign Pontiff show himself more infallible than in deciding the question whether a council is indispensable, and never can temporal power do better than refer to him the decision of this question.

The French people are not aware, perhaps, that the most reasonable thing that can be said in regard to the Pope and general councils has been written by two French theologians, in two passages of a few lines, distinguished by good sense and ingenuity—passages well known and appreciated in Italy by the wisest defenders of legitimate monarchy. Let us hear, in the first place, the great champion of the sixteenth century:

"By the infallibility which is supposed to belong to Pope Clement, as to the sovereign tribunal of the Church, is not understood that he is assisted by the Spirit of God so as to have the light necessary for deciding all questions whatsoever, but his infallibility consists in this, that he is privileged to judge all questions in regard to which he feels himself sufficiently enlightened to decide, whilst those in regard to which he does not conceive himself sufficiently enlightened to pass judgment he refers to the council."[18]

This is exactly the theory of states-general, which every right-thinking mind is constantly obliged to adopt.

*Ordinary questions, in regard to which the king knows that he is sufficiently aided with light, he decides himself; others, in regard to which he does not understand that he is sufficiently enlightened, he refers to the states-general over which he presides.* But he is always sovereign. The other French theologian is Thomassin, who thus expresses himself in one of his learned dissertations:

"Let us no longer contend whether an œcumenical council is superior or inferior to the Pope. Let us be satisfied to know that the Pope, in the midst of the council, is above himself; and that the council, deprived of its chief, is beneath itself."[19]

Never was language more to the purpose. Thomassin, particularly, embarrassed by the declaration of 1682, has acquitted himself admirably, and has given us to understand sufficiently well what he thought of *beheaded* councils; and the two passages united concur with many others in making known to us the *universal* and *invariable* doctrine of the clergy of France, so often invoked by the apostles of the four articles. . . .

## 15. Infallibility de Facto

If from the question of right we pass to that of facts, which are the touchstone of right, we cannot avoid the conclusion that the Chair of St. Peter, considered in the certainty of its decisions, is naturally an incomprehensible phenomenon. Replying to the whole world for eighteen centuries, how often have the Popes been found to be *incontestably* wrong? Never. Cavils have been raised, but never has it been found possible to allege anything decisive.

Among Protestants and even in France, as I have often remarked, the idea of infallibility has been amplified to such a degree as to render it a ridiculous bugbear. It is therefore quite essential to form a clear and perfectly well defined idea of it.

The defenders of this great privilege say, then, and say nothing more than, *that the Sovereign Pontiff, speaking in freedom*[20] *to the Church, and as the schools say, "ex cathedrâ," never erred, and never will err, in matter of faith.*

By what has occurred until now, I do not see that this proposition has been refuted. All that has been said against the Popes in order to make out that they have erred is either without solid grounds or beyond the range which I have just defined.

The criticism which has taken delight in counting the faults of the Popes loses not a minute in ecclesiastical history but proceeds at once to St. Peter. With him it begins its catalogue, and although the fault of the Prince of the Apostles be a fact wholly foreign to the question, it has not been the less adverted to by all the books of *the opposition* as the first proof of the fallibility of the Sovereign Pontiff. I shall cite on this point a writer the most recent, if I mistake not, amongst Frenchmen of the episcopal order who have written against the great prerogative of the Holy See.[21]

He had to repel the solemn and embarrassing testimony of the clergy of France, declaring, in 1625, *that infallibility has always remained firm and immoveable in the successors of St. Peter.*

To get rid of this difficulty, see what the learned prelate has fallen upon: "The indefectibility," says he, "or infallibility which has remained until this day firm and immoveable in the successors of St. Peter, is not undoubtedly of another kind than that with which was invested the Chief of the Apostles by virtue of the prayer of Jesus Christ. Now, the event proved that indefectibility, or infallibility in faith, did not shield him from a fall; therefore," etc. And, lower down, he adds, "Falsely exaggerated are the effects of Christ's intercession, which was the pledge of the stability of the faith of Peter, without, nevertheless, hindering his humbling fall."

Behold thus theologians, bishops even (I cite only one, as representing all who hold similar views), advancing or at least supposing without the least doubt that the Catholic Church was established and that St. Peter was Sovereign Pontiff before the death of our Saviour.

They had read, notwithstanding, just as we have done, that "where there is a testament the death of the testator must of necessity come in. For a testament is of force after men are dead; otherwise it is as yet of no strength whilst the testator yet liveth."[22]

They could not fail to know that the Church had its birth in the cenaculum and that before the descent of the Holy Ghost there was no Church.

They had read the great oracle, "It is expedient to you that I go; for if I go not, the Paraclete will not come to you; but if I go, I will send him to you. But when the Paraclete cometh . . . he shall give testimony of me; and you shall give testimony, because you are with me from the beginning."[23]

Before this solemn mission, therefore, there was no Church nor Sovereign Pontiff nor Apostolate properly so called; all was in germ, in a state of possible and expectative existence, and in this state even the heralds of the truth gave proof only of ignorance and weakness.

Nicole has called attention to this truth in his catechism: "Before having received the Holy Ghost," says he, "on the day of Pentecost, the Apostles appeared weak in faith, timid in regard to men, etc. . . . But since Pentecost, we behold only their confidence, their joy in sufferings, etc."[24]

We have just heard the truth speak; we shall now hear it thunder: "Was it not astonishing, miraculous, to behold the Apostles, the moment they received the Holy Ghost, as penetrated with the light of God, as they had been until then ignorant and full of errors . . . so long as they had Jesus Christ alone for their teacher! O, adorable, unfathomable mystery; Jesus Christ, all God that he was, had not sufficed, it appears, to make them comprehend the heavenly doctrine he came to establish on the earth . . . 'and they understood none of these things.'[25] Why? because they had not yet received the Spirit of God, and because all those truths are such as only the Spirit of God can teach. But, at the very moment the Holy Ghost is given to them, those truths, which had appeared to them so incredible, became clear to them," etc.[26] That is to say, the *testament is opened,* and the Church begins.

If I have insisted on this miserable objection, it is because it is the first which presents itself and because it serves admirably to place in its full light the spirit which governs this discussion on the part of the adversaries of the great prerogative—a spirit of cavil, envious to death of being in the right—quite natural, indeed, in every dissenter but in Catholics wholly inexplicable.

The plan of my work does not permit me to discuss one by one the pretended errors with which the Popes are reproached—and the more so as everything has been said on this subject. I shall allude only to the two points which have been discussed with the greatest ardour and which appear to me capable of being put in a clearer light; *the rest does not merit the honour of being adverted to.*

The Italian doctors have observed that Bossuet, who in his *Defence of the Declaration*[27] had at first argued, like all the rest from the fall of Pope Liberius, to establish the principal of the four propositions, retrenched the whole chapter relating thereto, as may be seen in the edition of 1745. I am not at present in a position to verify this statement, but I have not the least reason to mistrust my authors, and the new History of Bossuet, moreover, leaves not the slightest doubt as to the repentance of this great man.

We there read that Bossuet in the confidence of conversation said one day to Abbé Ledieu, "I have effaced from my *Treatise on Ecclesiastical Power* all that regards Pope Liberius, *as not proving very well what I intended to establish in that place.*"[28]

It was a great misfortune for Bossuet to have to retract on such a point, but he saw that the argument founded on Liberius could not be sustained.

So little could be made of it, indeed, that the Centuriators of Magdeburg not only did not venture to condemn this Pope but even absolved him.

"Liberius," writes St. Athanasius, quoted word for word by the Centuriators, "overcome by the sufferings of two years' banishment and by the threat of punishment, subscribed at last the condemnation which was required of him, but violence did everything and the aversion of Liberius to heresy is not less undoubted than that his opinion was in favour of Athanasius; this sentiment he would have manifested if he had been free." St. Athanasius concludes with this remarkable sentence: "Violence proves clearly the intention of him who makes another tremble, but by no means that of him who trembles"—a maxim decisive in this case.

The Centuriators quote with the same exactness other writers who show themselves less favourable to Liberius, without, however, denying *the sufferings of exile*. But the historians of Magdeburg evidently lean towards the opinion of St. Athanasius: "It appears," say they, "that all that has been related regarding the subscription of Liberius nowise concerns assenting to the Arian dogma but only the condemnation of Athanasius. That he subscribed with his tongue rather than his mind, as Cicero said of the oath of someone, is abundantly evident. That Athanasius excused him, clearly proves that he remained firm in the profession of the Nicene faith."[29]

What a spectacle is not that of Bossuet accusing a Pope who stands exculpated by the elite of Calvinism! Who could refrain from applauding the sentiments he confided to his secretary?

The plan of my work not admitting of details, I refrain from inquiring whether the passage of St. Athanasius just quoted be open to suspicion in some points—whether the fall of Liberius can be denied purely and simply as an "ingenious device"[30]—whether, on the contrary supposition, Liberius subscribed the first or the second formula of Sirmium. I shall limit myself to quoting a few lines of the learned Archbishop Mansi, who made a collection of the Councils; they will prove, perhaps, to some prejudiced minds that "there is a little sound sense within the borders of Italy."

"Supposing that Pope Liberius did subscribe to Arianism (which he by no means granted), did he speak on that occasion as Pope, *ex cathedrâ*? What Councils did he convene previously in order to examine the question? If none, what doctors did he summon around him? What congregations did he institute to define the dogma? What public and solemn prayers did he appoint for invoking the aid of the Holy Ghost? If he did not take these preliminary steps, he no longer taught as the master and teacher of all the faithful. And when he does not so act, be it known to Bossuet, the Roman Pontiff is not acknowledged by us to be infallible."[31]

Orsi is still more precise and exacting.[32] A great number of similar testimonies are found in Italian books, *sed Græcis incognita, qui sua tantum mirantur.*

The only Pope who can occasion legitimate doubts, less on account of his faults than because of the condemnation to which he has been subjected, is Honorius. What signifies, however, the condemnation of a man and a sovereign pontiff pronounced forty-two years after his death? One of those wretched sophists who too frequently dishonoured the patriarchal throne of Constantinople, a scourge of the Church and of common sense, Sergius, in short, patriarch of Constantinople, fell upon inquiring, at the commencement of the seventh century, *whether there were two wills in Jesus Christ.* Determined on maintaining the negative, he consulted Pope Honorius in ambiguous terms. The Pope, who perceived not the snare, thought that there was question of two human wills, that is to say, of the double law which afflicts our unfortunate nature and which was certainly wholly foreign to our Saviour. Honorius, moreover, outstepping, perhaps, the general maxims of the Holy See, which dreads above all things new questions and precipitate decisions, desired that there should be no mention of two wills and wrote in this sense to Sergius. By thus proceeding, he may have fallen into what may be termed a *fault of administration,* for if he was wanting in anything on this occasion it was in regard to the rules of government and of prudence. He miscalculated, it may be admitted; he saw not the fatal consequences of the measures he considered it fitting and in his power to have recourse to; but in all that he did we discover not any derogation from the dogma of the Church—any theological error. That Honorius understood the question as here supposed is at once demonstrated by the direct and irrefragable testimony of the very man whose pen he employed in writing his letter to Sergius, the cleric John Sympon, who only three years after the death of Honorius wrote thus to the Emperor Constantine, son of Heraclius: "When we spoke of one will in our Lord we had not in view *his twofold nature* but only his humanity. Sergius, indeed, having maintained that there were in Jesus Christ two contrary wills, we said that these two wills, that of the *flesh* and that of the *spirit,* as in ourselves from original sin, could not be recognized in him."[33]

And what more decisive can there be than these words of Honorius himself, quoted by Saint Maximus: "There is but one will in Jesus Christ; since, *without doubt,* the Divinity had clothed itself with our nature but not with our sin; and that thus all *carnal* thoughts were wholly foreign to him."[34]

If the letters of Honorius had really contained the venom of Monothelism, how imagine that Sergius, who had taken his stand, would not have made haste to give to his writings all the publicity in his power? This, however, he did not do. He concealed, on the contrary, the letters (or the letter) of Honorius during the whole lifetime of this pontiff, who yet survived two years—a circumstance which must not be overlooked. But immediately after the death of Honorius, which happened in 638, the patriarch of Constantinople, no longer under restraint, published his explanation or *ecthesis,* so famous in the ecclesiastical history of the period. Nevertheless, and this is also very remarkable, he quoted not the letters of Honorius. During the forty-two years which followed the death of this Pontiff the Monothelites never spoke of the second of these letters *for the good reason that it was not yet conceded.* Pyrrhus, even, in the celebrated dispute with St. Maximus, dares not maintain that *Honorius had imposed silence on the subject of one or two operations.* He confines himself to saying vaguely that *this Pope had approved the sentiments of Sergius on one will only.*

The Emperor Heraclius, exculpating himself in the year 641 to Pope John IV on account of the part he had taken in the affair of Monothelism, observes silence with regard to these letters, as does also the Emperor Constans II in his apology addressed in 619 to Pope Martin on the subject of the *type*—another imperial folly of that period. Now, once more, how can it be imagined that these discussions and so many others of the same description should not have induced some public appeal to the decisions of Honorius if they had been looked upon at that time as infected with the Monothelite heresy!

Let us add that if this Pontiff had observed silence after Sergius had declared himself, an argument might have been taken from his silence inasmuch as it would have been considered a culpable commentary on his letters; but he ceased not, as long as he lived, to raise his voice against Sergius, to threaten him, and to condemn him. St. Maximus of Constantinople is yet another illustrious witness on this interesting fact:

"We cannot but laugh," says he, "or rather to speak more appropriately, weep over those unfortunate men (Sergius and Pyrrhus) who dare to quote pretended decisions favourable to their impious *ecthesis,* endeavour to place in their ranks the great Honorius, and fortify themselves in the eyes of the world with the authority of a man eminent in the cause of religion. . . . Who could have inspired those forgers with so much audacity? What pious and orthodox man, what bishop, what

Church has not conjured them to abandon heresy? And, above all, what has not the *divine* Honorius done?"[35]

Here, it must be owned, we have rather a singular heretic!

And moreover Pope St. Martin, who died in 655, says in his letter to Arnaud d'Utrecht, "The Holy See has not ceased to exhort them (Sergius and Pyrrhus), to warn, to reprimand, to threaten them, in order to bring them back to the truth which they had betrayed."[36] Now, chronology shows that there can be question here of no other than Honorius, since Sergius survived him only two months and after the death of Honorius the pontifical chair was vacant during nineteen months.

Before writing to the Pope, Sergius wrote to Cyrus of Alexandria "that, for the sake of peace, it appeared useful to observe silence on the two wills, on account of the twofold danger of shaking, on the one hand, the dogma of the two natures, or of opposing two opposite wills in Jesus Christ, if profession were made of two wills."[37]

But where would the contradiction be if there were not question of a twofold human will? It appears evident, therefore, that the discussion first arose on the human will and that there was question only of knowing whether our Saviour in clothing himself with our nature had subjected himself to that double law which is the punishment of original guilt and the torment of our life.

In matters so elevated and so subtle, ideas meet and are easily confounded together if we are not much upon our guard. Is it inquired, for instance, without any explanation, whether there are two wills in Jesus Christ? It is clear that the Catholic can reply yes, or no, without ceasing to be orthodox. Yes, if we contemplate the two natures united without confusion; no, if we consider only the human nature exempt by its august association from the twofold law which degrades us; no, if there be question solely of excluding the twofold human will; yes, if we desire to confess the double nature of the man-God.

Thus, the word *Monothelism* of itself expresses not a heresy; we must explain and show what is the subject matter of the word. If it relates to the humanity of our Saviour, it is legitimate; if applied to the person of the God-man, it becomes heterodox.

In reflecting on the words of Sergius such as we have just read them, we feel inclined to believe that after the fashion of all other heretics he started not from a fixed point and that he had not a very distinct idea of his own views, which the keen disputes that afterwards ensued served to clear up and determine.

This same confusion of ideas which we observe in the writing of Sergius had some place in the mind of the Pope, who was not prepared. He shuddered on perceiving, even indistinctly, the advantage the Greek spirit was about to take of this question, once more to unsettle the Church. Without pretending to exculpate him altogether, since great theologians have thought that he was wrong in employing on this occasion too much political wisdom, I acknowledge, nevertheless, that I am not much astonished he should have endeavoured to stifle this dispute at its commencement.

However, this may be, since Honorius said solemnly to Sergius in his second letter, produced in the sixth council, "Take great care you do not publish that I decided anything as to one or two wills,"[38] how can there be question of the error of Honorius, who decided nothing? Surely, to be mistaken, one must affirm something. Unfortunately, his prudence deceived him more than he could have imagined; the question becoming embittered every day more and more, in proportion as the heresy was developed, men began to speak harshly of Honorius and his letters. At last, forty-two years after his death, these letters are produced in the twelfth and thirteenth sessions of the sixth council, and without any defence beforehand or preliminary proceeding whatsoever, Honorius is anathematized, at least according to the acts of the council such as they have come down to us. Nevertheless, when a tribunal condemns a man to death it is customary that it should say on what grounds it does so. If Honorius had lived at the time of the sixth council, he would have been cited, he would have appeared, he would have adduced in his favor the reasons which we are bringing forward today, and many more besides, which time and the malice of men have suppressed. . . . But, what do I say? he would have come himself to preside over the council; he would have said to the bishops so desirous of avenging on a Roman Pontiff the hideous stains of the patriarchal see of Constantinople, "My brethren, God abandons you most assuredly, since you presume to judge the chief of the Church, who is established judge over yourselves. I need not your assembly to condemn Monothelism. What can you say which I have not already said? My decisions suffice to the Church. I withdraw from the council, and so dissolve it."

Honorius, as we have seen, ceased not till his last breath to profess, to teach, to defend the truth, to exhort, to threaten, to reprimand those same Monothelites whose opinions, it is desired to make us believe, he had embraced; Honorius in his second letter (let us take it, word for word, as authentic) expresses the dogma in a manner which extorted the approbation of Bossuet.[39] Honorius died in possession of his see and of his dignity, without having ever since the unfortunate correspondence with Sergius written a line or uttered a word which history has marked as affording ground for suspicion. His remains reposed peacefully, and with honour, in the Vatican; his images continued to shine in the church, and his name in the sacred dyptics. A holy martyr, whose relics enrich our altars, called him, soon after his death, a *divine man.* In the eighth general council held at Constantinople the fathers, that is, the entire East, presided over by the Patriarch of Constantinople, profess solemnly *that it was not permitted to forget the promises made to Peter by our Saviour, and the truth of which was confirmed by experience, since the Catholic faith had always subsisted without stain, and the pure doctrine had been taught* invariably *in the Apostolic See.*[40]

Since the affair of Honorius, and on all possible occasions of which the one just alluded to is the most remarkable, the Popes have never ceased to claim this praise and to behold it generally attributed to them.

After that, I must own I can no longer understand the condemnation of Honorius. If some Popes, his successors—Leo II, for instance—have appeared not to raise their voice against the Hellenisms of Constantinople, we must praise their honesty, their modesty, and above all, their prudence, but all they may have said in this way is by no means dogmatical, and so the facts remain worth what they are worth.

Everything well considered, the justification of Honorius is far from appearing to me the greatest difficulty, but I have no mind to raise the dust and expose myself to the risk of clouding the path.

If the Popes had frequently laid themselves open to attack by *hazarding* decisions, I should not be astonished to hear both sides of the question discussed and would be much inclined in doubtful cases to assume the negative, for with doubtful arguments we cannot rest satisfied.

But the Popes, on the contrary, having never ceased during eighteen centuries to pronounce on all kinds of questions with prudence and accuracy truly miraculous, inasmuch as their decisions have invariably been independent of the moral tendency of the passions of the oracle—that oracle a man—a small number of circumstances, more or less open to doubt, cannot be construed to the prejudice of the Popes without violating all the laws of probability, which, nevertheless, must always be held as sovereign throughout the world.

When any power, of what order soever it may be, has always acted consistently, and if there should be found a very small number of cases in which it may appear to have derogated from its custom, we ought not to admit anomalies before having endeavoured to bend those phenomena to the general rule; and even though there should not be means of perfectly clearing up the problem, we ought never to come to any other conclusion than that we are ignorant.

It is, therefore, very unworthy of a Catholic, a man of the world even, to write against this magnificent, this divine, privilege of the Chair of St. Peter. As to the priest who indulges in so great an abuse of talent and erudition, he is blind and worse; if I am not fearfully deceived, he derogates from his character. Even that man who without reference to his state of life should hesitate as to the theory ought always to acknowledge the truth of the fact and agree that the Sovereign Pontiff never fell into error; he ought at least to lean cordially towards this belief, instead of lowering himself to college wranglings in order to shake it. We are tempted to say in reading certain writers of this description that they are defending a personal right against a foreign usurper, whilst in reality there is question of a privilege as favourable to them as it is well founded—an invaluable gift imparted to the universal family as much as to the common father.[41]. . .

## 18. No Danger in the Consequences of a Recognized Supremacy

Read the books of Protestants: you will there find infallibility represented as a fearful despotism which enthrals the human mind, which crushes it, deprives it of its faculties, which commands it to believe, and forbids it to think. The prejudice against this idle scarecrow has been carried to such a height, that we find Locke seriously maintaining *that Catholics believe in the real presence on the faith of the Pope's infallibility.*[42]

France has, in no slight degree, increased the evil by becoming in a great measure an accomplice in these extravagances. Germany has also lent the aid of its exaggerations. In short, there has been formed beyond the Alps, in regard to Rome, an opinion so strong, although exceedingly erroneous, that it is no easy enterprise to bring men to understand merely what there is question of. This formidable jurisdiction of the Pope over the mind is confined within the limits of the Apostles' Creed; the circle, as everyone knows, is not immense, and the human mind has quite enough whereon to exercise itself beyond this sacred perimeter.

As to discipline, it is either general or local. The first is not very extensive, for there are few points absolutely general and which may not be altered without any danger to what is essential in religion. The second depends on particular circumstances, on localities, privileges, etc. But it is matter of notoriety that, on both the former and the latter points, the Holy See has always given proof of the greatest condescension towards all the churches; frequently even, and almost always, it has gone beyond their wants and their desires. What interest could the Pope have to give needless vexation to the nations united in his communion?

There is, moreover, in the genius of the people of the West, an indescribably exquisite sense—a delicate and unerring tact—which proceeds at once to the essence of things, neglecting everything else. This is seen chiefly in the religious forms or rites in regard to which the Roman Church has always shown all imaginable condescension. It has pleased God, for instance, to attach the work of human regeneration to the sensible sign of water for reasons by no means arbitrary but, on the contrary, very profound and altogether worth being inquired into. We profess this dogma in common with all Christians, but we consider that there is water in a cruet as well as in the Pacific Ocean, and that everything depends on the mutual contact of water and man, accompanied by certain sacramental words. Other Christians pretend *that for this rite a basin at least is indispensable; that if a man goes into the water he is certainly baptized, but that if water falls upon man, the result becomes doubtful.* On this head may be said to them what an Egyptian priest addressed to them two thousand years ago, *You are but children!* After all, they are masters of their choice; nobody interferes with them. If they desired a river even, like the English Baptists, they would be allowed the privilege. One of the principal mysteries of the Christian religion has *bread* for its essential matter. Now a *wafer* is bread, as well as the most bulky loaf that ever was baked; we have, therefore, adopted the *wafer.* Do other Christian nations believe that there is no other bread properly so called than that which we eat at table, nor any real *manducation* without *mastication?* We respect exceedingly this oriental reasoning, and [are] quite sure that those who employ it today will gladly do as we do as soon as they have attained the same degree of certainty. It does not even occur to us to disturb them, whilst we are satisfied to retain for ourselves the light unleavened bread, which has in its favour the analogy of the ancient Pasch, that of the first Christian Pasch, and the propriety, greater perhaps than is supposed, of devoting a particular kind of bread to the celebration of such a mystery.

Do those same sticklers for immersion and leavened bread, by erroneous interpretation of the scriptures, and from obvious ignorance of human nature, maintain that the sacred tie of marriage is dissolved by its profanation, which is in fact a formal exhortation to guilt. We have not chosen to have any cavilling with our adversaries, even whilst they obstinately persist, and on the most solemn occasion we simply said to them, "We shall pass you over in silence, but in the name of reason and peace say not that we understand nothing of the matter."[43]

After these instances, and so many others that might be adduced, what nation can fear for its particular privileges on account of the Roman supremacy? The Pope will never refuse to listen to all, nor will he deny satisfaction to the rulers of the world in anything that is in a Christian sense possible. There is no pedantry at Rome, and if there were anything to fear as regards condescension, I should be inclined to dread excess rather than deficiency.

Notwithstanding these assurances, derived from considerations that are quite decisive, I doubt not but prejudice will still hold out; I make no doubt even but very shrewd minds will exclaim, "But if nothing checks the Pope, where will he stop? History shows us how he can use this power; what guarantee is given us that the same events will not be reproduced?"

To this objection, which will undoubtedly be made, I answer first, in general, that the examples taken from history against the Popes are of no value and ought not to inspire the least dread for the future, because they belong to quite another order of things from that with which we are conversant. The power of the Popes was excessive in regard to us when it was necessary that it should be so, and that nothing in the world could supply its place. This I hope to prove in the course of this work, in a way that must satisfy every impartial judge.[44]

In the next place, dividing in idea those men who honestly fear the enterprises of the Popes into two classes, that consisting of Catholics and that composed of all those who are not Catholics, I say to the first, "By what blindness, by what ignorant and culpable mistrust, do you look upon the Church as a human edifice of which it may be said, *Who will sustain it?* and its chief as an ordinary man of whom it can be said, *Who will preserve him?*" This is a distraction common indeed, yet by no means excusable. Never will any inordinate pretension be entertained by the Holy See; never will injustice and error be able to take root there and abuse the faith of mankind to the profit of ambition.

As to those who by birth or by system are without the Catholic circle, if they address to me the same question, *What can check the Pope?* I will answer, *Everything*—the canons, the laws, the customs of nations, sovereignties, the great tribunals, national assemblies, prescription, representations, negotiations, duty, fear, prudence, and above all, opinion, *which rules the world.*

Thus let me not be made to say that I would, *therefore, make the Pope a universal monarch.* Assuredly I desire nothing of the kind, whilst I am nowise astonished to hear this *therefore* always a ready argument when all others are wanting. But as the very serious faults certain princes have been guilty of against religion and its chief by no means derogate from the respect I owe to temporal monarchy, the possible offences of a Pope against this same sovereignty will not hinder me from acknowledging it for what it is. All the powers of the universe set limits to one another by their mutual resistance. It has not been the will of God to establish greater perfection on the earth, although in one way he has given marks sufficiently distinct to make his hand be recognized. There is not in the world any one power in a position to bear all possible and arbitrary suppositions, and if they are judged by what they can do (without allusion to what they have done), they must all be abolished.

## 19. Continuation of the Same Subject: Further Explanations in Regard to Infallibility

How liable are not men to blind themselves as regards the most simple ideas! The essential thing for every nation is to preserve its particular discipline, that is to say, those usages which without being connected with dogma constitute, nevertheless, a portion of its public law and have been for a long time amalgamated with the character and the laws of the nation so that they cannot be touched without causing disturbance and serious discontent. Now, those usages and those particular laws it may defend with respectful firmness if ever (and this is merely a supposition, for the sake of argument) the Holy See undertook to derogate from them, all being agreed that the Pope, and even the Church together with him, may be deceived in regard to everything that is not dogma or fact connected therewith, so that on everything in which are interested patriotism, affections, customs, and to say all in one word, national pride, no nation ought to dread the Pope's infallibility, which is applicable only to objects of a higher order.

As to dogma, properly so called, it is precisely on this point that we have no interest to call in question the infallibility of the Pope. Should there occur one of those questions of divine metaphysics which must necessarily be referred to the decision of the supreme tribunal, it concerns not our interests that it be decided in such or such a way but that a decision be pronounced without delay and without appeal. In the celebrated affair of Fénelon, of twenty examinators at Rome, ten were for him and ten against him. In a general council, five or six hundred bishops might likewise have been divided.

Those who believe that by multiplying deliberative voices doubt is diminished know little of human nature and have never sat in the midst of a deliberative body. The Popes have condemned several heresies in the course of eighteen centuries. When were they contradicted by an œcumenical council? Not one instance can be alleged. Never were their dogmatical bulls opposed, except by those whom they condemned. The Jansenist fails not to call that which struck him down "the too famous bull, *Unigenitus*," whilst Luther discovered, no doubt, that the bull *Erurge, Domine*, was also "too famous." We have been often told *that general councils are useless, since they have never reclaimed anyone.* This observation Sarpi has thought proper to place at the head of his History of the Council of Trent. The remark is undoubtedly not to the purpose, for the principal end of councils is by no means to reclaim innovators, whose invincible obstinacy was never unknown, but to show they were in the wrong and to tranquillize the minds of the faithful by a solemn dogmatical decision.

The resipiscence of dissentients is a result more than doubtful, which the Church ardently desires but scarcely hopes for. However, I allow the objection, and I say, *Since general councils are neither useful to us who believe nor to innovators who refuse to believe, why convene them?*

Despotism over thought, with which the Popes are so much reproached, is a mere chimera. Suppose that in our days it be asked in the Church, *Whether there be one or two natures, one or two persons in the Man-God? whether his body be contained in the Eucharist, by transubstantiation or by impanation?* etc., where is the despotism which says *yes* or *no* on these questions? Would not the council which should decide them *impose a yoke on thought* no less than the Pope? Independence will always complain of the one as well as of the other. All appeals to councils are only inventions of the spirit of revolt, which ceases not to invoke the council against the Pope, with no other view than to laugh at the council also as soon as it shall have spoken as the Pope.[45]

Everything recalls us to the great truths already established. No human society can exist without government, nor government without sovereignty, nor sovereignty without infallibility; and this last privilege is so absolutely necessary that we are obliged to suppose infallibility even in temporal sovereignties (where it is not), on pain of beholding society dissolved. The Church requires nothing more than other sovereignties, although it possesses an immense superiority over them inasmuch as infallibility is on the one hand *humanly supposed,* and on the other *divinely promised.* This indispensable supremacy can only be exercised by one organ; to divide it is to destroy it. Even though these truths should be less incontestable than they are, it would always be indisputable that every dogmatical decision of the Holy Father ought to be law until the Church make opposition to it. When this phenomenon occurs, we shall see what must be done; meanwhile, there is no other course for us than to abide by the judgment of Rome. This necessity is invincible, because it arises from the nature of things and the very essence of sovereignty. . . .

## NOTES

1. See André Duval (1564–1638), *De Suprema Potestate Romani Pontificis in Ecclesiam Disputatio Quadripartita* (Paris, 1614), part 1, question 1.

2. Robert Bellarmine, S.J., "De Summo Pontifice" (chap. 3 of *De Controversiis Fidei: Tertia Controversia Generalis*), in *Opera Omnia* (Paris: Fèvre, 1870; Frankfurt am Main: Minerva, 1965), 2:467–68.

3. Johann Lorenz Mosheim (1694?–1755), *De Gallorum Appellationibus ad Concilium Unitatem Ecclesiae Spectabilem Tollentibus* (Helmstedt, 1726), in the work of Dr. Marchetti, 2:208. (The work referred to is presumably that mentioned below in n. 6.—ED.)

4. Claude Fleury (1640–1723), *Discours sur les libertés de l'église gallicane*, in *Nouveaux opuscules* (Paris, 1807, in 12mo.), 30.

5. Louis-François Cardinal de Bausset, *Histoire de Jacques-Bénigne Bossuet* (Versailles, 1814), vol. 2, *Pièces justificatives* for book 6.

6. The first appeal to a future council is that made by Thaddeus in the name of Frederick II, in 1245. There is said to be some doubt as to this appeal, because it was addressed *to the pope and a more general council*. It is sought to be shown that the first undoubted appeal is that of Duplessis, made June 13, 1303, but it is like to the former and evinces excessive embarrassment. It is made *to the council, and to the holy apostolic see, and to him and to those* before whom it can and ought to be best carried of right. See Natalis Alexander [Noël Alexandre, 1639–1724], *In Seculis XIII et XIV*, art. 5, sec. 11 (apparently in his *Historia Ecclesiastica* [Paris, 1699]—ED). In the eighty years which follow are found eight appeals, worded thus: *To the holy see, to the sacred college of cardinals, to the future pope, to the pope better informed, to the council, to the tribunal of God, to the most holy trinity, to Jesus Christ* in fine. See Giovanni Marchetti (1753–1829), *Critique de l'histoire ecclésiastique de Claude Fleury*, appendix, 257, 260. (A third edition, revised by the author, appeared in Venice in 1787, and there were also editions in 1803 and 1818; I am not able to ascertain which edition de Maistre had before him—ED.)

7. Gottfried Wilhelm Leibnitz, *New Essays on Human Understanding*, trans. and ed. Peter Remnant and Jonathan Bennett (New York and Cambridge: Cambridge Univ. Press, 1981), 519 (chap. 20).—ED.

8. Not that I pretend to liken everything in the government of the Church to that of Great Britain, where the states-general are permanent. I only adopt whatever in the comparison tends to support my argument.

9. Guiseppe Agostino Cardinal Orsi (1692–1761), *De Irreformabili Romani Pontificis in Definiendis Fidei Controversiis Judicio* (Rome, 1772, in 4to.), 3:183–84 (book 2, chap. 20).

10. Fleury, *Nouveaux opuscules*, 138.

11. First, at the time of the Constitutional Church and of the civic oath. The respectable prelates, who believed themselves bound to resist the pope at this latter epoch, believed that the question was *whether the pope was mistaken*, whilst the point really was to know *whether they were bound to obey, even in the case that he was wrong*. This would have much abridged the discussion.

12. Nicolas Sylvestre Bergier (1718–1790), "Conciles," no. 4, in *Dictionnaire de théologie*. But lower down, in no. 5, sec. 3, he classes among the marks of oecumenicity convocation by the sovereign pontiff, or his consent. (An augmented edition of this work was published at Liège in 1789–92.—ED.)

13. De Maistre refers to the regency in the latter part of the reign of George III.—ED.

14. De Maistre refers to the opening of the Council of Constance in 1414.—ED.

15. Letter 55, to Procopius. (See *Poèmes et lettres,* trans. Paul Gallay, ed. Edmond Devolder [Namur, 1963], 118.—ED.)

16. David Hume, *The History of England* (New York, 1850), 4:531 (n. F to p. 61).

17. I recommend this observation to the attention of all thinking men. Truth in combating error never grows angry. In the enormous press of our controversial writings it requires a microscope to discover any sallies of ill humour proceeding from human weakness. Such men as Bellarmine, Bossuet, etc., have been able to combat all their lifetime without permitting themselves, I say not an insult, but even the slightest personality [that is, personal remark]. Protestant doctors share this privilege, and deserve the same praise whenever they combat incredulity, but in this case it is the Christian who does battle with the deist, the materialist, the atheist, and consequently it is still truth combating error; but the moment they turn against the Roman Catholic Church they insult, for error is never calm in contending with truth. This twofold character is as visible as it is decisive. There are few demonstrations that speak so directly to conscience. (The ecumenical movement is far in the future; cf., earlier in this volume, Möhler's remarks on symbolics.—ED.)

18. "Infallibility," in *Perroniana,* cited by Cardinal Orsi in *De Romani Pontificis Auctoritate* (Rome, 1772, in 4to.), 100 (book 1, chap. 15, art. 3). (The book *Perroniana, sive Excerpta ex Ore Cardinalis Perronii* [Jacques Davy du Perron, 1556–1618], was a hoax, the real authors being Pierre Dupuy and Jacques Dupuy [The Hague, 1669].—ED.)

19. Louis Thomassin (1619–95), *Dissert. de conc. chalced.,* no. 14 [contained in *Dissertationum in Concilia Generalia et Particularia Tomus Singularis* (Lucca, 1728)?]; see also Orsi, *De Romani Pontificis Auctoritate,* 184 (book 2, chap. 20). (It would seem that the same book of Orsi is being cited under two different titles in nn. 9, 18, 19.—ED.)

20. By this word *freely* I mean that neither torments, nor persecution, nor violence in any shape shall have been able to deprive the sovereign pontiff of the liberty of mind which ought to preside over his decisions.

21. Louis-Mathias de Barral (1746–1816), *Défense des libertés de l'église gallicane et de l'assemblée du clergé de France, tenu en 1682* (Paris, 1817, in 4to.), 327–29. (The Gallican spirit remained strong under the Bourbon restoration.—ED.)

22. Heb. 9:16–17.

23. John 16:7; 15:26–27.

24. Pierre Nicole (1625–95), *Instruction théologique et morale sur les sacrements* (Paris, 1723), 1:87.

25. Luke 18:34.

26. Louis Bourdaloue (1632–1704), "Sermon pour la fête de la Pentecote," part 1, in *Oeuvres* (Paris: Lefèvre, 1834), 2:342.

27. Jacques-Bénigne Bossuet, *Defensio Declarationis Cleri Gallicani de Ecclesia Potestate,* part 3, chap. 34, in *Oeuvres complètes* (Paris: Vivès, 1885), 22:228–31.

28. Vol. 2, *Pièces justificatives* for book 4, p. 390. (De Maistre appears to refer to *Histoire de Jacques-Bénigne Bossuet;* see above, n. 5. On Bossuet's view of Liberius see Aimé-Georges Martimort, *Le Gallicanisme de Bossuet* [Paris, 1953], 656–57. François Ledieu was Bossuet's secretary for twenty years; concerning him, see Martimort, p. 746. The first edition of Ledieu's memoirs was

published in 1856. According to E. E. Reynolds [*Bossuet* (Garden City, N.Y.: Doubleday & Co., 1963), 279], the work of Cardinal de Bausset is still—or was still, in 1963—the only full-scale biography of Bossuet.—ED.)

29. See *Centuriae Ecclesiasticae Historiae per Aliquos Studiosos et Pios Viros in Urbe Magdeburgica* (Basel, 1562–74), cent. 4, chap. 10, p. 1184.

30. Some learned men have thought this opinion could be held. See [Anon.?] *Dissertation sur le Pape Libère, dans laquelle on fait voir qu'il n'est pas tombé* (Paris: Lemesle, 1726, in 12mo.); and Francisco Antonio Zaccaria, S.J. (1714–95), *Dissertatio de Commentitio Liberii Lapsi*, in *Thesaurus Theologicus* (Venice, 1762, in 4to.), 2:580ff. (The *Thesaurus* [1762–63] was a collective work, including material by Natalis Alexander and others.—ED.)

31. See the note of Mansi in the work cited, p. 568. (Presumably the reference is to n. 36 below.—ED.)

32. Orsi, 1:118 (book 3, chap. 26). (See above, n. 19. The Latin may be translated, "But unknown to the Greeks [i.e., the French], who marvel only at what is their own."—ED.)

33. Carlo Sardagna (1731–75), *Theologia Dogmatica-Polemica*, 2d ed. (Polotiae, 1810), 1:293 (controv. IX, in appendix on Honorius, no. 305).

34. Extract from the letter of Maximus to the priest Marinus; see Jacques Sirmond, S.J. (1559–1651), *Opera Varia* (Paris, 1696, in fol.), 3:481.

35. Quoted in Sirmond's *Opera Varia* 3:489. Great attention is necessary to read this letter, of which we possess only a Latin translation executed by a Greek who did not know Latin. Not only is the Latin phraseology extremely confused but the translator allows himself, moreover, the privilege of fabricating words for his convenience. . . .

36. Giovanni Domenico Mansi (1692–1769), ed., *Sacrorum conciliorum nova et amplissima collectio* (Florence, 1764, in fol.), 10:1186.

37. These are the very words of Sergius in his letter to Honorius; see Pietro Ballerini (1698–1769), *De Vi ac Ratione Primatus Summorum Pontificum &c.* (Verona, 1766, in 4to.), 305 (chap. 15, no. 35).

38. Ibid., 306. It would be superfluous to call attention to the Greek turn of these expressions, translated from a translation. The most precious Latin originals have perished. The Greeks wrote what they liked.

39. But the manner in which he expresses himself is remarkable. Bossuet agrees: "Honorii verba orthodoxa *maxime* videri" (*Defensio,* part 3, book 7, chap. 22, p. 53). Jamais homme dans l'univers ne fut aussi maître de sa plume. On croirait, au premier coup de l'oeil, pouvoir traduire en français: *L'expression d'Honorius semble très-orthodoxe.* Mais l'on se tromperait. Bossuet n'a dit *maxime orthodoxa videri.* Le *maxime* frappe sur *videri*, et non sur *orthodoxa.* Qu'on essaie de rendre cette finesse en français. Il faudrait pouvoir dire, *l'expression d'Honorius très-semble orthodoxe.* La vérité entraîne le grand homme qui *très-semble* lui résister un peu. (The pith of this note would be entirely lost in an English version.—TRANS.)

40. Mansi, *Sacrorum conciliorum* 16:27. See Natalis Alexander, *Dissertatio de Photiano schismate et VIII Syn. C. P.,* in *Thesaurus theologicus* (Venice, 1762, in 4to.), 2:657 (§13).

41. Chap. 15 continues with a discussion of understanding, and establishing the authenticity of, ancient documents.—ED.

42. "Let the idea of infallibility, and that of a certain person, come to be inseparably united in the minds of some men, and you will soon behold them

*swallowing* the dogma of the simultaneous presence of the same body in two different places, without other authority than that of the infallible person who commands them to believe *without examination*" (Locke, *On the Human Understanding*, book 2, chap. 33, no. 17). . . .

43. Council of Trent, session 24, on matrimony, canon 7.

44. Cf. Möhler's remarks above on the variations in papal power, bearing in mind that Möhler was concerned chiefly with the popes' religious authority.—ED.

45. "We believe that it is allowed to appeal from the pope to a future council, notwithstanding the bulls of Pius II and Julius II, who have forbidden it; but such appeals ought to be very rare, and only for the most weighty reasons" (Fleury, *Nouveaux opuscules,* 52). In the first place, here is a *we* of which the Catholic Church ought to make very little account; and besides, what is a *most weighty* occasion? what tribunal will decide upon it? and in the meantime, what will it be our duty to do or to believe? Councils ought to be established *as a regular ordinary tribunal above the pope,* in opposition to what Fleury himself says in the very same page. It is, indeed, a very strange thing to see Fleury refuted by Mosheim on a point of such importance (see above, n. 3), as we have beheld a Bossuet on the point of being led into the right way by the Centuriators of Magdeburg (see above, n. 28). To what lengths are not men carried by ambition to say *we*—that pronoun so portentous in theology! (I assume that in the sentence "Councils ought to be established . . . ," de Maistre is speaking ironically, that is, "If you want parliamentary governance of the church, you ought, on your principles, to want it all the time."—ED.)

# 9

# Our Lady of Lourdes

*Orestes Brownson*

It has been suggested that it is easier to count the churches Orestes Brownson did not join than those he did. Be that as it may, the record shows that Brownson, born in Stockbridge, Vermont, in 1803, was in turn a Presbyterian, a Universalist, a Unitarian, an evangelist of his own "Church of the Future," a member (with Emerson) of the Transcendentalist Club, and in 1844, a lay Roman Catholic. At least he was a Roman Catholic latest and longest, though he went through several phases in his view of the relation between religion and various social questions. His principal occupation was religious journalism, his chief production *Brownson's Quarterly Review*, which he edited from 1844 to 1864, and again from 1873 to 1875. In 1853 Newman invited him to join the (abortive) Catholic University of Ireland but later withdrew the invitation. Brownson died in Detroit in 1876, where his son Henry subsequently (1882–87) published his collected works in twenty volumes. Ten years after his death Brownson's remains were transferred to the crypt of the chapel of the University of Notre Dame. American Catholics have always honored him as the New England transcendentalist who really did see the light.

The essay given here is a review of *The Wonders of Lourdes*, "translated from the French of Mgr. de Ségur by Anna T. Sadlier (New York, 1875)," which review appeared in Brownson's *Journal* in the issue for July 1875. Lourdes is a town in southern France (Hautes-Pyrénées, twelve miles southwest of Tarbes) where in 1858 Bernadette Soubirous, a teen-ager (later a nun, later a canonized saint), allegedly witnessed eighteen apparitions of Mary the mother of Jesus. (These happenings included dialogue between Mary and Bernadette, and the uncovering of a spring that sometimes displays curative properties.) The site of the apparitions became a renowned place of pilgrimage, where as the *Westminster Dictionary of Church History* chastely reports, "several thousand seemingly miraculous cures have been recorded." Let it be noted that the cult of Our Lady of Lourdes, though a quite arresting instance of nineteenth- and twentieth-century folk piety, has been conducted at the shrine itself with great sobriety, and quite sophisticated Catholics have joined in it. Archbishop John J. Keane, the great friend and ally of Archbishop Ireland in many a go-around with Rome, and the founding rector of the Catholic University of America, in Washington, D.C., twice went to Lourdes seeking the cure of serious eye problems. (Unfortunately, his quest was only partially successful.) Let it also be noted, however, that the popes, while encouraging devotion to Mary at sites of alleged apparitions, have never attempted to pass judgment on the factuality of the apparition stories, it being standard Catholic practice in regard to postapostolic or "private" revelations merely to assess whether such supposed communications do or do not conform to Catholic teaching as a whole.

Brownson's essay, though by no means downplaying the Lourdes story, lays bare a far deeper meaning in the Lourdes cult. In the first place. Brownson reminds us that we cannot in principle exclude the miraculous and the supernatural. All exists by the power of divine omnipotence, and to know what God can do would require divine omniscience. In any case, as Scheeben would so splendidly argue, the true destiny of humankind has been supernatural all along: the realm of the supernatural is where human beings really dwell. In Brownson's words, "The natural order is not separated from the supernatural, but is, so to speak, immersed in it, forming only one complete whole with it." Brownson continues, affirming a kind of cosmic romanticism, "The saints and the angels . . . dwell in the bosom of God, . . . and he is everywhere present. . . . We are apt to forget that space and time are nothing in themselves." Space, for Brownson, is the externalization of divine creativity, time the successive or progressive dimension of that externalization. So if the holy ones appear to us, the apparitions are but slight further movements by those who are always there. As Jacques Maritain's friend Léon Bloy said—voicing a thought dear to generations of Catholic novelists—each of us is at the center of infinite and mysterious combinations. Science fiction? To some, perhaps—but Brownson and millions of Catholics with him believed it, and believe it still.

In the second place, Brownson sees in the cult of Mary, at Lourdes or elsewhere, due recognition of what is arguably the most Catholic characteristic of the Catholic: synergism, or the sense that human beings work with God in the process of human salvation, what Brownson in another happy phrase calls the "mediatorial character of the kingdom of God." Mary who believed, but who also gave human form to the Son of God, is the archetypal Christian, the Catholic model both of the individual and of the church as a whole. To be sure, even if Mary is the greatest of saints, and in that sense is divinized, she is never literally divine; rather, in honoring her and in seeking her powerful prayers Catholics honor God's plan for all humankind. Here we touch the deepest insight of Catholicism as a religious system, namely, its emphasis that God is a loving God, a God who joyously makes room for synergism. (Synergism is a kind of ever-present clue to this deeper truth.) Brownson's God does not need creatures, but as the medieval doctors said, being—God's being—conceptualized as good, is "diffusive of itself." So Brownson's God, "in his superabounding goodness," bestows on creatures the "honor and blessedness of sharing in his work . . . and meriting his approbation and reward."

Perhaps it is clearer now why, after extended, worldwide consultation of the bishops, Pius IX in 1854 defined the dogma of Mary's lifelong (and Christ-merited) sinlessness, or the immaculate conception. At one stroke he honored Mary and reasserted the transcendence over circumstance of that which Mary symbolizes, the synergistic church, and in it the divinely sustained role of the pope. What an extraordinary confluence of religious symbols! The bishops at Vatican I would be asked to define in theory what had already to some extent been exercised in fact: papal infallibility. The mysterious Lady at Lourdes had told Bernadette, "I am the Immaculate Conception." Many a pious Catholic would later observe with satisfaction, "Well, there you are: Pius IX got it right."

But the implications of the Lourdes story do not end even here. Catholic women's-rights advocates have wondered about an all-male hierarchy's determining of the place of Mary: the noblest daughter of Eve is forever enshrined as the recipient of being and grace from the male-conceptualized Father and Son. For the record, Scheeben thought that the Holy Spirit might well be conceptualized as female (see *The Mysteries of Christianity,* trans. Cyril Vollert, S.J. [St. Louis: B. Herder, 1946], 95–96, 181–89). Where the matter will end we cannot say, but in the nineteenth-century context Catholic Christians did at least acknowledge that the greatest of Christians is a woman.

There is to the Christian mind, or to the mind that believes in God,[1] the Creator of heaven and earth and all things therein, no a priori difficulty in believing any duly attested miracle, or presumption against it, for God, as Creator, must be distinct from his works, independent of, and supreme over them, their sovereign Lord and Proprietor. They, then, can interpose no obstacle to his working a miracle, if he chooses or judges it proper. To pretend, as some do, that God is tied up by the so-called laws of nature, or is bound in his free action by them, is to mistake entirely the relation of Creator and creature. God, if at all, is super-cosmic, and cosmic laws are dependent on him, and subject to his will. They are, therefore, incapable of binding him, or impeding his free action. Creation itself is a miracle, and our personal existence is a standing miracle, for we exist at any moment only by virtue of the continuous creative act of God. God, being free in all his acts *ad extra,* can perform any act he pleases, not intrinsically impossible, or that does not imply a contradiction.

The Christian order, though it supposes nature and completes it, is itself supernatural, and a manifestation of the supernatural power and action of the Creator. Miracles, which are the direct and immediate acts of the Creator, are in some sense in the Christian order. Man and the universe are perfected, or fulfil their destiny, only in the supernatural, that is, in the Christian, order. This order being supernatural and the expression of the supernatural providence of God, miracles have in them nothing anomalous, nothing illogical, or not concordant with it, and hence are as credible as any other class of facts. They serve the purpose or end of the Christian order, and therefore tend to perfect or fulfil the design of God in creation. Being supernatural as to their cause, they express the supernatural order; but being in the natural and even sensible order as to their effects, they are as provable, as facts, by ordinary testimony, as if they were natural facts as to their cause. They prove of themselves their supernatural origin and character.

Our Lord promised that miracles should always remain in the church and they always have remained. It is of faith that miracles continue with the faithful; and whoever has paid any attention to the subject is well aware that nothing is or can be better authenticated or more conclusively proved than the fact that miracles have never ceased in the Christian Church.[2] Yet we are slow in crediting any particular alleged miraculous fact. Every alleged miracle stands, so to speak, on its own bottom, and is

From *Works* (Detroit, 1884), 8:104–17.

to be received or rejected according to the direct proofs in the case. If we are asked to believe the reality of this or that alleged miracle, we must have proofs which conclusively establish it, and leave no room for a reasonable doubt. We find amongst good people, whose faith is lively and strong, hundreds of things passing as miracles, which, while we by no means deny them to be miraculous, we do not accept as miracles, because we do not find them to be proved as such. The Christian temper inclines neither to incredulity nor to credulity.

The alleged appearance to the shepherds of our Lady of La Salette we have never seen proved to our satisfaction, yet it may have been a real appearance; for we know no reason why our Lady should not appear to mortals, if such is the pleasure of her divine Son. That she has so appeared at different times cannot be doubted, unless we doubt all historical testimony. We know no reason why she should not so appear, if such appearance enters the divine economy, for nothing hides her or any of the saints from us but a mimetic veil, which nothing hinders our Lord from withdrawing as he did in his own case and that of Moses and Elias, in his transfiguration on the mount in presence of Peter, James, and John.

The Blessed Virgin, the saints, and the angels are not separated from us by space, or hidden from our view by physical distance, as with our false views of space and time we are apt to imagine. The state of the blessed is changed, but not their place, for they dwell in the bosom of God, are made one with him: and he is everywhere present, dwells not in space, but in immensity, and inhabits not time, but eternity. We are apt to forget that space and time are nothing in themselves. Ideal space has been well defined to be the power of God to externize his act, or to create *ad extra*; and ideal time, his power to externize his act successively or progressively. We should never think of God as physically remote from us; or of the Blessed Virgin, the saints, and the angels, as separated from us by distance, unless it be, unhappily, by a moral distance. In all other respects, they are present with us, as is our Lord himself. If we see them not, it is not because they are distant, but because the mimetic veil is before our eyes. Yet we must remember, as Dr. Watts sings, heretic as he was, that

> Angels, and living saints and dead
> But one communion make.

We all profess in the creed to believe in "the communion of saints." They who are separated do not commune. We think of God as here, and of him and the saints and angels as ever present with us. Our God is nigh unto every one of us, if haply we seek after him. The natural order is not separated from the supernatural, but is, so to speak, immersed in it, and forming only one complete whole with it. The natural proceeds from the supernatural, lives in it, is sustained by it, and completed only by returning to it, and becoming one with it, as the Creator and the creature become one in the incarnate Word.

There is nothing incredible in the supposition that, from time to time, the blessed show themselves to the living in furtherance of the gracious designs of God to individuals or nations. We do not reject modern spiritism, falsely called *Spiritualism,* because we doubt that the souls of the departed are still really living, or because we hold it impossible for them to appear by divine permission to persons in the flesh; but because we have no proofs that the spirits that appear are the spirits of the dead, and not evil spirits, fallen angels, who personate them. The literal facts alleged by the spiritists, or facts of the same order, we do not dispute, though there is connected with them much fraud, and no little jugglery. The proofs of miracles are not more conclusive than are the proofs of the satanic prodigies, that is, as simple facts; and in either case they are sufficient, if we accept historical testimony at all. What we deny in regard to spiritism is, not the facts as alleged, but the induction from them, that the spirits are really the spirits of the departed.

Nothing is more certain than that Satan imitates, as far as in his power, genuine miracles, and seeks to deceive by his prodigies. We must never assume that the superhuman, or what surpasses the power of man, is supernatural and divine. Satan, though a creature, has a superhuman power, and is able to work, not miracles, but prodigies, which imitate miracles, and which the unwary may mistake for them. But Satan, being a creature, has no creative, and, therefore, no supernatural power. He can operate only within the cosmos, and can never exhibit any real supercosmic power; whereas every real miracle is a manifestation of supercosmic, and, therefore, of creative power. There are certain diseases that Satan can heal—diseases which demand for their cure only the vitality of the diseased; but those which demand more, or a *vis* the system has lost, he cannot heal. Hence he cannot raise the dead, or restore a dead person to life, for that demands a creative power, as much as the production of an existence from nothing. In all cases where there is an exhibition of creative power, we must see the finger of God, not a satanic prodigy; a real miracle, not a lying wonder.

Many of the alleged cures related of persons visiting holy shrines do not surpass the power of Satan; and corresponding cures are recorded as having been effected in the temples of Aesculapius and other heathen shrines. They cannot, therefore, be taken as conclusive proofs, in themselves, of the divine interposition. They are such proofs only when effected under such circumstances as exclude the supposition of their being effected by satanic infuence.

We reject the induction of the spiritists, that the spirits they profess communicate with them, because their communications are not truthful, and they prove themselves lying spirits. They teach what we know to be false, and hurtful to the soul. They deviate from the apostolic doctrine, and lead to separation from the apostolic communion. Everything about them indicates that they are lying spirits, are trying to pass for what they are not, and are practising a gross imposition upon their dupes. In fact, spiritism is only a revived demonism, or the renewed effort of Satan to get himself worshipped as God. Saints and angels, when they appear, come as the messengers of the living God, show themselves to be engaged in his work, in promoting his worship, and leading souls to union with him: the supernatural end for which they are created. Their mission is to enlighten, to elevate, and perfect, or to help man to fulfil his destiny. They calm, they soothe, and they give peace to the troubled soul. They exert a directly contrary influence from that exerted by the lying spirits followed by the spiritists.

Though, as we have said, we are slow to believe this or that alleged miracle, we cannot help believing this of our Lady of Lourdes. The evidence in the case seems to us absolutely conclusive that she actually appeared to the poor girl Bernadette, and that she honors the shrine consecrated to her. We cannot doubt the perfect truthfulness of M. Henri Laserre's book, or that of Mgr. de Ségur, so beautifully translated by our young friend, Anna T. Sadlier, now before us; and which we have read with a renewal of our love and devotion to our blessed Mother, conceived without original stain, who is all fair, without spot or blemish. We cannot doubt the reality of the appearance, or the fact of the many marvellous cures related—cures often instantaneous and complete; and which are undeniably beyond the greatest medical science or skill, and also beyond any known natural therapeutic agent. We cannot deny them as facts, and are utterly unable to account for them without the supposition of a supernatural intervention.

Yet, as we have already intimated, not all these alleged cures are to us conclusive proofs of miraculous intervention. We had a near relative who for six months had been rendered utterly helpless by inflammatory rheumatism. She was unable to move herself in bed, or even to raise her hand. A Mormon elder asked her husband for a night's lodging, which was refused on the ground of the illness of his wife. The elder replied that that was no reason for refusing his request, for, if he would let him see his wife, he doubted not he could cure her. He was led to her bedside, where he kneeled down and made a short prayer; at the end of the prayer she was completedly cured—as well as ever she was in her life. We do not believe that God wrought a miracle at the prayer of the Mormon elder, nor are we willing to suppose an intervention of the Evil One. There are moral or non-physical causes whose operation we but imperfectly understand, and which produce effects on the physical system that seem to us little less than miraculous. Till we know the extent of these causes, or the moral *vis medicatrix* of nature, we cannot take these sudden and inexplicable cures as conclusive proofs of a supernatural intervention.

But there is a class of facts and cures that are to us conclusive. None but God can work a real miracle, because in every real miracle there is an exhibition of creative power, or the production of something from nothing, or where nothing was before: and God alone has creative power. Now, in the wonders related of Lourdes, we find facts which seem to us to involve the act of creation. When Moses smote the rock and the water gushed forth it was a miracle, for there was no water in the rock; and it was as purely an act of creation to cause the water to flow from the rock where previously there was none, as if there had been no water in existence. So to us, the opening, by Bernadette of the fountain which continues to flow, in the rocks of Massabielle, or Massavielle, seems a miracle of the same kind, and impresses us much more forcibly than most of the cures related.

Taking, as we do, the fact as related, there is all that is necessary to constitute a real miracle, and, therefore, full proof of the actual apparition of the Blessed Virgin, the *Immaculate Conception*, as she named herself, to the poor child. The continuousness of the fountain, and its copious flow of water still, is a standing proof of the reality of the miracle, or what seems to us an unmistakable miracle, though we are forbidden, if we mistake not, to pronounce it positively a miracle, till declared to be such by the judgment of the Holy See, which, so far as we are aware, has not been rendered in this case, though we are told that it has sanctioned the devotion to our Lady of Lourdes.

When our Lord raised the widow's son to life, or restored Lazarus to his weeping sisters, after he had lain four days in the grave, it was a miracle, and as much an act of creative power as the original production of life itself, for it was the production of life where there was no life. No power but that which can give life can restore the dead to life. Now, we find a case in these wonders of Lourdes that is marvellously the restoration of the dead to life. Supposing the facts in the case of the little Justin Bouhohorts to be as narrated,[3] this is virtually a restoration of the dead to life, and therefore a real miracle.

It must not, however, be supposed because we single out this case, that we recognize no supernatural intervention in the numerous other cures related, and, no doubt, truthfully related, but that this and the opening of the fountain are to our mind decisive. The fountain was supernaturally opened through the instrumentality of the Blessed Virgin; and as the water of the fountain possesses in itself no medicinal properties, the cures effected by its use must be ascribed to the same instrumentality, and therefore be held to be effected by supernatural intervention. They are to be considered as parts of one whole, or integral elements of one and the same supernatural manifestation or event. The fact of the reality of the apparition of our Lady to the child Bernadette, and the opening of the miraculous fountain under her auspices, removes the whole question from the order of facts adduced by the spiritists, places it in the order of divine and supernatural facts, and justifies the faith of those who use the water, or resort to it in their physical maladies. There is no superstition in resorting to it, for, springing from a supernatural cause, and, therefore, an omnipotent cause, the effects sought are from an adequate, not an inadequate, cause.

Why our Lady should seek a special shrine at Massabielle, or why she should favor one spot, or grant her favors at one spot more than another, or why certain pictures and images of her should receive greater marks of her favor than others, we do not know, and by no means attempt to explain. Perhaps, in reality, she does not confine her favors to them, but is equally ready to show favor to her clients anywhere, wherever they invoke her patronage with equal love and devotion to her divine Son, with equal concentration of faith and fervor. These sacred shrines, perhaps, serve chiefly to fix the attention, to intensify faith, kindle fervor, inflame devotion, and prepare the heart for the reception of supernatural favors.

We wish Mgr. de Ségur had judged it advisable to hint, at least, to his readers that the Blessed Virgin, however powerful as the mother of God with her divine Son, has of herself no miracle-working power. She is, though exalted above all below the ineffable Trinity, still a creature, and as destitute of creative power as any other creature. Not she, but our Lord, wrought the miracle of Cana of Galilee. She has power with her divine Son to obtain from him a miracle by her prayers, for she can ask nothing not in strict accordance with his will, or not inspired by him. Moreover, the relation of mother and son subsists, and ever must subsist, between them. But though she may, by her prayers, obtain favors, and even miracles, for us, it is God who works the miracles and bestows the favors. Every Catholic knows this, and Mgr. de Ségur has probably neglected to state it, because assured that it is a point on which no Catholic can fall into a mistake. But, as it is a point on which non-

Catholics suppose or pretend that we do fall into a mistake, and a most grievous mistake, too, that of giving to the creature the glory that belongs to the Creator, we think the author should have expressly guarded, not against our falling into the mistake, but against others supposing it possible for us to do so.

We do not, we may remark by the way, ask the Blessed Virgin to pray for us because we cannot pray directly to God for ourselves, or because we feel that she loves us better than does her Son, and is more ready to favor us, or, as far as depends on her, to hear and grant our petitions.[4] He is as near us as she is, and no less tender and merciful to us, since he loved us well enough to die for us on the cross. It is not because we can more easily approach them, because they have a greater, a tenderer, sympathy with us, or are more ready to help us, that we pray to Mary and the saints, and ask them to intercede with our Lord for us, or to bear for us our petitions to the throne of grace, for our Lord is perfect man as well as perfect God, and God himself is the fountain of all love, mercy, tenderness, and compassion to which we appeal in them. The reason is, the mediatorial character of the kingdom of God, as we have so often done our best to explain. The principle of the order founded by the incarnation of the Word is the deification of the creature, to make the creature one with the Creator, so that the creature may participate in the divine life, which is love, and in the divine blessedness, the eternal and infinite blessedness of the holy and ineffable Trinity, the one ever-living God. Creation itself has no other purpose or end; and the incarnation of the Word, and the whole Christian order, are designed by the divine economy simply as the means to this end, which is indeed realized or consummated in Christ the Lord, at once perfect God and perfect man, indissolubly united in one divine person.

The design of the Christian order is, through regeneration by the Holy Ghost, to unite every individual man to Christ, and to make all believers one with one another, and one with him, as he and the Father are one. All who are thus regenerated and united, are united to God, made one with him, live in his life, and participate in his infinite, eternal, and ineffable bliss or blessedness. Herein we see the superabounding goodness of the Creator. God is infinite, perfect, in all respects sufficient for himself, and therefore is and must be infinitely happy in himself. He could, therefore, have been moved to create only by his infinite goodness, in order to diffuse his own life, which is the light of men, love, and happiness, *ad extra,* as say the schoolmen. Creation is a manifestation of the love and goodness of the Creator; and as the purpose of God in creating was to give to creatures a share in his own infinite life and blessedness, he must be infinitely more loving, tender, compassionate than any creature, however exalted or glorified. It is from him that the glorified saints and angels draw whatever of love, tenderness, or compassion we appeal to in them.

But the goodness of God does not stop here.[5] He not only permits the glorified creature to participate in his own life, love, and happiness, or beatitude, but he also permits his creatures to be co-workers with him in his work, and to participate in the glory of its accomplishment. He makes, in some sense, the creature a medium of effecting its perfection; that is to say, he uses created agents and ministers in effecting his purpose, and in gaining the end for which he creates them, and thus enables them to gain the signal honor of sharing in the glory of the Creator's and the Redeemer's work, that is, in the glory of the kingdom of God. Hence it is that the true followers of Christ enter into glory with him, or participate in the glory of his kingdom; which they could not do, if they had done nothing towards founding and advancing it. It is not that he needs them for himself; but because, in his superabounding goodness, he would bestow on them the honor and blessedness of sharing in his work, and of being, so to speak, employed in his service, and meriting his approbation and reward. It is his love to his blessed mother that makes her the channel of his grace; his love to his saints, his friends, that leads him to employ them in his service, that gives them the high honor of being intercessors for us. This is not only a high honor to them, but a great joy and blessedness, for they are filled with his love, and, like him, overflow with love and goodness to all his creatures. The *cultus sanctorum* flows naturally, so to speak, from the principle of the Incarnation, the deification of man or the creature; and in it we not only honor the saints, but show forth our faith in the superabounding love and goodness of God, which permits them to work with him for the fulfilment of his design in creation, and to participate in its glory.

The fact, that God does employ the saints and angels as agents and ministers in carrying on his mediatorial work, is indisputable. If any thing is clear and certain from the Holy Scriptures, it is this. It is implied in the very fact of the Incarnation, which makes the creature one with the Creator. It is only the universal extension of the sacerdotal principle which underlies all religion, and cannot be denied without denying the very principle of the Christian order. Most Protestants would seem to reject it; but most Protestants, whatever they intend, really reject the Incarnation, and cannot be held to be believers in Christ the Mediator of God and men. Yet Protestants, when they send, as most of them do, a note to their minister asking him to pray, and the congregation to pray, for a sick or dying friend, or for a family, or an individual in great affliction, recognize, whether they know it or not, the sacerdotal principle—the very principle on which rests the invocation of saints. When a Protestant, writing to a friend, concludes with the request, pray for me, he does the same.

Indeed, the whole system of creation is a system of means to ends, and, in fact, could not be otherwise, since its prototype is in the ever-blessed Trinity, which it copies, or faintly expresses *ad extra,* as the three divine persons express the divine essence *ad intra.* In the Holy Trinity, the Holy Triad, we have principle, medium, and end. The Father is principle, the Son is medium, and the Holy Ghost is end—the consummator. As the *idea exemplaris,* or type of creation, is in the eternal essence of God, it must, through the free act of the Creator, express in a faint degree, *ad extra,* the Triad which expresses that eternal essence *ad intra,* or which, if we may so speak, constitutes that essence. Then everything in creation must express, in some degree, principle, medium, and end; and the end is unattainable without the medium or means, as we see all through even the natural world. We are promised seed-time and harvest, but we must cultivate the soil, and sow the seed, or no crop will be obtained. In no case is the end gained but by the proper use of the divinely appointed means.

Now, in the Christian world, founded by the Incarnation, the appointed means to the end is prayer. God grants his favors only to those who ask for them, perhaps because only those who ask have the internal disposition to profit by them. We can, of course, ask him directly for whatever we think we have need of; but when we ask also the saints to ask him for us, we act in accordance with his love for them, and unite with him in honoring them, by engaging them in working out his designs. We also give them the opportunity of serving him in us, and showing forth their love both for him and us. We honor God in honoring with our love and confidence those whom he delights to love and honor; and, in invoking their prayers, we use the appointed means of gaining the blessings we crave, and we enlist, in aid of our own prayers, the prayers of those whose sanctity renders them dear to our Lord and God.

If we have made ourselves understood, we have shown why it is we, in the old sense of the word, worship Mary and the saints, and why it is that God himself, in fulfiling his design in creation, especially the "new creation" or teleological order, uses the ministry of saints and angels, and chiefly, as their queen, his blessed mother, from whose chaste womb he took his human nature. The pretence of Protestants, that, in honoring Mary or the saints, we are robbing God of the honor that is his due, and putting the creature in the place of the Creator, shows, if not absolute want of faith in Christ an absolute ignorance of the Christian system, or the theological principles revealed in the Holy Scriptures. It overlooks the mediatorial character of the Gospel, and the fact that all in the Gospel grows out of the incarnation of the Word, who was with God in the beginning, and is God. The Protestant objection denies that creation has its prototype in the divine essence, and expresses it *ad extra*. It denies that the divine economy of creation, so to speak, was, by a free creation, to communicate, *ad extra,* his own life and blessedness, as they are realized *ad intra* in the generation of the Son and the procession of the Holy Ghost. It denies that the end or fulfilment of creation, in the supernatural order, is the deification of man, or the union in one of the creature and the Creator. It denies that God, to honor and bless the creature, admits him to a share in the fulfilment of his design, and, therefore, to a participation in his own divine life and blessedness. The Protestant either knows nothing, or believes nothing, of the Christian system. He fails to perceive that it is in accordance with the divine intention, that of diffusing his own divine life and blessedness, to employ the agency or ministry of saints and angels, who are honored and blessed in being so employed. In invoking that ministry in the *cultus sanctorum,* we only love and honor those whom he loves and honors, and give them, as it were, the opportunity to work with God, and participate in the glory of his kingdom.

The Blessed Virgin is the queen of saints and angels, and, as the mother of God, is exalted above every other creature, and is only below the ineffable Trinity. Whom, then, should God more delight to honor, or more delight to have honored by us? She is the spouse of the Holy Ghost, she is his mother; and nothing seems more in accordance with his love and goodness, and the very design, the very idea, if we may use the term, of his mediatorial kingdom, as revealed in the Gospel, than that he should do her the honor of making her his chief agent in his work of love and mercy—the medium through which he dispenses his favors to mortals. There is joy in heaven among the angels of God, we are told, over one sinner that repenteth. The saints and angels, filled with the spirit of God, and in perfect concord with the divine purpose in creation, and with the Word in becoming incarnate, are full of love to all the creatures of God, and join with him into whose glory they have entered, in seeking the blessedness of those he has redeemed by his own precious blood. They take an interest in the salvation of souls, the repentance of sinners, and the growth and perfection of the regenerated, and consequently love their mission, and perform their task with their own good-will, and with joy and alacrity. This love, this interest, this good-will, must be greatest in their queen, the ever-blessed Virgin. As she is exalted above every other creature, only God himself can surpass her in his love for his creatures.

We understand, then, why Mary holds so distinguished a place in Christian worship, and performs so important a mission in furtherance of the mediatorial work of her divine Son. Her love is greater, for she is full of grace, greater than that of any other creature. She is more intimately connected with the Holy Trinity, and holds a relation to God which is held and can be held by no other creature. In some sense, as the mother of the incarnate Word, she is the medium through which is effected the deification of man—the end of the supernatural order. She cannot be separated from that end. We can easily understand, then, why God should assign her a part assigned to no other creature. Her love is only less than his, and her heart is always in perfect unison with the sacred heart of her Son, and mother and Son are strictly united and inseparable. Equally easy is it now to understand why the Christian heart overflows with love and gratitude to Mary; why Christians recur to her with so much confidence in the efficacy of her prayers, the success of her intercession; and why Catholics offer her the highest worship below the supreme worship offered in the holy sacrifice, but never offered except to God alone.

We have not given, or attempted to give, a complete discussion of the great subject we have opened, or rather which the appearance of our Lady of Lourdes has opened. We have only aimed to throw out a few thoughts and suggestions, which, if followed up, will show that such appearances, that miracles, that the love and veneration of the blessed Mary, and the *cultus sanctorum,* as practised by Catholics, are not anomalous, but grow out of the very principles of the supernatural or Christian order, the mediatorial kingdom of God's dear Son; and are in strict accordance with the design or purpose of the ever-blessed Trinity, and tend to further and realize it as appropriate means to an end. The doubts or difficulties of non-Catholics on this subject originate in their rejection or ignorance of the Incarnation, and their never having considered the Christian system as a whole. The heathen retained the primitive revelation, but only in a broken and piecemeal state. Protestants do the same with the Christian revelation as preserved and taught by the church. They have lost the perception of the relation of the several parts to the whole, and fail to recognize their interdependence and strict logical consistency one with another, and with the whole, of which they are integral parts. They—in fact, the best of them—understand nothing of Christian theology. Even Catholics, while their faith and worship is right, do not always grasp the profound and eternal principles which underlie the dogmas they hold, and the worship in which they join.

We repeat, all in Christianity proceeds from, depends on, and clusters around, the Incarnation, in which the design of God in creation, the deification of the creature, is consummated. The devotion to Mary, the veneration of the saints, grow out of the Incarnation, as does the church herself, and tend to keep alive faith in that crowning act of the Creator. We need, then, place no restraint on our love to Mary, or our love and veneration for the glorified saints of God. In loving, venerating, and invoking them, we are acting in accordance with the design of the Holy Trinity.

## NOTES

1. Brownson apparently uses *believes* here in a loose, conversational sense, as people often do. Strictly speaking, the educated Catholic holds that there is a God on the basis of philosophical inference. Still, Vatican I did concede, following Thomas Aquinas, that those without the time or talent to philosophize might very properly take on faith truths that are in fact accessible to reason; see below, selection 11, sec. 1786—ED.

2. The chief, and unceasing, miracle is the church itself; see below, selection 11, sec. 1794—ED.

3. Gaston de Ségur, *The Wonders of Lourdes*, trans. Anna T. Sadlier (New York, 1875), 81–86. (The other book referred to is Henri Laserre's *Notre-Dame de Lourdes* [Paris, 1868]—ED.)

4. Cf. Vatican II, *Dogmatic Constitution on the Church*, secs. 66–69—ED.

5. In the Möhler-Scheeben tradition of the single-volume, hefty-handbook presentation, we now have *Catholicism*, by Richard McBrien of the University of Notre Dame (Minneapolis: Winston Press, 1981). Synergism turns up as expected at the conclusion of the volume, albeit engagingly paraphrased as *sacramentality, mediation, and communion*. Thus, McBrien states that "no theological principle or focus is more characteristic of Catholicism or more central to its identity than the principle of *sacramentality*. . . . The visible, the tangible, the finite, the historical—all these are actual or potential carriers of God's presence. . . . A corollary of the principle of sacramentality is the principle of *mediation*. [This means that] a sacrament . . . causes what it signifies. . . . Finally, Catholicism affirms the principle of *communion:* that our way to God and God's way to us is . . . a communal way" (pp. 1180–81). In a passage that echoes Brownson's words McBrien continues, "Catholics have always emphasized the place of the Church as both the *sacrament* of Christ, *mediating* salvation through the sacraments, ministries, and other institutional elements and forms, and as the *Communion of Saints*, the preview or foretaste, as it were, of the perfect communion to which the whole of humankind is destined in the final Kingdom of God." For a shorter presentation of these themes, see Lawrence Cunningham's excellent textbook, *The Catholic Experience* (New York: Crossroad, 1986). By far the best *Protestant* discussion of them is Langdon Gilkey's *Catholicism Confronts Modernity: A Protestant View* (New York: Seabury Press, 1975).— ED.

# 10

# An Address
# in Opposition to
# Papal Infallibility

### Archbishop Peter Richard Kenrick

The reader may wonder why two American archbishops, Peter Kenrick and John Ireland, have been included in this collection of theologians. To answer a question with a question, Is there any reason why a bishop cannot be a theologian? Perhaps twentieth-century bishops suffer unjustly by comparison, for in the nineteenth century the population was smaller, administrative tasks less complex, and travel and communication much slower. Whatever the reason, individual literary bishops of the nineteenth century were altogether willing to submit their thoughts to the discipline that book publication requires, and to the protracted examination by others that it entails. The great names, the two just mentioned, as well as John England, Peter Kenrick's elder brother Francis, Martin Spalding and his nephew John Lancaster Spalding, and Cardinal Gibbons, can be *read*. For these men, writing on religion and social questions was an important part of the role of bishop as teacher. We must also recognize that their organizational prominence made them spokesmen for American Catholicism in a way not equaled by academic or lay theologians of the time, with the possible exception of Brownson.

One may examine, at the article devoted to Peter Kenrick in the *New Catholic Encyclopedia*, a reproduced engraved portrait: it shows a youngish, benign, happy-looking bishop. Now turn to the engraving in John J. O'Shea's 1904 study, *The Two Kenricks* (which portrait is reprinted in A. B. Hasler's *How the Pope Became Infallible*): here you will find a troubled-looking old man. Between these two portraits lies a perplexing story.

Peter Richard Kenrick was born in Dublin in 1806. After preparing for the priesthood at Maynooth he accepted his brother Francis's invitation to Philadelphia, where his brother was then bishop. (Francis later became archbishop of Baltimore.) In Philadelphia, Peter held several major diocesan appointments, including the vicar-generalship, and also published several books, including one on the validity of Anglican orders. In 1841 he was made coadjutor bishop of St. Louis (i.e., assistant with the right of succession), in 1843 bishop, and in 1847, when the level of the see was raised, archbishop. He presided over a huge expansion of St. Louis, as city and diocese. When the time came he played an extremely interesting part at the First Vatican Council, being one of the minority of bishops who held that defining papal infallibility was highly inopportune—a needless challenge to governmental authority or the sensibilities of the educated public—or theologically erroneous.

To judge from the speech given here, Kenrick would seem to have been in the opposition on both counts. Kenrick wrote this speech but was not given the opportunity actually to deliver it, so he had it printed up (in Latin, of course)—and printed in Naples, which was outside the secular jurisdiction of the pope. Kenrick, with, it seems, some sixty other bishops, then left the council. By the time he arrived back in St. Louis the dogma had been defined and his assessment of events was eagerly awaited. In an address given upon his arrival he stated his acceptance of the dogma, saying, "The motive of my submission is simply and singly the authority of the Catholic Church. . . . Simply and singly on that authority I yield obedience and full and unreserved submission to the definition concerning the character of which there can be no doubt as emanating from the Council, and subsequently accepted by the greater part even of those who were in the minority on that occasion." In other words, the Catholic world, led by the episcopate, largely *had* accepted the dogma, and on his own principles Kenrick could not then refuse acceptance.

Kenrick himself now received a coadjutor, Patrick J. Ryan. In the article on Kenrick in the *New Catholic Encyclopedia*, John J. Leibrecht writes, "For reasons not altogether clear from extant sources, Ryan performed all episcopal functions in the archdiocese. . . . Meanwhile Kenrick . . . went into what was equivalent to retirement." But twelve years later, when in 1884 Ryan was made archbishop of Philadelphia, Kenrick resumed the active leadership of his archdiocese. (In 1893 the archdiocese received an administrator and in 1895 another coadjutor, no doubt because of Kenrick's great age.) Kenrick died in St. Louis in 1896. Leibrecht continues, assessing Kenrick's character and actions, "A judgment . . . is difficult to make and is complicated by the fact that much of Kenrick's correspondence has been lost; at times what is available is not conclusive, and may even be contradictory."

Kenrick's arguments in the speech given here are quite straightforward: neither Scripture nor the traditional practice of the church, especially in the English-speaking world, will support raising the notion of papal infallibility to the level of dogma. The reader will understand that a speech such as Kenrick's can only refer to scriptural and historical problems, not investigate them in detail; in fact, at the end of the speech Kenrick pleads that discussion be deferred until more investigation can be carried out.

It has been noted that before the emancipation of Irish Catholicism a significant number of the Irish clergy were French-trained, and doubtless picked up Gallican ideas of church polity from their teachers. This would help explain the mixed feelings of a number of Irish-American bishops when confronted with the necessity of voting on infallibility. On the other hand, some historians of Vatican I incline to the view that the American bishops in the minority opposed the definition more out of a sense that it was inopportune than from the conviction that it would be a doctrinal error. But such a pacific evaluation surely cannot apply to the pages that here follow.

MOST EMINENT PRESIDENTS; MOST EMINENT AND RIGHT REVEREND FATHERS:

The Most Reverend the Archbishop of Dublin,[1] in his speech from this platform, has said some things by which my honor is solely wounded. It was in vain that I begged permission of His Eminence the president to reply at once, at the close of his speech, or at least at the close of that day's general congregation. Therefore it is that, contrary to my previous purpose, I take the floor to-day to speak on the schema in general that is offered for our adoption; for I had taken for granted that everything pertinent to the subject would be more fully and forcibly said by others than I could say it. I entreat your pardon, most eminent and right reverend fathers, if I seem to weary you with a longer speech than I am wont to make. I only ask that you will grant me that liberty which (as Bossuet says) well becomes a bishop addressing bishops in Council, and having respect rather to the future than to the present—in the confidence that I will not wander from the scope of the schema, nor say anything which can give just offence to any one—least of all to the most eminent the archbishop of Dublin, to whom I acknowledge my very great obligations, to whom I have always looked up with respect, for these thirty years and more, and whom I hope and trust I shall continue to respect to my latest breath. With which preliminary words I come to the subject. . . .

1. I said [in my previous statement] that all the other apostles were designated by the same name of *foundation* which was applied to Peter; which seemed to him to impair the proof of the primacy of the Roman pontiff deduced by theologians from that word. The blame of this, to be sure, should not be laid on me, but on St. Paul and St. John. But that this was the furthest possible from my intention is proved by the words which I used, as follows: "The words of Christ, *Thou art Peter,* etc.,[2] certainly show that a privilege was conferred by Christ on Peter above the other apostles, so that he should be the primary foundation of the church; which the church has always acknowledged, by conceding to him the primacy both of honor and of jurisdiction." I denied, indeed, that by virtue of that word *foundation* the gift of infallibility was conferred upon Peter above the other apostles; since no mortal ever thought of claiming

From *Concio . . . in Concilio Vaticano Habenda at Non Habita* (Naples, 1870); photographic reprint in *Sacrorum Conciliorum Nova et Amplissima Collectio,* ed. J. D. Mansi et al., vol. 52 (Graz: Akademische Drück- u. Verlagsinstitut, 1961), 453–81. The translation is from *Speech . . . Prepared for Speaking but Not Spoken in the Vatican Council,* in *An Inside View of the Vatican Council,* ed. L. W. Bacon (New York: American Tract Society, n.d.), 95–166.

this privilege for the other apostles and their successors from the mere fact that they too had been honored with the same title of *foundation.* I then showed it to be a false inference that the stability of the church was derived from the strength of the foundation, since Christ had signified that he would provide for each of these in some other way; that is, in the words, addressed to all the apostles, Peter with the rest, "Lo, I am with you always, even to the end of the world."[3] It is hardly fair to say that by this line of reasoning I had either assailed or meant to assail the common arguments for the primacy derived from Christ's words, "Thou art Peter," etc. But I shall show, by-and-by, that the most reverend archbishop himself, by the line of reasoning which he adopts in speaking of the other apostles, and their successors the bishops, not only impeaches this argument for the primacy, but utterly destroys it. . . . The most reverend archbishop calls me to account for what I said concerning the word *faith* in Luke 22:32;[4] that that word was never used by our Lord to mean the system of doctrines (in which sense alone it can afford any ground for an argument in support of papal infallibility) and not more than once or twice to mean that act of supernatural virtue with which we believe in God making revelation of himself. I asserted that by that word (as may be gathered from the discourses of the Lord) was almost always meant *trust* or *confidence.* I showed that, in the passage cited, the word had this sense and no other, holding to the rule that the customary meaning of a word is to be retained, unless the context requires a different one—and in the present case the context favors the usual meaning. The most reverend archbishop said—perhaps not measuring the force of his words—that this assertion of mine smacked of the Calvinistic heresy; in proof of which he adduced John 11:27, the words in which Martha professes her belief in Christ, which we are compelled to understand concerning faith in the Catholic sense of the word.

But the excellent bishop did not notice that in my [previous statement] the question was not how to define the true nature of gracious faith as a "theological virtue," but only as to the force of the word *faith* in its customary usage in the discourses of Christ. Out of twenty-nine passages in the gospels in which this word occurs (which may be easily seen by consulting the concordance of the Latin Bible) there are only two—Matt. 23:23,[5] and Luke 18:8[6]—in which the word *faith* can possibly be taken in the sense of the theological virtue of faith. All the other passages give the meaning of *trust* or *confidence,* or *faith of miracles.* In Luke 22:32, which is the passage in question, this seemed, and still seems, to me to be proved to be the true meaning, both by the customary usage of the word and by the context. And the most reverend archbishop has brought forward nothing in disproof of this statement.

2. I now proceed to show that the archbishop of Dublin, by his course of reasoning, has emptied the words, "Thou art Peter," etc., of all the force which theologians have commonly thought them to contain. He denies that the bishops, as successors of the apostles, have that universal jurisdiction in the church which the apostles received from Christ; which indeed is true if we speak of the individual bishops outside of a general council, but is not true if understood of the body of bishops, whether in council or not. If the power given to the apostles, of preaching the gospel in the whole earth, is to be restricted to themselves, although it was given by Christ to continue "to the end of the world," it is impossible to prove that the privilege, whatever it may have been, conferred upon Peter in the words, "Thou art Peter," etc., descended to his successors, the popes. The argument, therefore, derived from these words in Matthew 16:18, 19, falls to the ground from the fact that the words of Christ in the 28th chapter, verses 18, 20, of the same evangelist, receive a less literal interpretation; for the question, in both passages, is on the power belonging to the sacred ministry, and not on any sign of their divine mission, such as working miracles, speaking with tongues, or some other such gift. Either, then, the whole of this power of the ministry passed to their successors, or none of it; and surely this last cannot be said. I have not, therefore, infringed upon the proof of the primacy from the words, "Thou art Peter," etc.; on the contrary, I have explicitly acknowledged that proof. But the archbishop, by denying that the universal jurisdiction granted to the apostles has descended to their successors, has done that very thing himself.

I thus prove that all the ministerial privileges granted, whether to Peter or to the rest of the apostles, have descended to their successors; making no inquiry at present what was the nature of these privileges, or by what sort of evidence they are proved to have been conferred.

Whatever belongs to the sacred ministry in the church of Christ by the institution of its Founder, must belong to it always; otherwise the church would not be such as he instituted it. Therefore those privileges granted to the apostles which concern the function committed to them, are the same now as when they were first conferred. This is equally true of those which were given to all, including Peter, and of that which was granted to Peter individually. On the day of the resurrection, Christ gave commission to all the apostles, always including Peter, in the words, "As the Father hath sent me, even so send I you";[7] and afterwards, when he was about to ascend into heaven, in the words, "Go, teach all nations," etc.[8] But these words, addressed to all, concern them, not as if spoken to them individually, but to them, as constituting a sort of college of apostles; which is clear from the fact that Thomas, thought absent when

Christ appeared to the apostles on the resurrection day, received (as all admit) the same commission and the same power of remitting sins as the rest. This apostolic college is constituted a *moral person,* which is to continue to the end of the world; whose identity is no more diminished by the perpetual succession of its members, than our personal identity is affected by the constant change of the elements that compose our bodies. Thus it stands ever before men a living eye-and-ear witness of those things which Christ did and taught; so that it may always use the words of John, "What we have seen and heard declare we unto you."[9] Whatever power, then, it had at its origin it has now: divine commission ("as the Father hath sent me") and universal jurisdiction ("Go, teach all nations") must be acknowledged to belong now to the apostolic college. And if this be denied or even weakened, the whole Christian religion falls to the ground.

From which I infer that the successors of Peter and the rest of the apostles, constituting the apostolic college, have every power now which they had when the college was first instituted by Christ. The individual bishops, taken singly, receive, by the ordinances of the college itself, only an ordinary local jurisdiction in their several dioceses. But the bishops, taken universally, have a universal jurisdiction; not in that sense exactly that the universal jurisdiction is made up by the sum of the local jurisdictions; but that the bishops universally, whether dispersed and separated from each other, or united in a general council, constitute the apostolic college. Hence the words of Cyprian, "There is one episcopate, an undivided part of which is held by every bishop,"[10] receive light and a ready explanation. If the most reverend archbishop of Dublin is not prepared to admit all this, at least he must confess that the several bishops united in General Council have universal jurisdiction. . . . But the school of theologians to which I adhere considers all episcopal jurisdiction to be held by the bishops by immediate derivation from Christ, but that the ordinary local restriction of it had no other origin than the ordinance of the church, in due subordination, nevertheless, to the Roman pontiff as the head alike of the apostolic college and of the universal church. I say, therefore, that the words of Christ spoken to the apostles lose none of their force to the successors of the apostles; and in this I lay down nothing which tends to weaken the argument which theologians are accustomed to deduce from Matt. 16:18, in proof of the primacy of the Roman pontiff. This argument I now proceed to examine.

3. I beg you so far to indulge me, most eminent and reverend fathers, as to give me your calm attention while I say things which doubtless will not be agreeable to many of you. I am not about to set forth anything

heretical or savoring of heresy (as the remarks of the archbishop of Dublin may have led you to fear), nor anything opposed to the principles of the faith, nor anything but what, so far as my slender abilities permit, I shall endeavor to sustain with solid argument. One thing I wish to give warning of: I speak for myself only, not for others; and I do not know but that what I am about to say may give dissatisfaction even to those with whom I take sides in the discussion of this question. If, in the course of my speech, I happen to speak too sharply on any point, remember and imitate the example of those leaders who were persuaded to patience by the famous saying, "Strike, but hear." I shall pay due respect to Their Eminences the moderators of the congregation; but I will not be put down by commotions.

The primacy of the Roman pontiff, both in honor and in jurisdiction, in the universal church, I acknowledge. Primacy, I say, not *lordship.* But that the primacy is vested in him as the succesor of Peter, all the tradition of the church testifies, from the beginning. And on the sole strength of this testimony I accept it as an absolutely certain principle and dogma of faith. But that it can be proved from the words of Holy Scripture, by any one who would be faithful to the rule of interpretation prescribed to us in that profession of faith which we have uttered at the opening of this Council, and so often on other occasions, I deny. . . .

The rule of Biblical interpretation imposed upon us is this: that the Scriptures are not to be interpreted contrary to the unanimous consent of the fathers. It is doubtful whether any instance of that unanimous consent is to be found. But this failing, the rule seems to lay down for us the law of following, in their interpretation of Scripture, the major number of the fathers, that might seem to approach unanimity.[11] Accepting this rule, we are compelled to abandon the usual modern exposition of the words, "On this rock will I build my church." . . .

Either no argument at all, or one of the slenderest probability, is to be derived from the words, "On this rock will I build my church," in support of the primacy. Unless it is certain that by *the rock* is to be understood the apostle Peter in his own person, and not in his capacity as the chief apostle speaking for them all, the word supplies no argument whatever, I do not say in proof of papal infallibility, but even in support of the *primacy* of the bishop of Rome. If we are bound to follow the majority of the fathers in this thing, then we are bound to hold for certain that by *the rock* should be understood the faith professed by Peter, not Peter professing the faith. . . .

It seems to me, after some thought upon the diversity of interpretations, that they may all be resolved into one, by taking into consideration the distinction between the foundation on which a house is built, and the foundation which is laid in the building of it. The builder of a house, especially if it is to be a great house, and to stand a long time, begins with digging down until he comes, as the phrase goes, "to the live rock"; and on this he lays the foundations, that is, the first course of the building. If we admit this double meaning of foundation, all the diversity of interpretations disappears; and many passages of Scripture, which at first might seem difficult to reconcile with each other, receive great light. The natural and primary foundation, so to speak, of the church, is Christ, whether we consider his person, or faith in his divine nature. The architectural foundation, that laid by Christ, is the twelve apostles, among whom Peter is eminent by virtue of the primacy. In this way we reconcile those passages of the fathers, which understand him on this occasion (as in the instance related in John 6, after the discourse of Christ in the synagogue of Capernaum) to have answered in the name of all the apostles, to a question addressed to them all in common; and in behalf of all to have received the reward of confession.[12]

In this explanation of the word *rock,* the primacy of Peter is guarded, as the primary ministerial foundation; and the fitness of the words of Paul and John is guarded, when they call all the apostles by the common title of the foundation; and the truth of the expression used with such emphasis by Paul, is guarded: "Other foundation can no man lay than that is laid, even Christ Jesus," 1 Cor. 3:2; and the adversaries of the faith are disarmed of the weapon which they have so effectively wielded against us, when they say that the Catholics believe the church to be built, not on Christ, but on a mortal man; and (a matter of no small account in the present discussion) the underpinning is taken out from the argument which the advocates of the infallibility of the pope by himself alone are wont to derive from a figurative expression of doubtful meaning—riding the metaphor to death—to prove that he received from Christ an authority not only supreme, but absolute. But whatever may be thought of this opinion of mine, it is obviously impossible to deduce from the words, "Thou art Peter," etc., a peremptory argument in proof even of the primacy.[13]

As to the other words of Christ to Peter, "Feed my lambs," and "Feed my sheep," it may be said that by that threefold commission Christ showed that Peter had not fallen, by his threefold denial, from the privilege by which he had been called to partnership with the apostles; and that this was continued to him in reward for the greater love he bore towards his Lord above the rest. As Augustine says, "The triple confession answers to the triple denial, so that his tongue might give no less service to his love than to his fear, and so that impending death should not seem to have drawn out more from him than present life."[14] The argument adduced by Bellarmine, that the words "my sheep" and "my lambs" include the whole flock of Christ, and therefore show that the power conferred by them extends to all, proves nothing at all. For they are no more general, nor do they any more express the idea of government, than those which Paul addressed to the elders at Miletus collectively: "Take heed to yourselves and to *all the flock*[15] over which the Holy Ghost hath made you bishops, to rule ($\pi o\iota\mu\alpha\acute{\iota}\nu\epsilon\iota\nu$)[16] the church of God which he hath purchased with his own blood."[17] . . .

The words, "I have prayed for thee," etc., do not have the sense commonly attributed to them, but are to be understood of Peter's fall at the time of the passion, and his subsequent conversion. . . . So the words were understood through the first six centuries of the church. The fact that they afterwards received another meaning seems to have grown out of the common usage of ecclesiastical writers, of interpreting the words of Scripture in an accommodated sense instead of the literal sense. . . .

From the fact that the Saviour, after speaking to all the apostles and informing them that Satan had sought them, to sift them as wheat, turns then to Peter with the words, "I have prayed for *thee*"—which must necessarily be understood of him alone, to the exclusion of the rest, since, after being converted, he was to strengthen the others—it is inferred that some peculiar thing was promised to Peter in these words. In fact this is true, but something considerably different from the extraordinary gift commonly understood to have been promised to Peter in them.

Can it be said that Christ prayed for Peter alone, but that he provided no safeguard for the others, about to encounter so great a peril? How then does it come to pass that the others stood firm, unsustained by any extraordinary assistance, while Peter, for whom singly Christ prayed, so grievously fell? The true reason why the Saviour addressed the words to him alone seems to be this: He prayed indeed for all, as we cannot but take for granted. But to Peter he intimated, by directing his words exclusively to him (just as, after Peter's answer in verse 33, he proceeded to say it more plainly in verse 34) that he would deny his Master. Thus he warned him of his approaching fall, and foretold his conversion, and that by him the rest were to be confirmed. The Lord's words so understood give a clear sense. Beside the repeated warning given to Peter, they contain the prophecy of his conversion; so that when Peter, having come to himself, clearly recollected it, it left no doubt in his mind of the pardon which he should obtain, and thus saved him, it may be, from despair in view of his most grievous sin.

Besides, the successive words addressed by Christ to Peter cannot be understood of his successors without involving an extraordinary absurdity. The words, "When thou art converted," certainly refer to Peter's conversion. If the foregoing words, "I have prayed for thee," and the following, "Strengthen thy brethren," prove that the Divine assistance and the office have descended to his successors, it does not appear why the intermediate words, "when thou art converted," should not belong to them too, and in some sense be understood of them.

In saying these things, I am not greatly affected by the accusation lately levied against me, without mentioning my name, by the right reverend bishop of Elphin[18] (treading in the footsteps of the archbishop of Dublin) when he gave vent to his grief of heart that there should be any among the bishops who would not scruple to take the texts of Holy Scripture and other citations in proof of papal infallibility, and interpret them in the sense accepted by heretics! "If these things," said that excellent man, "are done in the green tree, what shall be done in the dry?" My answer to him and to others is this: Following the example of Irenæus, Tertullian, Augustine, and Vincent of Lerins, I believe that the proofs of the Catholic faith are to be sought rather in tradition than in the interpretation of the Scriptures.[19] "Interpretation of Scripture," says Tertullian, "is better adapted to befog the truth than to demonstrate it." Of the testimonies derived from tradition, there are some which, I think, will have to be given up; as in the phrase of Irenæus on the superior authority which he is commonly thought to have claimed for the Roman church. But I have taken the responsibility of this concession, alleging substantial reasons, which ought to be met, not with abuse, but with other reasons.

It has seemed to me that nice refinements upon figures of speech had better be laid aside: but I have appealed to the faith of the Councils and the fathers, which shows that such subtleties do not agree with the ancient doctrine and practice of the church universal, but rather contradict them. This method of reasoning is better fitted for bringing back Protestants into the bosom of the church than arguments the very principles of which they reject, and which, although they may seem impregnable to less intelligent Catholics, nevertheless are proved by the experience of the last three centuries to be ill adapted for putting an end to controversies.

I close this part of my speech with a brief summing up of the argument:

We have in the Holy Scriptures perfectly clear testimonies of a commission given to all the apostles, and of the divine assistance promised to all. These passages are clear, and admit no variation of meaning. We have not even one single passage of Scripture, the meaning of which is undisputed, in which anything of the kind is promised to Peter separately from the rest. And yet the authors of the schema want us to assert that to the Roman pontiff as Peter's successor is given that power which cannot be proved by any clear evidence of holy Scripture to have been given to Peter himself except just so far as he received it in common with the other apostles; and which being claimed for him separately from the rest, it would follow that the divine assistance promised to them was to be communicated only through him, although it is clear from the passages cited that it was promised to him only in the same manner and in the same terms as to all the others. I admit indeed, that a great privilege was granted to Peter above the rest; but I am led to this conviction by the testimony, not of the Scriptures, but of all Christian antiquity. By the help of this testimony it appears that he is infallible; but on this condition, that he should use the counsel of his brethren, and should be aided by the judgment of those who are his partners in this supreme function, and should speak in their name, of whom he is head and mouth. And yet there is no one but sees how far this privilege falls short of the desires of those who, not without abuse of their opponents that stand in the old paths of the church, desire that the papal power, great by its divine origin, and since that, in the course of ages, enormously augmented, should be the *sole* power in the church.[20]

4. At the opening of his speech, the archbishop of Dublin spoke in terms of the highest praise of an English work by my late brother archbishop of Baltimore, on "The Primacy of the Apostolic See"; for which I made due acknowledgments. But in the course of his speech it appeared to me that his commemoration of the dead was a reproach to the living; for he related how that thirty years ago, more or less, he learned by the reading of it, that the doings of the Sixth Council in the condemnation of Honorius were nowise opposed to the notion of papal infallibility. The most reverend the present archbishop of Baltimore afterwards made honorable mention of him, and quoted somewhat from his dogmatic theology, from which it might appear that there was no difference between the opinion which he himself so stoutly defends, and that which, in my letter to him, I asserted to have been my brother's opinion. I have a few things to say of each of these bishops.

I might prefer a serious complaint against the archbishop of Baltimore for having presented in a garbled and mutilated form, from this rostrum, the passage which has lately so often been brought before the public. My brother's complete sentence is as follows:

"On the other hand, that way of speaking is not to be approved, according to which the pope is declared to be infallible *of himself alone;* for scarcely any Catholic theologian is known to have claimed for him as a private teacher the privilege of inerrancy. Neither as pope is he alone, since to him teaching, the college of bishops gives its adhesion, which, it is plain, has always happened."

Thus far the archbishop of Baltimore quotes. The words immediately following on these he thinks best to omit, although, as will at once be manifest, they are absolutely necessary to the full expression of the writer's meaning:

"But no orthodox writer would deny that pontifical definitions accepted by the college of bishops, whether in council or in their sees, either by subscribing decrees, or by offering no objection to them, have full force and infallible authority."

These words leave no doubt of the mind of the writer. Hereafter they should not be omitted when the previous sentence is quoted, lest a false impression of his sentiments be conveyed.

It is clear that this is no chance utterance of his opinion, from what he says in that English work of his from the reading of which his eminence the archbishop of Dublin testified that he had derived such great profit. I read from the work itself belonging to the library of the English college in this city. I give a closely literal Latin version, lest I weaken the force of it by being ambitious of elegance:

"The personal fallibility [of the pope] in his private capacity, writing or speaking, is freely conceded by the most ardent advocates of papal prerogatives, but his official infallibility *ex cathedrâ* is strongly affirmed by many: while some, as the French Assembly of 1682, contend that his judgment may admit of amendment, as long as it is not sustained by the assent and adhesion of the great body of bishops. Practically there is no room for difficulty, since all solemn judgments hitherto pronounced by the pontiff have received the assent of his colleagues; and in the contingency of a new definition it should be presumed by the faithful at large that it is correct, as long as the body of bishops do not remonstrate or oppose it."[21]

5. Before proceeding to other points, I feel bound to say that I do not agree in all respects with my brother's opinion, which, I am aware, is the common opinion of theologians. The assent of the church dispersed, as the phrase is, I consider to have a negative rather than a positive authority. The church, whether dispersed or assembled in Council, can not assent to any error that *contradicts* revealed truth; otherwise, the gates of hell might be said to have prevailed against it. Nevertheless it has the divine assistance, in *those things alone* which were taught by Christ to the apostles, all which things—that is, all revealed truth—"all things whatsoever I have told you"—the Holy Spirit brought to their recollection by illuminating their minds with his own divine light (for this is the end to which he is given) rather than by revealing new things.

In order that the apostles and their successors may bear testimony of these things as ear-witnesses, it is necessary that they should be unable to approve, even by silence, of any opinion contradictory to them.

But when the question is on a new definition of faith, I consider that a Council which truly represents the church universal is of necessity required. For it is there alone that inquiry can be made, in case any doubt should arise. In certain matters only, and in these only under favorable circumstances, may silence be taken for assent; but not in all matters, especially when dissent might turn out to be either useless or perilous. Take the present controversy, for example. If the pope had thought fit to define himself as infallible in the sense of the schema, there would have been no opportunity given for the great investigation which we have seen instituted, now that the Council is convened and the bishops assembled, affording light and courage to each other. Very few of those who have stood out so stoutly against the new definition, in the most difficult circumstances, would have ventured to resist the pope, or, if they had had the courage for that, would have known where to lay their hands on weapons fit and effective for the protection of their rights, so gravely imperilled.

A signal instance in proof that the silence of the church is not, at least in all cases, to be taken for consent, is supplied by the history of the opinion concerning the power of the Roman pontiff against realms not subject to his government. For four centuries after the bull *Unam Sanctam* this opinion prevailed. I am not aware that any document is extant which shows that there was any remonstrance against it except on the part of persons who suffered some damage from it; and these must be considered as having demurred not so much to the power as to the exercise of it to their injury. From the fulmination of the bull of Boniface VIII, down to the beginning of the seventeenth century—for four whole centuries—this definition of the papal power seems to have been in force, and was said even by the most learned theologians of the seventeenth century to be matter of faith. I once used to think that the language of the bull *Unam Sanctam* was capable of being reconciled with the view I then held of papal infallibility. But I do not now think so. It used to seem to me a special act of divine providence which had kept the pope from declaring all mankind to be subject to him in temporals, by reason of sin; but on more mature reflection I saw that this explanation was a mere subterfuge, utterly unworthy of an honest man. Words derive their meaning from the intent of the speaker and the acceptation of the hearers. No man can deny that the purpose of Boniface in that bull was to claim for himself temporal power, and to propound this opinion to the faithful, to be held under pain of damnation. No man can deny that the words of the bull were received in this sense by all then living. If it was withstood by the subjects of Philip the Fair, these were extremely few in number compared to the whole of Christendom, for it was only a little part of modern France that was under his sceptre, and these few may be considered as having opposed rather the exercise of the power than its divine right. The church, then, through all that period seems to have approved by its assent the bull *Unam Sanctam,* hardly a single bishop having objected to it.

But at the present time the opinion so solemnly enunciated in that bull is repudiated by all, not excepting even the most ardent advocates of papal infallibility. I summon certainly a most unimpeachable witness in this case, namely, his grace the most reverend Martin John Spalding, archbishop of Baltimore, who, in a work (of which I shall have more particular occasion to speak hereafter) printed at Baltimore in 1866, after three other editions of the same had been exhausted and this fourth edition had been issued to meet the demand of the faithful, speaks as follows:

"But the papacy invested itself with temporal power; and in the middle ages it claimed the right to depose princes, and to absolve their subjects from the oath of allegiance. Be it so; what then? Was this accession of temporal power ever viewed as an essential prerogative of the papacy? Or was it not considered merely as an accidental append-age, the creature of peculiar circumstances? Are there any examples of such alleged usurpations during the first ten centuries of its history? Has this power been exercised, or even claimed, by the Roman pontiffs for the last three centuries? If these two facts are undoubted—as they certainly are—then how maintain that a belief in the papacy involves a recognition of its temporal power? The latter was never, certainly, a *doctrine* of the church. If it was, where is the proof?—where the church definition that made it a doctrine? Five leading Catholic universities (Sorbonne, Louvain, Douay, Alcala, and Salamanca) when officially called on by Mr. Pitt, prime minister of Great Britain (1789), solemnly and unanimously disclaimed this opinion and maintained the contrary. Did the Catholic church, did the popes, ever rebuke them for the disclaimer? Do not Catholics all over the world now almost unanimously disclaim it? and are they the less Catholic for this? I fearlessly assert—and I do so advisedly—that there are very few Catholics at the present day who do not reject this opinion; that there are still fewer who maintain it; and that it is not defended, at least publicly, even in Rome itself."[22]

The tacit assent of the bishops, therefore, for no less than four centuries, did not have the effect to constitute the opinion of the power of the popes in temporals into a doctrine of the Catholic faith, which is obvious of itself, since otherwise the rejection of it now would be equivalent to defection from the unity of the Catholic church.

In this opinion two things are to be distinguished: the power itself, and the reason of the power. The power itself had its ground in circumstances; and for the most part it tended to the public good. The reason of the power was not, as the popes asserted, divine authority, divinely granted to them as holding the primacy in the church; but it originated in circumstances, by the consent of Christendom. It was recognized by public law, and was, so far, legitimate. It was vested in the popes, not because as popes they had received it from Christ, but because there was no one else who could exercise it at that time, when the need for it arose. In ascribing it to the ordinance of God, the popes were laboring under something of human infirmity—a fact with which it would be unjust to reproach them. That it has now fallen into desuetude is admitted by all. Few persons think of it as a thing possible to be revived; although this may not be impossible, if the pope is to be held infallible, and if we may put confidence in the words of the most reverend archbishop of Westminster, in a speech delivered by him at London some years ago, before his promotion to the episcopate.

This distinguished man asserted in that speech—if I remember correctly what I read in the newspapers, and I certainly am not mistaken as to the substance of it—that the pope, as Christ's vicegerent, ought to be a king; and that the fact of his having been for centuries without secular dominion was no argument against this assertion, for he had always possessed the right to it. If this is true (which I vehemently deny), it follows that the pope possesses not only the petty domain of his Roman territory, but a sort of universal right over the whole world. Since Christ is king of kings, the pope, who as his representative ought to be a king (according to the archbishop of Westminster),[23] ought to represent him throughout the whole realm of Christ himself: that is, throughout the entire world. We know what a happy talent for drawing inferences, even out of figures of speech, is shown by the advocates of papal authority. What if they have for a premise so pregnant a principle as this of the archbishop of Westminster? It can be no more of an objection to this right that for a number of centuries it was never claimed, than that for many centuries from the beginning it was not possessed, and even that no one dreamed of its belonging to the pope. I refer to this not to excite prejudice against this eminent man, but in order to show him that the consequence which necessarily follows from a principle evidently erroneous, the falsity of which I shall try to prove in the course of this speech—a consequence which he himself would reject—ought to make him cautious not to know more than it is worth while to know about papal infallibility.

For these reasons I am compelled to differ from what is at least a common way of speaking, when the question arises about defining some new dogma of the Catholic faith. It is my opinion that this can not be done without a Council truly representing the church universal.

I now return to the subject, with which, after all, what I have said is by no means disconnected.

6. There is no great difference, if perchance there is any, between my brother's opinion and that expressed by the most reverend Martin John Spalding, archbishop of Baltimore, in his History of the Reformation; from the fifth edition of which, revised by the author and published at Baltimore in 1866, I quote the following, which I translate into Latin with the same fidelity as I did my brother's language. I premise that it had first appeared twenty-six years before, and that it was originally written in reply to the History of the Reformation by D'Aubigné. This book is to be found in the hands of almost all the Catholics in the United States, not only on account of the amount of information which it contains and the familiar style in which it is written, but also on account of the high esteem in which the author is held among us, as the occupant of the primatial see, and as a man of wide celebrity for learning and genius. This fifth edition appeared in the same year in which he drew up, in the name of the Council of Baltimore, a letter to the pope, from which both he and others would have it inferred that the bishops of the United States favor the designs of the infallibilists. It is contained in the library of the American College in this city, having been presented by the author, with his name in it in his own handwriting, in 1867, when he was at Rome; on which occasion he, with the other bishops, signed a letter to the pope, surely with no intention of settling or enunciating a doctrine, but only of manifesting their own veneration and affection towards the pope. The archbishop of Baltimore's words are as follows:

"In what, in fact, consists the difference between the authoritative teaching of the first body of Christ's ministers, the apostles, and that body of pastors who by divine commission succeeded them in the office of preaching, teaching, and baptizing, and who in the discharge of these sacred duties were promised the divine assistance all days, even to the consummation of the world? And if the latter was opposed to rational liberty, why was not the former? Besides, we learn, for the first time, that the Roman Chancery decided on articles of faith. We had always thought that this was *the exclusive province of General Councils,* and when they were not in session, of the Roman pontiffs *with the consent or acquiescence of the body of bishops dispersed over the world.* We had also in our simplicity believed that even these did not always decide on controverted points, but only in cases in which the teaching of revelation was clear and explicit; and that in other matters they wisely allowed a reasonable latitude of opinion. But D'Aubigué has taught us better! He would have us to believe that Roman Catholics are bound hand and foot, body and soul, and that they are not allowed even to reflect."[24]

It remains to say a few words of my brother's views about the case of Honorius. It is no wonder that, educated at the College of Urban, and being full of zeal for the Holy See, he should have judged him very mildly. For the case was not of any such importance before the rise of the present controversy, and therefore had not been so thoroughly cleared up as it now is. I take this opportunity to say a word of the bishop of Rottenburg's[25] opinion expressed in his profoundly learned History of Councils. The archbishop of Dublin, who has perhaps acquired his information from the French translation instead of from the work itself, says that there will be some difficulty in reconciling this opinion with that which the bishop of Rottenburg now advocates. A year ago I read the original work, and it was from that that I first learned—what my own examination has since confirmed—that the letters of Honorius to Sergius do contain some things which cannot be reconciled with sound doctrine.

7. It was with great delight that I listened to the recent speech of the archbishop of Westminster in this assembly. I was at a loss which most to admire, the eloquence of the man, or his fiery zeal in moving, or rather commanding us to enact the new definition. The lucid arrangement of topics, the absolute felicity of diction, the singular grace of elocution, and the supreme authority and candor of mind which were resplendent in his speech, almost extorted from me the exclamation, "Talis cum sis, utinam noster esses!"[26] And yet, while I listened, I could not help thinking of what used to be said of the English settlers in Ireland—that they were more Irish than the Irishmen. The most reverend archbishop is certainly more Catholic than any Catholic I ever knew before. He has no doubt himself of the infallibility—personal, separate, and absolute— of the pope, and he is not willing to allow other people to have any. He declares it to be a doctrine of faith, and he does not so much demand as he does predict, that the Vatican Council shall define it as such; something perhaps in the style of those prophets who go to work to bring about the fulfillment of their own predictions. As for myself—whom the experience of well nigh sixty years, since I first began to study the rudiments of the faith, may perhaps have made as well informed upon this subject as one who has been numbered with the church for some twenty years—I boldly declare that that opinion, as it lies in the schema

is not a doctrine of faith, and that it cannot become such by any definition whatsoever, even by the definition of a Council. We are the keepers of the faith committed to us, not its masters. We are teachers of the faithful intrusted to our charge, in just so far as we are witnesses. The great confusion of ideas which prevails throughout this controversy seems to me to arise from an inaccurate notion of certain terms, and from the neglect of the distinction, which should never be lost sight of, between theology as a science, and the revealed truths of which it treats, as an object of our faith. Let me briefly explain my meaning.

All truths divinely revealed are to be believed with divine faith, which are propounded as such to the faithful by the church, whether in councils or through its ordinary government. Among these truths some are explicitly revealed, others implicitly. These last are to be restricted to those truths only which are necessarily connected with truths explicitly revealed, so that one who should deny the former would be held to have denied the latter also. Thus the church in its acts of definition is always a *witness*, and formulates a judgment only by witnessing. It condemns errors which openly *contradict* doctrines explicitly revealed, and besides these, errors opposed to corollaries *necessarily* deduced from such doctrines. It is the general opinion of theologians that it may happen that arguments of doubtful value shall be adduced in proof of truths of faith, even in General Councils; although in declaring the faith itself, the Councils cannot err. The reason is, that in *declaring* the faith—an act of which all bishops, learned and unlearned alike, are capable—the church acts as witness: in *proving* the faith, whether from reason or from Scripture, she sustains the part not so much of a witness as of a theologian.

It is within the limits above enunciated that that faith divinely revealed is contained, concerning which the church as witness is capable of pronouncing a formal judgment, and of anathematizing gainsayers as heretics. Among these truths explicitly or implicitly revealed, those which have been defined by a solemn judgment of the church are said to belong to the Catholic faith, in distinction from those which, although revealed, and necessary to be believed, have not been enunciated or defined by decree of Council. But this distinction is merely scholastic, and implies no difference at all between the two kinds of truth, so far as respects the obligation of believing them.

Theology as a science is to be carefully distinguished from faith or the body of *credenda*. It sets forth the truths of faith in systematic order, and proves them, in its way of proving, either positively or scholastically, and deduces sundry conclusions from truths explicitly or implicitly revealed, which, for distinction's sake, are called theological conclusions. These conclusions, not being immediately and necessarily connected with revealed truths, so that the denial of them would be deemed a denial of those truths themselves, cannot be elevated to the rank of truths of faith, or propounded as such to the faithful at cost of their everlasting salvation. Propositions contradictory of them may be condemned as erroneous, but not as heretical.

In the Vatican Council, this distinction does not seem to have been observed. The result—a thing unknown hitherto in Councils—has been that the bishops are divided among diverse opinions, disputing, certainly not about doctrines of faith of which they are witnesses and custodians, but about opinions of the schools. The Council-chamber has been turned into a theological arena, the partisans of opposite opinions, not only on this question of the infallibility of the pope, but on other subjects, exchanging blows back and forth with the hot temper which is more common in theologians than in bishops, and is not becoming to either; for all acknowledge the Roman pontiff, united with the body of bishops, to be infallible. Here we have a doctrine of faith. But not all acknowledge him to be infallible by himself alone; neither do all know what is meant by that formula; for different parties offer different interpretations of it. Here we have the opinions or views of the schools, about which (as is fair enough) there are all sorts of mutual contradictions.

It may be objected that by this line of argument I assail the definition of the immaculate conception of the blessed Virgin by the bull *Ineffabilis Deus*;[27] since this opinion was for centuries freely denied by many, and was afterwards erected into an article of faith by the bull aforesaid, with the consent and applause of the body of bishops, as appears from their acts and writings, many of them having been present at the pontifical definition. Speaking for myself alone, I give the following frank reply, which perhaps will meet the approval neither of my friends nor of others. . . . I admit that the blessed Virgin Mary through the singular favor of God, and in view of the merits of her Son Jesus Christ, was kept in her conception from all guilt of Adam's sin. I do not deny that this sentiment belongs to the deposit of faith; nevertheless, I have never been able to discover it therein, so far as that deposit is set forth in the Scriptures and the writings of the fathers; neither have I ever found the man who could show it to me there. The assent of "the Church Dispersed" (as it is called) proves that the definition to which that assent is given is not in contradiction to any revealed truth; since, as I have already remarked, the church, whether in council or dispersed, can tolerate nothing which contradicts the faith. The pious opinion was always cherished among the faithful—an affection which the church encouraged, and by the institution of the Feast of the Conception, almost sanctioned. But it never delivered it as a doctrine of faith, and popes have strictly forbidden that the opposite opinion should be branded with the mark of heresy by its opponents. If any one should deny that it is a doctrine of faith, I do not see what answer could be made to him; for he would reply that the church could not so long have tolerated an error contrary to truth divinely revealed, without seeming either ignorant of what the deposit of faith contained or tolerant of manifest error.

8. I now proceed to show that the opinion of the infallibility of the pope in the sense of the schema, whether true or false, is not a doctrine of faith, and cannot be propounded as such to the faithful, even by the definition of a Council.

Definitions of faith are not incitements to devotion, much less are they the triumphal exaltation of the opinions of schools of theology, according as one or another of these gets the upper hand. They are authoritative expositions of the doctrines of faith, generally designed to guard against the subterfuges of innovators, and they never impose upon believers a new faith.

This being settled, I say that the infallibility of the pope is not a doctrine of faith.

[a] It is not contained in the symbols of the faith; it is not presented as an article of faith in the catechisms; and it is not found as such in any document of public worship. Therefore the church has not hitherto taught it as a thing to be believed of faith; as, if it were a doctrine of faith, it ought to have delivered and taught it.

[b] Not only has not the church taught it in any public instrument, but it has suffered it to be impugned, not everywhere, but, with the possible exception of Italy, almost everywhere in the world, and that for a long time. This is proved by a witness above all impeachment—the approbation of Innocent XI twice conferred upon Bossuet's Exposition of the Faith, a work in which not only no mention of this doctrine occurs, but in which the notion is plainly referred to in the remarks upon matters in dispute among theologians, on which opinion is free.

To speak only of the English-speaking nations, it may be observed that in no one of their symbolical or catechetical works is this opinion found set down among truths of faith.

The whole supply of books treating of faith and piety, down to the beginning of the present century, and later, has been imported into Ireland and the United States from England. In many of them the opposite opinion is given. In none of them is the opinion itself found as a matter of faith. A year ago, indeed, in England and the United States,

there came out sundry books—two or three of them to my knowledge—
intended to prepare men's minds to receive the opinion as belonging to
the faith. As for that one which was published in the United States, and
afterwards translated into French and German,[28] written by a pious and
extremely zealous but ignorant man, I may say that it abounded in such
grave blunders, at least in the first edition in English, as to excite more
laughter than indignation in others beside me, holding different opinions
on the pending question. When I was solicited by the author to give
some sort of commendation to the little book, which is measurably
damaging to the bishops, I did not wish to trouble the good man with a
debate, and so, in an unguarded moment, I promised him the charity of
silence.

It was known, indeed, among us that the school of theologians
commonly called by us *Ultramontanes,* upheld the opinion of papal
infallibility in a sense more favorable to papal privileges than the other
theologians. And that opinion, after the translation into English of the
distinguished Joseph De Maistre's work on The Pope, widely prevailed
among clergy and laity, and still prevails, yet not as a doctrine of faith,
but as a free opinion which seems to have in its favor important reasons
and weighty names. But to return to the point.

For almost two centuries there has been in use among English-
speaking Catholics a little book entitled *Roman-catholic Principles in
Reference to God and the King.* So widely circulated is this little book,
that from 1748 to 1813 were printed thirty-five editions of it, in a
separate form; besides that, being very brief, it was often appended to
other works. The Very Reverend Vicar Apostolic Coppinger, in England, at the opening of the present century, had it printed twelve times
over; and another vicar apostolic, Walmesley, a man of the highest
erudition, left his written opinion of this book, commending it to his
friends for its clearness and good judgment. On the present question it
speaks as follows:

"It is no matter of faith to believe that the pope is in himself infallible,
separated from the church, even in expounding the faith. By consequence papal definitions or decrees, in whatever form pronounced,
taken exclusively from a General Council or universal acceptance of the
church, oblige none, under pain of heresy, to an interior assent."[29]

The work is printed in full in the Appendix to Charles Butler's
Historical Memoirs, which may be found in the library of the English
college in this city.

We have with us a witness from the United States of North America,
in the person of the most reverend archbishop of Baltimore, who has
expressed his opinion on this point, not in the historical work from

which I have quoted, which, as likely to meet the eye of other than Catholic readers, might seem, perhaps, to permit a more liberal explanation of the subject; but in a lecture delivered to the faithful in his own cathedral church, while he was bishop of Louisville. To the great benefit of the church, he collected the lectures into a volume, and published them. The volume has been often reprinted, and a copy of the fourth edition, printed at Baltimore in 1866, is preserved in the library of the American college in this city, having been presented to the library by the author, with an inspection in his own handwriting, in the year 1867, when he was here.

He delivers many admirable arguments on the infallibility of the church; then, refuting the objections commonly made against it, he says:

"Do we mean to say that even the pope is impeccable or infallible in his private and individual capacity? No Catholic divine ever so much as dreamed of saying or thinking so. Do we mean to say that the pope, viewed in his public and official capacity, when he speaks out as the organ and visible head of the church, is gifted with infallibility? No Catholic divine ever defended his infallibility, even under such circumstances, unless when the matters on which he uttered his definitions were intimately connected with the doctrines of faith and morals, and when, if he should be permitted by God to fall into error, there would be danger of the whole church being also led astray. Those numerous and learned Catholic theologians who maintain the infallibility of the Roman pontiff in this particular case, consider it as if matter of *opinion* more or less certain, not as one of Catholic *faith* [the Italics are by the archbishop himself] defined by the church and obligatory on all. Though not an article of Catholic faith, it is, however, the general belief among Catholics; and I myself am inclined strongly to advocate its soundness, chiefly on account of the intimate connection between the pontiff and the church, as will be shown in a subsequent lecture. Still, it is an opinion, for all this, and no Catholic would venture to charge the great Bossuet, for example, with being wanting in orthodoxy for denying it, while he so powerfully and so eloquently established the infallibility of the Church."[30]

It is scarcely necessary to remark that the scholastic distinction between "doctrines of the faith" and "doctrines or dogmas of the Catholic faith," cannot be brought in to break the force of the conclusion, derived from sources so numerous and so important, that the opinon of the infallibility of the pope has not been delivered to the faithful as a thing to be believed with divine faith. This notion is never mentioned except when it becomes necessary to refer to it in meeting the objections of opponents, and it is always asserted that it does not belong to the faith.

It is not to be admitted that in those circumstances, men of the weightiest character, distinguished with the office of priest or bishop, would have made use of verbal quibbles which it would be hardly possible for their opponents to understand; such a quibble would be that scholastic distinction between a doctrine of the faith and a dogma of the Catholic faith. The bishop of Elphin said, in reply to the archbishop of Cincinnati, that Catholics had not denied the opinion of the infallibility of the pope as a doctrine of faith, but had denied that it was a dogma of the Catholic or defined faith. If this is true, which I by no means believe, the reproach is justly and deservedly to be applied to us, that in a matter of the gravest consequence we have not been ashamed to hide our meaning by making use of scholastic distinctions.[31] . . .

10. The archbishop of Westminster holds infallibility to be a spiritual gift, or *charisma*. If that is true, I agree to it in the case of the person making good his claim to the gift; for in the strict sense of the word it is predicable only of a *person*. The usage has prevailed, indeed, of predicating infallibility, of the church, but it would be better to use the word *inerrancy*.[32]

God only is infallible. Of the church, the most that we can assert is, that it does not err in teaching the doctrines of faith which Christ has committed to its charge; because the gates of hell are not to prevail against it. Therefore infallibility absolute and complete cannot be predicated of it; and perhaps it would be better to refrain from using that word, and use the word *inerrancy* instead. But the church's inerrancy does not seem to be a positive thing, infused into it from heaven—which could not be intelligently said of a "moral person" like the church—although it is always so aided by the grace of the Holy Spirit that it may faithfully keep and set forth the truths which Christ had taught. For this end it has a fit means—but not at all a miraculous means—in the tradition of the particular churches of which it consists. Therefore the inerrancy, or infallibility, of the church is not a charisma infused from heaven, as the archbishop of Westminster would have it, by which it may discover and distinguish truths divinely revealed. It is nothing else, in my opinion, than the tradition of the church divinely founded and kept by the divine indwelling, so that it shall not tolerate errors contradicting revealed truths and their immediate and necessary corollaries, nor propound to the faithful, by its supreme authority, anything that is not true.

As I was saying this, not long ago, a Catholic objected that infallibility though not a miraculous, was a supernatural gift; that is, a grace annexed to the office of pope, by means of which, without any miraculous intervention of God he can discern true from false and revealed truth from natural.

Since the Roman pontiff, as bishop, has no other grace of ordination than his brethen who share the same Episcopal office, the supposed grace can only be a personal one. But that kind of grace does not preserve from error those even to whom it is granted in the largest measure, as appears from the saints who in the great schism were found on both sides, although eminent in virtue and splendid with the glory of miracles. If papal infallibility is a personal grace or charisma, as the archbishop of Westminster calls it, it demands a miraculous intervention of God, that the pope, when he means to define anything of faith or morals, may be kept free from error.

It may be shown in another way that this novel invention of the charisma ought to be rejected, from the consequences which it involves. Granting that infallibility is a charisma, in what does it differ from that special private inspiration by which certain persons think themselves led, and which is rejected by theologians on this precise ground, that no means is granted, outside of the person who considers himself to be led by the divine Spirit, by which it may be proved whether the spirit really is divine. Not one word will the archbishop of Westminster listen to, of fixing the conditions for the exercise of the pope's infallibility. He asserts that He who gave the charisma will give the means for its due exercise, or will bring it about that such means shall be used.

Verily this is a royal road to the discovery of the truths of faith! And yet it is not without its dangers both for pope and for church. Once imbued with this conviction, the holier in life, the purer in purpose, the more fervent in piety the pope should be, the more dangerous he would prove both to himself and to the church, which (according to this system) derives its infallibility from him; especially would this be true if he should find even one of his advisers laboring under the same illusion. What need would there be, to a pope who accepted this notion, of the counsel of his brethren, the opinions of theologians, the investigation of the documents of the church? Believing himself to be immediately led by the divine Spirit, and that this Spirit is communicated through him to the church, there would be nothing to hold him back from pressing on in a course on which he had once entered. These consequences of the principle laid down by the archbishop of Westminster prove it to be false. Nevertheless if infallibility is a charisma, we must be able to follow out the fact to its conclusions.

11. Among other things which utterly astounded me, it was said by the archbishop of Westminster that by the addition made at the end of the decree *De Fide,* passed at the third session, we had already admitted the doctrine of papal infallibility, at least by implication, and that we were no longer free to recede from it.[33]

If I rightly understand the right reverend relator of the committee, who, when this addition had once been moved in the General Congregation, then withdrawn, and finally, while we were wondering what the matter was, suddenly moved a second time, he said, in plain terms, that no doctrine at all was taught by it, but that it was placed at the end of the four chapters of which the decree was composed, in order to round them off handsomely; and that it was rather disciplinary than doctrinal in its character. Either he was deceived, if what the archbishop of Westminster said was true; or else he intentionally led us into error—which we are hardly at liberty to suppose of so honorable a man. However it may have been, many of the bishops, confiding in his assurance, decided not to refuse their suffrages to the decree on account of that clause; while others, of whom I was one, were afraid that there was a trap set, and yielded reluctantly on this point to the will of others.

In saying all this, it is not my intention to accuse any of the right reverend fathers of bad faith. I treat them all, as is meet, with due reverence. But it is said that we have among us, outside of the Council, certain "religious" men—who are perhaps pious as well as "religious"— who have a vast influence upon the Council; who, relying rather on trickery than on fair measures, have brought the interests of the church into that extreme peril from which it has risen; who at the beginning of the Council managed to have no one appointed on the committees of the Council but those who were known or believed to be in favor of their schemes; who, following hard in the footsteps of certain of their predecessors, in the schemata that have been proposed to us, and which have come out of their own workshop, seem to have had nothing so much at heart as the depreciation of the authority of the bishops and the exaltation of the authority of the pope; and seem disposed to impose upon the unwary with twists and turns of expression, which may be differently explained by different persons. These are the men who have blown up this conflagration in the church; and they do not cease to fan the flame by spreading among the people their writings, which put on the outward show of piety, but are destitute of its reality.

With more zeal than knowledge, these excellent men would like to cover up the design of the divine Architect with another and, as they may think, a better and stronger one. For He had consulted at once for the unity of the whole, and the liberty of every part; nor had he conferred the entire fulness of his own power on the vicar appointed by himself; knowing what was in man, and not wishing that any one should have lordship over the *clergy*, that is, his "portion," [κλῆρος], the church.

Already in vain the petition has been offered that this painful contro-

versy might not be started in the Council. Equally in vain the petition
has been urged that there might be no definition until after an examination which should leave no room for doubt as to the testimony of
tradition on this point. In order to such an examination, the request was
presented, nearly three months ago, to their eminences the presidents of
the general congregation, in a petition from prelates of distinguished
sees, that there might be a committee of fathers, taken in equal number
from each party, and appointed by the votes of those agreeing with them
in opinion. This request was repeated over and over again by others in
the General Congregation; and is said to have had the approval of some
even of the advocates of papal infallibility. For the question is one which
calls for an investigation of the records of the entire church, and should
be dealt with in a calm rather than an excited temper. The archbishop of
Dublin says, indeed, that such an examination would last too long—that
it would reach till the day of judgment. If this be so, it were better to
refrain from making any definition at all, than to frame one prematurely.
But it is said the honor and authority of the Holy See demand a
definition, nor can it be deferred without injury to both. I answer in the
words of Jerome, substituting another word for the well-known word
*auctoritas.*

                    MAJOR EST SALUS ORBIS QUAM URBIS[34]

I have done.

## NOTES

1. Paul Cardinal Cullen. Made a cardinal in 1866, he was the first Irish bishop
ever to receive that honor. The sequence of events to which Kenrick refers ran
thus: (1) During a council recess, February 22–March 18, 1870, a number of
bishops submitted written comments on the draft proposals dealing with papal
primacy and infallibility, among them Kenrick; these comments were collected
and published by council officials in a document entitled *Synopsis animadver-
sionum.* At the end of April, Kenrick also wrote, and had printed in Naples, a
forty-two-page pamphlet on the same subject, *De pontificia infallibilitate qualis
in Concilio Vaticano definienda proponitur dissertatio theologica.* (2) Cullen
spoke on May 19, criticizing Kenrick's views. (3) No less a personage than Lord
Acton "delivered a parcel to the railroad station for the archbishop, a thick
manuscript which Kenrick was sending to be printed at Naples" (James Hennesey, S.J., *The First Vatican Council: The American Experience* [New York:
Herder & Herder, 1963], 244, referring to a letter from Acton to Döllinger, June
8); this "thick manuscript" is what is given (without its appendixes) here in
English translation. Kenrick had not had the chance to give it orally because of a
cloture vote on June 3. In the text as given here, Kenrick's mention of his
remarks in the *Synopsis* has been altered to read "previous statement."—ED.

2. Matt. 16:18.
3. Matt. 28:20.
4. "I have prayed for thee, that thy faith fail not."
5. ". . . the weightier matters of the law, judgment, mercy, and faith."
6. "When the Son of man cometh, shall he find faith on the earth?"
7. John 20:21.
8. Matt. 28:19–20.
9. 1 John 1:3.
10. Cyprian *On the Unity of the Church* 5.
11. The rule is contained in the *Creed of Pius IV*, or *Professio Fidei Tridentina*, 1564; see *Enchiridion Symbolorum, Definitionum et Declarationum de Rebus Fidei et Morum*, ed. Heinrich Denzinger, 29th ed. (Freiburg im Breisgau: Herder & Herder), nn. 994–1000.—ED.
12. Jerome *Commentary on Matthew* 16, 15–16 (*C.C.L.* 77.140); Augustine *On the Psalms* 108.1 (Latin enumeration); Augustine *On the Gospel of John* 118.4; and Ambrose *On the Psalms* 38.37 (*P.L.* 14.1057).
13. See . . . Paschasius Radbertus *Commentary on Matthew* 8.16 (*P.L.* 120.560).
14. Augustine *On the Gospel of John* 123.5. (The Mansi edition erroneously has 122.—ED.)
15. In the Vulgate, *universo gregi.*—ED.
16. In the Vulgate, *regere.*—ED.
17. Acts 20:28. See Basil *Constitutiones Monasticae* 22, n. 5; and Augustine *De Agone Christiano* 30 (*P.L.* 40.308). (Basil's authorship is considered doubtful.—ED.)
18. Lawrence Gillooly. Elphin is a suffragan see of the archbishopric of Tuam, Ireland.—ED.
19. No citation is given for Tertullian, but similar remarks may be found in *On Prescription* 15–18. See Irenaeus *Against Heresies* 3.3.2.—ED.
20. In his Letter to the Archbishop of Paris, dated October 24, 1865, the pope claims for himself the ordinary power in the particular dioceses. In the schema [that is, draft proposal] *De Romano Pontifice* it is said that he has ordinary and immediate jurisdiction in the universal church. Since this is said without making any distinction between ordinary or episcopal power and ordinary patriarchal or primatial power, it would seem to follow that the pope is actually ordinary or bishop of each several diocese in the Christian world. According to the author of the book *On the Roman Curia,* who lived at Rome for fifteen years, the pope is the *exclusive* ordinary of all the missions under the sacred congregation *de Propaganda Fide,* so that there is no difference between vicars apostolic and the titular bishops set over those missions, except that the latter are *ordinary* and the former are *extraordinary* vicars of the pope (Johann Heinrich Bangen, *Die Römische Curie* [Münster, 1854], 253). After the Concordats have been done away, which will not be long after the infallibility of the pope is established, all episcopal sees will be at the disposal of the pope alone, *ad nutum;* and thenceforth all bishops will be vicars of the pope, liable to be removed at his nod—*ad nutum ejus.* Thus the church, from which civil society borrowed the form of representative government to which it owes the rights it has acquired, will exhibit an example of absolutism, both in doctrine and administration, carried to the highest pitch. A right reverend orator said, no long time since, that the papal power is, in government, absolute indeed, but not

arbitrary, because it is always guided by reason—which evidently implies that the pope is *impeccable.* In fact, this is necessarily inferred from his infallibility; for infallibility is a quality of the intellect, and the intellect is affected by the character.

21. Francis P. Kenrick, *Primacy of the Apostolic See* (Philadelphia, 1845), 357.

22. Martin J. Spalding, *Lectures on the Evidences of Catholicity,* 4th ed. (Baltimore, 1866), 377–78. [As to whether belief in the pope's temporal power is a matter of church doctrine] the author is certainly mistaken. It does not require a definition to constitute a doctrine. It is enough that there should be truth divinely revealed, and propounded as such to the faithful by the ordinary magistery of the church. But that power was propounded as a doctrine by Boniface VIII, when he declared that it must be held by all *sub salutis dipendio.* Furthermore, Suarez has it for a defined doctrine. [Further in the quotation] the expression *at least publicly* is too incautious. (Spalding ultimately voted *for* infallibility. Concerning the evolution of his view, see the many references to him in Hennesey's *First Vatican Council,* esp. 104–5, 200–201, 281.—ED.)

23. The leader of the British Roman Catholic episcopate, Henry Edward Manning. A former Anglican priest, converted to Roman Catholicism in 1851, Manning was one of the strongest advocates of defining papal infallibility. He was made a cardinal in 1875. In *Eminent Victorians,* Lytton Strachey presented an unfavorable portrait of him; a kinder estimate is given by Gordon Wheeler, in *The English Catholics, 1850–1950,* ed. G. A. Beck (London, 1950), 150–64.— ED.

24. Martin J. Spalding, *History of the Reformation,* 5th rev. ed. (Baltimore, 1866), 1:318.

25. Karl von Hefele, a distinguished church historian who studied with Möhler.—ED.

26. "If such you be, would that you were on our side."—ED.

27. I.e., Pius IX's proclaiming the dogma of the immaculate conception in 1854, which Kenrick had discussed in his *Synopsis* remarks.—ED.

28. Franz Xaver Weninger, S.J., *On the Apostolical and Infallible Authority of the Pope When Teaching the Faithful, and on His Relation to a General Council* (New York, 1868).—ED.

29. Charles Butler, *Historical Memoirs of the English, Irish, and Scottish Catholics, from the Reformation to the Present Time,* 3d ed. (London, 1822), 3:501–2. (*Taken . . . from here means considered apart from.*—ED.)

30. Spalding, *Evidences,* 263–64.

31. Omitted here is Kenrick's discussion of eighteenth- and nineteenth-century Irish anti-infallibility opinion, and sec. 9, about the ethical responsibility of each bishop at the council to make a careful personal examination of the evidence.—ED.

32. Kenrick's suggestion has been taken by twentieth-century theologians— e.g., by Hans Küng, in *Infallible? An Inquiry* (Garden City, N.Y.: Doubleday & Co., 1971).—ED.

33. The addition was as follows: "Since it is not enough to avoid heretical pravity, unless at the same time those errors are diligently avoided which more or less tend to it, we warn all persons of the duty of observing also the constitutions and decrees in which such erroneous opinions, which themselves are not expressly enunciated [here], have been proscribed and prohibited by this

Holy See." (The same text, in a somewhat different translation, is given in selection 11 of this volume, sec. 1820. Examples of such proscription and prohibition would be Pius V's condemnation of the errors of Michael Baius [1567]. Innocent X's [1653] and Alexander VII's [1656] condemnations of Jansenism, and Pius IX's own lengthy list of the errors of the nineteenth century, the celebrated *Syllabus* of 1864. Catholic authors differ as to what the "duty of observing" might consist of, ranging from a respectful tone when publicly disagreeing, to full internal assent. Similarly, the duty-engendering "weight" of documents has received considerable attention; there is, above all, some disagreement as to when, or how many times, in the history of the church the pope's gift of infallibility has been used *in relative independence from the bishops.* Critics of the doctrine of papal infallibility have pointed out that if the pope is acting in concert with the bishops a definition of the pope's infallibility is a tautology, whereas if a pope acts independently from the bishops his own orthodoxy and, hence, legitimacy are open to question. The interested reader may wish to examine the only instance *after 1870* in which a pope defined a dogma, Pius XII's definition of the assumption of Mary, in 1950. As was the case in 1854, this dogma bears not only on Mary but also on ecclesiology.—ED.)

34. "It is better to save the world than the city."

# 11

# The Dogmatic Constitutions on the Catholic Faith and on the Church of Christ

## The First Vatican Council

As noted in the Introduction, there seems to be no compelling reason to deny that the First Vatican Council was the high point of the Catholic nineteenth century. We say that today, and so did nineteenth-century Catholics from 1870 on. Such was their self-interpretation. But what of Catholics reflecting on the state of the church before December 1864, when Pius IX indicated his desire to hold an ecumenical council? However they interpreted themselves and their church, we can say of them that, conscious of it or not, they were caught up in a process of increasing centralization. In the reign of Pius VII (1800–1823) the papacy was disrupted by, then recovering from, the Napoleonic upheaval of Europe. It could be described as somnolent during the next two reigns, those of Leo XII (1823–29) and Pius VIII (1829–30). But under Gregory XVI the Vatican began to take account of the European scene—as well as of the expansion of the church in North America—with increasing vigor. Yet more vigor appeared with Pius IX in 1846, and among the many challenges confronting this relatively young pope—he had the longest reign in the history of the papacy— two call for particular attention. First, a significant number of European governments were either antireligious or anti-Catholic; it thus happened that Catholics in those countries, bishops included, often wanted a strong central power in the church to serve as a counterpoise to the power of their own governments. Second, as Pius IX's reign unfolded, it became increasingly clear that the papal states as such would not survive the movement for Italian unification. It looked as though papal authority would be deprived of its supranational physical base and therefore the relationship of the pope to the Catholic world would have to be put on a different footing. If we now add the challenges that Catholicism faced from new forms of philosophy and psychology, from Protestant biblical criticism, and from militant apostles of the natural sciences, it is plain that convening the first ecumenical council in three hundred years was scarcely an illogical thing for Pius to do.

The council lasted from December 8, 1869, to October 20, 1870, when it was adjourned *sine die* by reason of the Franco-Prussian War and the concomitant

Italian occupation of Rome. The council fathers produced two constitutions, or formal teaching documents: *Dei Filius,* on faith and reason, and *Pastor Aeternus,* on the primacy and infallibility of the pope. The former was approved on April 24, 1870, by a vote of 667 to 0; the latter, which as was objected then and later, was far from being a full statement on the church, was approved on July 18 by a vote of 533 to 2. The difference in the number of votes arises from many fathers' having gone home—for a variety of reasons, not the least of them an unwillingness to vote for infallibility. A number of accounts of the council debates are listed in the Bibliography; the reader will likely find those by Dom Cuthbert Butler and James Hennesey particularly helpful.

In the text as presented here it should be noted that the headings in italics have been supplied by the editors of the English translation. The marginal numbers are from the twenty-ninth edition of the Denzinger anthology (see note on p. 271); later editions of Denzinger, with new numbers, retain the twenty-ninth edition's numbers in the inside margins. It should also be noted that the footnotes have been omitted; they can be found in Mansi or Denzinger. Finally, the reader must keep in mind a crucial difference between Vatican I and Vatican II. In the latter, the council fathers were concerned to offer the world an updated, essentially pastoral presentation of Catholicism, the famous *aggiornamento* of Pope John XXIII. At Vatican I, however, the fathers intended to define dogmas, that is, credal articles, the opposite of which would be heresy. The text contains "chapters" and "canons": the chapters are explanatory, but the canons are dogma—and thus one who cannot accept them is "anathematized," or "put out" of the body of the Catholic faithful.

Several points would seem to require special comment. First, the council was at pains not to define a special philosophical method for showing that there is a God. In sections 1785 and 1806, the text says only that God's existence can be known with certitude by the light of natural reason (Latin, *certo cognosci posse*). Second, the canons in sections 1812–13 do, it must be admitted, create a problem for the twentieth-century Catholic exegete or theologian. Since the council also stressed that faith is a free assent, and an assent given in response to divine grace, it would appear that the purely natural effect of motives for assent is at best a so-called moral certitude. Third, in sections 1827–28 it is not altogether clear how papal and episcopal jurisdiction are related. As was pointed out in the council debates, often very sharply, if the pope has immediate jurisdiction over every Catholic, does this make the bishops merely papal deputies, and not successors of the apostles in their own right? Fourth, it is stated in sections 1830 and 1839 that papal acts clearly do not require the consent of the other bishops: Gallicanism is condemned as heresy. One must remember that prior to the council no Catholic doubted the infallibility of the bishop of Rome acting in concert with his brother bishops; what was in question was what he could do without seeking their consent. This leads us to a fifth point, namely, that the reader must recognize that the actual definition of infallibility is very limited. The charism of the pope is given him for the sake of the church. He cannot originate new doctrines. His infallibility bears only on questions of faith or morals, and it is the "infallibility with which the divine Redeemer wished his Church to be endowed." Finally, only the highest, most solemn papal acts are infallible, certainly not the pope's statements as an individual theologian nor even his day-by-day or year-by-year teaching speeches and documents except insofar as those pronouncements contain dogmas held on other grounds.

It would be utterly to misunderstand *Pastor Aeternus* if one thought that by it the pope became some sort of magic problem-solver. In more positive terms, what the bishops of 1870 wanted to say is that God will be faithful to his church through the organizational structure they conceived it to have. Note also that no more than minor schismatic cracks appeared after Vatican I. Still, a frequent theme in twentieth-century Catholic commentary on this council is that it was tragically suspended before its work was done, before more could be said of the ecclesiological context of the papal office.

# THE DOGMATIC CONSTITUTION ON
# THE CATHOLIC FAITH

*1781* . . . Now, therefore, with the bishops of the whole world being associated with Us and concurring in judgment, assembled for this ecumenical council by Our authority in the Holy Spirit, We have determined to profess and declare the saving doctrine of Christ from this Chair of Peter in view of all men. We do so, relying on the word of God in writing and in tradition, as We have received it from the Catholic Church, religiously guarded and authentically explained. All opposing errors We proscribe and condemn by the authority given to Us by God.

## 1. God the Creator of All Things

*The one living and true God and his distinction from the universe*
*1782* The holy, Catholic, apostolic Roman Church believes and professes that there is one true and living God, the creator and lord of heaven and earth. He is all-powerful, eternal, unmeasurable, incomprehensible, and limitless in intellect and will and in every perfection. Since he is one unique spiritual substance, entirely simple and unchangeable, he must be declared really and essentially distinct from the world, perfectly happy in himself and by his very nature, and inexpressibly exalted over all things that exist or can be conceived other than himself (see canons 1–4).

*The act of creation in itself and in opposition to modern errors, and the result of creation*
*1783* In order to manifest his perfection through the benefits which he bestows on creatures—not to intensify his happiness nor to acquire any perfection—this one and only true God, by his goodness and "almighty power" and by a completely free decision, "from the very beginning of time has created both orders of creatures in the same way

---

From *Sacrorum Conciliorum Nova et Amplissima Collectio*, ed. J. D. Mansi et al. (Graz: Akademische Drück- n. Verlagsinstitut, 1961), 51:429–36, 52:1330–34; the same text is also found in *Enchiridion Symbolorum, Definitionum et Declarationum de Rebus Fidei et Morum*, ed. Heinrich Denzinger et al. (Freiburg im Breisgau: Herder & Herder, 29th ed.), 1781–1840. The translation is from *The Church Teaches: Documents of the Church in English Translation*, ed. John F. Clarkson, S.J., et al. (Rockford, Ill.: TAN Books, 1973), 27–35, 47–48, 94–102, 151–53.

out of nothing, the spiritual or angelic world and the corporeal or visible universe. And afterwards he formed the creature man, who in a way belongs to both orders, as he is composed of spirit and body" (see cans. 2 and 5).

*The sequel to creation*
1784   Furthermore, by his providence God watches over and governs all the things that he made, reaching from end to end with might and disposing all things with gentleness (see Wisd. 8:1). For "all things are naked and open to his eyes" (Heb. 4:13), even those things that are going to occur by the free action of creatures.

## 2. Revelation

*The fact of positive, supernatural revelation*
1785   The same holy Mother Church holds and teaches that God, the origin and end of all things, can be known with certainty by the natural light of human reason from the things that he created; "for since the creation of the world his invisible attributes are clearly seen, being understood through the things that are made" (Rom. 1:20); and she teaches that it was nevertheless, the good pleasure of his wisdom and goodness to reveal himself and the eternal decrees of his will to the human race in another and supernatural way, as the Apostle says: "God, who at sundry times and in divers manners spoke in times past to the fathers by the prophets, last of all in these days has spoken to us by his Son" (Heb.1:1–2; see can. 1).

*The need for revelation*
1786   It is owing to this divine revelation, assuredly, that even in the present condition of the human race, those religious truths which are by their nature accessible to human reason can easily be known by all men with solid certitude and with no trace of error. Nevertheless, it must not be argued that revelation is, for that reason, absolutely necessary. It is necessary only because God, out of his infinite goodness, destined man to a supernatural end, that is, to a participation in the good things of God, which altogether exceed the human mental grasp; for "eye has not seen nor ear heard, nor has it entered into the heart of man, what things God has prepared for those who love him" (1 Cor. 2:9; see cans. 2 and 3).

*The source of revelation*
1787   Furthermore, according to the faith of the universal Church,

declared by the holy Council of Trent, this supernatural revelation is "contained in written books and in the unwritten traditions that the apostles received from Christ himself or that was handed on, as it were from hand to hand, from the apostles under the inspiration of the Holy Spirit, and so have come down to us." Those books of the Old and the New Testament must be accepted as sacred and canonical in their entirety, with all their parts, just as they are listed in the decree of that Council and are contained in the ancient Latin Vulgate. Those books, however, are held to be sacred and canonical by the Church, not on the grounds that they were produced by mere human ingenuity and afterwards approved by her authority; nor on the mere score that they contain revelation without error. But they are held to be sacred and canonical because they were written as a result of the prompting of the Holy Spirit, they have God for their author, and as such they were entrusted to the Church (see can. 4).

### The interpretation of Sacred Scripture

1788 However, the norms for the interpretation of divine Scripture which, to good purpose, were decreed by the holy Council of Trent with a view to restraining undisciplined minds are being explained in a distorted sense by certain men. Therefore, We renew the same decree and declare that this is its meaning: in matters of faith and morals affecting the structure of Christian doctrine, that sense of Sacred Scripture is to be considered as true which holy Mother Church has held and now holds; for it is her office to judge about the true sense and interpretation of Sacred Scripture; and, therefore, no one is allowed to interpret Sacred Scripture contrary to this sense nor contrary to the unanimous agreement of the Fathers.

## 3. Faith

### The definition of faith

1789 Because man depends entirely on God as his creator and lord and because created reason is wholly subordinate to uncreated Truth, we are obliged to render by faith a full submission of intellect and will to God when he makes a revelation (see can. 1). This faith, however, which is the beginning of human salvation, the Catholic Church asserts to be a supernatural virtue. By that faith, with the inspiration and help of God's grace, we believe that what he has revealed is true—not because its intrinsic truth is seen with the natural light of reason—but because of the authority of God who reveals it, of God who can neither deceive nor be deceived (see can. 2). For, on the word of the Apostle: "Faith is the substance of things to be hoped for, the evidence of things that are not seen" (Heb. 11:1).

*Faith and reason are in harmony*
    1790   Nevertheless, in order that the submission of our faith might be consonant with reason (see Rom. 12:1), God has willed that external proofs of his revelation, namely divine acts and especially miracles and prophecies, should be added to the internal aids given by the Holy Spirit. Since these proofs so excellently display God's omnipotence and limitless knowledge, they constitute the surest signs of divine revelation, signs that are suitable to everyone's understanding (see cans. 3–4). Therefore, not only Moses and the prophets but also and pre-eminently Christ our Lord performed many evident miracles and made clear-cut prophecies. Moreover, we read of the apostles: "But they went forth and preached everywhere, while the Lord worked with them and confirmed the preaching by the signs that followed" (Mark 16:20). And likewise it is written: "We have the word of prophecy, surer still, to which you do well to attend, as to a lamp shining in a dark place" (2 Pet. 1:19).

*Faith is essentially a gift of God*
    1791   However, even though the assent of faith is by no means a blind impulse, still, no one can "assent to the gospel preaching" as he must in order to be saved "without the enlightenment and inspiration of the Holy Spirit, who gives all men their joy in assenting to and believing the truth." Hence, faith itself is essentially a gift of God, even should it not work through charity (see Gal. 5:6); and the act of faith is a work that has a bearing upon salvation. By this act man offers to God himself a free obedience inasmuch as he concurs and cooperates with God's grace, when he could resist it (see can. 5).

*The object of faith*
    1792   Moreover, by divine and Catholic faith everything must be believed that is contained in the written word of God or in tradition, and that is proposed by the Church as a divinely revealed object of belief either in a solemn decree or in her ordinary, universal teaching.

*The need for embracing and keeping the faith*
    1793   Yet, since "without faith it is impossible to please God" (Heb. 11:6) and to enter the company of his sons, no one has ever obtained justification without faith and no one will reach eternal life, unless "he has persevered to the end" in faith (Matt. 10:22; 24:13). However, in

order to enable us to fulfill our obligation of embracing the true faith and steadfastly persevering in it, God established the Church through his only-begotten Son and endowed it with unmistakable marks of its foundation, so that it could be recognized by all as the guardian and teacher of the revealed word.

*External graces for fulfilling the obligation to believe*
1794 For all the many marvelous proofs that God has provided to make the credibility of the Christian faith evident point to the Catholic Church alone. Indeed, the Church itself, because of its marvelous propagation, its exalted sanctity, and its inexhaustible fruitfulness in all that is good, because of its catholic unity and its unshaken stability, is a great and perpetual motive of credibility and an irrefutable proof of its own divine mission.

*Internal graces for fulfilling the same obligation*
Consequently, the Church, like a standard lifted up for the nations (see Isa. 11:12), not only calls to herself those who have not yet believed, but also she proves to her own children that the faith they profess rests on a most solid foundation. To this testimony is added the efficacious help of supernatural power. For the most merciful Lord stirs up and helps with his grace those who are wandering astray, so that they can "come to the knowledge of the truth" (1 Tim. 2:4); and, never abandoning anyone, unless he is abandoned, he strengthens with his grace those whom he has brought out of darkness into his marvelous light (see 1 Pet. 2:9), so that they may remain in this light. Therefore, the position of those who have embraced the Catholic truth by the heavenly gift of faith and of those who have been misled by human opinions and follow a false religion is by no means the same, for the former, who have accepted the faith under the teaching authority of the Church, can never have any just reason for changing that faith or calling it into question (see can. 6). In view of all this, let us give thanks to God the Father, "who has made us worthy to share the lot of the saints in light" (Col. 1:12), and let us not neglect so great a salvation, but "looking towards the author and finisher of faith, Jesus" (Heb. 12:2), "let us hold fast the confession of our hope without wavering" (Heb. 10:23).

4. Faith and Reason

*The two kinds of knowledge*
1795 Furthermore, the perpetual universal belief of the Catholic

Church has held and now holds that there are two orders of knowledge, distinct not only in origin but also in object. They are distinct in origin, because in one we know by means of natural reason; in the other, by means of divine faith. And they are distinct in object, because in addition to what natural reason can attain, we have proposed to us as objects of belief mysteries that are hidden in God and which, unless divinely revealed, can never be known (see can. 1). This is why the Apostle asserts that God is known by the Gentiles "through the things that are made" (Rom. 1:20); yet, when he is discoursing about the grace and truth that "came through Jesus Christ" (John 1:17), he declares: "We speak the wisdom of God, mysterious, hidden, which God foreordained before the world unto our glory, a wisdom which none of the rulers of this world has known. . . . But to us God has revealed them through his Spirit. For the Spirit searches all things, even the deep things of God" (1 Cor. 2:7ff.). And the Only-begotten himself praises the Father for having hidden these things from the wise and prudent, and having revealed them to little ones (see Matt. 11:25).

### Reason's part in the study of supernatural truth

1796   It is, nevertheless, true that if human reason, with faith as its guiding light, inquires earnestly, devoutly, and circumspectly, it does reach, by God's generosity, some understanding of mysteries, and that a most profitable one. It achieves this by the similarity with truths which it knows naturally and also from the interrelationship of mysteries with one another and with the final end of man. Reason, however, never becomes capable of understanding them the way it does truths which are its own proper object. For divine mysteries of their very nature so excel the created intellect that even when they have been given in revelation and accepted by faith, that very faith still keeps them veiled in a sort of obscurity, as long as "we are exiled from the Lord" in this mortal life, "for we walk by faith and not by sight" (2 Cor. 5:6f.).

### No disagreement between faith and reason

1797   Nevertheless, although faith is above reason, yet there can never be any real disagreement between faith and reason, because it is the same God who reveals mysteries and infuses faith and has put the light of reason into the human soul. Now God cannot deny himself any more than the truth can ever contradict the truth. However, the chief source of this merely apparent contradiction lies in the fact that dogmas of faith have not been understood and explained according to the mind of the Church or that deceptive assertions of opinions are accepted as axioms of reason. Therefore, "We define that every assertion opposed to the enlightened truth of faith is entirely false."

*1798*   Moreover, the Church, which received the office of safeguarding the deposit of faith along with the apostolic duty of teaching, likewise possesses, according to the divine will, the right and duty of proscribing so-called knowledge (see 1 Tim. 6:20) so that none may be deceived by philosophy and vain deceit (see Col. 2:8 and can. 2). Hence, all faithful Christians are forbidden to defend as legitimate conclusions of science such opinions that are known to be opposed to the doctrine of faith, especially if they have been censured by the Church; rather, they are absolutely bound to regard them as errors that treacherously wear the appearance of truth.

*Faith and reason aid each other; and human knowledge is free in its own domain*
*1799*   Faith and reason can never disagree; but more than that, they are even mutually advantageous. For right reason demonstrates the foundations of faith and, enlightened by the light of faith, it pursues the science of divine things; faith, on the other hand, sets reason free and guards it from errors and furnishes it with extensive knowledge. Hence, far from opposing the study of human arts and sciences, the Church helps and furthers this study in many ways. For it is neither ignorant nor scornful of the advantages for human living that result from those pursuits. Indeed, it asserts that just as they have their source in God, the lord of all knowledge (see 1 Kings 2:3), so too, if properly pursued, they lead men back to God with the help of his grace. And it certainly does not forbid these sciences to use their own principles and method within their own field. But while recognizing this due liberty, it is carefully on the watch to see that they do not admit errors by going contrary to divine doctrine, or step beyond their own boundaries and cause confusion by assuming authority in the domain of faith.

*Genuine progress in natural and revealed knowledge*
*1800*   For the doctrine of faith as revealed by God has not been presented to men as a philosophical system to be perfected by human ingenuity; it was presented as a divine trust given to the bride of Christ to be faithfully kept and infallibly interpreted. It also follows that any meaning of the sacred dogmas that has once been declared by holy Mother Church, must always be retained; and there must never be any deviation from that meaning on the specious grounds of a more profound understanding (see can. 3). "Therefore, let there be growth . . .

and all possible progress in understanding, knowledge, and wisdom whether in single individuals or in the whole body, in each man as well as in the entire Church, according to the stage of their development; but only within proper limits, that is, in the same doctrine, in the same meaning, and in the same purport."

### Canons on Chapter 1

*Against all errors about the existence of a God who is creator*
      *1801*   1. If anyone denies that there is one true God, creator and lord of things visible and invisible: let him be anathema.

*Against materialism*
      *1802*   2. If anyone dares to assert that nothing exists except matter: let him be anathema.

*Against pantheism*
      *1803*   3. If anyone says that God and all things possess one and the same substance and essence: let him be anathema.

*Against particular forms of pantheism*
      *1804*   4. If anyone says that finite things, both corporeal and spiritual, or at least spiritual, emanated from the divine substance;
      or that the divine essence becomes all things by a manifestation or evolution of itself;
      or, finally, that God is universal or indefinite being, which by determining itself makes up the universe which is diversified into genera, species, and individuals: let him be anathema.

*Against both pantheists and materialists*
      *1805*   5. If anyone does not admit that the world and everything in it, both spiritual and material, have been produced in their entire substance by God out of nothing;

*Against the followers of Günther*
      or says that God did not create with a will free from all necessity, but that he created necessarily, just as he necessarily loves himself;

*Against the followers of Günther and Hermes*
      or denies that the world was made for the glory of God: let him be anathema.

## Canons on Chapter 2

*Against those who deny natural theology*
   *1806* 1. If anyone says that the one and true God, our creator and lord, cannot be known with certainty with the natural light of human reason by means of the things that have been made: let him be anathema.

*Against the deists*
   *1807* 2. If anyone says that it is impossible or useless for man to be taught through divine revelation about God and the service to be rendered to him: let him be anathema.

*Against the progressionists*
   *1808* 3. If anyone says that man cannot be elevated by the divine power to a knowledge and perfection that surpasses natural knowledge and perfection, but that he can and should by his own efforts and by continual progress eventually arrive at the possession of every truth and good: let him be anathema.

*Against those who deny the inspiration of Holy Scripture*
   *1809* 4. If anyone does not admit as sacred and canonical the complete books of Sacred Scripture with all their parts, as the holy Council of Trent enumerated them, or denies that they were divinely inspired: let him be anathema.

## Canons on Chapter 3

*Against false freedom of reason*
   *1810* 1. If anyone says that human reason is so independent that it cannot be commanded by God to believe: let him be anathema.

*There are some truths that reason left to itself cannot know*
   *1811* 2. If anyone says that there is no distinction between divine faith and natural knowledge about God and morals and, therefore, that for divine faith it is not necessary that revealed truths be believed on the authority of God who reveals them: let him be anathema.

*The reasonableness of faith*
   *1812* 3. If anyone says that it is impossible for external signs to render divine revelation credible and that, therefore, men ought to be

impelled towards faith only by each one's internal experience or private inspiration: let him be anathema.

*The demonstrability of revelation*
*1813*   4. If anyone says that all miracles are impossible and, hence, that all accounts of them, even though contained in Sacred Scripture, should be classed with fables and myths; or that miracles can never be recognized with certainty and that the divine origin of the Christian religion cannot be successfully proved by them: let him be anathema.

*The freedom of faith and the necessity of grace, against Hermes*
*1814*   5. If anyone says that the assent of Christian faith is not free, but necessarily results from arguments of human reason; or that the grace of God is only necessary for living faith, which works through charity (see Gal. 5:6): let him be anathema.

*Against the positive doubt of Hermes*
*1815*   6. If anyone says that the position of the faithful and of those who have not yet reached the only true faith is the same, so that Catholics could have good reason for suspending their assent and calling into question the faith that they have already accepted under the teaching authority of the Church, until they have completed a scientific demonstration of the credibility and truth of their faith: let him be anathema.

Canons on Chapter 4

*1816*   1. If anyone says that in divine revelation there are no true mysteries properly so called, but that all the dogmas of faith can be understood and demonstrated from natural principles by a well-trained mind: let him be anathema.
*1817*   2. If anyone says that human sciences can be pursued with such liberty that their assertions may be held as true, even though they are opposed to revealed doctrine, and that they cannot be condemned by the Church: let him be anathema.
*1818*   3. If anyone says that as science progresses it is sometimes possible for dogmas that have been proposed by the Church to receive a different meaning from the one which the Church understood and understands: let him be anathema.

*Concluding exhortation*
*1819*   Therefore, exercising the duty of Our supreme pastoral office,

through the heart of Jesus Christ We beseech all the Christian faithful and especially those who hold authority or who have the duty of teaching, and We command by the authority of the same God and our Savior, that they unite their zealous endeavors in order to repel and eliminate these errors from the holy Church and to spread abroad the light of purest faith.

*1820*   However, since it is not enough to shun the malice of heresy if those errors that more or less approach it are not also carefully avoided, We admonish all of their further duty of observing the constitutions and decrees by which suchlike perverse opinions, which are not expressly specified here, have been condemned by this Holy See.

## THE DOGMATIC CONSTITUTION ON
## THE CHURCH OF CHRIST

*The institution and foundation of the Church*
*1821*   The eternal Shepherd and Guardian of our souls (see 1 Pet. 2:25), in order to render the saving work of redemption lasting, decided to establish his holy Church that in it, as in the house of the living God, all the faithful might be held together by the bond of one faith and one love. For this reason, before he was glorified, he prayed to the Father not for the apostles only, but for those also who would believe in him on their testimony, that all might be one as he, the Son, and the Father are one (see John 17:20ff.). Therefore, just as he sent the apostles, whom he had chosen for himself out of the world, as he himself was sent by the Father (see John 20:21), so also he wished shepherds and teachers to be in his Church until the consummation of the world (see Matt. 28:20). Indeed, he placed St. Peter at the head of the other apostles that the episcopate might be one and undivided, and that the whole multitude of believers might be preserved in unity of faith and communion by means of a well-organized priesthood. He made Peter a perpetual principle of this twofold unity and a visible foundation, that on his strength an everlasting temple might be erected and on the firmness of his faith a Church might arise whose pinnacle was to reach into heaven. But the gates of hell, with a hatred that grows greater each day, are rising up everywhere against its divinely established foundation with the intention of overthrowing the Church, if this were possible. We, therefore, judge it necessary for the protection, the safety, and the increase of the Catholic flock to pronounce with the approval of the sacred council the true doctrine concerning the establishment, the perpetuity, and the

nature of the sacred apostolic primacy. In this primacy all the efficacy and all the strength of the Church are placed. We judge it necessary to pronounce what all the faithful must believe in its regard and what they must hold according to the ancient and constant belief of the universal Church. Likewise We judge it necessary to proscribe with sentence of condemnation the contrary erroneous opinions so detrimental to the Lord's flock.

### 1. The Establishment of the Apostolic Primacy in St. Peter

*Against heretics and schismatics*

*1822*    We teach and declare, therefore, according to the testimony of the Gospel that the primacy of jurisdiction over the whole Church of God was immediately and directly promised to and conferred upon the blessed Apostle Peter by Christ the Lord. For to Simon, Christ had said, "Thou shalt be called Cephas" (John 1:42). Then, after Simon had acknowledged Christ with the confession, "Thou art the Christ, the Son of the living God" (Matt. 16:16), it was to Simon alone that the solemn words were spoken by the Lord: "Blessed art thou, Simon Bar-Jona, for flesh and blood has not revealed this to thee, but my Father in heaven. And I say to thee, thou are Peter, and upon this rock I will build my Church, and the gates of hell shall not prevail against it. And I will give thee the keys of the kingdom of heaven; and whatever thou shalt bind on earth shall be bound in heaven, and whatever thou shalt loose on earth shall be loosed in heaven" (Matt. 16:17–19). And after his Resurrection, Jesus conferred upon Simon Peter alone the jurisdiction of supreme shepherd and ruler over his whole fold with the words, "Feed my lambs. . . . Feed my sheep" (John 21:15, 17). In open opposition to this very clear teaching of the Holy Scriptures, as it has always been understood by the Catholic Church, are the perverse opinions of those who wrongly explain the form of government established by Christ in his Church; either by denying that Peter alone in preference to the other apostles, either singly or as a group, was endowed by Christ with the true and proper primacy of jurisdiction; or by claiming that this same primacy was not given immediately and directly to St. Peter, but to the Church and through the Church to Peter as to an agent of the Church.

### Canon

*1823*    Therefore, if anyone says that the blessed Apostle Peter was not constituted by Christ the Lord as the Prince of all the Apostles and the visible head of the whole Church militant, or that he received immediately and directly from Jesus Christ our Lord only a primacy of honor and not a true and proper primacy of jurisdiction: let him be anathema.

## 2. The Continuation of St. Peter's Primacy in the Roman Pontiffs

*1824* Now, what Christ the Lord, supreme shepherd and watchful guardian of the flock, established in the person of the blessed Apostle Peter for the perpetual safety and everlasting good of the Church must, by the will of the same, endure without interruption in the Church which was founded on the rock and which will remain firm until the end of the world. Indeed, "no one doubts, in fact, it is obvious to all ages that the holy and most Blessed Peter, Prince and head of the Apostles, the pillar of faith, and the foundation of the Catholic Church, received the keys of the kingdom from our Lord Jesus Christ, the savior and the redeemer of the human race; and even to this time and forever he lives," and governs, "and exercises judgment in his successors," the bishops of the holy Roman See, which he established and consecrated with his blood. Therefore, whoever succeeds Peter in this Chair holds Peter's primacy over the whole Church according to the plan of Christ himself. "Therefore, the dispositions made by Truth endure; and St. Peter still has the rocklike strength that has been given to him, and he has not surrendered the helm of the Church with which he was entrusted." For this reason, "because of its greater sovereignty," it was always "necessary for every church, that is, the faithful who are everywhere to be in agreement" with the Roman Church. The outcome of this will be that in this See, from which "the bonds of sacred communion" are imparted to all, the members will be joined as members under one head and thus coalesce into one compact body.

### Canon

*1825* Therefore, if anyone says that it is not according to the institution of Christ our Lord himself, that is, by divine law, that St. Peter has perpetual successors in the primacy over the whole Church; or if anyone says that the Roman Pontiff is not the successor of St. Peter in the same primacy: let him be anathema.

## 3. The Power and the Nature of the Primacy of the Roman Pontiff

### *Declaration of the primacy*

*1826* Therefore, relying on the clear testimony of the Holy Scriptures and following the express and definite decrees of Our predecessors, the Roman Pontiffs, and of the general councils, We reaffirm the definition of the ecumenical Council of Florence. According to this definition all the faithful of Christ must believe "that the holy Apostolic See and the Roman Pontiff have the primacy over the whole world, and that the same Roman Pontiff is the successor of St. Peter, the Prince of the Apostles, and the true vicar of Christ, the head of the whole Church, the father and teacher of all Christians; and that to him, in the person of St. Peter, was given by our Lord Jesus Christ the full power of feeding, ruling, and governing the whole Church; as is also contained in the proceedings of the ecumenical councils and in the sacred canons."

*Consequences that the Reformers deny*

1827    And so We teach and declare that, in the disposition of God, the Roman Church holds the pre-eminence of ordinary power over all the other churches; and that this power of jurisdiction of the Roman Pontiff, which is truly episcopal, is immediate. Regarding this jurisdiction, the shepherds of whatever rite and dignity and the faithful, individually and collectively, are bound by a duty of hierarchical subjection and of sincere obedience; and this not only in matters that pertain to faith and morals, but also in matters that pertain to the discipline and government of the Church throughout the whole world. When, therefore, this bond of unity with the Roman Pontiff is guarded both in government and in the profession of the same faith, then the Church of Christ is one flock under one supreme shepherd. This is the doctrine of Catholic truth; and no one can deviate from this without losing his faith and his salvation.

*The jurisdiction of the Roman Pontiff and the bishops*

1828    This power of the Supreme Pontiff is far from standing in the way of the power of ordinary and immediate episcopal jurisdiction by which the bishops who, under appointment of the Holy Spirit (see Acts 20:28), succeeded in the place of the apostles, feed and rule individually, as true shepherds, the particular flock assigned to them. Rather this latter power is asserted, confirmed, and vindicated by this same supreme and universal shepherd in the words of St. Gregory the Great: "My honor is the honor of the whole Church. My honor is the solid strength of my brothers. I am truly honored when due honor is paid to each and every one."

*The right to deal freely with all the faithful*

1829    Furthermore, from his supreme power of governing the whole

Church, the Roman Pontiff has the right of freely communicating with the shepherds and flocks of the whole Church in the exercise of his office so that they can be instructed and guided by him in the way of salvation. Hence, We condemn and disapprove the opinions of those who say that it can be licit to hinder the communication of the supreme head with the shepherds and flocks; or those who make this communication subject to the secular power in such a way that they claim whatever is decreed for the government of the Church by the Apostolic See or by its authority has no binding force unless it is confirmed by the placet of the secular power.

*The right of recourse to the Roman Pontiff as supreme judge*
*1830* And because, by the divine right of apostolic primacy, the Roman Pontiff is at the head of the whole Church, We also teach and declare that he is the supreme judge of the faithful; and that one can have recourse to his judgment in all cases pertaining to ecclesiastical jurisdiction. We declare that the judgment of the Apostolic See, whose authority is unsurpassed, is not subject to review by anyone; nor is anyone allowed to pass judgment on its decision. Therefore, those who say that it is permitted to appeal to an ecumenical council from the decisions of the Roman Pontiff (as to an authority superior to the Roman Pontiff) are far from the straight path of truth.

Canon

*1831* And so, if anyone says that the Roman Pontiff has only the office of inspection or direction, but not the full and supreme power of jurisdiction over the whole Church, not only in matters that pertain to faith and morals, but also in matters that pertain to the discipline and government of the Church throughout the whole world; or if anyone says that he has only a more important part and not the complete fullness of this supreme power; or if anyone says that this power is not ordinary and immediate either over each and every church or over each and every shepherd and faithful member: let him be anathema.

4. The Infallible Teaching Authority of
   the Roman Pontiff

*Argument based on public documents*
*1832* Moreover, this Holy See has always held that the supreme power of teaching is also included in this apostolic primacy which the

Roman Pontiff, as the successor of St. Peter, the Prince of the Apostles, holds over the whole Church. The perpetual practice of the Church confirms this; and the ecumenical councils have declared it, especially those in which the Eastern and Western Churches were united in faith and love.

*1833* For the fathers of the Fourth Council of Constantinople, following closely in the footsteps of their predecessors, made this solemn profession: "The first condition of salvation is to keep the norm of the true faith. For it is impossible that the words of our Lord Jesus Christ who said, 'Thou art Peter, and upon this rock I will build my Church' (Matt. 16:18), should not be verified. And their truth has been proved by the course of history, for in the Apostolic See the Catholic religion has always been kept unsullied, and its teaching kept holy. From this faith and doctrine we by no means desire to be separated; and we hope that we may deserve to be associated with you in the one communion which the Apostolic See proclaims, in which the whole, true, and perfect security of the Christian religion resides."

*1834* Furthermore, with the approval of the Second Council of Lyons, the Greeks professed "that the holy Roman Church has supreme and full primacy and jurisdiction over the whole Catholic Church. This it truly and humbly recognizes as received from the Lord himself in the person of St. Peter, the Prince or head of the Apostles, whose successor in the fullness of power is the Roman Pontiff. And just as the holy Roman Church is bound more than all the others to defend the truth of faith, so, if there arise any questions concerning the faith, they must be decided by its judgment."

*1835* Finally, the Council of Florence defined "that the Roman Pontiff is the true vicar of Christ, the head of the whole Church, the father and teacher of all Christians; and that to him, in the person of St. Peter, was given by our Lord Jesus Christ the full power of feeding, ruling, and governing the whole Church."

*Argument based on the agreement of the Church*
*1836* To satisfy this pastoral duty, Our predecessors have always expended untiring effort to propagate Christ's doctrine of salvation among all the people of the world. And with similar care they have watched that the doctrine might be preserved genuine and pure wherever it was received. Therefore, the bishops of the whole world, sometimes singly, sometimes assembled in councils, following the long-standing custom of the churches and the form of the ancient rule, reported to this Apostolic See those dangers especially which came up in matters of faith, so that here where the faith can suffer no diminution, the harm

suffered by the faith might be repaired. However, the Roman Pontiffs on their part, according as the condition of the times and the circumstances dictated, sometimes calling together ecumenical councils or sounding out the mind of the Church throughout the whole world, sometimes through regional councils, or sometimes by using other helps which divine Providence supplied, have, with the help of God, defined as to be held such matters as they had found consonant with the Holy Scripture and with the apostolic tradition. The reason for this is that the Holy Spirit was promised to the successors of St. Peter not that they might make known new doctrine by his revelation, but rather, that with his assistance they might religiously guard and faithfully explain the revelation or deposit of faith that was handed down through the apostles. Indeed, it was this apostolic doctrine that all the Fathers held, and the holy orthodox Doctors reverenced and followed. For they fully realized that this See of St. Peter always remains untainted by any error, according to the divine promise of our Lord and Savior made to the prince of his disciples, "I have prayed for thee, that thy faith may not fail; and do thou, when once thou hast turned again, strengthen thy brethren" (Luke 22:32).

1837   Now this charism of truth and of never-failing faith was conferred upon St. Peter and his successors in this Chair, in order that they might perform their supreme office for the salvation of all; that by them the whole flock of Christ might be kept away from the poison of error and be nourished by the food of heavenly doctrine; that the occasion of schism might be removed, the whole Church preserved as one, and, secure on its foundation, stand firm against the gates of hell.

### The definition of infallibility

1838   But since in this present age, which especially requires the salutary efficacy of the apostolic office, not a few are found who minimize its authority, We think it extremely necessary to assert solemnly the prerogative which the only-begotten Son of God deigned to join to the highest pastoral office.

1839   And so, faithfully keeping to the tradition received from the beginning of the Christian faith, for the glory of God our Savior, for the exaltation of the Catholic religion, and for the salvation of Christian peoples, We, with the approval of the sacred council, teach and define that it is a divinely revealed dogma: that the Roman Pontiff, when he speaks ex cathedra, that is, when, acting in the office of shepherd and teacher of all Christians, he defines, by virtue of his supreme apostolic authority, doctrine concerning faith or morals to be held by the universal Church, possesses through the divine assistance promised to him in the person of St. Peter, the infallibility with which the divine Redeemer willed his Church to be endowed in defining doctrine concerning faith or morals; and that such definitions of the Roman Pontiff are therefore irreformable because of their nature, but not because of the agreement of the Church.

Canon

*1840*    But if anyone presumes to contradict this Our definition (God forbid that he do so): let him be anathema.

# PART FOUR

# An Uncertain Future: Americanism, Neo-Scholasticism, and Modernism

# 12

# The Mission of
# Catholics in America

*Archbishop John Ireland*

In the nineteenth century the official Bible of the Catholic church was the Latin Vulgate, wherein John 3:21 reads, Qui facit veritatem venit ad lucem, "He who does the truth comes to the light." But matters do not always go so smoothly as these Gospel words seem to suggest. "Doing things" is not always the same as "doing the right things," and the increment of knowledge brought about by doing things—or as this is more grandly styled today, praxis—may not turn out to be *the* light. Or perhaps we should say that pragmatically generated truth may hold some surprises, may be difficult to reconcile with what we have heretofore held to be true.

Just as the late-twentieth-century papacy has had difficulties with liberation theology, so the late-nineteenth-century papacy had difficulties with the philosophical pragmatism of the American William James and the Frenchman Edouard LeRoy—and also with the so-called Americanist views of Archbishop John Ireland, who led the faithful of St. Paul, Minnesota, from his appointment as coadjutor in 1875 to his death in 1918. Throughout the United States, Ireland was a highly respected public figure, and it is certainly arguable that his Americanism was in good part an independently arrived-at Catholic version of the social-gospel program. The reader may wish to compare Ireland's *The Church and Modern Society* with, for example, the *Theology for the Social Gospel* of his contemporary Walter Rauschenbusch.

Pope Leo XIII (reigned 1878–1903) wanted the teaching of Thomas Aquinas to be normative for Catholics. In his letter *Aeterni Patris* (1879) he told the bishops, "We earnestly exhort you that, for both the protection and the adornment of the Catholic faith, for the good of society, and for the advancement of all the sciences, you restore and as widely as possible propagate the golden wisdom of St. Thomas." That golden wisdom was a blend of realist philosophy and supernaturally caused faith. Thomist textbooks offered this realist definition of philosophical truth: *adaequatio intellectus cum re,* the correspondence of the intellect with the thing. This harmless-sounding conception of truth could, however, easily be used as the point of departure for a quite conservative world view: the things to which intellect must open itself would seem to be already existing things, not those still in the process of being discovered. (Here we have an element of what Bernard Lonergan, S.J., was to call a classicist world view.) It seems fair to say that Leo XIII was ambivalent about "modernity." Perhaps moved in part by the urging of the leader of the American hierarchy, the great conciliator James Cardinal Gibbons, Leo did uphold the rights of labor (in the letter *Rerum Novarum*, 1891). Still, he was suspicious of the separation of church and state. (In the letter *Longinqua Oceani* [1895] he actually affirmed that the American Catholic church would "bring forth more abundant fruits if, in addition to liberty, she enjoyed the favor of the laws and the patronage of public authority." The letter is to be found in *Documents of American Catholic History,* ed. John Tracy Ellis [Milwaukee: Bruce Pub. Co., 1956; Wilmington, Del.; Michael Glazier, 1987].)

In his letter *Testem Benevolentiae* (1899; also in *Documents of American Catholic History*) Leo condemned Americanism. (Supposedly Americanism was to be found in Walter Elliott's biography of Isaac Hecker, the founder of the Paulist community, and in the remarks of Félix Klein prefaced to the French translation of that biography. Devotees of clerical infighting will find interesting blow-by-blow accounts in Moynihan's life of Ireland, Ellis's life of Gibbons, and McAvoy's study of Americanism.) Americanism as described by the pope turned out to be a kind of phantom heresy: Archbishops Corrigan of New York and Katzer of Milwaukee thanked Leo for condemning this clear and present danger to Catholicism, whereas Gibbons and Ireland asserted that Americanism, while certainly damnable, was also mostly imaginary. Ireland wrote to Leo, "It is the enemies of the Church in America and the faithless interpreters of the faith who 'imagine' that there exists, or that some desire to establish, in the United States a Church differing in one iota from the Holy and Universal Church which other nations recognize, . . . and which Rome . . . recognizes" (James H. Moynihan, *The Life of Archbishop John Ireland* [New York: Harper & Bros., 1953], 126).

So what was Americanism? The least confusing description of what was condemned lies in the condemnatory letter itself. Salient emphases in Americanism do, however, include the beliefs that *(a)* "the Church ought to . . . show some indulgence to modern, popular theories and methods"; *(b)* ordinary human ("natural") virtues, particularly of the active, or "muscular," kind, are preferable to the supernatural virtues of faith, hope, and love, and to the exercise of the latter in prayer and the contemplative life; and *(c)* the church should be democratized, with the laity relying much less than before on the guidance of the clergy. If one reads quickly, these emphases will seem to appear in the address by Ireland given here. Perhaps on any reading they will appear; it was a question, in 1899, of how much is too much. Leo feared that already discernible changes in practice would entail changes in doctrine.

But what a wonderful occasion it was in 1889 for a man born in 1838 in County Kilkenny and taken to Minnesota as a boy, for the one-time Civil War chaplain, to stand before a distinguished audience—Ireland was a fine orator— and to celebrate the glories past and yet to be of the American church. Ireland foresaw that the United States would become a superpower, and he thought that American Catholics would be the best guardians of the Constitution, the best apostles of America's mission to the world. He called for expanded educational opportunities at all levels and "material comfort" for the masses. In other addresses (not that given here) he called for full civil rights for American blacks.

("Untimely today," he told critics of his racial views in 1891, "my words will be timely tomorrow. My fault, if there be a fault, would be that I am ahead of my day.") The list of Ireland's achievements is a long one. He got the railroader James J. Hill to build and endow his diocesan seminary. In St. Paul he built a great "modified Renaissance" cathedral for all to behold. He thought big.

The hundredth anniversary of the establishment of the Catholic hierarchy in the United States was celebrated with pomp and ceremony in the Cathedral of Baltimore on the tenth day of November, 1889.

Nearly all the bishops of the country, together with hundreds of priests and distinguished laymen, had come to Baltimore to take part in the festivities. Bishops and priests from Canada, Mexico, and England were also present. The Sovereign Pontiff, Leo XIII, was represented in the person of Monsignor Francis Satolli.

The celebration was worthy of the event that it commemorated.

The brief of Pius VI, erecting the episcopal see of Baltimore and giving to the United States its first bishop, bore the date November 6th, 1789. Before that time the Church in the United States had been governed by the Vicar Apostolic of London, England. Whatever the works of zeal which Catholic priests and laymen attempt or do in any country where the episcopate is not established, the Church is not rooted in that country, nor can she attain there her full growth. The episcopate was instituted by Christ as the ordinary government of the Church, and to the episcopate alone Christ has attached the graces of divine government. The brief of Pius VI was the creation of the American Church, the infusion into her of the fullness of life, and of the forces through which she was to prosper and conquer.

The first century of the Church in America was one of marvelous growth. From John Carroll, first Bishop of Baltimore, the only bishop in the vast territory between the Atlantic and the Pacific, to James Gibbons, the ninth Bishop of Baltimore, the primate of a Church that numbers seventy-seven bishops, a Cardinal of the Church Catholic— what wondrous changes a hundred years have brought about!

The hundredth anniversary of the establishment of the hierarchy was an occasion of rejoicing and of thanksgiving. It was something more. It was an occasion that suggested to the Catholics of 1889—clergymen and laymen—solemn thoughts as to the possibilities of work for the Church in the second century of her history in the United States and the obligations which those possibilities impose. The completeness of the celebration demanded that the coming century be considered and meditated upon no less than the past.

Great, indeed, the possibilities for the Church, and great the obligations of Catholics! The opening of the second century of the history of

From *The Church and Modern Society: Lectures and Addresses,* 2 vols. (St. Paul: Pioneer Press, 1904–5), 1:67–104.

the Church in the United States finds in the United States a population of sixty-five millions, of whom ten millions are Catholics, and finds the world on the eve of a new age, the twentieth century! On the morning of the anniversary celebration, the Archbishop of Philadelphia spoke of the glories and the triumphs of the century that was then closing; at the evening service, the Archbishop of St. Paul spoke of the possibilities and the duties of the century that was then opening:

> For thy soul strive for justice, and even unto death fight for justice, and God will overthrow thy enemies for thee. (Ecclesiasticus 4:33)

A century closes; a century opens. The present is for Catholics in America a most solemn moment. Another speaker has reviewed the past, evoked from its shades the spirits of its heroes, and read to you the lessons of their labors. I bid you turn to the future. It has special significance for us. The past our fathers wrought; the future will be wrought by us. The next century of the life of the Church in America will be what we make it. It will be our own, the fruit of our labors. Oh, for a prophet's eye to glance adown the unborn years, and from now to read the story of God's Church on this continent as generations a hundred years hence may read it! But no prophet's eye is needed. As we will it, so shall the story be. Brothers—bishops, priests, laymen—in what words shall I tell the responsibility which weighs upon us? There is so much at stake for God and souls, for Church and Country! There is so much in dependency upon our coöperation with the divine action in the world![1] The duty of the moment is to understand our responsibility, and to do the full work that Heaven has allotted to us—for our souls to strive for justice, and even unto death to fight for justice.

I would sink deeply into your souls the vital truth that the work which is to be done is our work. With us it will be done; without us it will not be done. There is to-day sore need that we ponder well this truth; for in practice, though not in theory, the error obtains among us, that in religious matters man has scarcely aught to do, the work having been done by the Almighty God. Do not imagine that I am losing sight of the necessity of the divine. The lesson of faith is not forgotten: "Unless the Lord build the house, they labor in vain who build it."[2] But it is no less the teaching of faith that in producing results the human blends with the divine, and that the absence of the one renders the other sterile. Too often we refuse to do our part; we seem to wish that God would do all. God will not alter the rulings of His providence to make up for our inaction.

There are times in the history of the Church when it is imperative that stress be laid on the supernatural in the work of religion. There are times when it is imperative that stress be laid on the natural. Singular phenomenon of our days! In all matters outside religion, the natural has unlimited play, and summons into action its most hidden energies; in religion, it seems as if the natural sought to extinguish itself so as to leave the entire field to the supernatural. There are countries where faithful Catholics pray, administer, or receive sacraments, but fear to go further. I cannot name a country where they are fully alive to their opportunities and their duties. Do Catholics in America put into the work of religion the sleepless energy and the boundless earnestness that characterize them in secular affairs? As Catholics too often are and too often do, failure in religion is inevitable. God will save His Church in all times. This He has promised. But no promise was given as to the splendor of her reign, or as to the permanency of her dwelling among a particular people. The apocalyptic candlestick has been often moved from its place. There are bright and there are dark lines in the Church's history. God's work is always done; man's work is often left undone. When saints walked on earth, their pathway sparkled with rays of light from heaven, and the surrounding atmosphere became ablaze. In our own country, what will be the lines of the Church's history? God demands that we make answer.

Let me state, as I conceive it, the work which, in God's providence, the Catholics of the United States are called to do within the coming century. It is twofold: To make America Catholic and to solve for the Church universal the all-absorbing problems with which religion is confronted in the present age.[3] Never, I believe, since the century the dawn of which was the glimmer from the Eastern Star, was there prepared for Catholics of any nation of earth a work so noble in its nature and so pregnant with consequences as that which it is our mission to accomplish. The work defines the measure of the responsibility.

The work is to make America Catholic. As we love America, as we love the Church, it suffices to mention the work, and our cry shall be, "God wills it," and our hearts shall leap towards it with Crusader enthusiasm. We know that the Church is the sole owner of the truths and graces of salvation. Would we not that she pour upon the souls of friends and fellow-citizens the gifts of the Incarnate God? The touch of her sacred hand will strengthen and sublimate the rich heritage of nature's virtues, which is the portion of America and of America's children; it will add the deifying treasures of supernatural life. The Catholic Church will preserve as no human power, no human church can preserve, the liberties of the Republic. We know that by the command of the Master it is the bounden duty of the Church to teach all nations. To lose the apostolic spirit were, on her part, to give proof that she is unconscious of the truths which she owns and of the commission under which she exists. The conversion of America should ever be present to the minds of Catholics in America as a supreme duty from which God will not hold them exempt. If we are loyal to duty, the record of our second century of Church history will tell of the wondrous spread of Christ's Church over the United States of America.

The value of America to the cause of religion cannot be overestimated. This is a providential nation. How youthful and yet how great! How rich in glorious promise! A hundred years ago the States hardly exceeded the third million in population; to-day they approach the sixty-fifth million. Streams of immigration from the lands of the earth are turned toward us. There is manifestly much in our soil and air, in our social and political institutions; for the world's throngs are drawn to us. The country must grow and prosper. In the solution of social and political problems, no less than in the development of industry and commerce, the influence of America will be dominant among nations. There is not a country on the globe that does not borrow from us ideas and aspirations. The spirit of American liberty wafts its spell across seas and oceans, and prepares distant continents for the implanting of American ideas and institutions. This influence will grow with the growth of the nation. Estimates have been made as to our population a century hence, placing it at 400,000,000, due allowance being had in this computation for diminution in the numbers of immigrants. The center of human action and influence is rapidly shifting, and at a no distant day America will lead the world. The native character of the American people fits them to be leaders. They are earnest, deliberate, aggressive. Whatever they believe, they act out; whatever they aim for, they attain. They are utterly incapable of the indifference to living interests and of the apathy which, under the specious name of conservatism, characterize European populations. The most daring elements of other lands have come hither to form a new people—new in energy, new in spirit, new in action—in complete adaptation to a new epoch in the world's history. We cannot but believe that a singular mission is assigned to America, glorious for itself and beneficent to the whole race, the mission of bringing about a new social and political order, based more than any other upon the common brotherhood of man, and more than any other securing to the multitude of the people social happiness and equality of rights. With our hopes are bound up the hopes of the millions of the earth. The Church triumphing in America, Catholic truth will travel on the wings of American influence, and encircle the universe.[4]

The work of Catholics in America is also to solve for the Church
Universal the problems with which religion is to-day confronted.

We are advancing towards one of those great epochs of history, in
which mighty changes will be wrought. The world is in throes; a new age
is to be born—"Magnus ab integro saeclorum nascitur ordo."[5] The
traditions of the past are vanishing; new social forms and new political
institutions are arising; astounding discoveries are being made of the
secrets and the powers of nature; unwonted forces are at work in every
sphere over which man's control reaches. There is a revolution in the
ideas and the feelings of men. All things which may be changed will be
changed, and nothing will be to-morrow as it was yesterday, save that
which emanates directly from God, or which the Eternal Power decrees
to be permanent.

Amid the movements of the modern world the startling question has
been put: Will not the Church, herself an institution of past ages,
disappear with other legacies of those ages? Why should she alone
triumphantly withstand the billows that are sweeping all else into destruction?

Catholics are ready with the answer: No; the Church will not disappear, whatever else disappears, for the Church is divine, and was made
for all ages.

But proofs must accompany the answer; and the most effective
proof—the one to which the modern world is most disposed to hearken—is to show that the Church is truly of the present age, as she was of
other ages, that she understands its needs and sympathizes with whatever is true and good in its ambitions, and that with the Church and
through the Church those ambitions will be realized.

A study of the modern world leads us to say that its predominant
feature is a resolute assertion of the powers and the rights of natural, as
distinguished from revealed or supernatural order. Nineteen hundred
years ago the Christian religion displaced in the life of mankind
paganism, under whose reign corrupt nature was unrestrained. During
many subsequent centuries the supernatural was supreme, permeating
minds and hearts, extending its influence over social institutions and
governments, over arts and industries, the natural order, meanwhile,
acting in fullest harmony with its laws and spirit. At the opening of the
sixteenth century, signs of a new era appeared on the horizon. The
Renaissance, unconsciously perhaps, sowed the seeds of rebellion
against the supernatural. The inevitable reaction from the teachings of
the reformers, as to the total depravity of the fallen race, quickened in
man the spirit of self-assertion. Then came the wondrous feats and

discoveries of the past hundred years to embolden the intellect, and nature at last proclaimed its self-sufficiency and its independence. The watchwords of the age are reason, education, liberty, the amelioration of the masses.[6] Nor are these watchwords empty sounds. They represent solid realities which it is noble in the age to strive for. Rebellious nature lays claim to words and to realities, as if they were its exclusive property, obtained not only by its unaided self, but even in spite of the supernatural. In the name of every forward movement war is declared against the Church and revealed religion; and combatants, ranged under banners upon which seductive words are inscribed, easily gain popular applause. The purpose is to exclude Christ and His Church from the living world, to relegate them to ruins and to sepulchres, even as Christ and His Church at one time relegated paganism. The war is between the natural and the supernatural. I need not state what is the duty of Christians. It is to maintain in the world the supremacy of the supernatural, and to save the age to the Church.

The burden of the strife falls upon Catholics in America. In America the movements of the modern world attain their greatest tension. Here the natural order is seen at its best, and here it displays its fullest strength. Here, too, the Church, unhampered by dictate of government or by despotism of custom, can, with the freedom of the Son of Jesse, choose its arms, and, making straight for the opposing foe, bring the contest to a more speedy close.

I am aware that there are among us those who do not share my hopefulness. What can be done, they say, in America? Catholics are a handful—ten millions in sixty-five—the few among the many, struggling against prejudice. The mere preservation of the little flock in the faith is a herculean task. Ill prepared are we to attempt the conversion of our fellow-citizens; and ill disposed are they to hearken to our words. As to the burning questions agitating the world, the prospect of a solution that will satisfy the age is remote. They sky above us is cloud-laden, and no glimmer of light pierces through it. The days of failing faith are upon us. The refuge of each one is to flee for safety to the mountains, and to wait in silence and prayer the return of God's vivifying breath upon the nations.

Brothers, hold not the language of fear and distrust. Will Catholics say that the triumphs of other days are not possible in our times and our country? The Church is the same to-day as when she overthrew pagan Rome, or won to grace ferocious Northmen—the Church of divine truth and divine power. Her commission is the same to-day as then—to teach all nations—and Christ is with her, even unto the consummation of ages.

God's arm is not shortened. What, then, is wanting? Our own resolute will to put to profit God's graces and God's opportunities. "For thy soul fight for justice, and even unto death strive for justice, and God will overthrow thy enemies."

Why should we fear or hesitate? We number ten millions—in the arena of truth and justice a powerful army, if the forces be well marshaled, and their latent strength be brought into action. Catholics in America are loyal to the Church and devoted to her chieftains, brave in confessing the faith and self-sacrificing in its interests. They have waxed strong amid storms; they have none of the hot-house debility of character which not seldom marks Catholics in countries where faith seems to live only because of its environment.[7] Their labors and their victories in the first century of their history, a century of poverty, struggling, and spiritual destitution, show what they are capable of in a century of adult stature, conscious power, and completeness of hierarchical organization.

Non-Catholic Americans deserve, by their splendid natural virtues, that we labor to impart to them the plenitude of Christ's faith; and neither in disposition nor in act do they place obstacles in our pathway. They are clever, intelligent, ready to listen, anxious to know what is the truth. They are fast putting off the old traditional prejudices against the Church. If they still retain some prejudices, the fault is ours. Either we have not sufficiently proved our faith by our manner of life, or we have not presented the truth with due urgency, and by methods that captivate attention. The alienation of non-Catholics in America from the Church is an inherited misfortune. They have deeply religious instincts; vital Christian principles are rooted in their modes of thought and social practices. America is at heart a Christian country. As a religious system, Protestantism is in process of dissolution; it is without value as a doctrinal or a moral power, and it is no longer a foe with which we need to reckon. The American people are generous, large-minded and large-hearted, earnest in all things, sincerely desirous of moral and intellectual growth. To repeat the words of Orestes A. Brownson: "Never, since her going forth from that upper room in Jerusalem, has the Church found a national character so well fitted to give her civilization its highest and noblest expression."[8] The supernatural rests on the natural, which it purifies and ennobles, adding to it supernatural gifts of grace and glory. Where the natural is most carefully cultivated, there will be found the best results from the union of nature and grace. The American people made Catholic, nowhere shall we find a higher order of Christian civilization than in America.

It can be shown to the American people that they need the Church for the preservation and the complete development of their national character and their social order.[9] So far, their civilization has had its life through that strong Christian element which is permeating it, and which, notwithstanding their separation from the Church, has remained with them. This element, however, is rapidly losing its vitality amid the disintegrating processes to which the negations of Protestantism subject it. The Catholic Church is the sole living and enduring Christian authority. She alone has the power to speak; she alone has an organization by which her laws may be enforced. To her the American people must look to maintain for them in the consciences of citizens the principles of morality and of religion, without which a people will ultimately fall into chaotic anarchy, or become the prey of ambitious despotism.

An inestimable advantage to us is the liberty which the Church enjoys under the Constitution of the United States. Here no tyrant casts chains around her; no concordat limits her action, or cramps her energy. Here she is as free as the eagle upon Alpine heights, free to unfold her pinions in unobstructed flight, and to soar to loftiest altitudes. The law of the land protects her in her rights, and asks in return no sacrifice of these rights, for her rights are those of American citizenship. The Republic at its very birth guaranteed liberty to Catholics at a time when, in nearly all other lands, governments, both Protestant and Catholic, were oppressing the Church; and during its whole history the Republic has not failed to make good its guaranty. To-day, in how few countries outside our own, is the Church really free! If great things are not done by Catholics in America, the fault lies surely with themselves, and not with the Republic.[10]

The tendencies of the age, which affright the timid, are providential opportunities, opening the way to glorious victory. I am far from asserting that modern ideas and movements are in all respects deserving of approval. Not seldom do they betray, in one way or another, immoral and iniquitous tendencies, and Pius IX has warned us in his Syllabus that when they present themselves under those aspects the Church will not be reconciled to them.[11] And yet how much there is in those ideas and movements that is grand and good! Despite its defects and its mistakes, I love my age. I love its aspirations and its resolves. I revel in its feats of valor, its industries, and its discoveries. I thank it for its many benefactions to my fellow-men, for its warm affections proffered to the people rather than to prince and ruler. I seek no backward voyage across the sea of time; I will ever press forward. I believe that God intends the present to be better than the past, and the future to be better than the present.

Let us be fair to the age, discerning in it that which is good, as well as that which is bad. The good is the essence; the bad is the accident, the misdirection. The movements of the age have their origin in the deepest recesses of humanity. As they part from their source they are upward; they make for the elevation of the race, the betterment of the multitude, the extension of man's empire over nature. Pass in review the watchwords of the age—each covers a substantial good, finding favor in the eyes of God and of those who love Him. Knowledge—it is the nurture of our noblest faculty, the intellect. Science—it is the peering into the mysteries of nature, into the glorious works of the all-wise and all-powerful God. Liberty—it first came to men through gospel truth; the Church has made ceaseless war on slavery and despotism, and the trend of all Christianity has been to enlarge the race's heritage of civil and political liberty. The amelioration of the masses—it has been the constant aim of Christian charity; it is the practical application of the Christian doctrine of the brotherhood of man and the fatherhood of God. Material comfort—there is abundant room for it beneath the broad mantle of Christian love; asceticism, beyond that detachment in spirit which is enjoined upon all, is the privilege of the chosen few; the ideal, both for religion and reason, is a sound mind in a sound body, and whatever interferes with either, be it hunger or malady, be it overwork or tainted air, true godliness will labor to remove. Socialism—it is, in its first outburst, the shriek of despair from the hungering souls upon which presses the heavy hand of greed and injustice; reasons for many of its demands are found in Catholic theology, which teaches that the human race does not exist for the benefit of the few, and that private property becomes common property when death from starvation is at the door.[12] And so it is with other watchwords of the age. They express aspirations towards a perfect civilization, towards the enjoyment of God's gifts in full measure, and by the largest number of God's children. That at times the age runs riot and plunges into fatal errors, leading to misery and ruin, is, I repeat, the accident arising from the absence of proper direction. Why have but anathemas for the age, seeing only its aberrations, irritating it by continuous denunciations of its mistakes, never acknowledging the good in it, never striving to win its love to Holy Church?

We can, if we wish, make the age the relentless enemy of religion. By coldness and harshness it is possible to drive it to despair. Meanwhile, wise in their generation, irreligion and secularism steal sacred words, words which are ours together with the realities they represent, words which the age yearns to hear, and which we refuse to speak to it; and sounding aloud those words, they draw the age into desert wastes, to its misery and utter ruin. It is ours to lose the age to Christ's Church, or to make it her devoted and grateful child.

The age is eager for gifts which the Church alone can bestow. Its present energies and ambitions are the fruits of the work of the Church. Through Christian influences it has risen to such a degree of power and consciousness that it aspires to higher things. It was the religion of Christ that first whispered into the ears of the world the sacred words: charity, brotherhood, liberty. It was the religion of Christ that took to its bosom bleeding, agonizing humanity, warmed it with divine love, healed its sores and breathed into it health and vigor. And only under the blessed guidance of the religion of Christ can humanity proceed on the road towards greater progress. Irreligion has stolen only words; it did not steal realities; for the realities have no existence away from God's altars. Tell all this to the age, and say to it: "Passing by and seeing your idols, I found also an altar on which was written, 'To the unknown God.' What, therefore, you worship without knowing, that I preach unto you."[13]

Tell all this to the age, and work to make good your assertions. Bid science, beneath the spell of religion's wand, to put on brightest pinions and covet highest flights. Whisper in tender accents to liberty that religion cherishes it, and stands ready to guard it alike from anarchy and despotism. Go down in sympathy to the suffering multitude, bringing to them charity, and, what is more needed and more rarely given, justice. Let labor know that religion will ward off the oppression of capital, and will teach capital that its rights are dependent upon its fulfilment of duties. Let labor and capital understand that their respective rights are nowhere so safe as under the aegis of the religion which preaches ceaselessly to them their respective duties. In this manner you will give to the world the new religion for which it yearns and prays—the religion of humanity, the religion of the age, which will be the old religion— God's truths never changing, the householders simply bringing forth out of their treasure "new things and old"—and the age will rush into the arms of the Church, and, in ecstatic love, will proclaim her its teacher and its queen.

In all truth, the greatest epoch of human history, if we except that which witnessed the coming of God upon earth, is upon us; and of this epoch our wisdom and our energy will make the Church supreme mistress.

Permit me briefly to trace lines of duty, fidelity to which is a condition of the realization of our hopes for the new century.

I repeat: "For thy soul fight for justice, and even unto death strive for justice." Earnestness is the virtue of the hour. It is the characteristic of Americans in things secular; it should be their characteristic in things religious. Let Catholics elsewhere, if they will, move on in old grooves, and fear, lest by quickened pace, they disturb their souls or ruffle their garments. Our motto be: "Dare and Do." Let there be no room among us for the lackadaisical piety which lazily awaits a zephyr from the sky, the bearer of efficacious grace, while God's grace is at hand entreating to be made efficacious by our own coöperation. We must pray, and pray earnestly, but we must work, and work earnestly. We fail if we work and do not pray; and likewise we fail if we pray and do not work, if we are on our knees when we should be fleet of foot, if we are in the sanctuary when we should be in the highways and the market places. Earnestness will make us aggressive. There will be among us a prudent but manly assertion of faith whenever circumstances demand it, and a determination to secure to Catholics rightful recognition, whether in private or public life. We shall seek our opportunities to serve religion, and when we have discovered them we shall not pass them by unheeded. We are often cowards, and to cloak our cowardice we invoke modesty and prudence, as if Christ had ordered us to put our light under the bushel. If the Church is slighted, or treated unfairly, we complain— we are admirable at complaining—but we do not stir to prevent injustice in the future. There is a woeful lack of Catholic public spirit. We are devoted to religion on Sunday, or when we are saying our morning or evening prayers. In the world's battles we seem to lose sight of our faith, and our public men are eager to doff all Catholic vesture. In American parlance—let us go ahead. What if at times we do blunder? Success is not the test of valor or merit. If we never venture, we never win. The conservatism which wishes to be ever safe is dry-rot. Pay no attention to criticism; there is never a lack of it. It usually comes from men who are do-nothings, and who rejoice if failure follows action, so that they may have a justification for their own idleness. Do not fear what is novel, provided principles are well guarded. It is a time of novelties, and religious action, to accord with the age, must take new forms and new directions. Let there be individual action. Layman need not wait for priest, nor priest for bishop, nor bishop for pope.[14] The timid move in crowds, the brave in single file. When combined efforts are called for, be ready to act and prompt to obey the orders which are given; but never forget that vast room remains for individual action.

We should live in our age, know it, be in touch with it. There are Catholics, more numerous, however, in Europe than in America, to whom the present will not be known until long after it will have become the past. Our work is in the present, and not in the past. It will not do to understand the thirteenth century better than the nineteenth; to be more conversant with the errors of Arius or Eutyches than those of contemporary infidels or agnostics; to study more deeply the causes of Albigensian or Lutheran heresies, or of the French Revolution, than the causes of the social upheavals of our own times. The world has entered upon an entirely new phase; the past will not return; reaction is the dream of men who see not, and hear not; who, in utter oblivion of the living world behind them, sit at the gates of cemeteries weeping over tombs that shall not be reopened. We should speak to our age of things which it feels and in language that it understands. We should be in it, and of it, if we would have it listen to us.

For the same reasons, there is need of thorough sympathy with the country. The Church in America must be, of course, as Catholic as in Jerusalem or Rome; but so far as her garments may be colored to suit environment, she must be American.

There is danger: we receive large accessions of Catholics from foreign countries. God witnesses that they are welcome. I will not intrude on their personal affections and tastes; but these, if foreign, shall not encrust themselves upon the Church.[15] Americans have no longing for a Church with a foreign aspect; they will not submit to its influence. Only institutions to the manor born prosper; exotics have but sickly forms.

America treats us well; her flag is our protection. Patriotism is a Catholic virtue. I would have Catholics be the first patriots in the land. There are fitting occasions, when the Church should officially show forth her love of America, blessing the country, offering thanks in its name, invoking favors upon it. There are occasions without number when Catholics, as citizens, can prove their patriotism; and of such occasions they should be eager to avail themselves. The men most devoted to the institutions of the country, the most ardent lovers of its flag, should be they who believe in Catholic truth, who breathe the air of Catholic sanctuaries. Catholics should be models of civic virtue, taking an abiding interest in public affairs, bearing cheerfully their part of the public burdens, always free from selfishness and venality in the exercise of their privileges of citizenship.

This is an intellectual age. It worships intellect. It tries all things by the touchstone of intellect. By intellect, public opinion, the ruling power of the age, is formed. The Church herself will be judged by the standard of intellect. Catholics must excel in religious knowledge; they must be ready to give reasons for the faith that is in them, meeting objections from whatever source, abreast of the times in their methods of argument. They must be in the foreground of intellectual movements of all kinds. The age will not take kindly to religious knowledge separated from secular knowledge. The Church must regain the scepter of science, which, to her honor and to the benefit of the world, she wielded for ages in the past. An important work for Catholics in the coming century will be the building of schools, colleges, and seminaries; and a work more important still will be the lifting up of present and future institutions to the highest degree of intellectual excellence.[16] Only the best schools will give the Church the men she needs. Modern, too, must they be in curriculum and method, so that pupils going forth from their halls will be men for the twentieth century and men for America.

In love, in reverence, in hope I salute thee, Catholic University of America! Thy birth—happy omen!—is coeval with the opening of the new century. The destinies of the Church in America are in thy keeping. May heaven's light shine over thee and heaven's love guard thee. Be ever faithful to thy motto, *Deo et Patriae*. Hasten thy work, so that our youth, whatever be the vocation to which they aspire, may soon throng thy halls, and by thee be fitted to be ideal children of Church and country. Meanwhile, School of our Hopes, nurture well our youthful priesthood! The priests will be leaders, and as they are, so will the whole army of God's soldiers be amid the battles of life.[17]

I do not forget the vast importance of Catholic literature and of the Catholic press. They, too, are schools, and schools not only for the days of youth, but for the entire time of life; they deserve, and should receive, our warmest encouragement.

The strength of the Church to-day in all countries, particularly in America, is the people. Ours is essentially the age of democracy. The days of princes and of feudal lords are gone. Woe to religion where this fact is not understood! He who holds the masses, reigns. The masses are held by intellect and heart. No power controls them, save that which touches their own free souls. We have a dreadful lesson to learn from certain European countries, where, under the weight of tradition, the Church clings to thrones and classes, and loses thereby her power over the people.[18] Let us not make this mistake. In America we have no princes, no hereditary classes. Still, there is danger that in America there be formed a religious aristocracy, upon whom we lavish so much care that none remains for others. Are we not inclined to intrench ourselves within the sanctuary, and to see only the little throng of devout persons who weekly or monthly kneel around the altar-rail, or those whose title to nobility is that they are pew-holders and respond to the pastor's call with generous subscriptions? Pews and pew-holders may be necessary evils; but it were fatal not to look far beyond them. What, I ask, of the multitude who peep at us from gallery and vestibule? What of the thousands and tens of thousands, nominal Catholics and non-Catholics, who seldom or never open the church door? What of the uncouth and unkempt, the tenant of the cellar and alley-way, the mendicant and outcast? It is time to bring back the primitive gospel spirit, to go out into highways and byways, to preach on house tops and in market places.

Erect stately temples if you will; they are grand monuments to religion; but see to it that they be filled with people.

If people do not come to the temple, invite them to hear you beneath humbler roof. And if some yet remain outside, speak to them in the street or on the public road. The time has come for "salvation armies" to penetrate the wildest thicket of thorns and briars, and to bring God's word to the ear of the most vile, the most ignorant, the most godless.[19]

To save those who insist on being saved, is not the mission of the Church. "Compel them to come in,"[20] is the command of the Master. To sing lovely anthems in Cathedral stalls, and wear copes of broidered gold while no multitude throng nave or aisle, and while the world outside is dying of spiritual and moral starvation—this is not the religion we need to-day. Seek out men; speak to them not in stilted phrase or seventeenth-century sermon style, but in burning words that go to their hearts, as well as to their minds, and in accents that are familiar to their ears. Popularize religion, so far as principles permit; make the people chant in holy exultation canticles of praise and adoration; draw them to God by all "the cords of Adam." Save the masses. Cease not to plan and work for their salvation.

The care of the masses implies an abiding and active interest in the social questions that torment humanity at the present time. Our chieftain, Leo XIII, who knows his age, and whose heart-beatings are in sympathy with it, has told Catholics their duties on this point. About two years ago he recommended that social questions be made part of the special curriculum of studies which are to fit priests for their ministerial labors. Whatever be the cause there exist dreadful social injustices. Men, made in the image of the Creator, are viewed as pieces of machinery or beasts of burden. The moral instincts are ground out of them. Until their material condition is improved, it is futile to speak to them of supernatural life and duties. Men who suffer are conscious of their wrongs, and will hold as their friends those who aid them. Irreligion makes promises to them, and irreligion is winning them. They who should be the first and the last in promise and in deed are silent. It is deplorable that Catholics grow timid, take refuge in sanctuary and cloister, and leave the bustling, throbbing world with its miseries and sins to the wiles of false friends and cunning practitioners. Leo XIII speaks fearlessly to the world of the rights of labor; Cardinal Lavigerie pleads for the African slave; Cardinal Manning interposes his hand between the plutocratic merchant and the workingman of the docks; Count de Mun and his band of noble-minded friends devote time and talent to the interests of French laborers.[21] But, as a body, Catholics are

quietness itself. They say their prayers, they preach, they listen to
sermons on the love of God and on resignation in suffering; or, if they
venture at all into the arena, it is at the eleventh hour, when others have
long preceded them, and public opinion has already been formed.
Strange, indeed, is all this! Christ made the social question the basis of
His ministry. The evidence of His divinity which He gave to the disciples
of John was: "The blind see, the lame walk, the lepers are cleansed, and
the poor have the Gospel preached to them."[22] Throughout her whole
history the Church grappled with every social problem that came in her
way and solved it. The Church liberated the Roman slave, raised up
woman, civilized the barbarian, humanized medieval warfare, and gave
civic rights to the child of serfdom. What has come over us that we shun
the work which is essentially ours to do? These are days of action, days
of warfare. It is not the age of the timid and fugitive virtue of the
Thebaid. Into the arena, priest and layman! Seek out social evils, and
lead in movements that tend to rectify them. Speak of vested rights, for
this is necessary; but speak, too, of vested wrongs, and strive, by word
and example, by the enactment and enforcement of good laws, to
correct them. Glance mercifully into factories at etiolated youth and
infancy. Pour fresh air into the crowded tenement quarters of the poor.
Follow upon the streets the crowds of vagrant children. Visit prisons and
secure for the inmates moral and religious instruction. Lessen on rail-
ways and in public service the Sunday work which renders the practice of
religion impossible for the thousands. Cry out against the fearful evil of
intemperance which is hourly damning the bodies and souls of countless
victims, and which, at the present time, is, more than any other social
sin, bringing disgrace upon the Church and misery upon her children.
Into the arena, I repeat, to the work, which lies before you, in this age
and this country, caring not for customs of the dead, nor for sharp
criticisms from the living, fighting at every point for justice with bravery
and perseverance. This is "religion pure and undefiled."[23] This is the
religion that will win the age to God's Church.

I do not overlook our duty to our non-Catholic brethren. We must
earnestly desire their conversion, and earnestly work for it. Our prayers,
doubtless, our good example, the fulfillment of the duties I have mentioned, will be the surest means to success. Instruction should, nevertheless, be given, specially adapted to the intellectual needs of non-Catholics.[24] Efforts should be made to bring them to our temples, and kind
attention should be shown to them when they do come. Books should be
prudently distributed among them. Above all, we shoud know them,
and, sincerely loving them, desire their conversion. We sometimes repel
them through prejudice; we do not make sufficient allowance for their

good intentions; we do not acknowledge the degree of Christian truth and Christian practice which they possess. Let us be just; let us admit what they have and then tell them what they have not. If we do our duty, truth will make progress among our non-Catholic fellow-citizens, and, once made Catholics, they will, by their zeal and activity, rank among the most loyal and most devoted of the children of the Church.

What I have said applies to all—to priests, who, as leaders, must be the first to act, as well as to command; and, in great measure, to laymen. But lest I be misunderstood in a matter of such importance, I wish to make to laymen a special and emphatic appeal. Priests are officers, laymen are soldiers. The hardest fighting is often done by the soldier; in the warfare against sin and error the soldier is not always near the officer, and he must be ready to act without waiting for the word of command. Laymen are not anointed in confirmation to the end that they merely save their own souls, and pay their pew rent. They must think, work, organize, read, speak, act, as circumstances demand, ever anxious to serve the Church and to do good to their fellow-men. There is, on the part of the Catholic laymen, too much dependence upon priests. If priests work, laymen imagine that they themselves may rest. In Protestantism, where there is no firmly constituted ministerial organization, the layman is more keenly alive to his responsibility, and lay action is more common and more earnest. Lay action is to-day particularly needed in the Church. Laymen have in this age a special vocation.[25]

My words have borne on the exterior life of Catholics. This point I desired to emphasize. I am speaking to men of action, to soldiers, whom I would arouse to deeds of highest valor. God forbid that I forget the need of interior Christian life. Without it, however much we may plant and water, God will not give the increase. Nor do I forget that, however much you ought to do for others, your first and all-important duty is to yourselves, to the salvation of your own souls.[26]

And now the new century opens. O God, we pray Thee, grant us to understand its possibilities and its promises; grant us to be true to our responsibilities. Had I this night the power, as I have the will, I would bid the seraph touch with coal of fire from the altar of divine love hearts and lips of priests and laymen of America, and set them aglow with Pentecostal flame.[27] Oh, that we all be what God desires us to be, worthiest apostles of His blessed Gospel! If only we do with all our might the work appointed unto us, the new century has wondrous things in store for the Church in America.

O Saviour of men, who didst say: "I am come to send fire upon the earth, and what will I but that it be kindled?"[28]—to Thee we entrust this new century. By a superabundance of love and grace, make amends for the deficiencies which are in us. Bless us, that our labors fructify even a hundredfold. In Thy love of Holy Church, Thy spouse, which Thou hast purchased by the shedding of Thine own blood, widen out her tabernacles; gather unto her bosom tribes and nations; shed upon her brow glory and honor. O Saviour, we pray Thee, renew for Thy Church in America the miracles of love and piety of apostolic days. Look with gracious eyes upon our country, so fair, so rich in nature's gifts; add unto those gifts favors of grace, and let America be for long ages to come what our hearts bid her to be—first in civil liberty and social happiness, first in Christian loyalty among the nations of the earth!


## NOTES


1. Emphatic synergism. Cf. Leo's words in *Testem Benevolentiae:* "It is hard to understand how those who are imbued with Christian principles can place the natural ahead of the supernatural virtues as more in accordance with the ways and requirements of the present day, and consider it an advantage to be richly endowed with them, because they make a man more ready and more strenuous in action" (*Documents of American Catholic History,* ed. John Tracy Ellis [Milwaukee: Bruce, 1956], 2:558). But the comparison must not be pressed too far: Ireland did not say that the natural should be placed *ahead* of the supernatural.—ED.

2. Ps. 126:1.

3. Never, to be sure, would Ireland countenance anything stronger than persuasion in pursuit of this end. The non-Catholic reader should try to grasp, at least conceptually, what Ireland has in mind: the Catholicizing of the United States would be, for him, the bringing of an enormous benefit to a beloved nation. The Catholic reader will sense in Ireland's words a kind of turning point: no longer is a Catholic spokesman merely trying to show that Catholics can be acceptable citizens; instead, Catholics are here portrayed as *benefactors* of the republic. Many of Ireland's themes would be developed by John Courtney Murray, S.J., in his collected essays *We Hold These Truths* (New York: Sheed & Ward, 1960). Thus, Murray writes, "American government has not undertaken to represent transcendental truth in any of the versions of it current in American society. . . . In taking this course American government would seem to be on the course set by Pius XII for the religiously pluralist international community, of which America offers, as it were, a pattern in miniature" (pp. 74–75). American Catholics will as such be benefactors, as Ireland says, "of the Church universal," with their American solving of the "problems of the present age." An interesting nineteenth-century *Italian* plea for disestablishment is to be found in *Of the Five Wounds of the Holy Church,* by Antonio Rosmini-Serbati (1797–1855), trans. H. P. Liddon (London, 1883). In his summary statement, Rosmini writes, "Feudalism is in fact the only, or at all events, the principal source of all these evils. . . . Feudalism enslaved the Church with all her possessions" (pp. 301–2). The evils, or "wounds," that Rosmini describes in this book are the division of

clergy and people (not least in the *language* of worship), the poor education of the clergy, the lack of unity in the episcopate, the church's loss of the power of making ecclesiastical appointments, and excessive civil jurisdiction over church property and activities. Regarding the life and teachings of Rosmini, see Claude Leetham, *Rosmini: Priest and Philosopher* (Brooklyn, N.Y.: New City Press, 2nd ed., 1982)—ED.

4. "We have represented our countrymen as greatly in need of the Catholic religion, even under a political and social point of view, to cherish their patriotism and to preserve the republican spirit they so ardently love, and we have believed that, if once converted, they would carry into their Catholic life those natural virtues of boldness, energy, enterprise, and perseverance for which they are now so remarkable, because our religion does not destroy the natural, but elevates, purifies, and directs it" (*Works of Orestes A. Brownson* [Detroit, 1887], 20:59).

5. Virgil *Eclogue* 4.

6. Ireland did not, perhaps, perceive what might one day place the pope and the bishops in a peculiar position: the advocacy of liberty by a monarchical, or at least oligarchic, institution.—ED.

7. Ireland would doubtless have included the pope's and Msgr. Satolli's own Italy on a list of such countries.—ED.

8. *Works of Orestes A. Brownson,* 11:559.

9. Cf. Murray, *We Hold These Truths,* 42–43: If there should ever be widespread American dissent from our constitutional principles the American Catholic community would, however, "still be speaking in the ethical and political idiom familiar to them as it was familiar to their fathers, both the Fathers of the Church and the Fathers of the American Republic. The guardianship of the original American consensus, based on the Western heritage, would have passed to the Catholic community, within which the heritage was elaborated long before America was. And it would be for others, not Catholics, to ask themselves whether they still shared the consensus which first fashioned the American people into a body politic and determined the structure of its fundamental law." The thrust of Ireland's and Murray's argument would seem to be, not that at some providentially determined point the Catholics came along to help, but that the founding fathers, by their convictions about human nature, were to that extent unconsciously Catholic. By any standard they erected a noble work, but it should not be overlooked that they prepared a place for those who, in the mysterious design of providence, came later and were *consciously* Catholic. These reflections dovetail interestingly with a remark by Nelson W. Aldrich, Jr., in *Old Money: The Mythology of America's Upper Class* (New York: Knopf, 1988), 279: "WASP ethnocentrism dooms an ascendant social class even more surely than it dooms a ruling class. White Anglo-Saxon Protestants happen to have been the first group of rich men to import into American society the class values characterized as Old Money. But there is nothing in those values that genetically marks them as belonging to white Anglo-Saxon Protestants."—ED.

10. "The Church has lived under absolute empires, under constitutional monarchies, and in free republics, and everywhere she grows and expands. She has often, indeed, been hampered in her divine mission . . . but in the genial atmosphere of liberty she blossoms like the rose. For myself, as a citizen of the United States, and without closing my eyes to our shortcomings as a nation, I say with a deep sense of pride and gratitude that I belong to a country where the civil

government holds over us the aegis of its protection without interfering with us in the legitimate exercise of our sublime mission as ministers of the gospel of Christ" (Discourse of Cardinal Gibbons in his Titular Church in Rome, March 25, 1887).

11. The propositions reported in the *Syllabus* as at one time or another "censured" by Pius IX represent the excesses and extravagances of the movements of the age, and not the movements themselves, such as they are when properly understood and properly directed. Moreover, if through those propositions we would apprehend the mind of the Pope, we must read them not only in the brief and abrupt formulas of the *Syllabus,* but also in the original letters and discourses from which they were extracted. (Explanation did seem to be called for; in no. 80 of the eighty *condemned* propositions, e.g., it was stated that the pope should make his peace with progress, liberalism, and recent political systems. Apparently Pius IX and his advisers never quite grasped that in the English-speaking world democratic views did not necessarily include anticlericalism.—ED.)

12. "The institutions of human law cannot derogate from natural law or divine law. But according to the natural order established by Providence, inferior things are ordained to the end that out of them the needs of men may be relieved. . . . And therefore the things that some men have in super-abundance are claimed by the natural law for the support of the poor. . . . Secretly to take for use the property of another, in a case of extreme need, cannot properly be called theft, because what one takes for the support of his life becomes his because of such necessity" (Saint Thomas *Summa theologiae* II–II, q.66, a.7).

13. Acts 17:23.

14. Cf. *Testem Benevolentiae:* "We have . . . shown the difference between the Church, which is of divine right, and all other associations which subsist by the free will of men." It is "hostile to Catholic doctrine and discipline" to claim that "a certain liberty ought to be introduced into the Church, so that, limiting the exercise and vigilance of its powers, each one of the faithful may act more freely in pursuance of his own natural bent and capacity." (*Documents of American Catholic History,* ed. Ellis, 556).—ED.

15. Ireland refers to "Cahenslyism" and similar movements; he was among those who insisted that non-English-speaking immigrants be "Americanized" sooner rather than later. Many German and Polish clergy resisted the demand for rapid Americanization as pastorally unwise, and resented it as coming from an Irish-dominated episcopate. Ireland's building of a *major* (i.e., undergraduate and graduate) seminary was the fulfillment for him of one of an American bishop's dearest wishes, getting control of the education of his priests.—ED.

16. But cf. the famous essay by John Tracy Ellis, "American Catholics and the Intellectual Life," *Thought* 30 (1955): 351–88.—ED.

17. In 1889 the Catholic University of America was prepared to receive only ecclesiastical students; since that date it has added other departments to that of theology and is now doing its great work for laymen as well as priests.

18. See Ireland's lecture "America in France" (delivered in Paris, 1892), in *The Church and Modern Society: Lectures and Addresses,* 2 vols. (St. Paul: Pioneer Press, 1904–5), 1:361–95, esp. 383ff.—ED.

19. In the organization of the "Salvation Army" General William Booth recognizes, and forces others to recognize, the incontrovertible fact that multitudes of people—"the Submerged Tenth"—are outside the influences of the

Christian religion. We cannot approve the methods of the "Salvation Army"; but we ought to recognize the need of the work which the "Army" strives to do, and we should ourselves do that work with the methods which are Christ's. Meanwhile, if we do nothing, we should, at least, not despise and ridicule men and women who try in their own way and according to their own light to rescue the "Submerged."

20. Luke 14:23.

21. Charles Cardinal Lavigerie (1825–92) was the founder of the White Fathers, a missionary order originally devoted to working among the Muslims of the French colonial possessions in North Africa. Ireland no doubt mentions Lavigerie and de Mun because both advocated the reconciliation of French Catholics with the Third Republic. Concerning de Mun, see Theodore Zeldin, *France, 1848–1945,* vol. 5, *Anxiety and Hypocrisy* (New York: Oxford Univ. Press, 1981), 251–60. The study of Catholic social teaching and involvement is best begun by extended reading of secular historians. Catholic accounts tend to become mired in self-congratulation or apologetics, masking thereby the size and effectiveness of what is being described.—ED.

22. Matt. 11:4.

23. James 1:27.

24. Such was the intent of Cardinal Gibbons's popular *The Faith of Our Fathers* (1876); on a much broader front it was the work of the Paulist Fathers, the community founded by Isaac Hecker.—ED.

25. "In discussion the layman, under responsibility, we hold, may take the initiative, and not await it from authority. He may open such questions as he deems important, and the business of authority is not to close his mouth, but to set him right when and where he goes wrong. This is no more than princes and nobles have always been allowed or assumed unrebuked the right to do, and princes and nobles are only laymen. What a crowned or titled layman may do, a free American citizen, though uncrowned and untitled, may also do." (*Works of Orestes A. Brownson,* 20:271).

26. The casual reader might find, in the brevity of this paragraph, some occasion for the pope's concern. It is probably more accurate to take Ireland at his word when he states that *this address* is about the "exterior life"; the address did, after all, commemorate the centenary of an institution, the American episcopate.—ED.

27. *Pentecostal* is here simply the adjectival form of *Pentecost,* not a reference to pentecostal Christians.—ED.

28. Luke 12:49.

# 13

# Faith and Reason

*Matthias Joseph Scheeben*

Matthias Joseph Scheeben was born near Bonn, in 1835, and died in Cologne, in 1888. After theological study in Rome under the most highly regarded Italian and German masters, he was ordained a priest in 1858. Scheeben brought awesome industry and intelligence to the study of the entire history of theology, from the fathers, through the medievals, down to nineteenth-century German writers. He thus became a kind of model for what the Catholic dogmatician should be—particularly since, following the path commended by Leo XIII in *Aeterni Patris,* he gave prominence in his teaching to the thought of Thomas Aquinas. Most of Scheeben's career was spent as professor of dogmatics at the seminary of Cologne. The fruit of this teaching is the unfinished six-volume *Handbuch der katholischen Dogmatik* (1874–87) and a number of shorter works. Chief among the latter is his compendium of theology, *Die Mysterien des Christentums,* which originally appeared in 1865. To be sure, it is a very generous compendium, being over six hundred pages in length; given here is the tenth and last chapter, comprising sections 107–10. Though it does not do full justice to the breadth of Scheeben's outlook to call him merely a neo-scholastic, the reader may find it instructive to compare the chapter given here with Thomas's *Summa theologiae,* part 1, question 1.

It is worth pondering whether Scheeben's *Mysteries* might make the best point of departure for the study of Catholic theology in the *twentieth* century, for Scheeben clearly distinguishes things that later became murky indeed. Note that he distinguishes between the only goal that God has ever had for humankind, participation in the life of the Trinity, and our quite limited knowledge of that goal and the steps leading to it. From this distinction arises the notion of the supernatural—that which is but which man can know and participate in only by divine gift, or grace. Grace as affecting the life of the mind is the ability, quite beyond man's natural or philosophically knowable powers, to make an act of faith in revelation and to abide in that faith. Faith thus delivers to theological reason the materials upon which to work. Reason can then find further analogies for the realities revealed, discover how they are interconnected, and work out their practical consequences.

But Scheeben would lead us deeper, beyond academic theology not differing from other academic disciplines except in having its basic principles revealed. He points to the boundary line of theology and mysticism. (The reader might well compare Jacques Maritain's *The Degrees of Knowledge.*) Bear in mind that God's goal for human beings is inclusion, in heaven, in the life of the Trinity, and on earth, that same inclusion, in a real if provisional manner, by means of faith, hope, and love in the life of the individual, and by means of participation in the eucharist with other Christians. Does, then, greater progress toward the goal, greater holiness, make one a better theologian, other things being equal? Scheeben's answer is an emphatic yes. In the soul that is highly sensitive to the promptings of the Spirit reason works more effectively, for that soul is increasingly "connatural" with what is at once its personal goal and its object of study. In other words, the gifts of the Holy Spirit called understanding and wisdom perfect the study of theology.

Lest there be any confusion in the matter, it is worth noting that Scheeben and other orthodox nineteenth-century theologians would be appalled at a turn of language frequently heard among late-twentieth-century Catholics: that one can "experience" God. To Scheeben such an expression would unforgivably confuse sense, reason, and faith. Even the mystic does not literally experience God; he or she experiences the self, which self is deemed (by faith or reason or both) to be moved by God.

Scheeben, then, would part company with many twentieth-century born-again Christians by his insistence that the hidden workings of the Spirit not only do not take the place of but actually enhance the operations of critical reason. Theological reason is like Mary, who willingly received the Word and yet also gave it human sustenance. Theological knowledge, the product of revelation and reason, may well be compared to Jesus the Word himself, divine wisdom personified. Ultimately theology has every right to be considered a science; indeed, "the enlightened Christian need envy no one but the blessed in heaven, on account of the lucidity, the depth, and the fullness of their knowledge." And yet, in characteristic Catholic fashion, Scheeben has this whole splendid structure begin for us, on our side, with reason's function of providing the *praeambula,* or *prolegomena,* of faith—with demonstrating that there is a God, that humanity is capable of receiving a revelation from God, and that Jesus is the bearer of such a revelation. Theology was for Scheeben a "*scientia sapida,* a science full of delights," wherein reason and revelation were poised in harmonious balance. For us, Scheeben's synthesis of what he thought the best in patristic, medieval, and German romantic thought may seem a brief golden moment, almost a timeless celestial pause, before the onslaught of modern criticism.

## 107. The Organic Unity of Understanding and Faith in Theological Knowledge

The closing paragraph of the preceding chapter makes it clear that the *intellectus rerum creditarum,* the understanding of things accepted on faith, not only does not exclude belief in these objects, but necessarily supposes it. Full, scientific knowledge of the supernatural order of things is possible only in conjunction with faith. In addition to well-founded certitude about a truth, full scientific knowledge requires an apprehension of its ontological grounds. Similarly, a simple apprehension of objects without a certain judgment about their objective truth does not verify the notion of scientific knowledge. The conception of supernatural objects does not in itself include a positive guaranty of the truth of the objects conceived even in the ideal order, to say nothing of the real order. It does not do so in the real order: with the exception of the Trinity, supernatural objects are essentially contingent; hence any conviction I may have that they are conceivable does not entail their real existence. Likewise in the ideal order, with regard to the objective possibility of their realization: since I do not fully comprehend them with my analogous concepts, and can do no more than ascertain that I myself find no contradiction in them, I am not in a position to judge positively that they are objectively possible.

With all my inspection of supernatural objects, I cannot form a positive judgment as to their objective possibility and actual existence except by belief in divine revelation, which simultaneously proposes them for my conception and vouches for their objective truth. Hence, even though I may arrive at a concept as connected with another and as evidently proposed therein, I cannot judge of the objective truth of the former except through the faith whereby I assent to the objective truth of the latter; for I can never deduce one supernatural truth except from another that is likewise supernatural. And although in virtue of my understanding of revealed objects I may perceive the dependence of an object on its ontological grounds, I can acquire a sure knowledge of its objective truth only so far as I am apprised of the existence and the character of these grounds by faith.

Consequently I can mentally reconstruct the objective system of

*From Die Mysterien des Christentums,* vol. 2 of *Gesammelte Schriften,* ed. Joseph Höfer (Freiburg im Breisgau: Herder & Herder, 1941), 642–71. This edition is based on the author's 1887 notes for revision. The translation is from *The Mysteries of Christianity,* trans. Cyril Vollert, S.J. (St. Louis: B. Herder, 1946), 762–96.

supernatural truths with conviction of its objective verity, only to the extent that I hold fast in faith to the cardinal point around which it revolves, and the principles from which it develops. Often such a principle is directly expressed in the revealed truth; and then without further ado I can evolve the system from it. At times, however, the fundamental idea underlying one or more explicitly revealed truths can be ascertained only by an analysis of them. The former is the case, for example, in the Trinity. But in the Incarnation we were obliged, at least in part, to pursue a different route in order to discover the end it is meant to achieve.

In the Trinity we found our principle in the inner productivity and fruitfulness of the divine nature. All the other mysteries are contingent works of God. The principle leading to our knowledge of them is located in the purposes they are to realize; by realizing these purposes they become linked with the mystery of the Trinity as their ultimate end.

These principles supposed, all the truths issuing from them in theology may be explained with the strictest scientific precision, and may be deduced with the most rigorous scientific consistency. But the roots themselves, the first principles, cannot be inferred by the application of a strictly scientific process. Any explanation of their tenor must rest content with analogy, and their certainty can be guaranteed only by faith.

Nevertheless, if these principles are rightly grasped, our very apprehension of them renders them in some measure probable and acceptable to the intellect, at times even to the degree that we may come to look upon them as self-evident, and take their objective truth for granted.

We must give a somewhat more detailed explanation of this point. If it is put clearly, it closes off the source of most of the misunderstandings that arise with regard to the essential character of theological science.

If I rightly understand and weigh the import of a theological principle—for instance, that there are inner productions in God's knowledge and love, that God has destined man for the immediate vision of Himself, or that in the redemption He wills simultaneously to reveal His infinite mercy and justice—then with my unaided reason I can straightway become aware that I perceive no evident contradiction in these objects. I perceive no such contradiction among the objects themselves or with what reason by itself knows to be well established concerning the nature of God and man. Consequently I become aware that reason has no grounds for vetoing the acceptance of such principles. Reason does not pronounce upon the ideal truth of the principles. But, on the supposition of their objective conceivability, reason can perceive that, if they are brought to realization, God would be revealed both *ad intra* and *ad extra* in all the magnificent splendor of His infinity, and man would be elevated to an unimaginable height of dignity and blessedness. Hence reason sees that the lofty idea it has acquired of God by its own powers would be strikingly substantiated, and that the most extravagant cravings of human nature would be superabundantly satisfied. Reason must admit to itself that the infinity of God can and must embrace a host of perfections that are not reflected in the mirror of creation. And as soon as it has the slightest clue to go on, its very nature impels it continually to think as highly as possible of God in regard to His own being and to His activity in the outer world, and to expect for itself the best that it could receive from the infinite goodness of God.

Accordingly reason does not shrink from such truths; it even feels itself drawn to them and feels an inclination to presume their reality. Though but dimly grasped, the coherence of these truths with objects known and valued by reason, and therefore with reason itself, engenders a certain kinship between them and reason. On this kinship depends the attractive force whereby they charm our reason and sway it in their favor. This disposing of reason in favor of a truth rests not so much upon the intelligibility of the truth as upon the goodness and beauty of its content. It has an analogy with the *pius credulitatis affectus,* the pious disposition to believe, which is the starting point of positive, supernatural faith. Indeed, it is the natural stock on which the grace leading to theological faith is grafted, to elevate and sublimate it. Hence it is in itself a certain natural faith, a certain surrender of the will to the supernatural object. It inclines reason to accept the latter, although it can impart no definite certitude. Although it cannot of itself banish doubt, it sets up a bias in favor of the truth, and so makes impossible an absolute indifference on the part of reason toward that truth. However, this indifference is not completely eliminated except by positive belief in divine revelation, which undeniably vouches for the objective truth that had previously been presumed. Thus, too, the presumptive disposition itself acquires true vitality and efficacy only through supernatural grace, which exhibits the supernatural objects to us in a favorable light and causes our will to experience the power of attraction they exert. But even grace conduces to certitude only by inclining us to a willing surrender to divine revelation.

If we are not mistaken, this account gives us the best explanation of the psychological possibility and the true import of the utterances and the method of many great theologians who, while emphatically professing the absolute necessity of positive faith for a sure knowledge of the mysteries, often proceed as though they wished to raise such knowledge to certitude independently of faith. We may not ascribe either an over-optimistic esteem for man's intellectual powers or an obvious logical inconsistency to such learned and holy men as Anselm, Bonaventure, and Richard of St. Victor. Their mode of procedure may be partly explained on the ground that the power of faith as "the substance of things to be hoped for, the evidence of things that appear not,"[1] brought the mysteries so close to them. Or perhaps the power of faith unconsciously raised their spiritual vision so high that they thought they beheld the invisible, and supposed they could illuminate others with the abundance of their own light. They did not always clearly differentiate between the natural standpoint of the intellect and the level to which revelation raises the intellect. Yet, as we saw earlier,[2] St. Bonaventure and Richard sometimes make the proper distinctions. But we must not forget that the ideal disposition that we spoke of above was a prominent feature of their intellectual life, even apart from theological faith. Hence they thought that whatever was presented in the form of supreme goodness and perfection would be acceptable even to one who was as yet an unbeliever, in the genuine conviction that a person who once looked at the mysteries of faith from this angle would readily embrace external revelation, and so would in some measure have anticipated belief in it.

They speak of *rationes necessariae* with which, independently of Scripture, they desired to demonstrate revealed dogmas. But this is to be understood in the sense that they wished to establish the various teachings of faith with necessary, inescapable logic from causes and principles which, taken strictly, cannot be known with certitude except by belief in positive revelation, but which would not be denied by anyone of good will who has not closed his mind to the majesty of God and the sublimity of man's destiny. This is true particularly where there is question of justifying or explaining the data of revelation which depend on those causes and principles. Thus, for instance, St. Bonaventure could assume that no one would refuse to grant that the infinite divine goodness is essentially communicable in an infinite way, a principle from which he draws out the entire doctrine of the Trinity. Thus also St. Anselm did not think that anyone would care to dispute that there is a real production of a Word and a sigh in the divine knowledge and love, just as there is in human knowledge and love, on the analogy of which we conceive the divine. Nor did he think anyone would deny that man is destined for the intuitive vision of God, or that in the redemption God wished to assert His justice and His mercy alike in a perfect manner. Therefore with full confidence he could go on to deduce the details of the dogmas of the Trinity, original justice, and the Incarnation. With both doctors this procedure is all the easier to understand inasmuch as the genius of St. Bonaventure veered toward idealization rather than analysis, and St. Anselm, who was the first to break ground in the matter of treating dogma scientifically, was not yet in a position to devise a method that would be well defined and sound from every point of view. St. Thomas is more cautious. He found speculative theology in a higher and more complex stage of development and systematization and was able, in the full flight of his genius, to analyze everything supremely well. In countless passages he declares that the starting points of the mystical portion of theology can be rendered intelligible only by comparisons and analogies, and can in some measure be made plausible and acceptable only by their agreement with truths already mastered by reason. Often he goes so far as to draw attention to the dangers and drawbacks that may arise from the claim to have demonstrated these fundamental truths on rational grounds. This appears clearest of all in the Trinity, as we saw previously.

With regard to man's supernatural destiny, on the other hand, his procedure often resembles that of St. Anselm. He infers the existence of this destiny from man's natural cravings to behold the Cause of all things, a craving that cannot remain ungratified. And in the *Summa contra Gentiles* he even seems to place this destiny and all that follows from it in the category of natural truths. Indeed, it is not until the fourth book (he had treated of this subject in the third), after he has finished dealing with truths attainable by reason itself, that he takes up the roll of true mysteries. How this particular procedure is to be understood, we have tried to explain in another place.[3] It is enough to remark here that St. Thomas consistently bases the necessity and importance of supernatural faith on the fact that the intellect can be made ready for the attainment of the supernatural goal of the beatific vision and can be conducted to it only by faith. The intellect, by force of its very nature, aspires to a perfect knowledge of the ultimate reality, but it keeps this reality definitely in view only by supernatural faith. This view is the condition of that efficacious, dynamic striving which issues in attainment of the objective.[4]

Accordingly, whoever wishes to refrain from undermining knowledge of supernatural truths by depriving it of the first condition of scientific knowledge, the unshakable certainty of its principles, must of set purpose take belief in the principles as his foundation. Whatever understanding is possible in this sphere does not do away with faith or engender a knowledge independent of faith. On the contrary, the entire function of such understanding is discharged by the fact that it leans upon faith or leads to faith. And so by the science of faith is to be understood either the purely rational demonstration of the fact of revelation, which disposes to faith, or the scientific understanding of the objects revealed. This latter understanding conduces to faith or strengthens readiness to embrace it, but does not impart full conviction of the truth of the object apprehended except in faith and by faith. With respect to the objects of faith, therefore, such understanding of them as is possible should never be called a real knowing as distinct from faith, as if it constituted a proper, complete knowledge that would take its place at the side of faith. To be real knowledge, it must be as intimately associated with faith as faith is with it, if not more so. The profound observation, Fides quaerit intellectum, is adequately appreciated only in conjunction with another, Intellectus quaerit fidem. Both, faith and understanding, complement and postulate each other for the organic unity of a knowledge imparted by God concerning truths revealed by Him. By faith I accept the word of God; with my understanding I apprehend it. Only if I have both together do I make my own the knowledge which God has uttered in the Word, and thus become a true knower myself.

Without carefully qualifying our statement, we cannot say that through the activity of the intellect faith passes over into knowledge as a further stage of cognition, and that this is brought about not by self-surrender but by self-development. For ordinarily we give the name faith to that stage of supernatural knowledge in which we understand the truths we believe only so far as some grasp of them is indispensable for holding a definite object as true. In this sort of understanding the object is known only in vague outline; it is not known with clarity and precision in its various facets, its inner organism, its principles, and its connection with other objects. At this stage faith is naturally the predominant element, and understanding has scarcely any importance as compared with our acceptance of the truth. If, however, understanding is cultivated along the lines just indicated, the cognitive process inaugurated by faith enters upon another and higher stage, in which it is called knowledge. But one who thus knows and one who simply believes are not distinct as two individuals, the first being aware of a definite thing by ocular evidence, the second by receiving information about it from another person. Rather they are as two individuals, both of whom perceive a thing with their own eyes, hence through the same medium; but one stands in front of the object scarcely adverting to it, while the other scrutinizes it from all sides in a scientific spirit, examines the interrelation of the parts and studies their functions, and generally seeks to account both for the whole and for the details. Something of the sort would ensue, for instance, if the same plant were placed before an uneducated man and before a botanist. Or perhaps we should do better to say: they are in the position of two men who together listen to a report of a momentous event that is recounted in great detail. Both have to rely on the word of the narrator; but one of them catches only a few outstanding facts, while the other comprehends the logical coherence of the development and learns so much that he is able to appreciate both the motivation and the significance of each fact.

Moreover, the reasoned probability of theological principles which, as we said above, results from a deeper understanding of them, can be strengthened in yet another way. This other way is by detecting in the unfolding of the principles the wonderful coherence and harmony whereby all the truths of the supernatural order are related to one another and to the truths of the natural order. It seems that false principles cannot be at the basis of a system of truths in which not the slightest contradiction can be found, in which each detail is perfectly adapted to the whole, in which every fresh examination uncovers new unifying threads, a system which in the course of the centuries discloses an increasing fruitfulness, which exhibits itself not merely in one but in a thousand different departments as the consummation of natural truth, and with ever deeper perception reveals new points of contact with the latter.[5] This indirect proof can easily rise to certitude with a person who carefully surveys the whole vast sweep of the system. Yet it can never, by any process of demonstration, afford an insight into the principles themselves. It merely engenders the conviction that the principles of such a system, which man cannot reach by his own efforts, must be revealed by God, and therefore must be accepted by faith in the word of God.

## 108. The Supernatural Stimulus in Our Understanding of the Truths of Faith

Up to this point we have said nothing of the influence of supernatural grace on the *intellectus fidei;* and the same is true, at least in part, of our treatment of faith itself. We have regarded this understanding as a purely intellectual operation which, to be sure, is connected with the external revelation that has been accepted or is to be accepted on faith, but supposes no other light in the thinking subject than the light of reason itself.

If the reasoned conviction of the fact of revelation and of credibility, or the *intellectus credibilitatis,* is to lead to supernatural, theological faith, it must be elevated, transfigured, and stimulated by a supernatural light, the *lumen fidei.* In like manner, if the understanding of the truths of faith (the *intellectus rerum credendarum*) is to be at all vivid, and hence in junction with faith is to result in a truly vital grasp of the truths believed, there must be found in the believing subject something more than simple faith or the grace formally required for faith itself. There must be found a supernatural disposition that is more or less closely connected with faith and the grace of faith. It is this disposition which effects a certain spiritual kinship and harmony between the believer and the supernatural objects.

The logical operations by which an understanding of the supernatural is achieved with the aid of rational concepts, in themselves suppose no more than an external proposal of the objects and a sufficient cultivation and docility of the intellect on the part of the subject, without being absolutely dependent on a supernatural, inner light or on the moral disposition of the subject. Even in the sphere of the higher natural truths lying within the radius of reason, man often requires an auxiliary illumination from God, and must bring with him a good moral disposition of will, so that the light of his reason may not slumber ineffectually or be smothered as soon as it starts to rise. If this is so, then in the case of supernatural truths the natural receptiveness of the intellect for all truth will hardly suffice for a vivid and dynamic conception of them. A supernatural light will be needed to display the objects to their best advantage, and to elevate reason to their level. In the soul there will have to grow forth a life that will enable the objects to strike root in the soul itself.

This is the sense in which the Apostle says: "The sensual man perceiveth not these things that are of the Spirit of God; for it is foolishness to him, and he cannot understand, because it is spiritually examined. But the spiritual man judgeth all things."[6] By sensual man (that is, natural or animal man), is here meant the man who with his entire nature is opposed to the Spirit of God, whereas the spiritual man is the man who is not only raised above the animal man, but is animated and pervaded by the Spirit of God. Unless man is in some way or other moved, enlightened, and animated by the Spirit of God, he cannot actively grasp "the doctrine of the Spirit"[7] concerning the deep things of God, and the gifts that are drawn out of these depths.[8] Without the Spirit's illumination, supernatural objects must ever appear strange to us, and our relations with them must lack vitality. But this illumination makes them shine in our eyes with a favorable light, and brings them close to us. Even if it does not actually enable us to behold them, at any rate it places them before us so plainly and clearly that we could almost be persuaded we saw them.

By this illumination of the Holy Spirit, as has been indicated above, we understand first a more or less perfect, immediate enlightenment of our reason about the matter to be believed, an enlightenment normally connected with the grace of faith, or even conveyed by this grace. Secondly we understand by this illumination the radiation, through faith itself, of the love and life of the Holy Spirit. Therein our faith becomes a living faith, informed by sanctifying grace, and its objects come into close contact with the soul by a real manifestation of themselves.

In the first of these illuminations the Holy Spirit opens up "the ear of our heart," moving it to a willing, resolute surrender to the word of revelation, and at the same time "enlightens the eyes of our heart," that we may know, or correctly and vividly conceive, the objects of revelation, which the Apostle refers to as our supernatural calling, the riches of the glory of the divine inheritance, and in general as the exceeding greatness of the divine power over us.[9] It is chiefly this illumination that brings about the transfiguration of our natural concepts, so necessary for an apprehension of supernatural truths. Strictly speaking, such transfiguration and transformation can be undertaken by the unaided reason, acting in conformity with external revelation. But if no corresponding inner light illuminates our understanding, the concepts lose their vitality and precision in the very process of being recast, owing to the introduction of analogy. They are not of the same order as the objects, which they represent under forms that always remain unsuited to them.

The illumination we are speaking of can precede faith, and then it makes for a firmer and more cheerful acceptance of faith. Or, in the case of one who already believes, it can make its influence felt with increasing power later, whether in response to man's loyal cooperation or in pursuance of God's free choice of graces. In general, however, the dispensing of divine grace is mainly dependent on man's humble consciousness of his own powerlessness; and this is particularly true of this grace. The more man trusts in the power of his own reason, and boldly sets out with nothing but its murky lantern to explore the ocean of the divine mysteries, the more dimly will the supernatural light illuminate his way, and the more obscure and confused will his connection be.

In this connection, the word of the divine Savior holds: "Unless you become as little children, you shall not enter into the kingdom of heaven."[10] As we must become little in our persons if we wish to be reborn of God, so we must enroll in God's school as infants, and must allow ourselves to be led into the depths of His mysteries clasping His hand, and guided by His light. Indeed, whoever refuses to become little in this way will not even reach what he is actually capable of reaching with his natural faculties. God's curse will rest upon his undertaking, and under its weight his enterprise will inevitably founder. But where a childlike spirit prevails unspoiled, neither great intellectual culture nor a skilled human teacher is needed for a vivid conception of the most august truths; for the Holy Spirit's anointing teaches us concerning all things.[11] Grace often manifests its enlightening power preferably to those very people who are truly small in respect to their intellectual equipment, so that they not infrequently apprehend the mysteries of God more surely and clearly than the most learned philosophers, and the supernatural is as easily grasped by them as the natural. Indeed, their perception and clarity in the domain of the mysteries seem greater at times than their powers of comprehension in worldly and natural affairs.

Sometimes children, in whom we can scarcely instill the most ordinary notions of earthly matters, vividly conceive and, as it were, imbibe the most sublime truths that are placed before them. How can we explain this fact if not by the grace of the Holy Spirit who by His illumination stirs up a holy hunger in their hearts, and enables them to receive such truths as easily as the eye drinks in pictures of material objects? Of course, this supernatural light does not in itself engender any abstractly formulated and organically integrated conception of the mysteries, as true science demands. Ideas of this sort can be acquired only by study and a methodical cultivation of the intellect. But such study receives its higher efficacy and consecration, its blessing and its life, from that illumination.

We might add that the eye of the heart must be cleansed of pride, as well as of every other defilement, in order to have the power of acquiring a lively understanding of God's mysteries. An egotistical spirit, and especially sensual cravings which rule the heart, not only make the heart unworthy of God's enlightening grace, but paralyze grace and snuff out the very light that normally illuminates the intellect. Even in the natural sphere such vices darken the mind respecting quite evident truths, whenever they emerge beyond the circle in which concupiscence moves, or go so far as to oppose these truths in open hostility. How much more must the supernatural light presuppose a circumcised heart and a pure, consecrated eye, if it is to prove effectual! As only the pure of heart can see God, so they alone can here below grasp the mysteries with a clarity and vividness akin to vision, because they alone hold up a pure, untarnished mirror to the light of the Holy Spirit's grace.

Humility and purity of heart, as considered here, are obviously not independent of grace. On the contrary, they are produced by the Holy Spirit and by faith which is already operative. To that extent they have a certain analogy with the second kind of influence listed above, whereby the Holy Spirit graphically brings the truth of our faith home to us. But in themselves these two virtues do not positively raise us above nature, in such a way as to bring us closer to revealed truths than we were by nature. In themselves they merely remove the obstacles to our approach, and make us responsive to the double radiation of the light and the life-giving warmth of the Holy Spirit.

The second kind of radiation emanating from the Holy Spirit comes to this: by its light it causes the truths of faith to illuminate us from without, and by its warmth and energizing power it places us in a real, living communication with them. It makes these truths, so to speak, live in us, and us in them, and brings them to our consciousness in all their vibrant reality. The consequence of this influence is that we are enabled to grasp their content more readily, and can, in a way, confirm their existence by our own inner spiritual experience.

The supernatural life growing out of faith under the action of the Holy Spirit, the life whereby faith becomes objectively a living faith in its real and moral implications, further causes faith to become a living faith. What effects this is the illumination it confers by bringing the invisible objects of faith close to us. This takes place in a variety of ways.

First, if faith is animated by the love which the Holy Spirit infuses, this love sets up in us a relationship of intimate union with the objects of faith, for all of them reveal to us in many forms the infinite lovableness of God. By love that knows no distance, the lover is placed in the object loved, to embrace and permeate it. The mind is carried along in this flight of the heart. Its power of vision becomes keener and stronger in proportion as the heart craves to possess the object loved. And the attraction which the object of faith exercises upon the heart, as also the joy and rapture which every ray of its beauty arouses, is taken by the intellect as a proof of the splendor and reality of the object.

Secondly, the love infused by the Holy Spirit works in the soul itself a transformation whereby the soul is assimilated to the objects loved and becomes a mirror of them. Moreover, it is assimilated to the exalted goodness and love of God, the very foundation and root of all the mysteries. Indeed the mysteries are but revelations and fruits of the one truth that God is in all reality a *bonum summe communicativum,* a supremely communicable Good. To one who has clearly grasped this truth, even the greatest and most sublime mysteries will appear understandable and comprehensible. But only he who discerns in himself the power and the nature of divine love, on whom the Holy Spirit has lavished His own love, who has been, as it were, transformed by this love into God and Christ, and who, in the words of the Apostle, has in him the mind that was in Christ Jesus, will vividly perceive the full force of this truth. Such a one will understand how the infinite divine goodness could impel the Father to communicate His entire nature to the Son and the Holy Spirit, to send His Son into the outer world, and to surrender Him up to the most ignominious and agonizing death.

Lastly, in consequence of the inspiration of the Holy Spirit there grows out of faith the entire higher life in which we endeavor to regulate our conduct in conformity with the truths of faith and stamp their laws upon our souls. This higher life must be regarded as a sort of real revelation of those truths and a practical confirmation of their existence. As a result of believing in those truths, we can almost feel in ourselves a certain power, along with the spiritual peace and consolation conferred on us by our living in accord with them. This power enables us to experience their wonderful efficacy for satisfying the deeper needs and the nobler cravings of our nature. It reveals to us in our Christian life the truth of Christianity, and draws its mysteries down from their transcendental remoteness to the closest and most intimate proximity to us.

Thus in these three ways the faith which lives in love places us in vital relationship with the truths that are but dimly grasped by faith alone. It also imparts to us such a vivid conception of them that we can almost believe we are seeing them.

But no matter how keen such perception may become, it will never do away with faith itself or make faith superfluous, since at all points it supposes faith as its principle. Without the anchor of faith our heart is always in danger of leading us astray. If we insisted on heeding the thrust, the emotions, and the feelings of the heart alone, all our certitude about supernatural truths would evaporate into empty subjectivism. The voice of the heart may be listened to only in conjunction with faith and the objective criteria of external revelation. The heart may serve as proof and corroboration, but never as a substitute for revelation and faith.

The same holds with even greater urgency as regards the inner light which is joined to the grace of faith. This light may assist us to apprehend the truths of faith correctly; but it does not enable us actually to see them. Besides, it is psychologically impossible for us readily to ascertain with sureness that the light by which we think we behold a thing is really a true light, unless it pertains to the intellect as such. If, prescinding from the objective and external revelation to which it corresponds, we wish to follow that light alone, we are no more secure from visionary fanaticism than we are from emotional excess.

Hence we conclude: both the supernatural light shining in the grace of faith, and the union with the objects of faith that flows from faith, whereby we penetrate into the objects, and they become, as it were, a part of ourselves, both serve, and are even necessary, to acquaint us with the mysteries, and to turn the lifeless and artificial conception of them—

the only conception possible for unaided reason—into a living, graphic understanding; but they can never bring about an intuition in the proper sense.

That light is merely a faint glimmer in the night of our intellect, the dawn of the light of vision. It leads us securely only when we cling in faith to our divine Guide, who tells us what He has Himself beheld. That union does indeed establish a contact with the objects, and according to circumstances stirs us powerfully and fills us with anticipatory joy. However, in the darkness of our night, nothing but faith, in which we receive these objects from the hand of God, makes a firm and sure grasp of them possible for us.

Faith will be replaced only by the light of glory, in which alone we no longer need to cling to God's word, because God will flood us with the light in which He sees; it is from the fullness of this light that He speaks. He will take us to His bosom, the source and center of all the mysteries, and will place us in an immediate and real communication with them all.

However, since the light of grace and the life of grace are an anticipation of the light of glory and of life in the bosom of God, we can perhaps say that the natural understanding and supernatural faith are formed and vitalized by grace into a perfect, living knowledge. Hence we can also say that an anticipation of the future vision is germinally contained in faith, obscure though it may be of itself. But faith derives the principle of this vitality not from reason, but from the very divine source whence it itself arises. Faith brings it down from the infinite light of the divinity, in order to imbue the intellect with supernatural illumination, just as faith itself formally enriches reason with the certitude of supernatural principles. This principle of vitality comes down with faith, because it consists in two of the seven gifts of the Holy Spirit. All these gifts, in a higher or lower degree, accompany at least the faith that is animated by grace in the just, and are designed to guide the theological virtues to their full perfection. The two gifts we are speaking of are understanding (*intellectus*) and wisdom (*sapientia*): understanding, so far as it sharpens our sight in a supernatural way, enabling it to penetrate into the truths believed and to grasp them clearly and accurately; wisdom, so far as, in consequences of the affective unity contained in love and of our kinship with the objects of faith, it confers on us a certain spiritual discrimination and relish whereby our judgment about these objects is made easily and naturally.[12]

This supernatural acumen and this supernatural relish, standing at the head of the list among the gifts of the Holy Spirit, instill into unlearned souls that are, however, pure, unsophisticated, and God-loving, that instinctive clarity and assurance in the most august questions of theology, which frequently scholars can but marvel at in amazement. Yet these same gifts also guide the scholar most rapidly and securely in the use of his reason on the supernatural plane. At the same time they imbue his thoughts and words with that heavenly ointment which, by the light it gives and the perfume it emits, so powerfully quickens the eye and lovingly stirs the heart of the disciples and readers of the saintly doctors of the Church.

## 109. General Relation between Reason and Faith in the Genesis of Philosophical and Theological Knowledge

In accordance with this doctrine, we may readily determine the general relation between the factors that work together for the production of theological knowledge, that is, reason and faith. In dealing with this subject, we must touch upon the lively controversies enkindled in recent times by the revival of the adage, "philosophy is the handmaid of theology."

The metaphorical cast of this proposition has given rise to a number of misunderstandings, which only an accurate interpretation of its meaning can correct. We are of the opinion that in many respects this metaphor illustrates the true relation between philosophy and theology, but that it must be supplemented by another metaphor which brings out that relation more profoundly and adequately, and has the further advantage that it tones down the harsh and objectionable features of the first figure. In putting forth our view, we will at the same time proceed further and illustrate the relation with two analogies. These, drawn as they are from the very essence of Christianity, propose not a natural symbol, but the supernatural ideal according to which that relationship is objectively constituted.

First of all, we should note that philosophy and theology are not being compared here according to the nature and range of their respective objects. Nor are they compared subjectively as the sums of the correct elements of knowledge acquired by drawing out their respective principles of cognition. For under these two aspects they have only a static, not a dynamic, relation to each other, whereas the latter is expressed in the formula quoted above. There is question rather of the relation between the two principles of cognition, natural reason and supernatural faith, and also of the relation between the respective activities whereby theology and philosophy are built up into subjectively complete sciences. With this presupposed, it is easy to determine the sense in which philosophy is the handmaid of theology, or, more exactly, the sense in which reason is the handmaid of faith.

1. In the first place, natural reason is, in dignity and power, a lower cognitive principle than faith. It ranks below faith in a very important respect, namely, in the range and inerrancy of its illumination. Faith reaches as far as the communication of the divine knowledge and, in supernatural reliance thereon, shares in its infallibility. In a word, it represents the divine reason as opposed to human reason. This opposition between reason and faith does not formally imply the idea of the positive subordination of reason to faith. But, as soon as a real relationship is set up between them, reason is dependent on faith and proceeds from faith.

This occurs when man is called to faith, or actually receives the gift of faith. In this case reason has to work for the good of faith as for a higher principle, and in dependence on faith as on a higher principle. To this extent reason has to serve faith, or be its "handmaid."

Reason has to work for faith in two ways: first, to prepare a place in the soul for faith itself; secondly, once faith has taken possession, to bring about an understanding and development of its contents. Thus reason serves theological knowledge as a higher science by helping to impart it in its principle and in its subsequent development. In the first connection reason is a *praeambula* (forerunner), in the second a *pedisequa* (attendant) of faith.

As *praeambula*, reason goes before faith, exploring the natural order of things upon which is erected the supernatural order to be known by faith and from which must be acquired the notions that, when illuminated by analogy, are to be applied to the conception of the supernatural order. Again, reason precedes in order to convince the soul of the existence and credibility of supernatural revelation, and hence of the licitness and obligation of belief in it. In virtue of man's vocation to faith, reason may no longer work exclusively for itself when investigating natural things in its effort to win control over the domain of natural truths. It is called upon to build a throne for faith and to utilize its natural knowledge as a pattern for the higher knowledge to be gained through faith. Further, owing to this same vocation, reason is under orders not to ignore the facts by which revelation comes to its attention, but must ponder them carefully so as thereby to open the door of the soul to faith. Reason cannot, of course, inaugurate faith; for faith is ushered in and set upon its throne by the free will elevated by grace.

From this point on, reason is called upon to work for faith as *pedisequa,* so that faith can develop the rich resources of its own subject matter. Reason must strive more to promote the development of faith than its own good, since the object of faith is immeasurably nobler and more worthy than its own proper object, and comprises everything that reason longed for by nature, but could not reach by its own efforts. Therefore reason must place its natural concepts at the disposal of faith, and must endeavor to elucidate the objects of faith according to the norm of revelation by determining to what extent such concepts can be analogously applied to them. In the same way reason must devote its natural associative and discursive powers to the task of discovering the interconnection between the truths of faith and the motivation of the one by the other. It must also strive to bring out all the implications of each of the truths by unfolding the full wealth of the consequences potentially contained in them.

Thus reason is to serve faith by laboring in its behalf. Of course its assignment to this higher office does not deprive it of the right of working for itself. Far from losing this right, it can serve faith efficiently only by fully developing its own talent. Still less does it lose the physical power of exercising its own activity as before, and particularly of ruling its own domain. On the contrary, its higher destiny gives it the new power, in conjunction with faith, of rising above its own natural sphere. It is not degraded but ennobled by its assignment to the service of the higher science, just as the private citizen is ennobled when he enters the service of the state.

In exerting itself in behalf of faith, reason is dependent on faith in all its efforts, since every cause is dependent on the end to which its activity is to be directed; and also because it is influenced and ruled by faith in the exercise of its functions. This latter dependence flows from the former. For he who is under orders to labor for a definite end must so regulate his procedure as really to attain the objective, and of course he may not imperil it. Thus the maidservant who has agreed to place her services at the disposal of a master must first of all abstain from everything that would be contrary to his interest; secondly, the maidservant must do what will conduce to his advantage, as he desires, and not according to her own whims.

Moreover, so far as reason is to be active on behalf of faith, it may not pronounce any judgment, even in its own sphere, that would prejudice faith or would subvert faith, in the psychological impossibility of two simultaneously contradictory judgments. Further, when laboring in the specific domain of faith, reason must take faith as the basis and norm of its whole activity, since only thus can it really be of effective service for the cultivation of faith. For unless it had faith to sustain it, it could draw no certain conclusions; and unless it conformed to the norm of the revealed proposition, it would not be able to determine how far its concepts were analogously applicable, and consequently could not form correct ideas of supernatural things. Therefore it must take faith as the principle of its argumentation, and the proposition given by faith as the model for the recasting of its concepts. Accordingly there are two ways in which reason must exert itself in dependence on faith.

However, this sort of dependence of reason on faith does not destroy its natural liberty and autonomy, but rather imparts to it a higher freedom, and even raises it to a higher plane, although it can remain there only by clinging to faith. A higher sphere of activity is thereby opened up to it, which faith alone can authorize it to undertake. This does not mean that its natural range of action is curtailed, or that henceforth it can rule over its own domain only with the permission of faith. Within its own sphere it is prevented only from abusing its power, since for the future it is restrained from setting up errors against faith, and consequently from accepting falsehood for truth. The true liberty and autonomy of reason, its freedom to search for clear, untarnished truth in the light of its own principles, is but assured by the joint reign of faith over its province. This liberty is doubly assured if reason, in addition to being on its guard against pronouncing judgment prejudicial to the infallible authority of faith, endeavors to make the data of faith the goal of its own investigations, and thus lightens the task of discovering truth by itself.

Briefly, the dominion of faith over reason involves only the joint rule of faith over the natural sphere; and this joint regency is limited to the function of a protectorate set up for the maintenance and furtherance of reason's own natural freedom and sovereignty. On the other hand, the dominion of faith elevates reason to joint regency in the supernatural domain of faith, over which reason of itself had no dominion at all, and in any case can acquire no more than the dominion proper to a vassal.

Nowhere do we find more perfectly verified the profound truth of the wise adage, "to serve God is to reign." For the rule of faith is at bottom nothing but the rule of the divine reason, which takes possession of our souls in faith. If human reason submits to the demands of the divine reason or reverently follows its lead, divine reason assures human reason of its rightful dominion over natural truth, and admits it to a dominion, though only a dominion proper to a vassal, over a higher kingdom of truth. The full force of the Savior's statement applies here: "If you continue in My word . . . you shall know the truth, and the truth shall make you free."[13] Divine truth, which we take secure possession of in faith, can and will keep our reason free from the domination of any error that contradicts it, will aid it in its investigations to pursue an undeviating course toward truth, and will never permit it to be misled by a will-o'-the-wisp. And as the Son of God has made us free in the highest sense by endowing us with the liberty of the children of God, so our reason will be supremely free when, elevated above its natural limits, it not only overthrows error, but like the eagle, borne on the wings of faith, it can soar up to the heights of the most secret truth.

We may regard the relation involved in reason's service from the standpoint of the activity it exerts on behalf of faith, or from the standpoint of its dependence on faith in that activity. Then this relation is not that of a slavish subjection and subordination in which reason would no longer retain any rights or power for itself, nor is it the relation of a tyrant, to whom God might say, as Pharao said to Joseph: "Without thy commandment no man shall move hand or foot in all the land of Egypt."[14] It is not even the relation of an ordinary subject to his master, but the relation of a subject privileged and ennobled by special service to his prince. Assuredly it is not a slavish relation, for it can rise effectively and endure only so far as reason recognizes it voluntarily, and the will of man enters into it freely.[15]

2. Because of this element of freedom, the relation is conveyed far more profoundly, clearly, and adequately, and at the same time more nobly, if we describe it as the relation of a bride to her bridegroom. The preservation, enhancement, and elevation of reason's natural liberty by its union with faith, which is not explicitly brought out in the relation of the handmaid to her lord, is as fully stressed in our comparison as is reason's subordination and submissiveness to faith. For the wife must acknowledge the husband as her head and lord, particularly when she is originally of lower rank than the husband, and is called to union with him only because he is pleased to invite her to share his higher estate. This view of the matter also corresponds to the general relation between nature and grace (or God as the dispenser of grace), as we have suggested on several occasions, and is but a special application of this doctrine to the relations existing between the light of nature, reason, and the light of grace which operates through faith. Lastly, it gives a more accurate idea of the inner union and fusion, the intimate, real cooperation of reason and faith in the genesis of their common product, theological knowledge. This is not the case with the other metaphor, drawn as it is from a purely moral union between two persons.

Although pertaining to different spheres, the two illuminations are compatible, and are of the same species, since both issue from the same source, the depths of the divine wisdom. Hence they can come together again in close union. And they ought to be joined, to complement and sustain each other, especially for the production of theological knowledge of the divine mysteries, of which reason is by nature receptive, and in which it satisfies its deepest cravings and highest desires. Reason by itself cannot generate this knowledge. It requires the fructifying seed of faith, which must furnish reason with principles and a standard for fomulating its thought, and by the light of its accompanying grace must empower reason to cooperate effectively in the generation of theological knowledge. In a word, faith must convey to reason the subject matter and law of the higher knowledge, and provide the stimulus for pursuing it. But without reason, faith is no less unable to unfold and develop its content. That is why faith must deposit this content in the womb of reason, and cause it to be nurtured and formed there. Reason is doubt-less receptive as regards faith; but it conceives in order to clothe and develop the object it has conceived. Hence in the generation of the-ological knowledge reason and faith unite to constitute a single princi-ple; they operate in each other and through each other. With regard to this function, therefore, reason appears in all truth as the bride of faith. Reason is raised from its natural lowliness to a mysterious union with the divine light of faith. Since this union cannot take place unless reason freely acknowledges the superior dignity and the rights of faith, and willingly admits the entrance of faith into its womb, both the character of the union and the form it assumes must be envisaged as a marriage.

It is clear that by entering into this union with faith as bridegroom, reason must be subordinate to faith and must be submissive to it. This subjection of the bride to the bridegroom is the necessary consequence of the union, the natural correlative of the bridegroom's descent to the bride and of the bride's elevation to union with the bridegroom. Reason must be submissive to faith especially in their common activity in the theological sphere, by dedicating its entire effort to the service of faith, and by receiving from faith the law of its behavior. Even in its own proper actions and omissions, reason may not proceed as if it stood alone. It may utter no opinion that opposes the law of its bridegroom, and as a true bride must endeavor even in its own affairs to follow the path pointed out by faith's superior wisdom. Reason may no longer regard itself as isolated, because it is no longer isolated. Much less may it look upon the curtailment of the liberty it possesses in the abstract as a misfortune, for the enjoyment of true liberty is not thereby impeded, but is safeguarded and enhanced.

3. Like the nuptials of nature with grace, the yoking of reason with faith in the theological sphere has its fairest and most sublime ideal in the espousals of the noblest of purely human beings, the Virgin of virgins, with the Holy Spirit, whereby she became the mother of Him who is personal Wisdom incarnate.

Mary, bride of the Holy Spirit, conceived of Him the personal Word

of eternal Wisdom. Under the action of the Holy Spirit she gave her own
flesh to that Word, and in her womb fashioned the flesh that had been
animated by the Holy Spirit, thereupon to present Him to the world
embodied in visible form. In like manner reason, wedded in faith to the
same Holy Spirit by His grace, conceives, in the light of faith shed by
Him, the divine truth contained in the word of God. Reason offers to
that truth the matter required for its intellectual formulation, and
clothes it, so to speak, with the forms of its own natural ideas. Thereby
reason makes that truth intelligible and apt for embodiment in human
phraseology. For reason cannot reflect divine truth in its divine vastness
and splendor. This can occur only in the light of glory, where reason
contributes nothing but a potency for the reception of this light and for
its own transfiguration. Mary had to clothe the personal Wisdom of the
Son of God in the unpretentious raiment of the "form of a servant,"[16] so
that later this "form of a servant" might become the "form of God," not
of course by annihilation but by transfiguration. So likewise here below
reason has to invest divine truth with the garments of its own lowliness,
only to behold the veil drop later, and without the intermediacy of
earthly forms to gaze on the Divine in the full purity of its natural
brilliance.

As the summons to become the Mother of the God-man involved the
highest dignity for Mary, and raised her from a humble maid to be the
Queen of all creation, thus also there is no greater distinction for reason
than its vocation to cooperation with faith in the generation of theological knowledge, whereby it is elevated beyond its native lowliness to
the highest nobility. Mary rose to the dignity of Mother of God by the
humble obedience of a handmaid of the Lord. With this obedience she
assented to the invitation of her divine bridegroom, and even in her high
estate preserved the humility fitting for the Lord's handmaid. So too,
reason can receive faith only by the humble acknowledgment of the
rights of revelation and an obedient assent to God's call. Even in its
intimate union with faith, it must remain conscious of its subjection to
faith. With the humility of a maidservant, reason may not contradict
faith, but mistrustful of self, must gladly submit to the infallible guidance of faith. In both cases, however, the bride's dignity ensures that the
obedience will be a free and liberating, noble obedience, which is not
under the constraint of harsh subjection to a master. On the contrary,
this obedience proceeds from a tender devotedness that fittingly corresponds to the gracious kindness of the lord.

Therefore he who is repelled by the axiom, "philosophy is the handmaid of theology," should turn his thoughts to the handmaid of the Lord
and the merit of her humility; he should think of her who is the pinnacle

of human eminence and dignity in her attitude toward the divine. For by her humble submissiveness and by her sublime union she prefigures the perfect relationship of all that is human with the divine.

4. In line with our discussion up to this point, the God-man Himself would have to be considered not so much a type of the relation between reason and faith as a type of their joint product, theological knowledge. We will come back to this idea. Nevertheless, from the viewpoint of the two principles of activity, the divine and the human nature which enter into the composition of the God-man, I can also look upon Him as a figure of the relation between the two principles, faith and reason.

One of the chief features of marriage, the free union between the parties, cannot of course be found here, since the human nature of Christ has never had independent existence apart from the Logos. Besides, at first sight the autonomy of Christ's human nature almost seems to have vanished in the person of the Logos. This indeed is the case so far as hypostatic autonomy is meant. But neither do reason and faith possess hypostatic autonomy; for in our present supposition both pertain to one and the same subject. Hence their difference and their relation can be illustrated by this very comparison, according to a point of view that is completely lacking in the other analogies.

(a) The two natures in Christ, despite their hypostatic union, exist alongside each other unmingled, as the higher and the lower; for both together constitute the whole Christ. This, too, is the way reason and faith exist unmixed alongside each other in the believer, as the principles of the two highest sciences, philosophy and theology. These two taken together invest the knowing subject with proprietorship over the highest domain of knowledge.

(b) Owing to its integrity, the human nature in Christ preserves its own proper energy and mode of operation, its own activity that proceeds from the human nature itself and exists in its own right. Thus likewise reason keeps its own activity, even after it has been joined to faith in the same subject. Hence it has the power and the right to know, in virtue of its own principles, the truths that lie within its radius, that is, to cultivate pure philosophy.

(c) However, as Christ's human nature, owing to its union with the Logos, cannot and may not exercise its own activity as if it had separate existence, but must conform to the divine nature and will, so reason in a believing Christian cannot and may not philosophize independently of every other consideration, but must cherish harmony with faith in its philosophical speculations.

(d) On the other hand, in those activities which the human nature of Christ cannot carry through by its own power, it must not only be conformed to the divine nature, but must let itself be used by the latter as an instrument of its activity, so that the two natures may work in and through each other in theandric action. In like manner, whenever there is a question of cultivating knowledge that is not purely philosophical but is theological, reason must develop its activity in and through faith.

Would anyone contend that, in consequence of this close and necessary harmony and union between the operations of Christ's two natures, the natural freedom of the human nature is not elevated and transfigured, but curtailed? Or would anyone say that the activity of the human nature ceases to be truly human when it performs what is proper to it by its own power, although in accord with the divine nature? Why, then, should the natural freedom of man's reason be lost, when all it has to do is to seek and embrace truth in harmony with faith, and in common with faith to engender a knowledge of supernatural truths? Why should it cease to operate in a purely philosophical and a truly philosophical manner when, in developing and drawing out the principles placed in it by God, it strives to enter into accord and remain in accord with the wisdom of God that faith has revealed to it with the greatest certitude? And even if activity of this sort were no longer to be called purely philosophical, should reason on that account completely isolate itself from faith, to which it is joined in so close a union?

Thus the various natural figures and analogies, which a deep contemplation of the nature of Christianity yields, complement one another, and furnish us with a good illustration of the relations between reason and faith. In this relationship the sharp distinction between the two factors is preserved in unity, and necessary independence is maintained in subordination. Indeed, the union of both is based upon their very difference, and the subordination of the lower to the higher is shown to be the supreme elevation of the former.

### 110. Theology as Wisdom both Human and Divine

It remains for us but to cast a glance at theology itself, as the subjective science of faith already acquired or yet to be attained, in its relation to the sciences of pure reason, and to compare it with them from the standpoint of scientific excellence. In view of the foregoing discussion we can be quite brief. Let us begin by seeing to what degree theology verifies the conditions on which the absolute and relative perfection of a science depends.

These conditions are partly objective, partly subjective.

If we consider a science as objective, its perfection consists in the greatest possible universality, uniformity, and sublimity of its subject matter. For the perfection of any system is proportionate to the multitude and value of the items that make it up, and the order by which they are brought together in unity. Hence the unity of a science need not be sought exclusively in the unity of the cognitive principle from which all its truths may be deduced as conclusions. This sort of unity pertains to the subjective perfection of a science. Moreover, it is not attainable by us men in any physical science (such as physics, zoology, or psychology), and least of all in philosophy, if philosophy is not to lose itself in abstract formulas and degenerate into barren speculation. The essential objective conditions are admirably realized in the subject matter of theology. For theology embraces all things in heaven and on earth, the natural as well as the supernatural, although the former only with respect to the latter, and hence the most sublime objects. Primarily it contemplates the supreme and most simple unity, the divine nature, and secondarily all other beings, so far as they are taken up into a union with God so intimate that, according to the profound expression used by the Apostle, God is all in all.[17] Its proper subject matter is first and foremost the supernatural unity of the divine persons among themselves in the interior of the divine nature, and the union of all creatures with God and one another in a unity which, though reason could never respect it, is an imitation of the divine ideal. Objectively, therefore, by reason of its subject matter, theology is the most universal, unified, and sublime science that can be conceived.

The subjective perfection of a science is nothing but the perfection of the knowledge with which we comprehend the system as it is actually constituted. This perfection depends on three factors: (1) the logical connection between the various truths and their reduction to the fewest possible principles; (2) the certainty or evidence of these principles themselves; (3) the coincidence of the cognitive principles with the real principles or real foundations of the system. If these three conditions are verified, knowledge reaches its greatest simplicity, certitude, and profundity.

1. It would be unreasonable to require that all the truths known in any science should be reduced to a single principle. Yet it does unquestionably pertain to the greater perfection of its simplicity that the entire network of truths should be reducible as conclusions to the fewest possible premises, so that a formal unity in the mind of the knower may be established. This is actually the case in theology, no less than in philosophy. If we examine the *Summa theologica* of St. Thomas, we find that in almost every section dealing with supernatural truths he places at the beginning a single article of faith, from which, as from a premise, he

proceeds with mathematical rigor to infer all the truths connected with the topic in question. Thus at the head of his Trinitarian doctrine he places the single proposition taken from revelation, that there are real processions in God. From this proposition he derives, in a methodical and perfectly concatenated series, the entire profusion of those wonderful truths that revelation and theology have made accessible concerning this subject. In the *Prima Secundae* he starts with the supernatural destiny of man as his principle and leads up to the beatific vision as his end. He adopts this procedure in order scientifically to deduce all the conclusions bearing on man's supernatural progress toward God. On man's supernatural destiny he bases his whole theory of the meritorious virtues, the supernatural law, and grace.

2. Only in one detail does theology seem, at first sight, to rank below other sciences: the principles, the fundamental truths from which it proceeds, are not known by intrinsic evidence, but are accepted on faith. We spoke of this matter above. That the principles of theology are not evidentially known, but must be believed, is accounted for by their supernatural eminence, not by any uncertainty or unreliability on their part. Because of their eminence, they can be known clearly and evidently by God alone with the light natural to Him and by us only through the light of glory. But even in our present state we are more certain of them than we are of the principles of philosophy. Since, as regards the mastery of a science, there is as much question of the certainty as of the evidence of the principles, we can say that the higher certitude in theology amply compensates for any deficiency in intrinsic evidence.

3. The value of a science depends on a perception of the objective grounds on which its several truths are ultimately based, even more than it depends on the evidence of the principles or the connection of the conclusions with them. In philosophy this perfection is unattainable; our intellect mounts to a knowledge of a cause only from its effects, with the aim of returning with greater clarity from the cause to the effects. Transcendental philosophy alone makes the claim of being independent of effects in its investigation of causes. It would wish to transcend effects and penetrate into the cause immediately, so as to have an intuition of the effects in the light of the cause. But what is impossible for philosophy is, by the grace of God, possible for theology. Theology is the true transcendental science, and is able to employ the synthetic method in the highest perfection possible for us.

God alone, per se, knows immediately the ultimate foundation of all things, His own essence, and perceives how all things proceed therefrom by His free will. Through the light of glory He shares His knowledge with the blessed, admits them to immediate intuition of His essence, and in it enables them to perceive all the other objects of theology, and even those of philosophy. In faith we do not, of course, attain to intuitive knowledge; but our knowledge is based on God's vision, and so we anticipate the vision proper to the blessed. By faith we have an immediate knowledge of God Himself, the supreme Cause, of His omnipotence, and of the divine decree and plan according to which He is pleased to act in the outer world. And thus we are empowered to survey the whole vast range of theological truths from their heart and center, as is possible in no other science (except, perhaps, abstract mathematics), and also the domain of natural beings, to the extent that these, as explained above, are illuminated by supernatural revelation.

However, as at present we behold neither the divine essence, nor the power, the goodness, and the plan of God in the clearness of vision, but only in the dim light of faith, our understanding of the way God acts and communicates Himself is far from being a perfect knowledge. Nevertheless God has revealed to us the connection of the natural and supernatural orders with their causes, particularly their final and exemplary causes. From these supreme ends and exemplars which He pursues in His plan we can infer, if not all details, at any rate the chief elements of the supernatural order. God's ultimate aims and ideals, as is the case with everything that has to do with the planning and execution of His activity, are derived from Himself, from His own essence. From this essence, as made known to us by revelation, we can understand in turn how and why God has ordained the designs of His wisdom as He has, and not otherwise. Thus by faith we struggle through to the *rationes aeternae* of all temporal things; and these reasons comprise, in addition to the source, the motive and the norm of the wonderful structure of the universe.

Accordingly faith, which at first sight seems to negate science, actually establishes us in the possession of the most excellent of all sciences. When in faith we follow the theologians in their eagle flight under the guidance of the Evangelists, we share in God's own knowledge, and transcend all creation, so as finally to attain to the summit of all being. From there we command a view of all things in their utmost harmony and unity.[18]

From all this it follows that theology is more than simply one science out of many; it is the most excellent and precious of them all. Among the various sciences (*scientiae*) it is the one which as the wisdom (*sapientia*) par excellence, divine wisdom, towers majestically over all human sciences.

The qualities characterizing theology as a perfect science are identical with the qualities usually associated with wisdom. Its primary concern is not with created things, but with divine things, with God; it deals with created things only to the extent that they are related to God, proceed from Him, are united to Him, and serve for His glorification. Indeed, as regards God Himself, theology fastens its gaze chiefly on the interior mysteries of His bosom and His heart, and outside of God follows up mainly the extension of the Trinitarian productions and the assumption of creatures into the Trinitarian unity. It perceives and judges all things in the light of the most basic and certain principles, from the viewpoint of their deepest, most hidden causes and their highest ends. It contemplates the temporal only in the light of the eternal reasons (*rationes aeternae*), according to the eternal designs of God and the destiny of the temporal for reception into the divine eternity. To the dweller in time theology reveals his own ultimate and supreme destiny as well as the road that leads thereto, and hence instructs him to regulate his life and conduct in the wisest manner. It shows him the supreme Good in the possession of which he is to enjoy a superhuman happiness, and grants him even here below a faint foretaste of its heavenly sweetness. Consequently theology is, like no other science, a *scientia sapida,* a science full of delights.

At bottom theology is all this because it flows from the source of all wisdom, the divine wisdom, more directly and in purer and fuller flood than all the other sciences. Unlike these sciences, which do not rise above the level of human wisdom, it deserves to be called divine wisdom. As product of the natural reason, in whose womb it is conceived, formed, and brought to birth, it does not disown its earthly conception and generation, and so remains at the same time a truly human science: just as the Son of God is true man, because born of woman. But as Mary's Son, who was not conceived of earthly seed but came down into her womb from heaven, is a God-man, and therefore infinitely excels not only all the rest of the sons of men but His very mother herself, so, too, theology, generated as it is of divine light in the womb of reason, is not a purely human, but a divine-human wisdom and science. Like a heavenly queen, theology surpasses all merely rational sciences, and takes all of them, together with the very intellect from which it is sprung, into its service.

Between theology, considered as divine wisdom poured out upon man and, so to speak, taking human form in him, and the incarnate, personal Wisdom of God in Christ, a surprisingly close analogy and kinship is discernible.

The Incarnation of the personal Wisdom of God is, first of all, the source through which divine wisdom is communicated to us, according to the Apostle's phrase: "Christ Jesus, who of God is made unto us wisdom."[19] By taking our flesh, the personal Wisdom of God has flooded it with "all the treasures of wisdom and knowledge,"[20] thence to pour those treasures out upon all flesh. By His human speech and by the inner illumination which enables us to believe in His authority, He unlocks for us the fullness of His knowledge. Through faith we receive the incarnate, personal Wisdom of God into ourselves, so that He dwells in our hearts. By His presence in our souls He becomes, as it were, the sun which, diffusing its light and at the same time stimulating and sustaining our own personal activity, generates our divine-human wisdom as a reflection of Himself. Living on in this reflection, the divine Wisdom is reborn in our hearts, embodies us in Himself, and thus in a mysterious, ineffable way becomes our Wisdom, too.

The incarnate, personal Wisdom of God continues, so to speak, His Incarnation in the communication and generation of our own divine wisdom. Hence He is manifestly the ideal of our divine wisdom in regard to its origin and nature. For, as in the Incarnation the personal Wisdom of God was sent into human nature to be hypostatically united to it, so God sends Him, the sharer of His throne, down from His heaven into holy souls,[21] to enlighten them with grace and faith, and fill them with His own brilliance. And, as the personal Wisdom assumed human flesh and blood in Mary's womb and transfigured them with His divine power, so in the depths of our souls He assumes flesh and blood from our human thoughts and concepts, by suffusing and sublimating them with His higher light, by bringing Himself to conception in them, and thus making His riches our own.

For all that, He remains invisible here below under the form He thus assumes, as He did in the flesh that was united to the Godhead, but prior to the Resurrection was not perfectly illuminated with the splendor of divinity. And although even here below we can savor the sweetness of the Spirit of divine Wisdom, this is only a slight foretaste, which no more stills the aching desire of our heart for an unobstructed sight of Him than the beatific vision enjoyed by Christ's humanity excluded the capacity to suffer. The weakness attending our earthly nature continues to cling to our theological wisdom, as the infirmity of the flesh clung to the earthly Christ. Our wisdom can become wholly divine only when the weakness of nature, besides being fructified and imbued with divine light, is completely absorbed in it. Not until then can the sweet and lovable Spirit of divine Wisdom fill us with the fragrance of His undiminished sweetness and lovableness, and satiate us with the torrent of His bliss; just as the incarnate Wisdom did not send the Spirit to us until after the resurrection and glorification of His body.

Finally, the incarnate Wisdom of God is the supreme end and object of theology, and the focus of its continually evolving wisdom. For the God-man is the most concrete and the greatest objective revelation of God, and the junction point, if not the root, of the whole system of Christian truths. Theology bases itself on His visible manifestation, but with the aim of pressing on to His invisible glory and that of His Father; and from the divine eminence He occupies it descends again, to trace out the shaping and perfecting of His mystical body. On the one hand, God "hath shined in our hearts, to give the light of the knowledge of the glory of God, in the face of Christ Jesus,"[22] in the visible, human form of the invisible image of the Father. On the other hand, we find the sum and substance of the whole of theological wisdom in the wisdom of "the mystery of Christ" and of the "unsearchable riches" contained in Him, in the outpouring of which "the manifold wisdom of God" is made known.[23]

Of course the objective center, the root, and the summit of the entire supernatural order is the Triune God, or the bosom of the eternal Father, from which Christ Himself came forth, and to which He returns with His mystical body. But as long as we have not yet entered with Christ into the very bosom of the eternal Father, and must be content to behold the invisible in the visible, He Himself in His earthly form is the way upon which we must travel in our ascent to that summit. Our theological wisdom, which is at once human and divine, must attach itself to Him primarily in His humanity, in order to scale the heights to His divinity, to His unity with the Father.

Thus from every point of view our theological wisdom is bound up with incarnate, personal Wisdom of God, is conformed to Him, and receives from Him its characteristic divine-human signature. Subjectively as well as objectively it is specifically Christian; for it is the science of the great mystery of Christ, and is the result of divine anointing and illumination. Owing to the unpretentious form in which it appears, and the enigmatical obscurity in which its objects are revealed, it is scorned by the world, in the same way that the Son of God was despised when in the form of a slave He went down to death upon a cross. Like the cross of Christ, theology appears to haughty human wisdom as foolishness and weakness. But "the foolishness of God is wiser than men; and the weakness of God is stronger than men."[24] Therefore in facing the wisdom of this world we may, with the Apostle, in holy pride "speak the wisdom of God in a mystery, a wisdom which is hidden, which God ordained before the world unto our glory."[25] In the grace of God we may consider ourselves blessed by reason of "all riches of fullness of understanding, unto the knowledge of the mystery of God the Father and of

344 MATTHIAS JOSEPH SCHEEBEN

Christ Jesus, in whom are hid all the treasures of wisdom and knowledge," and in whom we, too, shall be filled to repletion.[26]

The enlightened Christian need envy no one but the blessed in heaven on account of the lucidity, the depth, and the fullness of their knowledge. But the same faith as that in which we anticipate their vision holds out to us the sure promise that its imperfections and obscurity will vanish if, following its directions, we strive devotedly and perseveringly to reach its divine object. Faith is the prophet within our very spirit, presaging the full unveiling of the mysteries of God, the morning star of the day of eternity, the bread of our childhood in the kingdom of God, which rears us to the maturity of the wisdom of Christ.

May the love of the Holy Spirit, which can never fall away, the love which forms the bond between time and eternity, between heaven and earth, between yearning anticipation and blissful vision, the love that surpasses understanding and even now plunges us into the depths of the heart of God, raise us up with its heavenly power to the bosom of "the Father of lights," that together with His Son we may behold Him face to face, and may "be like to Him, because we shall see Him as He is," and as we ourselves "are known by God."[27]


## NOTES

1. Heb. 11:1.
2. See p. 39 [of *The Mysteries of Christianity,* trans. Vollert].
3. See pp. 659–62 [ibid.]
4. See *Summa theologica* IIa IIae, q.4, a. 1 ff.; *De veritate* q.14, a. 11; and especially *In III Sent.* d.23, q.1, a.4, quaestiunc. 3 in corp: "All things that act in pursuance of an end must have a tendency toward that end, and a certain inception of it; otherwise they would not be acting for an end. However, the end to which the divine generosity has foreordained or predestined man, namely, the fruition of God Himself, completely surpasses the powers of created nature; for 'eye hath not seen, nor ear heard, neither hath it entered into the heart of man, what things God hath prepared for them that love Him' (1 Cor. 2:9). Man's natural equipment does not confer on him a sufficient inclination to such an end, and so something must be added to man to give him an inclination to that end, just as his natural powers impart to him an inclination to an end that is connatural to him. These superadded gifts are called theological virtues, for three reasons. First, as concerns their object: for, since the end to which we are ordained is God Himself, the required tendency consists in actions whose object is God Himself. Secondly, with regard to their cause: for, as that end is appointed unto us by God, and not by our nature, God alone produces in us an inclination toward the end; and so they are called theological virtues, in the sense that they are caused in us exclusively by God. Thirdly, from the point of

view of natural knowledge: for the tendency to this end cannot be known by natural reason, but only by revelation; and so they are called theological, inasmuch as they are made known to us by information that comes from God. Consequently philosophers have no knowledge of them."

5. Newman uses this argument to good advantage in his *Essay on the Development of Christian Doctrine* (London, 1878), 93, 437 ff.—TRANS.

6. 1 Cor. 2:14–15.

7. 1 Cor. 2:13.

8. 1 Cor. 2:10–12.

9. Eph. 1:17–19.

10. Matt. 18:3.

11. 1 John 2:27.

12. On the gift of understanding, see St. Thomas, *In III Sent.* d.35, q.2, a.2, quaestiunc. 1 ff.; *Summa theologica* IIa IIae, q.8. The Angelic Doctor discusses the gift of wisdom in *In III Sent.* d.35, q.35, a.1; a better treatment is found in the *Summa* IIa IIae, q.45, a.2: "Wisdom implies a certain rectitude of judgment that is in accord with the divine reason. Rectitude of judgment can be regarded in two ways: first, with reference to perfect use of reason; secondly, from the point of view of a certain connaturality with the object about which judgment is to be pronounced. Thus, in matters pertaining to chastity, he who has mastered the science of moral theology judges rightly, once he has investigated the question; but another person, who has the habit of chastity, judges rightly about the same matter because this virtue is, so to speak, connatural to him. Therefore, with regard to divine matters as investigated by reason, the ability to judge aright pertains to the wisdom which is an intellectual virtue. But the ability to pass correct judgment about such matters by a sort of connaturality with them belongs to wisdom as a gift of the Holy Spirit. Thus Dionysius says, in chapter 2 of *De divinis nominibus:* 'Hierotheus is perfect in divine things, because he not only learns, but experiences them.' This connatural sympathy with divine things is the result of charity, which unites us to God, according to 1 Cor. 6:17: 'He who is joined to the Lord is one spirit.' Therefore the wisdom which is a gift has its cause in the will, for its cause is charity; but its essence resides in the intellect, whose act is to judge correctly, as was stated above." The gift of knowledge belongs here, too; but its position is inferior to that of understanding or wisdom. On the relation of these gifts to faith, St. Thomas teaches (*Summa* IIa IIae, q.4, a.8 ad 3): "The perfection of the gifts of understanding and knowledge exceeds the perfection of that knowledge which is proper to faith, from the point of view of greater clarity, but not as regards firmer assent. For the whole certitude of understanding and knowledge, considered as gifts, arises from the knowledge that belongs to faith, just as the certitude of conclusions arises from the certitude of principles."

13. John 8:31f.

14. Gen. 41:44.

15. Our doctrine might, perhaps, appear to involve the consequence that faith is the servant of reason, no less than reason is the servant of faith; for faith can exist and operate only in a certain dependence on reason, and in any case is in a position to render notable services to reason. But this view is excluded by our definition of the relationship servitude entails, as given above. Not every kind of dependence is the basis for a relationship of subordination. The higher can be dependent on the lower, and require its services; indeed the lower, by its

very nature, is often a prerequisite for the higher. In this sense a king is dependent on his subjects, for he cannot defend and rule his kingdom all by himself; thus also a housewife may be dependent on her maid for the management of her establishment. In the same way theological knowledge, so far as it is possible for us during this life, is dependent on the activity of the intellect and on philosophical knowledge. There could be no question of faith without such activity, nor could the knowledge which rests on faith be cultivated without philosophical reasoning. But it does not follow, nor would such a conclusion occur to any thoughtful person, that theology is the servant of philosophy on that account. For theology remains the higher science; whatever it requires from philosophy it simply takes, as having a rightful claim to it. Nor is the higher in any way subordinate to the lower simply because it works for the good of the lower, or performs some service for the lower. Everything that is higher can be useful to the lower, since it possesses greater wealth and power. God himself, the All-highest, serves His creatures by procuring many goods for them; but He is not on that account subordinate to them. Accordingly, although faith brings advantages to philosophy, and to that extent serves reason, it does not in any sense occupy a menial position with respect to philosophy.

16. Phil. 2:7.

17. 1 Cor. 15:28.

18. The finest example of a theological treatise that gives methodical explanations throughout in the light of the attributes and plans of the first principle of all being, is the *Breviloquium* of St. Bonaventure.

19. 1 Cor. 1:30.

20. Col. 2:3.

21. See Wisd. of Sol. 9.

22. 2 Cor. 4:6.

23. Eph. 3:4, 8, 10.

24. 1 Cor. 1:25.

25. 1 Cor. 2:7.

26. Col. 2:2, 3, 10.

27. James 1:17; 1 John 3:2; Gal. 4:9.

# 14

# What Is a Dogma?

*Edouard LeRoy*

Leo XIII was sure the wisdom of Saint Thomas would benefit all the sciences. Scientists themselves, however, often failed to be persuaded, and writers on religion were starting to imitate "modern" scientists. It thus fell to Leo's successor, Pius X (reigned 1903–14), to condemn "Modernism," which, to oversimplify somewhat, may be understood as the application to religious studies of elements of "scientific method." Such elements included reliance on the experiential, freedom of research and expression, and the mutability of theories or hypotheses. As was the case with Americanism, the most manageable description of Modernism is to be found in the document that condemns it; for Modernism that was Pius X's letter *Pascendi Dominici Gregis* (1907). (It seems reasonable here, as in other areas of cultural history, to consider that the nineteenth century ended in 1914.) As part of the campaign against the Modernists the Vatican also specifically condemned LeRoy's *Dogme et critique,* a work consisting of a reprinted periodical article, given here, followed by 349 more pages of objections and responses to them.

Born in Elbeuf-sur-Seine, in 1870, the mathematician and philosopher Edouard LeRoy was a disciple of Henri Bergson and was later Bergson's successor at the Collège de France. He is a Janus figure in religious studies, looking backward over the nineteenth century's enormous confidence in science but also forward toward the preoccupations of major twentieth-century religious figures. In one case the connection is direct and personal. At LeRoy's death, in 1954, the priest-paleontologist Pierre Teilhard de Chardin wrote, "There are few men whom I have so deeply admired and loved as I did him. So serene, so completely human—and so deeply Christian. . . . I owed him a very great debt. It was not exactly that I owed any particular idea to him, but that, particularly between 1920 and 1930, he gave me confidence, enlarged my mind (and my feeling of loyalty to the Church), and served (at the Collège de France) as a spokesman for my ideas, then taking shape, on 'hominization' and the 'noösphere.'" For his part, LeRoy wrote in the preface of *L'exigence idéaliste et le fait d'évolution* (1928), "I have so often and for so long talked over with Père Teilhard the views expressed here that neither of us can any longer pick out his own contribution." (The quotations are from Claude Cuénot's *Teilhard de Chardin: A Biographical Study* [Baltimore: Helicon Press, 1965], 58–59.)

In the work before us LeRoy reminds the reader of a basic principle of apologetics: that the church must take people as they are. "Men of today," he says, "are within their rights in not consenting to be held down to the point of view of the thirteenth century." He then sets forth what have since become frequent objections to dogmatic propositions: (1) Such propositions are unverifiable (i.e., it is impossible to discover whether they are true). (2) They are extrinsicist, allegedly framed independently of any human process of discovery. (3) They are, as overly metaphorical or anthropomorphic, wanting in thinkable meaning. And (4) they are incommensurable with the whole of positive knowledge; they do not belong to the same system of knowledge as other propositions. LeRoy finds these objections to what he terms the "intellectualist" understanding of dogma to be irrefutable. As a loyal Catholic, however, he does not therefore reject dogma; he infers that there must be a better way of understanding it.

The better way comes to taking dogma negatively and, more important, pragmatically. The negative understanding is the traditional way of the mystic: since, strictly speaking, no human word can adequately express the divine, it must be that ecclesiastical language, even when cast in affirmative grammatical form, tells us what the divine is not. (Late-twentieth-century devotees of Thomas Merton may be surprised to find that logicians and mystics are often secret allies, but the evidence is undeniable.) The pragmatic meaning of dogmatic propositions is that they tell us how to act. Thus, to use the first of LeRoy's examples, to affirm that God is personal is really to affirm (a) that God is not impersonal (like a law, or like some unknown cosmic force diffused throughout the universe), and (b) that one must act toward God as toward a person, as if God were a person. This "as if," however, is not for LeRoy merely a benign fiction. On the contrary, "under the guise of metaphors and images" dogmatic language still affirms something about "supernatural reality," namely, that it "contains the wherewithal to make [it] obligatory . . . that our attitude and our conduct with regard to it should have such and such a character." Since human cultures change, the interpretation of dogma must also change. "What remains constant in the dogma is the orientation it gives to our practical activity."

In the same year that LeRoy died, Pope Pius XII canonized Pius X. Unaffected professionally by even a saint's disapproval, LeRoy had continued to teach at the Collège de France and to publish books on metaphysics and the philosophy of religion.

This title, "What Is a Dogma?" is only a simple question and by no means does it promise an answer. It is a question from the philosopher to the theologian calling for an answer from the theologian to the philosopher.

It would indeed be vain to pretend to give here a complete and definite answer to this complex question. Such problems cannot be solved in a few pages. Therefore the reader must not look for a settled doctrine in the short article which is to follow, nor even for categorical theses on any point. If he sometimes finds that I speak in too affirmative a tone let him be kind enough to admit that I do so only for the sake of greater clearness in my questions. In fact I wish to confine myself to simple suggestions which I present merely as rough drafts of solutions offered for the criticism of those who have authority to judge of the subject. And moreover I can justify this attitude of mine by an imperative reason, namely that I am not a theologian and do not like to decide matters in which I am not proficient.

Perhaps some one will ask, why then do I take the trouble to treat a subject of which I admit I have no particular knowledge? Here is my reason. In our day every layman is called upon to fulfil the duty of apostleship in the incredulous world in which he lives. He alone can serve efficiently as the vehicle and intermediary of the Christian message to those who would not trust the priests. Therefore it is inevitable that some problems of apologetics should be laid before him, problems whose solution is an absolute necessity for him if he does not wish to fail in the task which the force of circumstances has laid upon him without possibility of escape, if he wishes to be always ready, following the counsel of the Apostle, to satisfy those who ask him the reason for his faith. It is only natural therefore that I desire to be informed; and if I formulate my question publicly it is because I am not the only one in this situation, and because there is a general interest that the answer shall also be a public one.

Besides I have another motive for acting as I am. If I freely acknowledge my incompetence in a matter which is properly theological, yet on the other hand I consider that I am well situated to appreciate correctly the state of mind in contemporary philosophers that is opposed to the understanding of Christian truth. And it is to this that I bear witness in

From "Qu'est-ce qu'un dogme?" *La quinzaine,* April 16, 1905; later in *Dogme et critique* (Paris: Bloud, 1907), 1–34. The translation is from *What Is a Dogma?* trans. Lydia G. Robinson (Chicago: Open Court, 1918).

saying frankly, even brutally (if I must in order to be fully understood), what I know, what I have observed, what perhaps are not always sufficiently comprehended, namely the exact reasons why unbelieving philosophers of to-day repulse the truth that is brought to them and the legitimate causes (agreeing in this with the Christian philosophers themselves) why they are not satisfied with the explanations that are furnished them.

My ambition goes no farther than to point out certain opinions, perhaps to suggest certain reflections, especially to particularize the statement of certain problems. If the present work bring a useful contribution to the studies of religious philosophy, if it furnish documents and materials which others can turn to account, I shall have attained my end. It is not a question of upholding a system nor of aligning arguments for or against this or that school, but only of elucidating certain fundamental ideas whose consideration is imposed upon every system and upon every school. An effort toward light in the bosom of Catholic truth, faithfully accepted in its completeness and rigor—this is what I submit to the decision of those who have been charged with the duty of defining and interpreting it.

What I desire above all, I repeat, is to make better known the state of mind of those contemporaries who think, the nature of the questions they ask themselves, the obstacles that hinder them and the difficulties that perplex them. It cannot be denied that the classical replies no longer satisfy them; there is no use in disputing over so obvious a fact. The experience of cultivated non-Christian circles (I might even say a personal experience) has demonstrated to me that the proofs brought forward as traditional have no effect on intellects accustomed to the discipline of contemporary science and philosophy. Now why this new impotence of old methods which have sufficed so long? The reason appears to me to be, at least in great measure, that the old apologetics assumes the greater part of the problems to be solved in advance which the moderns, on the other hand, judge to be essential and primordial. The real difficulty for the moderns comes in altogether before the arguments begin by which the theologians flatter themselves they can convince them; it lies in the postulates taken for granted and in the very manner in which the investigation is approached.

It will be well to see how the questions ought to be put to-day; this should be the first result to be obtained. It is the chief result, for without it we would never arrive at anything serious. Thus is imposed the preliminary task of coming in contact with the minds whom one wishes to address and whom one claims to understand. It is necessary that the various chapters of the apologetic should be taken up successively from this point of view in order to be brought to general attention; and in examining here the idea of dogma[1] I only give a first example of the kind of work that I think ought to be generally undertaken. Let no one think such a task profitless or superfluous. On the contrary, nothing is of greater urgency to-day nor of more pressing necessity. It is strange and lamentable how little we on the Catholic side know or how greatly we fail to appreciate the state of mind of the opponents to whom we try to speak.[2] Nor are we listened to or understood. What we say has no response and carries no weight. We exert ourselves in silence and in a void without even giving rise to any criticism or refutation. In short we only reach those who do not need to be reached—I mean those who are convinced beforehand or whose difficulties are not of a theoretical kind. We must not deceive ourselves. Catholic thought at the present day is without notable influence on the various intellectual movements which are developing around us. It sometimes follows them at a distance and after having resisted them for a long time; but nowhere does it appear capable of directing them, much less of promoting them. There is nothing more sad than to confess so many efforts expended without result on the one hand, and on the other hand so many sincere questions asked which remain unanswered.

Doubtless one might say, and indeed some have said, that there is no need of taking into account modern demands because they proceed from a perverted and misguided judgment. Wretched subterfuge! What contemporaneous thought is asking for beyond what it receives is perfectly legitimate, and there is no justification in pretending to refuse to grant it. Men of to-day are within their rights in not consenting to be held down to the point of view of the thirteenth century. It would indeed be strange if any one should ask for a proof to support a truth of this kind.[3] After all, is it not the very mission and the raison d'être of apologetics to address itself to the disordered, if such there be? It must take people as they are and not require of them that they first come of their own accord where it may prefer. Once again, it would be strange if one had no right to make a cure except with certain remedies.

Hence there may be some interest and some profit in the testimony of those whose situation has put them in a position to know the modern mind, its needs and its requirements. These may try to tell how they have come to think what they believe, how they have succeeded in practically overcoming, and of their own accord, the difficulties that they have met like the others. I do not say that we must accept the conclusions of their experiences uncritically: but after all, these experiences offer the advantage of furnishing living documents, not dead opinions, and that is something. I here make no further claim.

One more word before I begin. Perhaps the reader will be surprised to find so long a preamble introducing so short an article. The reason is first of all that I wished to write a sort of general preface for other similar articles intended to follow this one, and also because I wished in this way to forestall any possible misunderstanding. Whatever opinion may be held on the ideas which I shall put forth, it must not happen that any one will try to answer me by charging me with heresy. I affirm nothing in this work except facts easily verifiable by everybody. As to the rest, that is to say the sketches of theories, whatever the form of the language which I have adopted in order to make myself clear, I give them expressly as simple *interrogations* addressed to whomsoever they may concern. In a word, I do nothing but state some problems; it is for the apologists and theologians to solve them.

We no longer live in the day of partial heresies. Formerly a purely logical and dialectic argumentation might suffice because certain common principles were always admitted on both sides. But the case is no longer the same to-day, when these principles go by default, when the fundamental difficulty is to establish a point of departure upon which both sides may agree. To-day denial does not attack one dogma any more than another. It consists above all in a preliminary and total demurrer. The question is not whether a proposition is a dogma or not; it is the very idea of dogma which is repugnant, which gives offense. Why is that?

When we examine the ordinary motives of this repugnance we find four principal ones which I shall briefly enumerate, endeavoring to present them in all their force:

1. A dogma is a statement presented as being neither proved nor provable.[4] Those who declare it to be true declare at the same time that it is impossible ever to arrive at the point of grasping the intimate reasons of its truth. Now modern thought, faithful to the precept of Leibniz, endeavors more and more to demonstrate the old so-called axioms. At least it wishes to justify them with Kant by a critical analysis which shows them to be necessary conditions of consciousness implied a priori in every act of reason. It is distrustful of those evidences, pretending to be direct, which were so numerous in former times. Often enough it discovers in them simple postulates adopted for an end of practical utility more or less unconsciously perceived.[5] In short everywhere and always it calls for long and detailed discussions before believing itself authorized to draw conclusions. And it is not just any more or less roundabout proof that it thus demands, but direct specific proofs. It does not like too general arguments which look upon vast assemblages as a

whole and proceed by wholesale demonstrations, because it has had experience too many times with the illusions, mistakes and oversights which they ordinarily conceal. Nor does it like any better external, extrinsic arguments which end in proofs of a negative character, in *reductiones ad absurdum* founded on judgments of contradiction or impossibility, because it has also had experience[6] too many times with their imprudent and hazardous character to declare either impossible or contradictory a thing which may appear so to us only from habit. Therefore it seems that in order to remain faithful to the tendencies which have assured its success in all domains modern thought can do no less than condemn absolutely the very idea of a strictly dogmatic proposition. In what system acceptable to reason could such a proposition find room without violence? Is not the first principle of scientific method incontestably, according to Descartes, that it must hold as true only what clearly appears to be true? What justification would there be for making an exception of just those propositions which pass as the most important, the most profound and the simplest of all? When affirmations are of the greatest consequence and refer to the most difficult and recondite subjects it is certainly not fitting to show oneself less attentive to the exactness of the rules which constitute our protection against error. On the contrary it is just then that it would be legitimate to be even more exacting, more scrupulous, more particular than usual.

2. It will doubtless be said that dogmatic propositions are never affirmed without proof. In fact an indirect demonstration has been attempted over and over again. One certain apologetic which is regarded as purely traditional[7] claims to prove that these propositions are true, although it realizes that it is incapable of bringing fully to light the how and the why of their truth. There is some analogy, it seems, between such a proceeding and that of the mathematician who limits himself at times to the theorems of simple existence, or that of the physicist who often accepts facts of which he cannot give any theoretical explanation, or yet again of the historian who always receives knowledge only by the path of testimony. Thus would end the first objection.

Yes, here we would have a very simple solution, but there is one misfortune, namely that the analogy pointed out proves upon reflection to be absolutely inaccurate. The difficulty we wish to avoid reappears in toto when we try to justify postulates on which the alleged indirect demonstration rests. When a mathematician is satisfied with establishing a theorem of simple existence, I mean a theorem affirming the existence of a solution inaccessible in itself, he reasons no less rigorously than in other branches of his science. Now here we have nothing like that. It would be necessary to prove *directly* that God exists, that he has spoken, that he has said this and that, that we possess his authentic teachings to-day. This amounts to the same thing as saying that the problem of God, the problem of revelation, of the inspiration of the Bible and of the authority of the Church, must be solved by a *direct* analysis. Now these are questions of the same kind as the strictly dogmatic questions, questions with reference to which it is indeed impossible to produce arguments comparable to those of the mathematician. Likewise when a physicist accepts a fact to which he can give no theoretical explanation this fact corresponds, at least for him, to certain definite experiences, to certain manipulations that can be practically carried out, in short to a group of motions of which he has direct knowledge. What similarity is there here? And finally even the historian does not consent to receive truth by testimony except because he is dealing with phenomena of the same kind as those of which he has a direct view by some other means. He still regards his science as always conjectural and uncertain so long as it treats of somewhat profound causes or of events that are more or less remote. How much more ought one to draw the same conclusion in the case of dogmas which reflect only facts that are mysterious, strange and disconcerting, and to which no analogy in our human experience corresponds! It has been well done. The alleged indirect proof has inevitably for its basis an appeal to the transcendence of pure authority. It claims[8] to introduce the truth into us fundamentally from the outside in the fashion of a ready-made "thing" which might enter into us forcibly. Thus any dogma whatever seems like a subservience, like a limit to the rights of thought, like a menace of intellectual tyranny, like a shackle and a restriction imposed from without upon the liberty of investigation—all of which is radically opposed to the very life of the spirit, to its need of autonomy and sincerity, to its generative and fundamental principle which is the principle of immanence.

Let us insist a little upon this last point, for the principle of immanence has not always been rightly understood. Too often it has been made out a monster, whereas nothing is more simple nor on the whole more clear. We may say that to have gained a clear consciousness of it is the essential result of modern philosophy. Who refuses to admit it is from that time forth no longer counted among the number of philosophers; who does not succeed in understanding it indicates thereby that he has not the philosophic sense. And this is what constitutes the principle of immanence. Reality is not made of separate pieces put in juxtaposition, but everything is within everything else; in the smallest detail of nature or of science analysis recognizes all of science and all of nature. Each of our states and of our actions comprises our entire soul and the totality of its powers. Thought, in a word, is wholly included in each of its moments or degrees. In short, there is never for us a purely external fact like some sort of raw material. Such a fact indeed would remain absolutely unassimilable, unthinkable; it would be a nonentity to us, for where could we take hold of it? Experience itself is not in the least an acquisition of "things" which previously were entirely unknown to us. No, it is much more a transition from the implicit to the explicit, a profound movement revealing to us the latent requirements and actual abundance in the system of knowledge already explained, an effort of organic development, putting to use its reserves or arousing needs which increase our activity. Thus no truth ever enters into us except as it is postulated by that which precedes it as a more or less necessary complement; just as an article of food to become valuable as nourishment presupposes in the one who receives it certain preliminary dispositions and preparations, for instance, the appeal of hunger and the ability to digest. In the same way the statement of a scientific fact presents this character, no fact having meaning nor, consequently, existing for us except by a theory in which it is born.

On these various points a critical examination of the sciences has recently come to confirm the reflection of the philosophers. It is obvious that I could not enter here into detail,[9] but the little that I have said will doubtless suffice to give a glimpse at least of how that which has been called *extrinsicism*[10] is opposed in spirit, attitude and method to modern thought.

3. In spite of what we have just said let us admit, however, the instruction of dogmas by simple affirmation of a doctrinal authority which is accepted almost without criticism. Nevertheless, in order to be acceptable these dogmas would need to be perfectly intelligible in their statements, leaving no room for any ambiguity of interpretation or any possibility of error with regard to their real meaning. Now this is not the case. In the first place their formulas often belong to the language of a particular philosophical system which is not always easily understood, which does not always escape the danger of equivocation or even of contradiction. There is no doubt, for instance, that the doctrine of the Word in origin and context is closely connected with Alexandrian neo-Platonism; that the theory of substance and form in the sacraments and that of the relations between substance and accidents in the dogma of the real presence are really closely connected with Aristotelian and scholastic conceptions. Now these diverse philosophies are sometimes doubtful as to their basis and obscure as to their expression. In any event they have long been antiquated, fallen into disuse among philosophers and scholars. Would it therefore be necessary, in order to be Christians, to commence by being converted to these philosophies? This would be a

difficult undertaking, before which many believers themselves would feel strangely embarrassed. And moreover even this would not suffice, for the confusion of many languages resulting from heterogeneous philosophies constitutes still another difficulty no less troublesome than the first.

But this is not all. Aside from this, dogmatic formulas contain metaphors borrowed from every-day matters, for instance when they speak of the Divine Fatherhood or Sonship. It is impossible to give an exact intellectual interpretation of these metaphors, and consequently to determine their precise theoretical value. They are images which cannot be converted into concepts. It would require anthropomorphism to take them literally, and at the same time it would be difficult to give them any deep significance. One cannot even handle them without reserve, nor follow them to a conclusion without arriving too quickly at ridiculous consequences and absurdities. Hence arises a great uncertainty that continues to increase the confusion of imaginative symbols with the abstract formulas of which we were just speaking.

After all, the first difficulty with regard to dogmas which many people find to-day consists in the fact that they do not succeed in discovering a thinkable meaning in them. These statements tell them nothing, or rather seem to them to be indissolubly connected with a state of mind which they no longer possess and to which they think they are no longer able to return without degenerating. Moreover many believers are virtually of the same opinion, and prefer to refrain from all reflection, foreseeing certain obstacles that they would meet in thinking what they believe under the forms laid before them. A contemporaneous philosopher has said: "What would most embarrass the greater number of believers would be if, before asking them for a *proof* of what they believe, one were simply to call upon them to *define* exactly what it is they *affirm* and what they *deny*."[11]

4. Finally, let us pass over these difficulties. Even after they are disposed of there still remains a last objection which seems very grave, namely that in any event dogmas form a group incommensurable with the whole of positive knowledge. Neither by their content nor by their logical nature do they belong to the same system of knowledge as other propositions. They therefore could not be arranged with others in a way to form a coherent system, so that if one accepts them the result is an inevitable breach of unity in the mind, a disastrous necessity of playing a double part. Being unalterable they appear foreign to progress, which is the very essence of thought. Being transcendent they exist without relation to effective intellectual life. They bring no increase of light to any of the problems which occupy science and philosophy. Thus the least

reproach that one can cast upon them is that they seem to be without profit, to be useless and barren—a very grave reproach in a period when it becomes more and more perceptible that the value of a truth is measured above all by the services that it renders, by the new results that it suggests, by the consequences which it brings forth, in short by the vivifying influence it exerts on the entire body of knowledge.

Such, briefly summed up, are the principal reasons why the idea of any dogma whatever is repugnant to modern thought. I have endeavored to present them in all their force, taking the same point of view in setting them forth as those who regard them as conclusive, and speaking, so to say, not in my own name but in theirs. It remains now to investigate some conclusions and some lessons which we ought to be able to derive from them.

These reasons, it must be recognized, are perfectly valid. I do not see any legitimate way of refuting the preceding line of argument.[12] The principles which it invokes seem to me no more contestable than the deductions which it draws from them. In fact I do not see that it has ever been answered except by worthless subtleties or rhetorical artifices.[13] But eloquence is not a proof, neither is diplomacy. Hence our only real resource is to prove that the idea of dogma which is condemned and rejected by modern thought, is *not* the Catholic idea of dogma.

Perhaps it will be found that in speaking in this way I depart from the role to which I have promised to confine myself, that this time decidedly I am stating theses and not asking questions. This would be a mistake. There is no doubt that I am affirming something here, but what? Nothing but *facts*. It is a fact that the unbelievers of to-day are halted in the face of dogmas by the foregoing objections. It is also a fact that whoever (even among believers) has truly comprehended the spirit and the methods of contemporary science and philosophy, cannot but give his assent to these objections. Now please note: those very people who submit most completely and most cordially to the authority established over them could not be affected by it. No authority indeed could bring it about or prevent that I find an argument valid or weak, nor especially that this or that notion has or has not any meaning for me. I not only say that no authority has any right in the world to do so, but that it is absolutely impossible; for after all it is I who do the thinking and not the authority that thinks for me. No argument could prevail against this fact. I can neither force myself to feel satisfaction nor prevent myself from feeling it at the evidence on one side or another. To be sure I admit that authority imposes upon me this or that belief with the result that it makes me follow this or that line of conduct, but how could it compel me by virtue of such a proof to believe what I do not regard as convincing?

And how would I be able to obey it if it commanded me to understand this or that declaration which I did not understand at all? As well might it require me to cease thinking. No *reason* can be founded on faith. Here we have an *identity* pure and simple. There is no such thing as *revealed logic*.

Hence I come back to what I said a while ago, and, *speaking as a philosopher,* I declare myself incapable of thinking differently from our adversaries on the above-mentioned points.

Moreover in making this declaration I consider that I am doing nothing but stating a problem. The state of mind which I have described exists, it is triumphant to-day; even those who believe the most firmly share it. These are the *facts* which it is impossible not to take into account and which constitute, I repeat, the statement of a question to be solved. Let us see exactly what this question is.

I shall henceforth regard it as granted that the objections summed up above cannot be evaded so long as the idea of dogma which they contain is preserved. Does this mean that we must conclude definitely that there is an absolute incompatibility between the idea of dogma and the essential conditions of reasonable thought? That in order to think as a Christian it is necessary to cease thinking altogether? I certainly do not believe so. But to avoid the objections in the case and to obtain the desired harmony I ask myself if it is not the very manner in which the idea of dogma is presented that is the real cause of the contention, and if consequently we have not reason to change this manner.[14]

Now when we examine the conception of dogma which the four objections above enumerated assume and imply, we are surprised to find that it is common to the greater number of Catholics and their opponents. It is a distinctly intellectual conception. It regards the practical and moral meaning of the dogma as secondary and derived and places in the first rank its intellectual meaning, believing that this constitutes the dogma whereas the other is merely a consequence of it. In a word, it makes of a dogma something like the statement of a theorem—an intangible statement of an undemonstrable theorem, but a statement having nevertheless a speculative and theoretical character and relating above all to pure knowledge. This is the common postulate that one discovers by analysis at the foundation of both of the two opposed doctrines, the one that accepts and the one that rejects the idea of dogma. Here I believe is the crux of the difficulty. From this unexpressed postulate and from the conception which flows from it originate, in my opinion, both the abuses to which the idea of dogma can give rise and the conscientious objections that it raises. Indeed it is inevitable that one would finally draw the conclusion that all dogma was illegitimate, for he would at the same time define it as a theoretical statement while never-theless attributing to it characteristics the very opposite of those which make statements correct. It is very curious that the apologists are not more often informed of a fact of such great importance as that their conception of dogma would destroy in advance the theses that they wish to establish. On the other hand, the same intellectualist idea of dogma leads to two very regrettable and unfortunately very frequent exaggera-tions: one consists of confusing dogmas properly so called with certain opinions and certain theological systems, that is to say, with intellectual accessory representations; the other, in failing to see that a dogma could never possess any scientific significance and that there are no more dogmas concerning for instance biological evolution than there are concerning the movements of planets or the compressibility of gas.

From a thorough study of these various points we reach the convic-tion that the problem of dogma is usually badly stated;[15] and perhaps we will see at the same time how it ought to be stated in order to render possible a satisfactory solution.

From this point I enter at once into the domain in which I must keep myself in an interrogatory attitude. This is my definite intention al-though to insure clearness I may keep the didactic tone. What follows must be taken as a simple exposition of what I ordinarily reply to those who ask me what I think of the idea of dogma. Am I wrong to speak in this way? I am quite ready to acknowledge it if any one will show me that it is not the right way in the eyes of the Church.

First of all I say that a dogma cannot be compared to a theorem, of which we only know the statement without its proof and whose proof can only be guaranteed by the assertion of a teacher. Nevertheless I know that this is the most common conception. We like to think of God in the act of revelation as a very wise professor whose word we must believe when he communicates to his audience results whose proof that au-dience is not capable of understanding. But this appears to me to be hardly satisfactory. We say that God has spoken. What does the word "speak" mean in this case? Most certainly it is a metaphor. What is the reality which it conceals? Herein lies the whole difficulty.

Without recurring to the general considerations I have already devel-oped let us take some examples that will serve to specify what we have hitherto looked upon only in large outlines.

"God is a person." Here we have a dogma. Let us try to see in it a statement having above all an intellectual meaning and a speculative interest, a proposition belonging first of all to the order of theoretical knowledge. I pass over the difficulties aroused by the word "God," but let us consider the word "person." How must we understand it?

If we grant that the use of this word bids us conceive the divine personality in the form shown to us by psychological experience on the model of what common sense designates by the same name, as a human personality, idealized and carried on to perfection, we have here a complete anthropomorphism, and Catholics would certainly agree with their opponents in rejecting such a conception. Moreover to carry such a thought to its extreme limits is a very delicate thing, very likely to induce error or at least mere verbiage, incapable in any event of producing anything more than very vague metaphors and perhaps even eventually contradictory results.

Shall we limit ourselves to saying that the divine personality is essentially incomparable and transcendent? Very well, but if so it is very badly named, and in a way which seems made expressly to induce delusion. For if we declare that the divine personality does not resemble in any respect that with which we are acquainted, what right have we to call it "personality"? Logically it should be designated by a word which would belong only to God, which could not be employed in any other instance. This word would therefore be intrinsically undefinable. Let us imagine any assemblage whatever of syllables deprived of all possible significance. Let A be this assemblage. Then by our hypothesis "God is a person" does not have any other meaning than "God is A." Is this an idea?

The dilemma is unsolvable for any one who is seeking an intellectual interpretation of the dogma "God is a person." Either he will define the word "personality," and then he is fatally sure to fall into anthropomorphism; or he will not define it, and then he will fall none the less fatally into agnosticism. Here we have a circle.

The same remarks hold with regard to the propositions "God is conscious of himself; God loves, wills, thinks, etc."

Let us take another example, the resurrection of Jesus. If this dogma, whatever may be eventually its practical consequences, has for its first aim to increase our knowledge in guaranteeing to us the accuracy of a certain fact, if it constitutes before all a statement of an intellectual character, the question to which it first gives rise is this: What precise meaning does it assume is to be attached to the word *resurrection?* Jesus, after having experienced death, has once more become alive. What does this mean from the theoretical point of view? Doubtless nothing except that after three days Jesus reappeared in a state identical with that in which he was before he was nailed on the cross. Now the Gospel itself tells us exactly the opposite. The resurrected Jesus was no longer subject to ordinary physical or physiological laws; his "glorified" body was no longer perceptible in the same conditions as before, etc. What does this mean? The idea of life has not the same content when applied to the period preceding the crucifixion as to that which followed it. Now what does the word represent with relation to this second period? Nothing that can be expressed by concepts. It is simply a metaphor which cannot be converted into specific ideas. Here again, to be exact, it would be necessary to create a new word, a word reserved for this single case, a word consequently to which it would not be possible to give any regular definition.

Let us borrow a final example from the dogma of the real presence. Here it is the term "presence" which must be interpreted. What does it usually signify? A being is said to be present when he is perceptible, or when though he himself cannot be grasped by perception he yet manifests himself by perceptible effects. Now according to the dogma itself neither of these two circumstances is realized in the case in hand. The presence in question is a mysterious presence, ineffable, unique, without analogy to anything that one ordinarily understands by that name. Now I ask what idea is there here for us? A thing that can neither be analyzed nor even defined could not be called an "idea" except by an abuse of the word. We wish a dogma to be a statement of an intellectual order. What does it state? It is impossible to say exactly. Does not this fact condemn the hypothesis?

Finally the pretension of conceiving dogmas as statements whose first function would be to communicate certain theoretical bits of knowledge would run against impossibilities on every hand. It seems to end inevitably in reducing dogmas to pure nonsense. Perhaps it must for this reason be resolutely abandoned. Let us therefore see what different kind of significance remains possible and legitimate.

First of all, if I do not deceive myself, a dogma has a *negative* meaning. It excludes and condemns certain errors instead of positively determining the truth.[16]

Let us once more take up our former examples. We shall first consider the dogma "God is a person." I nowhere see in it any definition of the divine personality. It teaches me nothing about that personality. It does not reveal its nature to me nor furnish me with any explicit idea. But I see clearly that it tells me, "God is not impersonal"; that is to say, God is not simply a law, a formal category, an ideal principle, an abstract entity, any more than he is a universal substance, or some unknown cosmic force diffused throughout the world. In short, the dogma "God is a person" does not bring to me any new positive conception nor does it any more guarantee to me the truth of any particular system among those which the history of philosophy shows to have been successively proposed, but it warns me that this or that form of pantheism is false and ought to be rejected.

I would say the same with regard to the real presence. The dogma does not tell me any theory about that presence, it does not even teach me in what it consists; but it tells me very clearly that it must not be understood in such or such a way as were formerly proposed, that for instance the consecrated host must not be regarded solely as a symbol or a figure of Jesus.

The resurrection of Christ gives rise to the same remarks. The dogma does not teach me in any degree what was the mechanism of this unique fact nor of what kind the second life of Jesus was. In short it does not communicate a conception to me. But on the contrary it excludes certain conceptions that I might be tempted to make. Death has not put an end to the activity of Jesus with reference to the things of this world. He still mediates and lives among us, and not at all merely as a thinker who has disappeared and left behind a rich and living influence and whose work has left results through the ages; he is literally our contemporary. In short, death has not been for him, as it is for ordinary mortals, the definite cessation of practical activity. This is what the dogma of resurrection teaches us.

Shall I insist further? It does not seem advisable at this time. The foregoing examples are sufficient to make the principle of interpretation that I have in mind clearly understood. Of course long expositions would be necessary if we would enumerate in detail all the consequences of this principle and all its possible applications, and an enumerative study of the different dogmas would therefore become indispensable. But this is not my real purpose. I wish to confine myself simply to indicating an ideal. This is why I do not undertake either to multiply examples or even to develop any one of them completely.

Moreover the idea is not a new one. It belongs to the most authentic tradition. Is it not indeed the classical teaching of theologians and scholars that in supernatural matters the surest method of investigation is the *via negationis?* Permit me to recall in this connection a well-known text of St. Thomas: "But the *via remotionis* is to be used chiefly in considering divine substance. For divine substance by its immensity exceeds every form which our mind can touch; and so we cannot grasp it by knowing what it is, but some sort of a notion of it we have by knowing what it is not."[17]

Nevertheless I ought to point out one objection which might occur to the mind. We will easily grant that the dogmatic formulation promulgated by the Church in the course of history has especially a negative character, at least when looked upon from an intellectual point of view as we are doing at this time. In fact, the Church itself declares that its mission is not in the least to produce new revelations but only to maintain the *depositum revelationis,* and the negative method here adopted is entirely suitable for this mission. And yet, of what does this *depositum* consist if not of a certain collection of original affirmations? Take the primary expression of Christian faith, the Credo. What could be more positive? Now here is the basis of doctrine, that which characterizes and constitutes it. Moreover when we say "revelation" we certainly say affirmation and not negation.

Certainly we do. I do not contradict it in the least, but we must make a distinction. The creed of Nicaea and Constantinople contains many traces of a negative dogmatic elaboration: for instance, on the divinity of Christ as against the Arian heresy; on the procession of the Holy Ghost in opposition to the Macedonians, etc.[18] Consequently there is nothing on this head to contradict our conclusions. It is only the grammatical form which is affirmative here; in reality we are treating of errors to be excluded rather than theories to be formulated. But let us take the Apostles' Creed. Here indeed we have nothing negative but neither do we have anything properly intellectual and theoretical, nothing which belongs properly to the order of speculative knowledge, nothing in short which resembles the statement of theorems. It is a profession of faith, a declaration of attitude. We shall soon examine dogmas from this practical point of view (which I hasten to say is in my eyes the principal point of view), yet we shall stop a moment at the intellectual point of view. The Apostolic Creed in its original form affirms the existence of realities of which it gives not even a rudimentary representative theory, hence its only role with reference to abstract and reflective knowledge is *to state objects and therefore problems.* Finally we see that the proposed objection is not valid and we can maintain our thesis until further notice.

Thus in so far as they are statements of a theoretical order dogmas have all a negative meaning. History proves this when it procures our assistance at the birth of one after another of them in relation to the several heresies.[19] The rise of all dogmas has always followed the same course, has always presented the same phases: at the beginning purely human speculations, some explanatory systems very similar to other philosophical systems, in short, attempts at theories relating to religious facts, to mysterious realities experienced by Christendom in its practical faith; then only come the dogmas for the purpose of condemning certain of these attempts, of taxing certain of these conceptions with error and of excluding certain of these intellectual representations. Hence it follows that dogmatic formulas often borrow expressions from different philosophies without taking the trouble to fuse together and unify these heterogeneous languages.

This offers no more disadvantages than does the use of concepts derived from different origins, from the moment that dogmas do not tend to constitute by themselves a rational theory, an intelligible system of positive affirmations, but confine themselves to opposing certain exceptions to certain hypotheses and conjectures of the human mind. On the other hand it is natural that each dogma should put itself in the point of view belonging to the doctrine that it lays under an interdict, in order to attack it directly without danger of ambiguity. Hence it also follows that dogmatic formulas can enact laws on the incomparable and the transcendent and yet not fall into the contradictions of anthropomorphism or of agnosticism. It is man who with his opinions, his theories and systems, gives to dogmas their intelligible substance;[20] these are confined to pronouncing a veto at times, to declaring at times that "such an opinion, such a theory, such a system, is not allowed," without ever pointing out why they should not be accepted, nor by what they must be replaced. Thus negative dogmatic definitions do not limit knowledge nor put an end to progress; in short they only close up false paths.

From the strictly intellectual point of view it seems to me that dogmas have only the negative and prohibitive sense of which I speak. If they formulated absolute truth in adequate terms (to assume that such a fiction has a meaning) they would be unintelligible to us. If they gave only an imperfect truth, relative and mutable, they would not be justified in obtruding. The only radical way to put an end to all the objections on principle against dogma is to conceive of them, as we have already said, as being undefinable in so far as they are speculative propositions, except with relation to previous doctrines upon which they promulgate an unwarranted judgment. Moreover is it not the teaching of theologians, including most intellectualists, that in a dogmatic statement the reasons which can be incorporated in the text are not in themselves objects of faith imposed upon belief?

There is one important consequence resulting from the foregoing, namely, that the true method of studying dogmas (from the intellectual point of view, understand) is the historical method. The science known as positive theology, or rather the history of dogma, seeks to perform this task. The method has an effective apologetic value much greater than purely dialectic dissertations. Because in any event it is impossible to comprehend dogmatic statements, there is the greater reason for justifying them if one would commence by plunging them once more into their natural historical environment without which their authentic meaning becomes more and more vague and finally ends by vanishing entirely.

Nevertheless dogmas do not have merely a negative meaning, and even the negative meaning that they offer when regarded from a certain direction does not constitute their essential and primary significance. This is true because they are not merely propositions of a theoretical character, because they must not be examined solely from the intellectual point of view, from the point of view of knowledge. This is what we shall now elucidate further.

Here more than ever I insist that the intention and tendency of the pages to follow must not be misunderstood. I repeat that the affirmative tone is used only as a means for clearness. At bottom the question is always the same as I specified at the beginning. Here, if I may say so, is the form in which experience has shown me that the notion of dogma is most easily assimilable to the minds of to-day:

A dogma has above all a *practical* meaning. It states before all a prescription of a practical kind. It is more than all the formula of a rule of practical conduct. This is its principal value, this its positive significance. This does not mean, however, that it must be without relation to thought, for (1) there are also certain duties concerned with the act of thought; (2) it is virtually affirmed by the dogma itself that under one form or another reality contains wherewith to justify the prescribed conduct as reasonable and wholesome.

I take pleasure in quoting in this connection the following passage from R. P. Laberthonnière:[21] "Dogmas are not simply enigmatical and obscure formulas which God has promulgated in the name of his omnipotence to mortify the pride of our spirits. They have a moral and practical meaning; they have a vital meaning more or less accessible to us according to the degree of spirituality we possess."

After all, when converts, in spite of good intentions, themselves create part of the theoretical difficulties under discussion do we not answer them daily: "Never mind all that, it is not important. Do not believe that God requires so many formalities. Come to him fairly, frankly, simply, according to the wise words of Bossuet. Religion is not so much an intellectual adherence to a system of speculative propositions as it is a living participation in mysterious realities." Why not then make theory agree with practice?

Let us keep the same examples. They represent well enough the different types of dogmas. "God is a person" means, "Conduct yourself in your relations to God as in your relations with a human person."

Likewise "Jesus has risen" means, "Be in relation to him as you would have been before his death, as you are with a contemporary." In the same way again the dogma of the real presence means that one must have the same attitude toward the consecrated host as one would have toward Jesus had he become visible, and so on. It would be easy to multiply these examples, and also to develop each of them farther.[22]

That dogmas can and ought to be interpreted in this way there is no doubt, and the fact will not be contested by any one. In fact, it cannot be repeated too often that Christianity is not a system of speculative philosophy but a source and regimen of life, a discipline of moral and religious action, in short the sum total of practical means to obtain salvation. What then is surprising in the fact that its dogmas primarily concern conduct rather than pure reflective knowledge?[23]

I do not think it is necessary to insist farther upon this point, but I wish to indicate in a few brief words the most important consequences of the principle here laid down.

First of all it is clear that the general objections summed up at the beginning of this article do not affect this conception of dogma to the same extent and in the same degree as they do the usual intellectualist conception, for that provokes the conflict and renders the difficulty insurmountable, whereas on the other hand we may now catch a glimpse of a possible solution. As there is no question of obtaining a theoretical statement in conditions radically opposed to those prescribed by scientific method, we no longer find ourselves face to face with a logical stumbling-block but only with a problem referring to relations between thought and action—a difficult problem certainly, but not unapproachable and one which at any rate does not appear absurd after it is stated.

Of course there are always important questions to be solved. It is necessary to supply the dogma in some way with a demonstration and justification, and this is by no means a perfectly easy matter. Nevertheless one of the greatest obstacles has been smoothed away. Practical truths are established differently from speculative truths. Recourse to authority which is entirely inadmissible in the realm of pure thought seems a priori less shocking in the domain of action, because if authority has legitimate rights anywhere it certainly has in the domain of practical affairs.

The Council of the Vatican tells us: "If any shall say that no true mysteries properly so called are contained in divine revelation, but that all the dogmas of faith can be comprehended and demonstrated through reason duly perfected by natural principles, let him be anathema."[24] Now if faith in dogmas were first of all knowledge, an adherence to some statements of an intellectual kind, one could not comprehend either that assent to unsolvable mysteries could ever be legitimate, or even simply possible, or in what it might consist, or what sort of utility or value it might have for us, or how it might constitute a virtue. On the other hand all this can be understood if faith in dogmas is a practical submission to commandments which have to do with action. Nothing is more normal than activity placing mysteries before intelligence.[25]

The Council of the Vatican tells us further: "If any shall say that assent to the Christian faith is not free . . . let him be anathema."[26] This text is generally explained by recognizing that the reasons for believing, the motives of credibility, are not of insuperable force, a mathematical evidence, and that in consequence a decisive act of the will or of the heart is always necessary to conclude the investigation definitely. Is this not virtually admitting that one cannot see in belief in dogmas an act which should first of all be intellectual without making it thereby inferior to the ordinary acts of thought? How would such an act—an act performed under conditions contrary to the nature of thought—be even legitimate or merely possible? But on the other hand it is easy to believe that the practical acceptance of commandments relating to action depends on our free will and gains in perfection by not being able to manifest itself by necessary consequence. Let us insist a little upon this point, for it is of highest importance in the problem of the relation between reason and faith.

From the beginning apologetics is confronted with a grave difficulty which perhaps cannot always be satisfactorily disposed of. On the one hand it is clearly understood that an act of faith is a free act and that its object, as well as its supreme motive, is supernatural. But on the other hand an act of reason ought to precede and prepare the act of faith, for it is by reason alone that the obligation and necessity of overreaching reason can be recognized. And an act of reason must also constantly accompany the act of faith, for it is necessary that the human mind shall have some sort of hold upon the dogma if it wishes to accept it. St. Thomas said well: "Those things which are under the faith . . . no one would believe unless he sees they ought to be believed."[27]

Now how shall we reconcile these two opposite requirements in a system of intellectualist interpretation? Either we would maintain (as there are some who do) that the apologetic proofs are absolutely positive and exact; and then what would become of the liberty of the act of faith? Or in order to safeguard that liberty we would call them insufficient and only more or less probable; and then our faith would lack any basis, for after all an insufficient proof is not an acceptable proof, especially in so important and difficult a matter. An intellectualist attitude becomes disarmed in the face of this dilemma since liberty does not belong to the domain of pure intelligence and has no place or part in the proceeding of discursive reason. But with the other attitude the dilemma can be solved because this time the dialectic in the case is action and life, not simply argument, and liberty revives with life and action.

Likewise we have here the objection relating to the intelligibility of dogmatic formulas. Although these formulas are hopelessly obscure, even inconceivable, when we want them to furnish positive determinations of truth from a speculative and theoretical point of view, they nevertheless show themselves capable of clearness if we are careful not to ask of them anything but instruction as to practical conduct. What difficulty, for instance, do we find in understanding the dogmas of the divine personality, of the real presence, or the resurrection, in the practical system of interpretation just outlined? Although these dogmas are mysteries for the intelligence that demands explanatory theories they are nevertheless susceptible of perfectly clear statement as to what they prescribe for our actions. Hence the language of common sense has its place as well as the use of anthropomorphic symbols and the employment of analogies or metaphors, and neither the one nor the other gives rise to unsolvable complications since this time it is a question only of propositions relating to man and his attitudes.

We also see now what the relation is between dogmas and efficient life. We predict for them a possibility of experimental study and of gradual research which has heretofore escaped us. Finally we understand how they can be common to all, accessible to all, in spite of the inequality between intellects, whereas to conceive them in the intellectualist way one would be inevitably led to make a distinction of an intellectual aristocracy. I have not room here to develop these different considerations as much as I should like, but I imagine that a simple indication after all may be sufficient for the time being, and that the reader can carry the process on for himself without any difficulty. Nevertheless it seems necessary to me to prevent a possible objection in order to avoid all misapprehension.

I have spoken of *practice*. This word must be rightly understood. I take it in the widest acceptation of the term. *Action* and *life* are here synonymous. Hence the word does not in the least mean a blind step, without relation to thought or consciousness. In fact there is an act of thought which accompanies all our actions, a life of thought which mingles throughout our life; in other words, to know is a function of life, a practical act in its way. This function, this act, is also called *experience*, a name which indicates at the same time that we are not at all dealing with actions performed without any sort of light but that the light in question is not that of simple argumentative reason.

I have also spoken of the activity which places mysteries before intelligence, and by way of elucidation I have cited the example of scientific facts. To comprehend what I mean by this, one must not forget that a scientific fact is not a thing to be submitted to passively. If there is any semblance of a purely external fact, of a mystery totally opaque, of a violent commandment from without, it is so with respect to argumentative understanding. But the thought-action of which I was just now speaking avoids this appearance. It infinitely exceeds the purely intellectual thought. I have not heard anything to affirm otherwise.[28]

Hence there is a necessary relation between dogmas and thought. It is at the same time both a right and a duty not to be content with a blind belief in dogmas but to strive also in proportion to one's strength to think them. The system of separation, of tight partitions, of the twofold accountability of conscience, is not desirable nor, to speak truthfully, possible. It is contrary to the demands of that faith which wishes to hold every man; it is contrary to the requirements of philosophy which desires a spiritual unity; and finally it is contrary to the requirements of morality which cannot approve an action that is systematically unconsidered.

But thought when applied to dogmas should not misunderstand their primarily practical meaning. The path to be followed is the test of practical experience and not an intellectual dialectic. The inspiring principle is perfectly expressed in the sacred word, *qui facit veritatem venit ad lucem.*

Thus translated into terms of action the traditional methods of *analogy* and *eminence* assume a very clear significance. Under the guise of metaphors and images they affirm that supernatural reality contains the wherewith[al] to make obligatory by law that our attitude and our conduct with regard to it should have such or such a character. The images and metaphors—which are hopelessly vague and fallacious when one tries to see in them any approximation whatever of impossible concepts—become on the other hand wonderfully illuminating and suggestive after one looks to find in them only a language of action translating truth by its practical echo within ourselves.

It remains finally to specify the relations of dogmas, understood in the way we have described them, to theoretical and speculative thought, to pure knowledge. In what respect do they govern our intellectual life? How does their intangible and transcendent character leave the full liberty of research intact as well as the undeniable right of the mind to repulse every conception which tries to impose itself from without? We shall easily see.

The Catholic is obliged to assent to the dogmas without reservation. But what is thereby imposed upon him is not in the least a theory, an intellectual representation. Such a constraint indeed would inevitably lead to undesirable consequences: (1) the dogmas would in that case be reduced to purely verbal formulas, to simple words whose repetition would constitute a sort of unintelligible command; (2) moreover these dogmas could not be common to all times nor to all intelligences.[29]

No, dogmas are not at all like that. As we have seen, their meaning is above all practical and moral. The Catholic, obliged to accept them, is not restrained by them except as regards rules of conduct, not as regards any particular conceptions. Nor is he condemned to accept them as simple literal formulas. On the contrary, they offer him a very positive content, explicitly intelligible and comprehensible. I will add that this content, having to do solely with the practical, is not relative to the variable degree of intelligence and knowledge; it remains exactly the same for the scholar and the ignorant man, for the exalted and the lowly, for the ages of advanced civilization and for the races still in barbarism. In short it is independent of the successive states through which human thought passes in its effort toward knowledge, and thus there is *only one faith for everybody*.

This being granted, the Catholic after having accepted the dogmas retains full liberty to make for himself whatever theory, or whatever intellectual representation he wishes of the corresponding objects—the divine personality, the real presence, or the resurrection, for instance. It remains with him to grant his preference to the theory which best agrees with his own views, to the intellectual representation which he deems the best. His position in this respect is the same as that toward any scientific or philosophical speculation, and he is free to adopt the same attitude in both cases. Only one thing is imposed upon him, only one obligation is incumbent upon him; his theory must justify the practical rules expressed by the dogma, his intellectual representation must take into account the practical edicts prescribed by the dogma. Thus in a word it appears almost like the statement of a fact with regard to which it is possible to construct many different theories but which every theory must take into account, like the expression of a truth many of whose intellectual representations are legitimate but of which no explanatory system can well be independent.[30]

From this naturally follows the step that we have recognized as usual with religious thought in its effort at elaboration. Let us take any dogma whatever, Divine Personality, the real presence or the resurrection of

Jesus. By itself and in itself it has only a practical meaning. *But there is a mysterious reality corresponding to it and therefore it presents to the intelligence a theoretical problem.* The human intellect at once takes possession of this problem; and obeying simply and solely the laws of its own nature it imagines the explanations, the answers, the systems codified in the precepts of scientific method and the principles of reason.[31] As long as the theory constructed in this way respects the practical significance of the dogma it is given carte blanche. Hence to pass judgment on the theories remains the task of pure human speculation, and any authority exterior to the thought itself has neither the right nor the power to interfere.[32] But once let a theory arise which makes an attack on dogma in its own domain by altering its practical significance, and the dogma would immediately array itself against it and condemn it, thus becoming a negative intellectual statement superimposed upon the rule of conduct which at first it was, purely and simply.

Hence one sees positively how the two meanings of a dogma, the practical meaning and the negative meaning, are reunited, the latter being subordinated to the former. Moreover we see how dogmas are immutable and yet how there is an evolution of dogmas. What remains constant in the dogma is the orientation that it gives to our practical activity, the direction in which it inflects our conduct. But the explanatory theories, the intellectual representations, change constantly in the course of the ages according to individuals and epochs, freed from all the fluctuations and all the aspects of relativity manifested by the history of the human mind. The Christians of the first centuries did not profess the same opinions on the nature and personality of Jesus as we, and they did not have the same problems. The ignorant man to-day does not have at all the same ideas on these lofty and difficult subjects as the philosopher does, nor the same mental preoccupations. But whether ignorant men or philosophers, men of the first or the twentieth century, every Catholic has always had and always will have the same practical attitude with regard to Jesus.

It is time to conclude, and I will do so in as few and brief words as possible.

Two main results seem to me to have been attained by the foregoing discussion:

1. The intellectualist conception which is current to-day renders the greater number of objections raised by the idea of dogma unsolvable.

2. On the other hand, a doctrine of primacy of action permits a solution of the problem without abandoning either the rights of thought or the requirements of dogma.

If these conclusions were admitted, the apologetics of our days would be under the irresistible necessity of modifying many of its arguments and methods.

Now, can these conclusions be admitted without loss to faith? It is for the theologians to tell us, and in case their response is negative to teach us how they expect otherwise to prepare to surmount the obstacles which perplex us.

## NOTES

1. I will say once and for all that by *dogma* I mean especially the "dogmatic proposition," the "dogmatic formula," not at all the reality which underlies it.

2. I would say the same, moreover, of our opponents with respect to us.

3. The object of faith always remains the same, but not the manner of thinking it or of complying with it.

4. I mean here to speak of *intrinsic* proof.

5. Cf. the Philosophie nouvelle edition of Bergson's works.

6. Especially in the sciences.

7. This method of *extrinsic* demonstration is regarded as traditional. Here is a historical point on which much might be said, but such a discussion is foreign to my subject.

8. Or at least appears to claim, which is the form under which it is too often presented.

9. See the *Bulletin de la société française de la philosophie*, meeting of February 25, 1904.

10. Blondel uses the term *extrinsécisme* together with *historicisme* to denote two kinds of apologetics which he condemns. See his article "Histoire et dogme," in *La quinzaine* of January 15, February 1, and February 15, 1904.

11. [Gustave?] Belot, *Bibliothèque du congrès internationale de philosophie de 1900* (Paris: Armand Colin [1902–3?]).

12. I say, "refuting," but it could be *cut short* by destroying the postulate which is its root.

13. It would be interesting to enter into a detailed discussion of these answers, but there is no room for it here.

14. I beg the reader to give heed to the limits within which this question is comprised. It does not discuss in any way the modification of the content of dogma, nor even its traditional religious interpretation, but only the determination of the modality of the dogmatic judgment and of the qualification it possesses.

15. At least in books in current use and in elementary education.

16. We shall shortly see how dogmas are more and greater than this. But at the start I shall place myself in a strictly intellectual point of view.

17. Saint Thomas Aquinas *Summa contra Gentiles* 1.14.

18. It would be easy to insist on the example of *consubstantialem* or of *Filioque*.

19. Cf. the usual formula of the decrees of councils: "If anyone shall say, . . . : let him be anathema."

20. From the theoretical point of view, understand. Dogmas are thought in terms of the human systems which they oppose.

21. Lucien Laberthonnière, *Essais de philosophie religieuse* (Paris: Lethielleux [1903]), 272.

22. I do not claim in the least that the foregoing comments exhaust the meaning of the dogmas mentioned: they will suffice to point out a line of enquiry.

23. This is why assent to dogmas is always a free act and not the inevitable result of a compelling line of argument.

24. *Constitution on the Catholic Faith,* canon 1 on chap. 4 [see above, sec. 1816].

25. Submission to dogmas, then, from one point of view, is for the believer what submission to facts is for the scholar.

26. *Constitution on the Catholic Faith,* canon 5 on chap. 3 [see above, sec. 1814].

27. LeRoy does not give the source of this quotation.—ED.

28. The reader who desires to pursue this point further may refer to several articles I have published since 1889, in the *Revue de métaphysique et de morale* and in the *Bulletin de la société française de philosophie.*

29. In the two words *esotericism* and *Pharisaism* would be the inevitable rock upon which they would split.

30. It is at this point that we must distinguish between *intellectual formula* and the *underlying reality* of dogma.

31. In this respect the Middle Ages had an independence and a boldness which we have forgotten.

32. Religious authority which has souls in its charge can indicate certain theories as dangerous, as long as they run the risk of being wrongly understood and thus of reacting injuriously upon conduct. Hence arise censures of an inferior note to those of heresy. But these condemnations are not properly dogmatic.

# Further Reading

## General Church Histories

Aretin, Karl Otmar, Freiherr von. *The Papacy and the Modern World.* Trans. Roland Hill. New York: McGraw-Hill, 1970. Excellent short introduction.

Chadwick, Owen. *The Popes and European Revolution,* esp. chaps. 6–8. New York and London: Oxford Univ. Press, 1981.

Dansette, Adrien. *Religious History of Modern France.* Trans. and abridg. John Dingle. 2 vols. New York: Herder & Herder, 1961.

Franklin, R. W. *Nineteenth-Century Churches: The History of a New Catholicism in Württemberg, England, and France.* New York: Garland, 1987.

Jedin, Hubert, and John Dolan, eds. *History of the Church.* Vols. 7–9. New York: Crossroad, 1981. Recommended.

MacCaffrey, James. *History of the Catholic Church in the Nineteenth Century.* 2d ed. 2 vols. Dublin, 1910. Gives much attention to the political and legal difficulties of Catholics in each country.

Phillips, C. S. *The Church in France, 1789–1848.* London, 1929; New York: Russell & Russell, 1966. Highly recommended.

———. *The Church in France, 1848–1907.* London, 1936; New York: Russell & Russell, 1967. Also highly recommended.

Rogier, Louis, et al., eds. *Nouvelle histoire de l'église.* Vols. 4 and 5. Paris: Éditions du Seuil, 1975. ET: *The Christian Centuries: A New History of the Catholic Church.* Vol. 5. New York: Paulist Press, 1978. An ET of volume 4 was projected.

## Histories of Catholic Theology

Cayré, Fulbert, A.A. *Patrologie et histoire de la théologie.* 2d ed. Vol. 3. Paris, 1950. Deals chiefly with French writers.

Chadwick, Owen. *From Bossuet to Newman: The Idea of Doctrinal Development.* 2d ed. New York and Cambridge: Cambridge Univ. Press, 1987.

Congar, Yves, O.P. *A History of Theology*. Trans. Hunter Guthrie. Garden City, N.Y.: Doubleday & Co., 1968.

Connolly, James M. *The Voices of France: A Survey of Contemporary Theology in France*. New York: Macmillan, 1961.

Dulles, Avery, S.J. *A History of Apologetics*. Philadelphia: Westminster Press, 1971.

Fries, H., and G. Schwaiger, eds. *Katholische Theologen Deutschlands im 19. Jahrhundert*. 3 vols. Munich, 1973.

Goyau, Georges. *L'Allemagne religieuse: Le catholicisme, 1800–1870*. 4 vols. Paris, 1905–9. A first-class presentation of doctrine in its social context; there is an additional volume, *Le protestantisme* (5th ed., 1906).

Grabmann, Martin. *Die Geschichte der katholischen Theologie seit dem Ausgang der Väterzeit*. 2d ed. Darmstadt, 1961. Short notices.

Hocedez, Edgar. *Histoire de la théologie au XIXe siècle*. 3 vols. Paris, 1947–52. Still the principal history.

McCool, Gerald A., S.J. *Catholic Theology in the Nineteenth Century: The Quest for a Unitary Method*. New York: Seabury Press, 1977.

Nédoncelle, Maurice, ed. *L'écclésiologie au XIXe siècle*. Paris, 1960.

O'Meara, Thomas Franklin, O.P. *Romantic Idealism and Roman Catholicism: Schelling and the Theologians*. Notre Dame, Ind.: Univ. of Notre Dame Press, 1982.

Reardon, Bernard M. G. *Liberalism and Tradition: Aspects of Catholic Thought in Nineteenth-Century France*. New York and Cambridge: Cambridge Univ. Press, 1975. Highly recommended.

_____. *Religion in the Age of Romanticism: Studies in Early Nineteenth Century Thought*. New York and Cambridge: Cambridge Univ. Press, 1985. Also highly recommended.

Scheffczyk, Leo, ed. *Theologie in Aufbruch und Widerstreit: Die deutsche katholische Theologie im 19. Jahrhundert*. Bremen, 1965. An anthology with a fine introduction, pp. xi–xlix.

Spencer, Philip. *Politics of Belief in Nineteenth-Century France: Lacordaire, Michon, Veuillot*. London, 1954; New York: Howard Fertig, 1973.

Werner, Karl. *Geschichte der katholischen Theologie seit dem Trienter Concil bis zur Gegenwart*. Munich, 1866; New York: Johnson Reprint, 1966.


## François-René de Chateaubriand

_____. *Oeuvres complètes*. 12 vols. Paris: Garnier, 1861.

_____. *Mémoires d'outre-tombe*. Ed. Maurice Levaillant and Georges Moulinière. 2 vols. Paris: Bibliothèque de la Pléiade, 1958. With bibliography.

_____. *The Genius of Christianity*. Trans. Charles I. White. Baltimore, 1856. Chateaubriand's *Genius* is directed against the "cultured despisers" of Christianity generally; a Spanish work of similar scope, directed, however, against a *Protestant* interpretation of European history (specifically, François Guizot's *History of Civilization in Europe*) is Jaime Balmes's *European Civilization: Protestantism and Catholicity Compared in Their Effects on the Civilization of Europe,* trans. C. J. Hanford and Robert Kershaw, corrected ed. (Baltimore, 1850). Yet another Spanish response to Guizot (and

Proudhon, too) is by Juan Donoso Cortés, Marqués de Valdegamas: *Essays on Catholicism, Liberalism, and Socialism,* trans. William M'Donald (Dublin, 1874). Both works are well worth reading as quite intelligent presentations of a very conservative point of view.

Dempsey, Madeleine. *A Contribution to the Study of the Sources of the "Genie du Christianisme."* Paris, 1928.
Giraud, Victor. *Le christianisme de Chateaubriand.* Paris, 1925.
Levaillant, Maurice. *Chateaubriand, prince des songes.* Paris, 1960.
Maurois, André. *Chateaubriand.* Trans. Vera Fraser. New York: Harper & Bros., 1938.
Painter, George D. *Chateaubriand: A Biography.* Vol. 1, *The Longed-For Tempests, 1768–1793.* New York: Alfred A. Knopf, 1978.

## Johann Sebastian Drey

_____. *Die Apologetik, als wissenschaftliche Nachweisung der Göttlichkeit des Christentums in seiner Erscheinung.* Mainz, 1838–47; Frankfurt am Main: Minerva, 1967.
_____. *Kurze Einleitung in das Studium der Theologie.* Tübingen, 1819; Frankfurt am Main: Minerva, 1966.

There are also assorted items in *Geist des Christentums und des Katholizismus,* ed. Josef Rupert Geiselmann (Mainz, 1940). Included, along with the work of other theologians, are "Revision des gegenwärtigen Zustandes der Theologie," "Aus der Tagebüchern über philosophische, theologische und historische Gegenstände," "Vom Geist und Wesen des Katholizismus," "Ideen zur Geschichte des katholischen Dogmensystems," "Über den Satz von der alleinseligmachenden Kirche," and "Der katholische Lehrsatz von der Gemeinschaft der Heiligen."

Burchtael, James T., C.S.C. "Drey, Möhler, and the Catholic School of Tübingen." In *Nineteenth Century Religious Thought in the West,* ed. Ninian Smart et al. 2:111–39. New York and Cambridge: Cambridge Univ. Press, 1985. Useful bibliography.
Fehr, Wayne L., S.J. *The Birth of the Catholic Tübingen School: The Dogmatics of J. S. Drey.* Chico, Calif.: Scholars Press, 1981.
Fitzer, Joseph. "J. S. Drey and the Search for a Catholic Philosophy of Religion." *Journal of Religion* 63 (1983): 231–46.
Geiselmann, Josef Rupert. "Die Glaubenswissenschaft der katholischen Tübinger Schule in ihrer Grundlegung durch Johann Sebastian von Drey." *Tübinger theologische Quartalschrift* 111 (1930): 49–117.
_____. *Die katholische Tübinger Schule: Ihre theologische Eigenart.* Freiburg im Breisgau, 1964.
Lachner, Raimund. *Das ekklesiologische Denken Johann Sebastian Dreys.* Frankfurt am Main: Peter Lang, 1986.
McCool, Gerald A., S.J. *Catholic Theology in the Nineteenth Century: The Quest for a Unitary Method,* 67–81. New York: Seabury Press, 1977.
Reardon, Bernard M. G. *Religion in the Age of Romanticism: Studies in Early Nineteenth Century Thought,* 130–45. New York and Cambridge: Cambridge Univ. Press, 1985.

Ruf, Wolfgang. *Johann Sebastian von Dreys System der Theologie als Begrundung der Moraltheologie.* Göttingen, 1974.

Welte, Bernhard. "Zum Strukturwandel der katholischen Theologie im 19. Jahrhundert." In *Auf der Spur des Ewigen.* Freiburg im Breisgau, 1965.

## Johann Adam Möhler

————. *Gesammelte Schriften und Aufsätze.* Ed. I. von Döllinger. 2 vols. Regensburg, 1839–40. See especially the long article on Anselm of Canterbury, 1:32–176. There is no complete edition of Möhler's works, but the books not edited by Geiselmann have been reprinted by Minerva (Frankfurt am Main, 1968–70). Not all of Möhler's articles were included by Döllinger; Scheele (below) gives a complete list.

————. *Athanasius der Grosse und die Kirche seiner Zeit.* Mainz, 1827. Möhler's Christology.

————. *Commentar zum Briefe an die Römer.* Ed. F. X. Reithmayr. Regensburg, 1845.

————. *Die Einheit in der Kirche; oder, Das Prinzip des Katholizismus, dargestellt im Geiste der Kirchenväter der drei ersten Jahrhunderte.* Ed. Josef Rupert Geiselmann. Cologne: Hegner, 1957.

————. *Kirchengeschichte.* Ed. Pius Bonifacius Gams. 3 vols. Regensburg, 1867–70.

————. *Neue Untersuchungen der Lehrgegensätze zwischen den Katholiken und Protestanten: Eine Vertheidigung meiner Symbolik gegen die Kritik des Herrn Professors Dr. Baur in Tübingen.* Mainz, 1834 (slightly enlarged, 1835). The 1834 edition was reprinted (see previous listing).

————. *Patrologie; oder, Christliche Literärgeschichte.* Ed. F. X. Reithmayr. Mainz, 1840.

————. *Symbolik; oder, Darstellung der dogmatischen Gegensätze der Katholiken und Protestanten nach ihren öffentlichen Bekenntnisschriften.* Ed. Josef Rupert Geiselmann. 2 vols. Cologne: Hegner, 1960–61. ET: *Symbolism; or, Exposition of the Doctrinal Differences between Catholics and Protestants, as Evidenced by Their Symbolical Writings.* Trans. James Burton Robertson. 2 vols. London, 1843. Includes "Memoir of Dr. Möhler," pp. xxvii–cxxxiv.

Congar, Yves, O.P. "Sur l'évolution et l'interpretation de la pensée de Möhler." *Revue des sciences philosophiques et théologiques* 27 (1938): 205–17.

Fitzer, Joseph. *Möhler and Baur in Controversy, 1832–1838: Romantic-Idealist Assessment of the Reformation and Counter-Reformation.* Tallahassee, Fla.: Scholars Press, 1974. Select bibliography.

Geiselmann, Josef Rupert. *Lebendiger Glaube aus geheiligter Überlieferung: Der Grundgedanke der Theologie Johann Adam Möhlers und der katholischen Tübinger Schule.* Mainz, 1942.

————. *Die theologische Anthropologie Johann Adam Möhlers.* Freiburg im Breisgau, 1955. Largely the same as Geiselmann's commentary in volume 2 of his edition of the *Symbolik.*

Goyau, Georges, ed. *Moehler.* Paris, n.d. (ca. 1910?). A French translation of large sections of *Einheit, Symbolik,* and *Neue Untersuchungen;* but see also the introduction, pp. 9–52.

Nienaltowski, Henry R. *Johann Adam Möhler's Theory of Doctrinal Development.* Washington, D.C.: Catholic Univ. of America Press, 1959.

Riga, Peter. "The Ecclesiology of J. A. Möhler." *Theological Studies* 22 (1961): 563–87.

Savon, Hervé. *Johann Adam Möhler: The Father of Modern Theology.* Trans. Charles McGrath. Glen Rock, N.J.: Paulist Press, 1966. Good short introduction to Möhler's thought.

Scheele, Paul-Werner. *Einheit und Glaube: Johann Adam Möhlers Lehre von der Kirche und ihre Bedeutung für die Glaubensbegründung.* Munich, 1964. Excellent bibliography.

Tristram, Henry. "Johann Adam Möhler et John Henry Newman: La pensée allemande et la renaissance catholique en Angleterre." *Revue des sciences philosophiques et théologiques* 27 (1938): 184–204.

Vigener, Fritz. *Drei Gestalten aus dem modernen Katholizismus: Möhler, Diepenbrock, Döllinger.* Munich, 1926.

## Georg Hermes

———. *Einleitung in die christkatholische Theologie.* Part 1, *Philosophische Einleitung.* Münster, 1819. Part 2, 1st division, *Positive Einleitung.* 2d ed. Münster, 1834. Both parts, Frankfurt am Main: Minerva, 1967.

———. *Untersuchungen über die innere Wahrheit des Christenthumes.* Münster, 1805; Frankfurt am Main: Minerva, 1967.

Braun, Johann, and Peter Elvenich, eds. *Acta Romana.* Leipzig, 1838.

Elvenich, Peter. *Der Hermesianismus und Johannes Perrone, sein römischer Gegner.* Breslau, 1844.

Eschweiler, Karl. *Die zwei Wege der neueren Theologie: Hermes—Scheeben.* Augsburg, 1926.

Goyau, Georges. *L'Allemagne religieuse, 1800–1870* 2:2–12. Paris, 1905.

Hocedez, Edgar. *Histoire de la théologie au XIXe siècle* 1:167–203. Paris, 1947.

McCool, Gerald A., S.J. *Catholic Theology in the Nineteenth Century: The Quest for a Unitary Method,* 59–67. New York: Seabury Press, 1977.

Perrone, Joannes. *Praelectiones Thelogicae quas in Collegio Romano S.I. Habebat.* 21st ed. 9 vols. Ratisbon, 1854–55.

———. *Kompendium der katholischen Dogmatik, zum Gebrauche für Theologen und gebildete Laien.* Trans. into German "von einem katholischen Geistlichen." 4 vols. Landshut, 1852–55.

Reardon, Bernard M. G. *Religion in the Age of Romanticism: Studies in Early Nineteenth Century Thought,* 117–27. New York and Cambridge: Cambridge Univ. Press, 1985.

Schwedt, Herman H. *Das römische Urteil über Georg Hermes.* Rome: Herder & Herder, 1980.

See also the article by A. Thouvenin in *Dictionnaire de théologie catholique* 6:2288–2303; and the articles by R. Schlund and E. Hegel in *Lexikon für Theologie und Kirche* 5:258–61, where additional bibliography is given.

## Anton Günther

———. *Gesammelte Schriften: Neue Ausgabe in 9 Bänden.* Vienna, 1882; Frankfurt am Main: Minerva, 1968.

Goyau, Georges. *L'Allemagne religieuse, 1800–1870* 2:43–53. Paris, 1905.

Hocedez, Edgar. *Histoire de la théologie au XIXe siècle* 2:39–59. Paris, 1952.

Knoodt, Franz-Peter. *Anton Günther: Eine Biographie.* 2 vols. Vienna, 1881.

McCool, Gerald A., S.J. *Catholic Theology in the Nineteenth Century: The Quest for a Unitary Method,* 88–112. New York: Seabury Press, 1977.

Minz, Karl-Heinz. *Pleroma Trinitatis: Die Trinitätstheologie bei Matthias Joseph Scheeben,* 219–60. Frankfurt am Main: Peter Lang, 1982. Excellent bibliographies.

Pritz, Joseph. *Glauben und Wissen bei Anton Günther.* Vienna, 1963. Anthology of texts by Günther, with an introduction.

Reardon, Bernard M. G. *Religion in the Age of Romanticism: Studies in Early Nineteenth Century Thought,* 125–34. New York and Cambridge: Cambridge Univ. Press, 1985.

Rondet, Henri. *Hégélianisme et christianisme,* esp. 121–35. Paris, 1965.

Schäfer, Theodor. *Die erkenntnis-theoretische Kontroverse Kleutgen—Günther.* Paderborn, 1961.

Wenzel, Paul. *Der Freundskreis am Anton Günther und die Gründung Beurons.* Essen, 1965.

_____. *Das wissenschaftliche Anliegen des Güntherianismus.* Essen, 1961.

Werner, Karl. *Geschichte der katholischen Theologie seit dem Trienter Concil bis zur Gegenwart,* 452–64. Munich, 1866; New York: Johnson Reprint, 1966.

Winter, E. K. *Die geistige Entwicklung Anton Günthers und seiner Schule.* Paderborn, 1931.

## Louis Bautain

_____. *La philosophie du christianisme.* 2 vols. Paris, 1835; Frankfurt am Main: Minerva, 1967.

Geiselmann, Josef Rupert. *Lebendiger Glaube aus geheiligter Uberlieferung: Der Grundgedanke der Theologie Johann Adam Möhlers und der katholischen Tübinger Schule,* 59–78. Mainz, 1942.

_____. *Die theologische Anthropologie Johann Adam Möhlers,* 243–51. Freiburg im Breisgau, 1955.

Hocedez, Edgar. *Histoire de la théologie au XIXe siècle* 2:69–82. Paris, 1952.

Horton, Walter Marshall. *The Philosophy of the Abbé Bautain.* New York: New York Univ. Press, 1926.

McCool, Gerald A., S.J. *Catholic Theology in the Nineteenth Century: The Quest for a Unitary Method,* 37–58. New York: Seabury Press, 1977.

Poupard, Paul. *Un essai de philosophie chrétienne du XIXe siècle: L'abbé Louis Bautain.* Paris, 1962.

Reardon, Bernard M. G. *Liberalism and Tradition: Aspects of Catholic Thought in Nineteenth Century Thought,* 113–37. New York and Cambridge: Cambridge Univ. Press, 1985.

## John Henry Newman

_____. *Apologia pro Vita Sua.* Ed. Martin J. Svaglic. New York and London: Oxford Univ. Press, 1967.

_____. *An Essay in Aid of a Grammar of Assent.* Ed. Ian Ker. New York and London: Oxford Univ. Press, 1985.

_____. *An Essay on the Development of Christian Doctrine*. Westminster, Md.: Christian Classics, 1968.

_____. *Fifteen Sermons Preached before the University of Oxford*. London: SPCK, 1970.

_____. *The Idea of a University*. Ed. Martin J. Svaglic. Notre Dame, Ind.: Univ. of Notre Dame Press, 1982.

_____. *Letters and Diaries*. Ed. C. S. Dessain et al. 31 vols. New York and London: Oxford Univ. Press, 1961–84.

_____. *On Consulting the Faithful in Matters of Doctrine*. Ed. and intro. John Coulson. London, 1961.

_____. *The Philosophical Notebooks of John Henry Newman*. Ed. Edward Sillem. 2 vols. Louvain, 1969–70.

_____. *The Theological Papers of John Henry Newman on Biblical Inspiration and on Infallibility*. Ed. J. Derek Holmes. Oxford: Clarendon Press, 1979.

_____. *The Theological Papers of John Henry Newman on Faith and Certainty*. Ed. J. Derek Holmes. Oxford: Clarendon Press, 1976.

Balmes, Jaime. "El Doctor Newman, el Puseísmo y una Retractación Extraordinaria." In *Obras Completas,* ed. Ignacio Casanovas, S.J., 13:101–14. Madrid, 1925. In this article from 1843 Balmes (1810–48) predicts Newman's "full" conversion to Catholicism.

Blehl, Vincent F., S.J. *John Henry Newman: A Bibliographical Catalogue of His Writings*. Charlottesville: Univ. Press of Virginia, 1978.

Boekraad, A. J. *The Personal Conquest of Truth*. Louvain, 1955.

Boekraad, A. J., and Henry Tristram. *The Argument from Conscience to the Existence of God according to John Henry Newman*. London, 1961.

Bouyer, Louis. *Newman: His Life and Spirituality*. Trans. J. Lewis May. London, 1958.

_____. *Newman's Vision of Faith*. San Francisco: Ignatius Press, 1986. A commentary on the *Plain and Parochial Sermons*.

Cameron, J. M. "John Henry Newman and the Tractarian Movement." In *Nineteenth Century Religious Thought in the West,* ed. Ninian Smart et al., 2:69–109. New York and Cambridge: Cambridge Univ. Press, 1985. Useful bibliography.

Casey, Gerald. *Natural Reason: A Study of the Notions of Inference, Assent, Intuition, and First Principles in the Philosophy of John Henry Newman*. New York: Peter Lang, 1984. Useful bibliography.

Church, R. W. *The Oxford Movement, 1833–1845*. London, 1891.

Coulson, John. *Newman and the Common Tradition*. New York and London: Oxford Univ. Press, 1970.

Coulson, John, and A. M. Allchin, eds. *The Rediscovery of Newman: An Oxford Symposium*. London, 1967.

D'Arcy, Martin, S.J. *The Nature of Belief.* London, 1931. For comment on the *Grammar of Assent* see pp. 107–202.

Dessain, C. S. *John Henry Newman*. 2d ed. London, 1971.

Faber, Geoffrey. *Oxford Apostles: A Character Study of the Oxford Movement*. 3d ed. London, 1974.

Lash, Nicholas. *Newman on Development: The Search for an Explanation in History*. Shepherdstown, W.Va.: Patmos Press, 1975.

MacDougall, Hugh, O.M.I. *The Acton-Newman Relations: The Dilemma of Christian Liberalism*. New York: Fordham Univ. Press, 1962.

Misner, Paul. *Newman and Development.* Leiden: E. J. Brill, 1976.

Nédoncelle, Maurice. *La philosophie religieuse de John Henry Newman.* Strasbourg, 1946.

Newman, Jay. *The Mental Philosophy of John Henry Newman.* Waterloo, Ont.: Wilfrid Laurier Univ. Press, 1986.

O'Faoláin, Seán. *Newman's Way: The Odyssey of John Henry Newman.* New York: Devin-Adair Co., 1952.

Ryan, Alvan S., ed. *Newman and Gladstone: The Vatican Decrees.* Notre Dame, Ind.: Univ. of Notre Dame Press, 1962.

Trevor, Meriol. *Newman.* 2 vols. London, 1963. This work and that of Ward, below, are the principal biographies.

Vargish, Thomas. *Newman: The Contemplation of Mind.* New York and London: Oxford Univ. Press, 1970.

Walgrave, J. H. *Newman the Theologian.* Trans. A. V. Littledale. London, 1962.

Ward, Wilfrid. *The Life of John Henry, Cardinal Newman.* 2 vols. London, 1912.

Weaver, Mary Jo, ed. *Newman and the Modernists.* Lanham, Md.: Univ. Press of America, 1986.

Yearley, Lee H. *The Ideas of Newman: Christianity and Human Religiosity.* University Park: Pennsylvania State Univ. Press, 1978.


## Joseph de Maistre

_____. *De l'église gallicane.* Vol. 3 of *Oeuvres complètes.* Lyon, 1891.

_____. *Du pape.* Ed. Jacques Lovie and Joannès Chetail. Geneva, 1966. ET: *The Pope.* Trans. Aeneas McD. Dawson. London, 1850.

Breton, Germain. *"Du pape" de Joseph de Maistre: Etude critique.* Paris, 1931.

Dermenghem, Emile. *Joseph de Maistre, mystique.* 2d ed. Paris, 1946.

Goyau, Georges. *La pensée religieuse de Joseph de Maistre d'après des documents inédits.* Paris, 1921.

Latreille, Camille. *Joseph de Maistre et la papauté.* Paris, 1906.

Lebrun, Richard Allen. *The Political and Religious Thought of Joseph de Maistre.* Ottawa, 1965.

Lively, Jack, ed. *The Works of Joseph de Maistre.* New York: Macmillan Co., 1965. Selected passages, with a good introduction, pp. 1–45.

Reardon, Bernard M. G. *Liberalism and Tradition: Aspects of Catholic Thought in Nineteenth-Century France,* 20–42. New York and Cambridge: Cambridge Univ. Press, 1985.

Triomphe, Robert. *Joseph de Maistre,* esp. 329–51. Geneva, 1968.


## Orestes Brownson

_____. *Works.* Ed. Henry F. Brownson. 20 vols. Detroit, 1882–1907.

_____. *The Convert; or, Leaves from My Experience.* New York, 1857.

Brownson, Henry F. *Orestes Brownson's Life.* 3 vols. Detroit, 1898–1900.

Gower, Joseph F., and Leliaert, Richard M., eds. *The Brownson-Hecker Correspondence.* Notre Dame, Ind.: Univ. of Notre Dame Press, 1979.

McSorley, Joseph, C.S.P. *Isaac Hecker and His Friends.* Rev. ed. New York: Paulist-Newman Press, 1972.

Malone, George K. *The True Church: A Study in the Apologetics of Orestes Brownson.* Mundelein, Ill.: St. Mary of the Lake Seminary, 1957.

Maynard, Theodore. *Orestes Brownson: Yankee, Radical, Catholic.* New York: Macmillan, 1943.

Ryan, Thomas R. *Orestes Brownson.* Huntington, Ind.: Our Sunday Visitor, 1976.

Schlesinger, Arthur M., Jr. *Orestes Brownson: A Pilgrim's Progress.* Boston, 1939.

Sveino, Per. *Orestes A. Brownson's Road to Catholicism.* New York: Humanities Press, 1970.

## Archbishop Peter Richard Kenrick

_____. *Concio . . . in Concilio Vaticano Habenda at non Habita.* Naples, 1870. ET in *An Inside View of the Vatican Council,* ed. Leonard Woolsey. New York: American Tract Soc., n.d.

_____. *The Validity of Anglican Ordinations and Anglican Claims to the Apostolical Succession Examined.* 2d rev. and augm. ed. Philadelphia, 1848.

Leibrecht, John J. "Kenrick, Peter Richard." *New Catholic Encyclopedia* 8:156–57. New York: McGraw-Hill, 1967.

O'Shea, John J. *The Two Kenricks.* Philadelphia, 1904.

Rothensteiner, John Ernest. *History of the Archdiocese of St. Louis.* 2 vols. St. Louis, 1928.

## The First Vatican Council

Mansi, Joannes Dominicus et al., eds. *Sacrorum Concilium Nova et Amplissima Collectio.* Vols. 49–53. Reprint. Graz, 1961.

Clarkson, John F., S.J., et al., eds., *The Church Teaches.* Rockford, Ill.: TAN Books, 1973.

Acton, John Emerich Dalberg, Lord. "The Munich Congress." In *Essays on Church and State,* ed. Douglas Woodruff, 159–99. London, 1952.

_____. "Ultramontanism." In *Essays,* ed. Woodruff, 37–85.

_____. "The Vatican Council." In *Essays on Freedom and Power,* ed. Gertrude Himmelfarb, 275–327. Cleveland: World Publishing Co., 1955.

Boÿs, Albert de. *Ses souvenirs du Concile du Vatican, 1869–1870.* Ed. Jacques Gadille. Louvain, 1968.

Bury, John Bagnell. *History of the Papacy in the Nineteenth Century, 1864–1878.* Ed. R. H. Murray. London, 1930.

Butler, Dom Cuthbert, O.S.B. *The Vatican Council: The Story Told from Inside in Bishop Ullathorne's Letters.* 2 vols. London, 1930. A slightly abridged, one-volume version has been edited by Christopher Butler (London, 1962). Recommended.

Gibbons, James Cardinal. *A Retrospect of Fifty Years.* Vol. 1. Baltimore, 1916.

Granderath, Theodor, S.J. *Geschichte des Vatikanischen Konzils.* Ed. K. Kirsch, S.J. 3 vols. Freiburg im Breisgau, 1903–06.

Hasler, August Bernhard. *How the Pope Became Infallible: Pius IX and the Politics of Persuasion.* Trans. Peter Heinegg. New York: Doubleday & Co., 1981. Takes the rather unusual view that Pius IX was mentally unbalanced.

Hennesey, James, S.J. *The First Vatican Council: The American Experience.* New York: Herder & Herder, 1963. Recommended.

Hergenröther, Joseph. *Anti-Janus: An Historico-Theological Criticism of the*

*Work Entitled "The Pope and the Council" by "Janus."* Trans. James Burton Robertson. New York, 1870.

"Janus" ( = Ignaz von Döllinger). *The Pope and the Council.* Authorized trans. Boston, 1870.

MacDougall, Hugh, O.M.I. *The Acton-Newman Relations: The Dilemma of Christian Liberalism,* esp. 108–39. New York: Fordham Univ. Press, 1962.

Manning, Henry Edward. *The True Story of the Vatican Council.* London, 1877.

———. *The Vatican Council and Its Definitions.* London, 1871.

———. *The Vatican Decrees in Their Bearing on Civil Allegiance.* London, 1875.

Portier, William L. *Isaac Hecker and the First Vatican Council.* Lewiston, N.Y.: Edwin Mellen Press, 1985. Appendix contains Hecker's *Exposition of the Church in View of Recent Difficulties and Controversies and the Present Needs of the Age.*

"Quirinus" ( = Ignaz von Döllinger). *Letters from Rome.* 2 vols. London, 1870; Jersey City, N.J.: Da Capo Press, 1973.

Ryan, Alvan S., ed. *Newman and Gladstone: The Vatican Decrees.* Notre Dame, Ind.: Univ. of Notre Dame Press, 1962. Contains Gladstone's "The Vatican Decrees in Their Bearing on Civil Allegiance" and Newman's "Letter to His Grace the Duke of Norfolk."

Sparrow Simpson, W. J. *Roman Catholic Opposition to Papal Infallibility.* Milwaukee, 1910.

## Archbishop John Ireland and Americanism

———. *The Church and Modern Society.* 2 vols. St. Paul, 1904–5.

Ahern, Patrick H. *The Life of John J. Keane,* esp. 244–89. Milwaukee: Bruce Pub. Co., 1955.

Dease, Dennis J. *The Theological Influence of Orestes Brownson and Isaac Hecker on John Ireland's Americanist Ecclesiology.* Ann Arbor, Mich.: UMI, 1978. Recommended; lists additional addresses by Ireland.

Elliott, Walter, C.S.P. *The Life of Father Hecker.* New York, 1891.

Ellis, John Tracy. *The Life of James Cardinal Gibbons,* esp. 2:1–80. 2 vols. Milwaukee: Bruce Pub. Co., 1952.

Holden, Vincent F., C.S.P. *The Yankee Paul, Isaac Thomas Hecker.* Milwaukee: Bruce Pub. Co., 1958. Hecker's life to 1858; Hecker died in 1888.

Klein, Félix. *Americanism: A Phantom Heresy.* Atchison, Kans.: Aquin Bookshop, 1951.

Leo XIII. *Longinqua Oceani.* In *Documents of American Catholic History,* ed. John Tracy Ellis, 514–26. Milwaukee: Bruce Pub. Co., 1956; The Ellis anthology was reprinted in three volumes by Michael Glazier, Wilmington, Del., 1987.

———. *Rerum Novarum.* In *The Great Encyclical Letters of Leo XIII,* ed. John J. Wynne, S.J., 208–48. New York, 1903. Many editions.

———. *Testem Benevolentiae.* In *Documents,* ed. Ellis, 1st ed., 553–62.

McAvoy, Thomas T. *The Americanist Heresy in Roman Catholicism, 1895–1900.* Notre Dame, Ind.: Univ. of Notre Dame Press, 1963. A reissue of *The Great Crisis in American Catholic History, 1895–1900* (Chicago: Henry Regnery Co., 1957).

Moynihan, James H. *The Life of Archbishop John Ireland.* New York: Harper & Bros., 1953. Excellent bibliography.

O'Connell, Marvin R. *John Ireland and the American Catholic Church.* St. Paul: Minnesota Historical Society Press, 1988.

Reher, Margaret Mary. *The Church and the Kingdom of God in America: The Ecclesiology of the Americanists.* Ann Arbor, Mich.: UMI, 1972.

Zwierlein, Frederick J. *The Life and Letters of Bishop McQuaid.* 3 vols. Rochester, N.Y., 1925–27. Bernard J. McQuaid (1825–1909), critical of Ireland, was bishop of Rochester. On McQuaid at Vatican I, see *Life and Letters* 2:48–66; and James Hennesey, S.J., *The First Vatican Council: The American Experience* (New York: Herder & Herder, 1963). On McQuaid and Ireland, see *Life and Letters* 3:160–251.

## Neo-Scholasticism and Thomism

Casper, Bernhard. "Der Systemgedanke der späten Tübinger Schule und in der deutschen Neoscholastik." *Philosophisches Jahrbuch des Görres Gesellschaft* 72 (1964–65): 161–79.

Chenu, M.-D., O.P. *Nature, Man, and Society in the Twelfth Century.* Trans. Jerome Taylor and Lester K. Little. Chicago: Univ. of Chicago Press, 1968.

_____. *Toward Understanding St. Thomas.* Trans. A. M. Landry and D. Hughes. Chicago: Henry Regnery Co., 1964.

Chesterton, G. K. *St. Thomas Aquinas.* New York, 1933. One of the best discussions of the concerns of the Thomist revival.

Copleston, Frederick, S.J. *A History of Philosophy* 7:387–89. Westminster, Md.: Newman Press, 1963. 9:250–70 ("Thomism in France"). London, 1975. A highly recommended history of philosophy.

Fabro, Cornelio, C.P.S. *Participation et causalité selon St. Thomas d'Aquin.* Louvain, 1961.

Gilson, Etienne. *Being and Some Philosophers.* 2d cor. and enl. ed. Toronto, 1952.

_____. *The Christian Philosophy of St. Thomas Aquinas.* Trans. L. K. Shook, C.S.B. New York: Random House, 1956.

_____. *Elements of Christian Philosophy.* Garden City, N.Y.: Doubleday & Co., 1960; Westport, Conn.: Greenwood Press, 1978.

_____. *Introduction à la philosophie chrétienne.* Paris, 1960.

Gilson, Etienne, Thomas Langan, and Armand Maurer. *Recent Philosophy: Hegel to the Present.* 330–54, 772–93. New York: Random House, 1966. Volume 4 of Gilson's *A History of Philosophy.*

John, Helen James, S.N.D. *The Thomist Spectrum.* New York: Fordham Univ. Press, 1966.

Leo XIII. *Aeterni Patris.* In *The Great Encyclical Letters of Leo XIII,* ed. John J. Wynne, S.J., 34–57. New York, 1903.

McCool, Gerald A., S.J. *Catholic Theology in the Nineteenth Century: The Quest for a Unitary Method,* 81–87, 129–240. New York: Seabury Press, 1977. Recommended.

Maritain, Jacques. *Approaches to God.* Trans. Peter O'Reilly. New York: Harper & Bros., 1954.

_____. *The Degrees of Knowledge.* Trans. Gerald B. Phelan. New York: Charles Scribner's Sons, 1959.

_____. *Existence and the Existent.* Trans. Lewis Galantière and Gerald B.

Phelan. New York: Pantheon Books, 1948; Westport, Conn.: Greenwood Press, 1975.

———. *The Range of Reason,* esp. 22–29, 66–102. New York: Charles Scribner's Sons, 1952.

———. *Ransoming the Time,* esp. 191–255. Trans. Harry Lorin Binsse. New York: Charles Scribner's Sons, 1946.

Rickaby, Joseph, S.J. *Scholasticism.* London, 1911. An earlier short—and intelligent—introduction. James MacCaffrey (*History of the Catholic Church in the Nineteenth Century,* 2d ed., 2 vols. [Dublin, 1910], 2:469 states that the British Jesuit "*Stonyhurst Philosophical Series,* . . . by Clarke, Rickaby, Boedder, and Maher, offers the best exposition of Scholasticism that has been published in English." Rickaby's contribution was his epistemology text, *First Principles of Knowledge* (4th ed., London, 1901).

## Matthias Joseph Scheeben

———. *Gesammelte Schriften.* Ed. Josef Höfer. 8 vols. Freiburg im Breisgau, 1943–67.

———. *The Mysteries of Christianity.* Trans. Cyril Vollert, S.J. St. Louis: B. Herder, 1946.

———. *Nature and Grace.* Trans. Cyril Vollert, S.J. St. Louis: B. Herder, 1954.

Bode, Franz-Josef. *Gemeinschaft mit dem lebendigen Gott: Die Lehre von der Eucharistie bei Matthias Joseph Scheeben.* Paderborn: Schöningh, 1986.

Eschweiler, Karl. *Die zwei Wege der neueren Theologie: Hermes—Scheeben.* Augsburg, 1926.

Fraigneau-Jullien, B., P.S.S. *L'Eglise et le caractère sacramentel selon Matthias-Joseph Scheeben.* Paris, 1958.

Klein, Klaus-Leo. *Kreatürlichkeit als Gottebenbildlichkeit . . . bei Matthias Joseph Scheeben.* Frankfurt am Main: Peter Lang, 1975.

Minz, Karl-Heinz. *Pleroma Trinitatis: Die Trinitätstheologie bei Matthias Joseph Scheeben.* Frankfurt am Main: Peter Lang, 1982. Excellent bibliographies.

Murray, John Courtney, S.J. *Matthias Joseph Scheeben on Faith.* Ed. Thomas Hughson, S.J. Lewiston, N.Y.: Edwin Mellen Press, 1987.

Paul, Eugen. *Denkweg und Denkform der Theologie von Matthias Joseph Scheeben.* Munich, 1970.

———, ed. *Matthias Scheeben.* Graz, 1976. Anthology of texts by Scheeben, with an introduction.

## Edouard LeRoy and Modernism

———. *Dogme et critique.* Paris, 1907.

———. *Esquisse d'une philosophie première,* esp. 2:861–75. 2 vols. Paris, 1956–58.

———. *Introduction à l'étude du problème religieux.* Paris, 1944.

———. "Notice générale sur l'ensemble de mes travaux philosophiques." *Etudes philosophiques,* 1955, 189–205.

Chaix-Ruy, Jules. "Edouard LeRoy." In *Les grands courants de la pensée mondiale contemporaine,* ed. M. F. Scicca, vol. 2, *Portraits,* 879–905. Milan, 1961.

Cuénot, Claude. *Teilhard de Chardin: A Biographical Study,* esp. 58–59, 138–39. Trans. Vincent Colimore. Baltimore: Helicon Press, 1965.

Fitzer, Joseph. "Tyrrell and LeRoy: Their Case Reopened." *Communio Viatorum* (1975) 4, pp. 201–24. A brief commentary on the piece by LeRoy reprinted in this volume and on George Tyrrell's *Christianity at the Crossroads.*

Mansini, Guy, O.S.B. *What Is a Dogma? The Meaning and Truth of Dogma in Edouard LeRoy and His Scholastic Opponents.* Rome: Editrice Pontificia Università Gregoriana, 1985. Recommended.

Pius X. *Pascendi Dominici Gregis.* In *All Things in Christ: Encyclicals and Selected Documents,* ed. Vincent A. Yzermans, 86–132. Westminster, Md.: Newman Press, 1954.

Poulat, Emile. *Histoire, dogme et critique dans la crise moderniste.* Paris, 1962.

Reardon, Bernard M. G. "Roman Catholic Modernism." In *Nineteenth Century Religious Thought in the West,* ed. Ninian Smart et al., 2:141–77. New York and Cambridge: Cambridge Univ. Press, 1985. Useful bibliography.

———, ed. *Roman Catholic Modernism.* Stanford, Calif.: Stanford Univ. Press, 1970. See Reardon's excellent introduction (pp. 9–67) to this anthology of Modernist writers.

Vidler, Alec R. *A Variety of Catholic Modernists.* New York and Cambridge: Cambridge Univ. Press, 1970. Good discussion of the controversy as a whole, but little on LeRoy.